SHADE THE CHANGING WOMAN

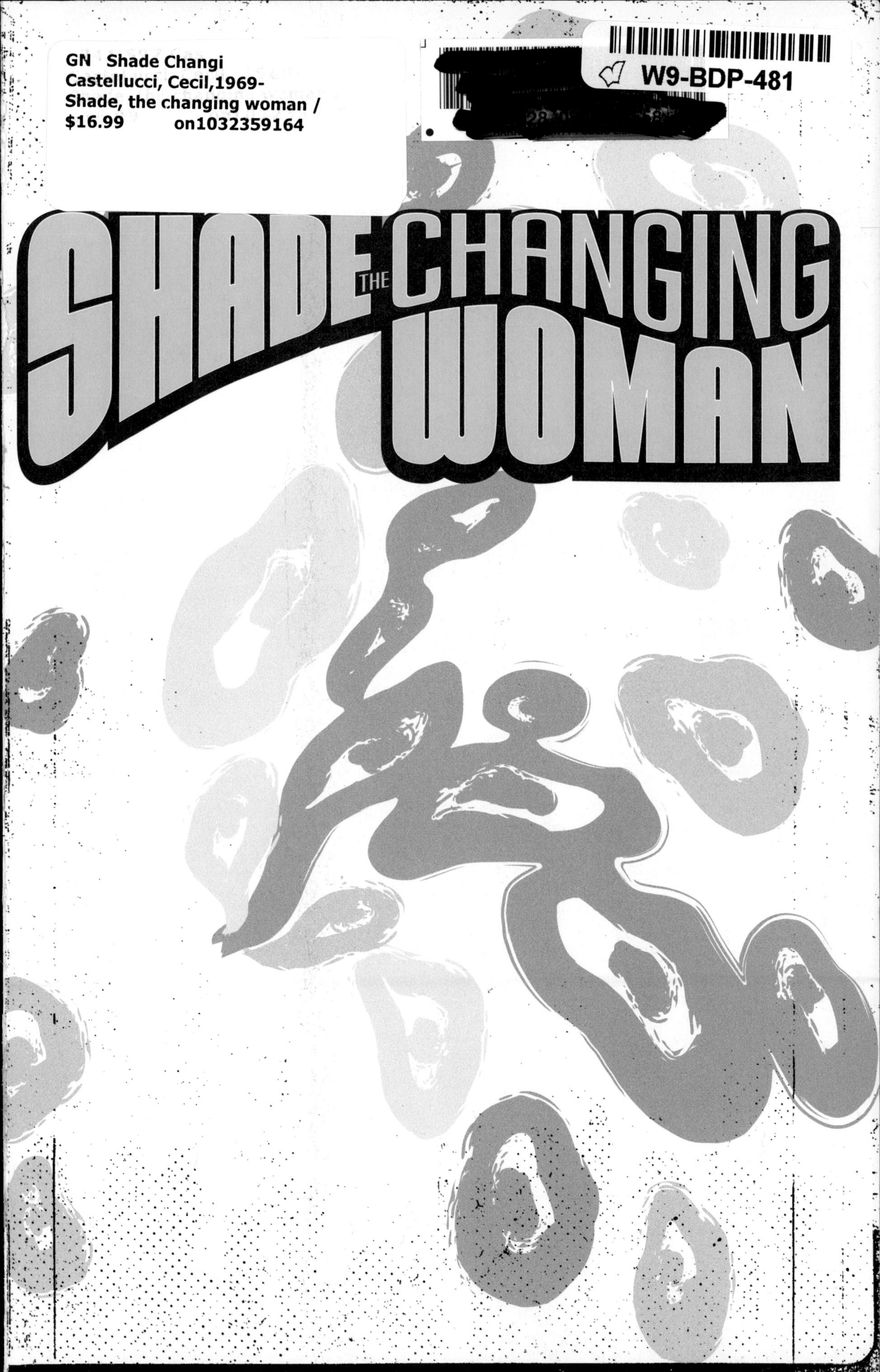

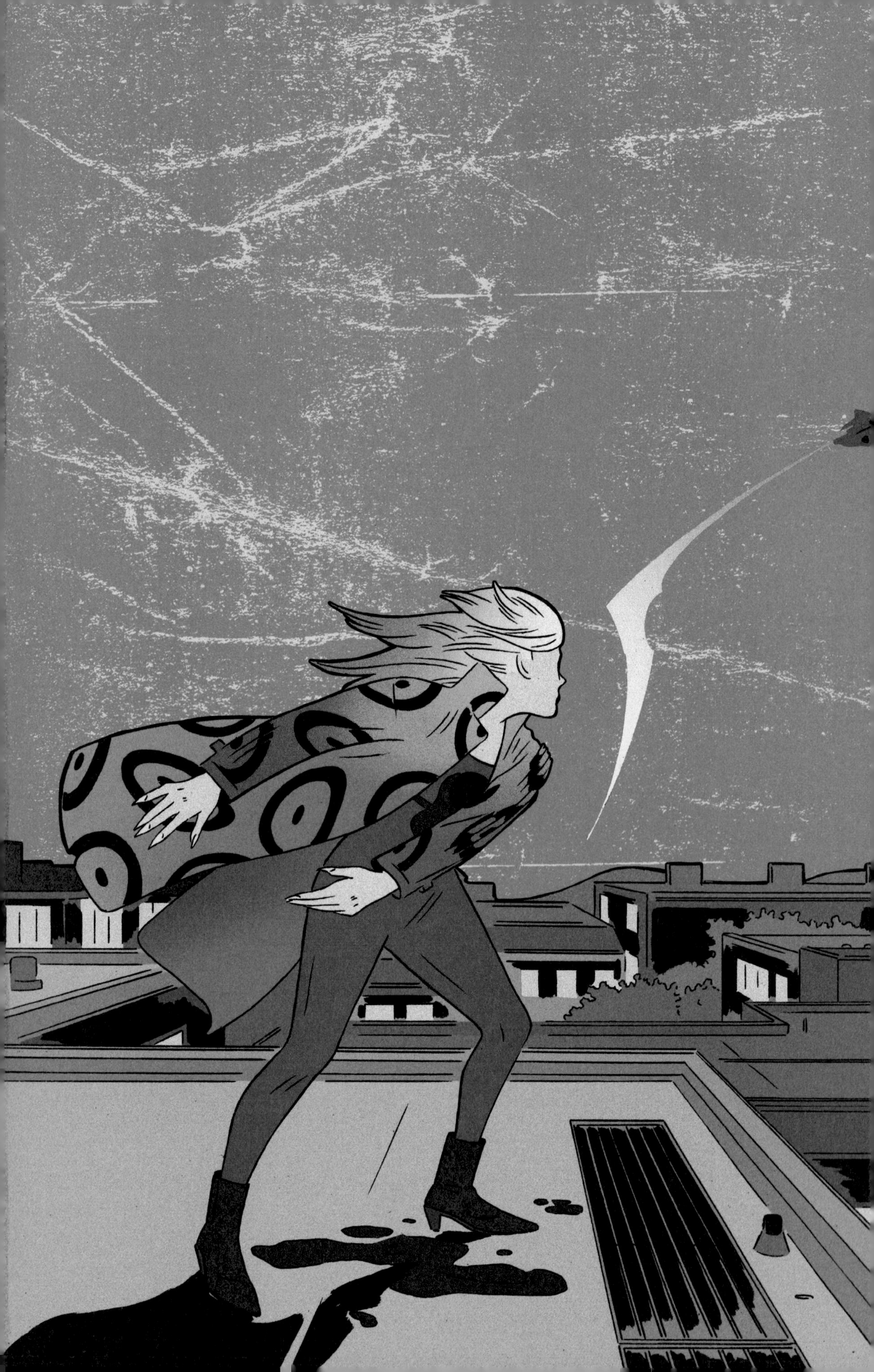

SHADE THE CHANGING WOMAN

CECIL CASTELLUCCI
Writer

MARLEY ZARCONE
ANDE PARKS
Artists

KELLY FITZPATRICK
Colorist

SAIDA TEMOFONTE
Letterer

BECKY CLOONAN
Cover Art and Original Series Covers

GERARD WAY
DC's Young Animal Curator

SHADE, THE CHANGING MAN created by
STEVE DITKO

JAMIE S. RICH, MOLLY MAHAN Editors – Original Series
JEB WOODARD Group Editor – Collected Editions
SCOTT NYBAKKEN Editor – Collected Edition
STEVE COOK Design Director – Books
MEGEN BELLERSEN Publication Design

BOB HARRAS Senior VP – Editor-in-Chief, DC Comics
MARK DOYLE Executive Editor, Vertigo & Black Label

DAN DiDIO Publisher
JIM LEE Publisher & Chief Creative Officer
AMIT DESAI Executive VP – Business & Marketing Strategy, Direct to Consumer
& Global Franchise Management
BOBBIE CHASE VP & Executive Editor, Young Reader & Talent Development
MARK CHIARELLO Senior VP – Art, Design & Collected Editions
JOHN CUNNINGHAM Senior VP – Sales & Trade Marketing
BRIAR DARDEN VP – Business Affairs
ANNE DePIES Senior VP – Business Strategy, Finance & Administration
DON FALLETTI VP – Manufacturing Operations
LAWRENCE GANEM VP – Editorial Administration & Talent Relations
ALISON GILL Senior VP – Manufacturing & Operations
JASON GREENBERG VP – Business Strategy & Finance
HANK KANALZ Senior VP – Editorial Strategy & Administration
JAY KOGAN Senior VP – Legal Affairs
NICK J. NAPOLITANO VP – Manufacturing Administration
LISETTE OSTERLOH VP – Digital Marketing & Events
EDDIE SCANNELL VP – Consumer Marketing
COURTNEY SIMMONS Senior VP – Publicity & Communications
JIM (SKI) SOKOLOWSKI VP – Comic Book Specialty Sales & Trade Marketing
NANCY SPEARS VP – Mass, Book, Digital Sales & Trade Marketing
MICHELE R. WELLS VP – Content Strategy

SHADE, THE CHANGING WOMAN

Published by DC Comics. Compilation and all new material Copyright
© 2018 DC Comics. All Rights Reserved.

Originally published in single magazine form in SHADE, THE
CHANGING MAN 26, 50 and SHADE, THE CHANGING WOMAN 1-6.
Copyright © 1992, 1994, 2018 DC Comics. All Rights Reserved.
All characters, their distinctive likenesses and related elements
featured in this publication are trademarks of DC Comics. The stories,
characters and incidents featured in this publication are entirely
fictional. DC Comics does not read or accept unsolicited submissions
of ideas, stories or artwork.

DC Comics
2900 West Alameda Avenue
Burbank, CA 91505
Printed by LSC Communications, Owensville, MO, USA.
12/7/18. First Printing.
ISBN: 978-1-4012-8570-8

Library of Congress Cataloging-in-Publication Data is available.

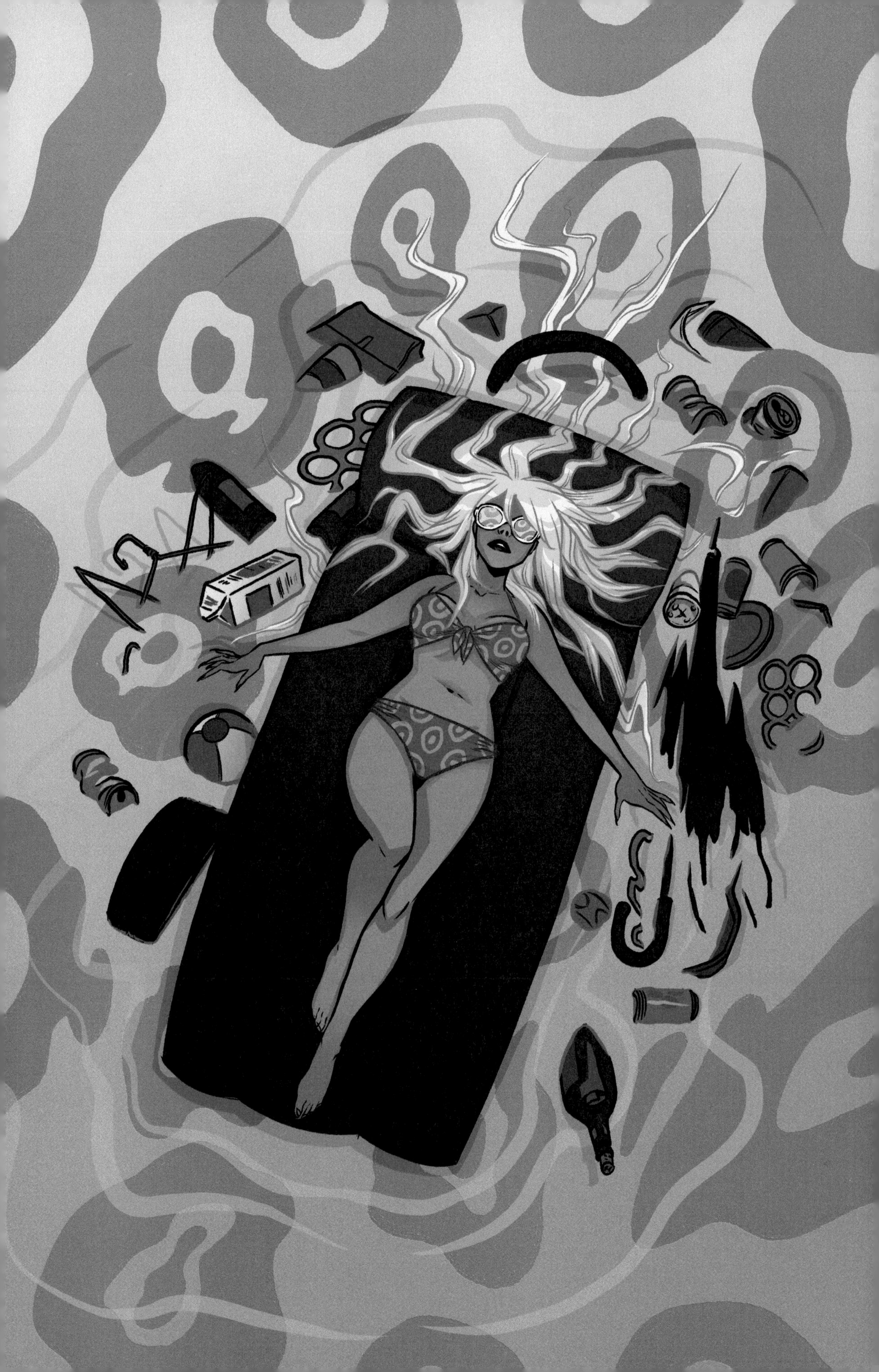

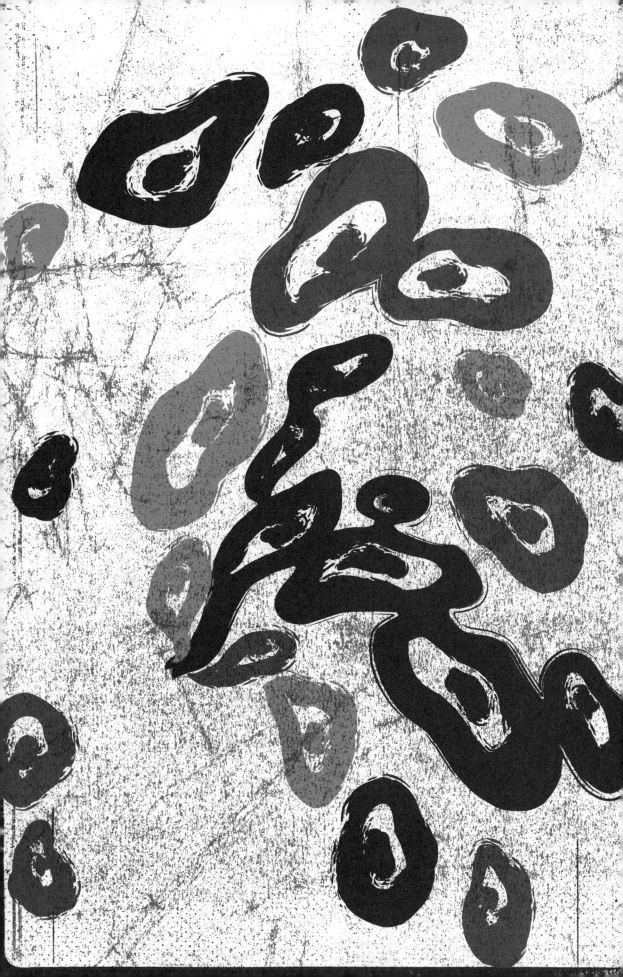

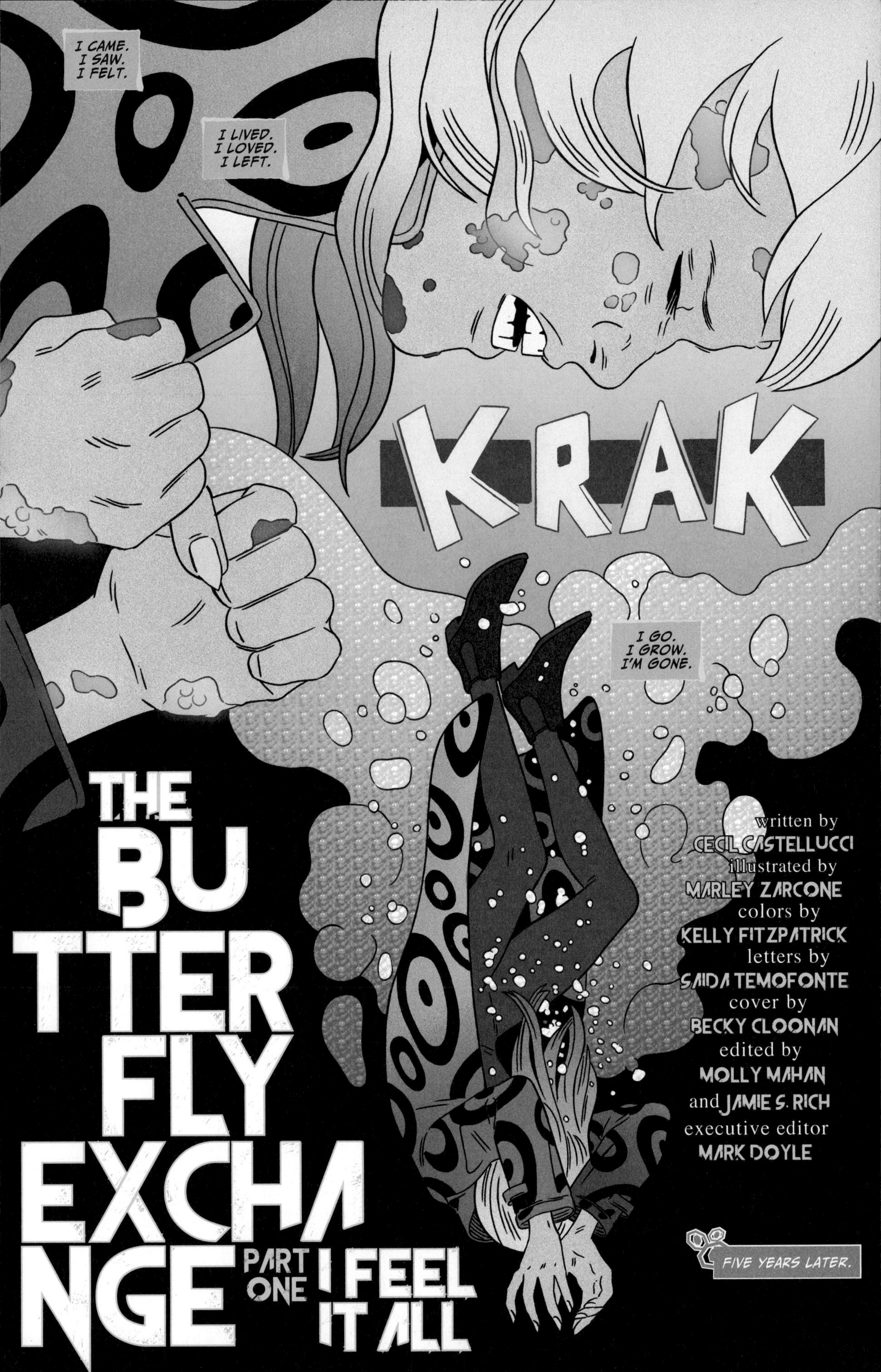

I CAME.
I SAW.
I FELT.
I LIVED.
I LOVED.
I LEFT.
KRAK
I GO.
I GROW.
I'M GONE.
THE BUTTERFLY EXCHANGE
PART ONE I FEEL IT ALL
written by CECIL CASTELLUCCI
illustrated by MARLEY ZARCONE
colors by KELLY FITZPATRICK
letters by SAIDA TEMOFONTE
cover by BECKY CLOONAN
edited by MOLLY MAHAN and JAMIE S. RICH
executive editor MARK DOYLE
FIVE YEARS LATER.

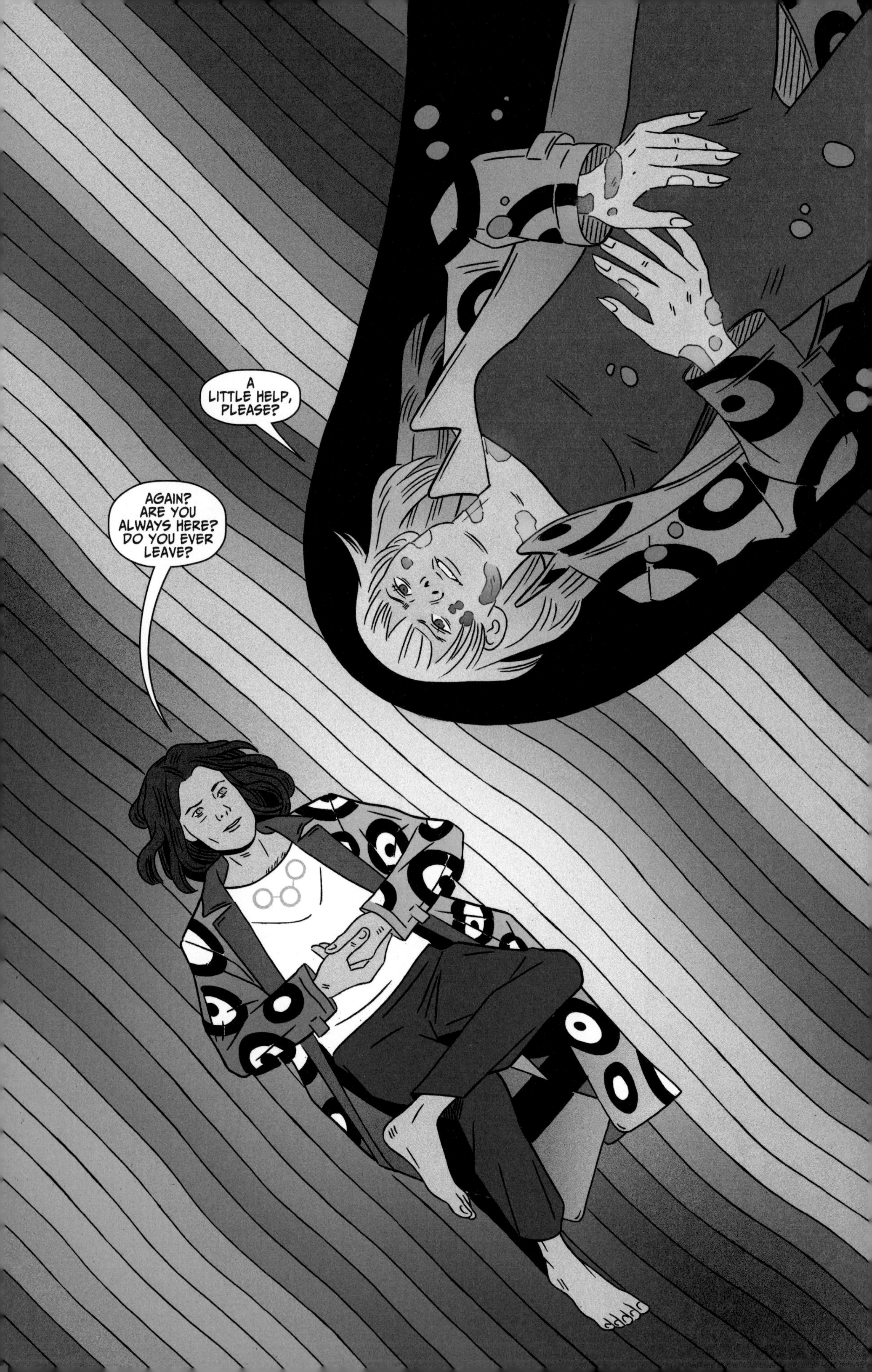
A LITTLE HELP, PLEASE?
AGAIN? ARE YOU ALWAYS HERE? DO YOU EVER LEAVE?

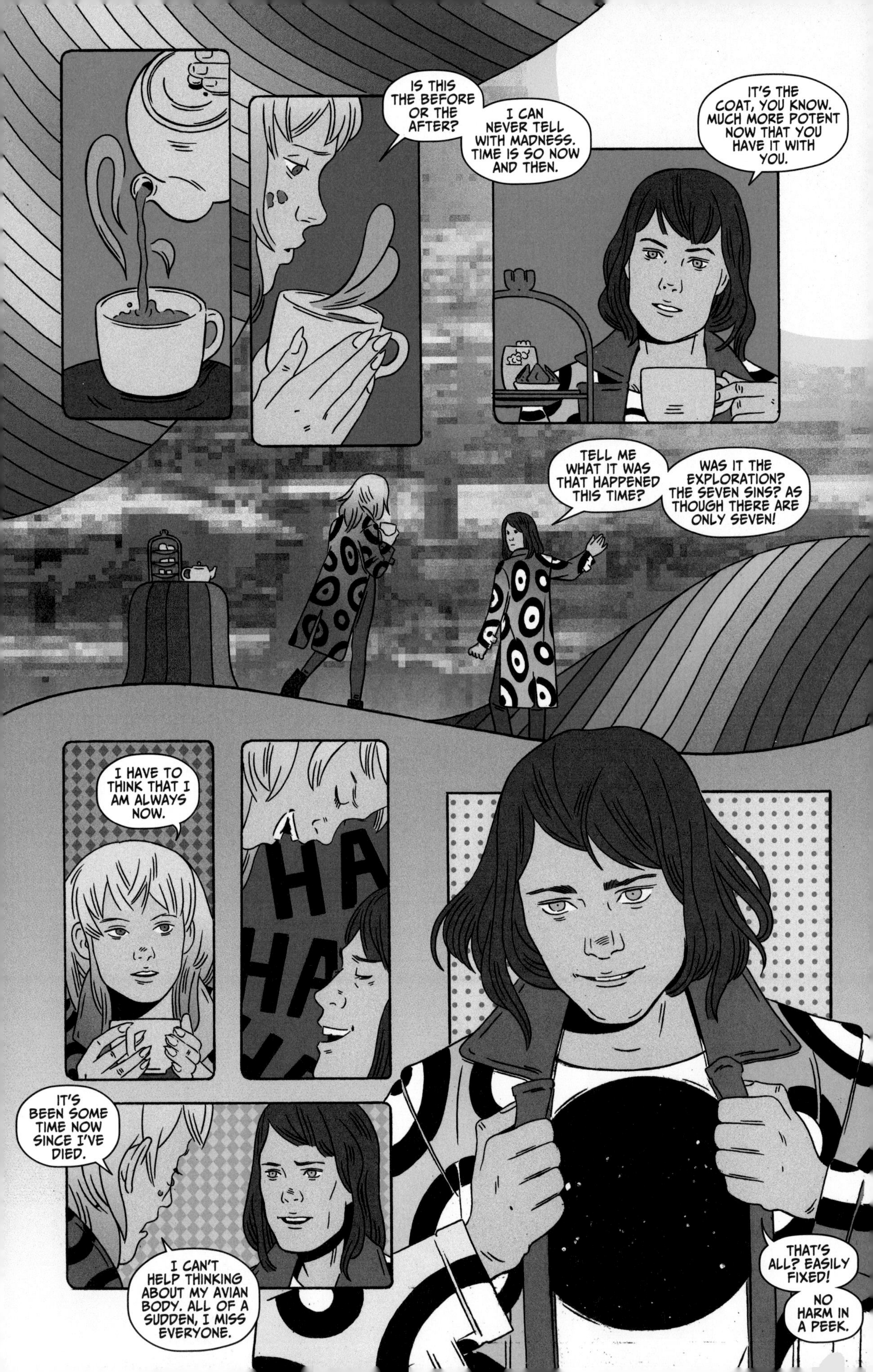
IS THIS THE BEFORE OR THE AFTER?
I CAN NEVER TELL WITH MADNESS. TIME IS SO NOW AND THEN.
IT'S THE COAT, YOU KNOW. MUCH MORE POTENT NOW THAT YOU HAVE IT WITH YOU.
TELL ME WHAT IT WAS THAT HAPPENED THIS TIME?
WAS IT THE EXPLORATION? THE SEVEN SINS? AS THOUGH THERE ARE ONLY SEVEN!
I HAVE TO THINK THAT I AM ALWAYS NOW.
HA HA
IT'S BEEN SOME TIME NOW SINCE I'VE DIED.
I CAN'T HELP THINKING ABOUT MY AVIAN BODY. ALL OF A SUDDEN, I MISS EVERYONE.
THAT'S ALL? EASILY FIXED!
NO HARM IN A PEEK.

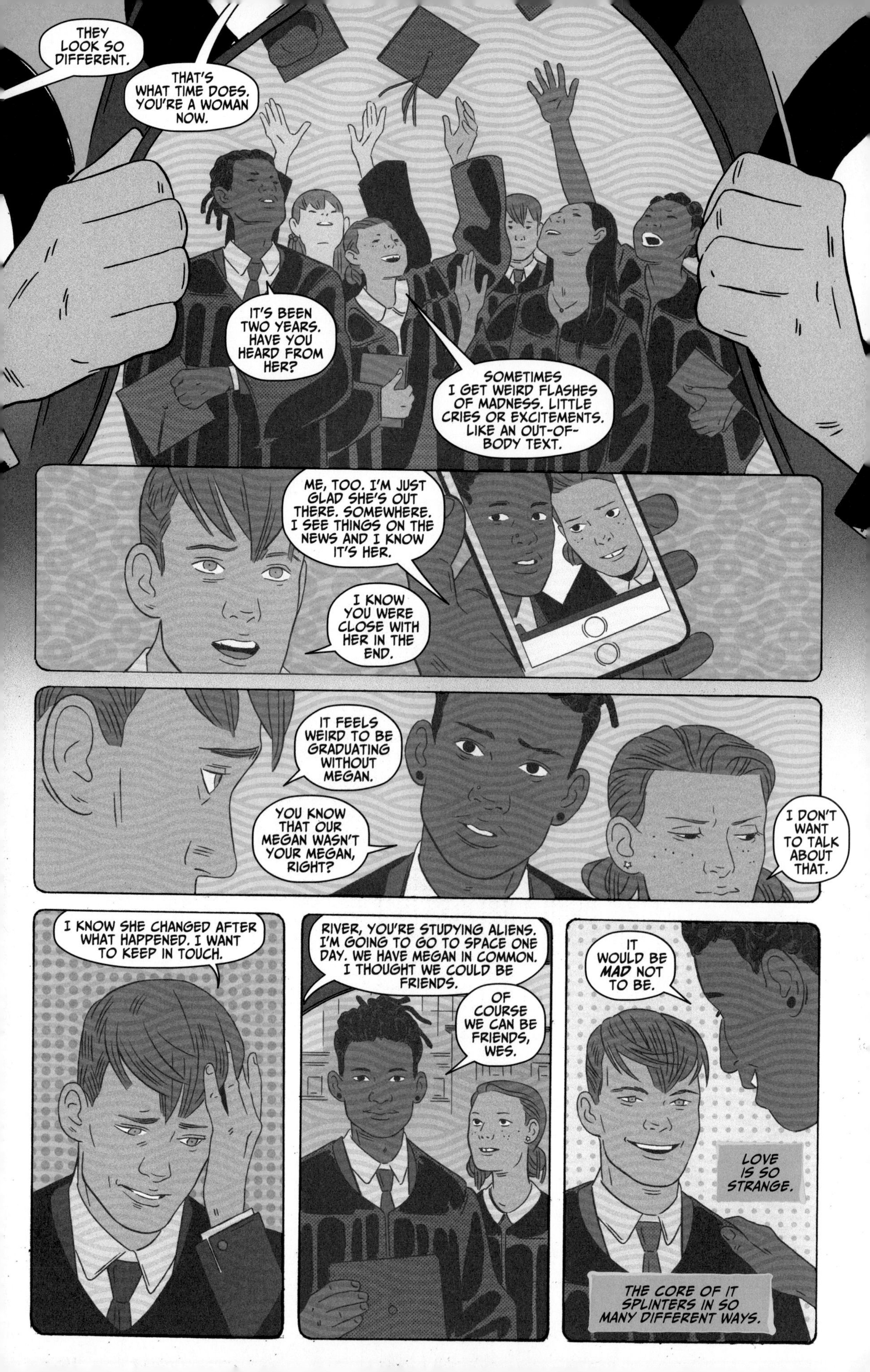
THEY LOOK SO DIFFERENT.
THAT'S WHAT TIME DOES. YOU'RE A WOMAN NOW.
IT'S BEEN TWO YEARS. HAVE YOU HEARD FROM HER?
SOMETIMES I GET WEIRD FLASHES OF MADNESS. LITTLE CRIES OR EXCITEMENTS. LIKE AN OUT-OF-BODY TEXT.
ME, TOO. I'M JUST GLAD SHE'S OUT THERE. SOMEWHERE. I SEE THINGS ON THE NEWS AND I KNOW IT'S HER.
I KNOW YOU WERE CLOSE WITH HER IN THE END.
IT FEELS WEIRD TO BE GRADUATING WITHOUT MEGAN.
YOU KNOW THAT OUR MEGAN WASN'T YOUR MEGAN, RIGHT?
I DON'T WANT TO TALK ABOUT THAT.
I KNOW SHE CHANGED AFTER WHAT HAPPENED. I WANT TO KEEP IN TOUCH.
RIVER, YOU'RE STUDYING ALIENS. I'M GOING TO GO TO SPACE ONE DAY. WE HAVE MEGAN IN COMMON. I THOUGHT WE COULD BE FRIENDS.
OF COURSE WE CAN BE FRIENDS, WES.
IT WOULD BE MAD NOT TO BE.
LOVE IS SO STRANGE.
THE CORE OF IT SPLINTERS IN SO MANY DIFFERENT WAYS.

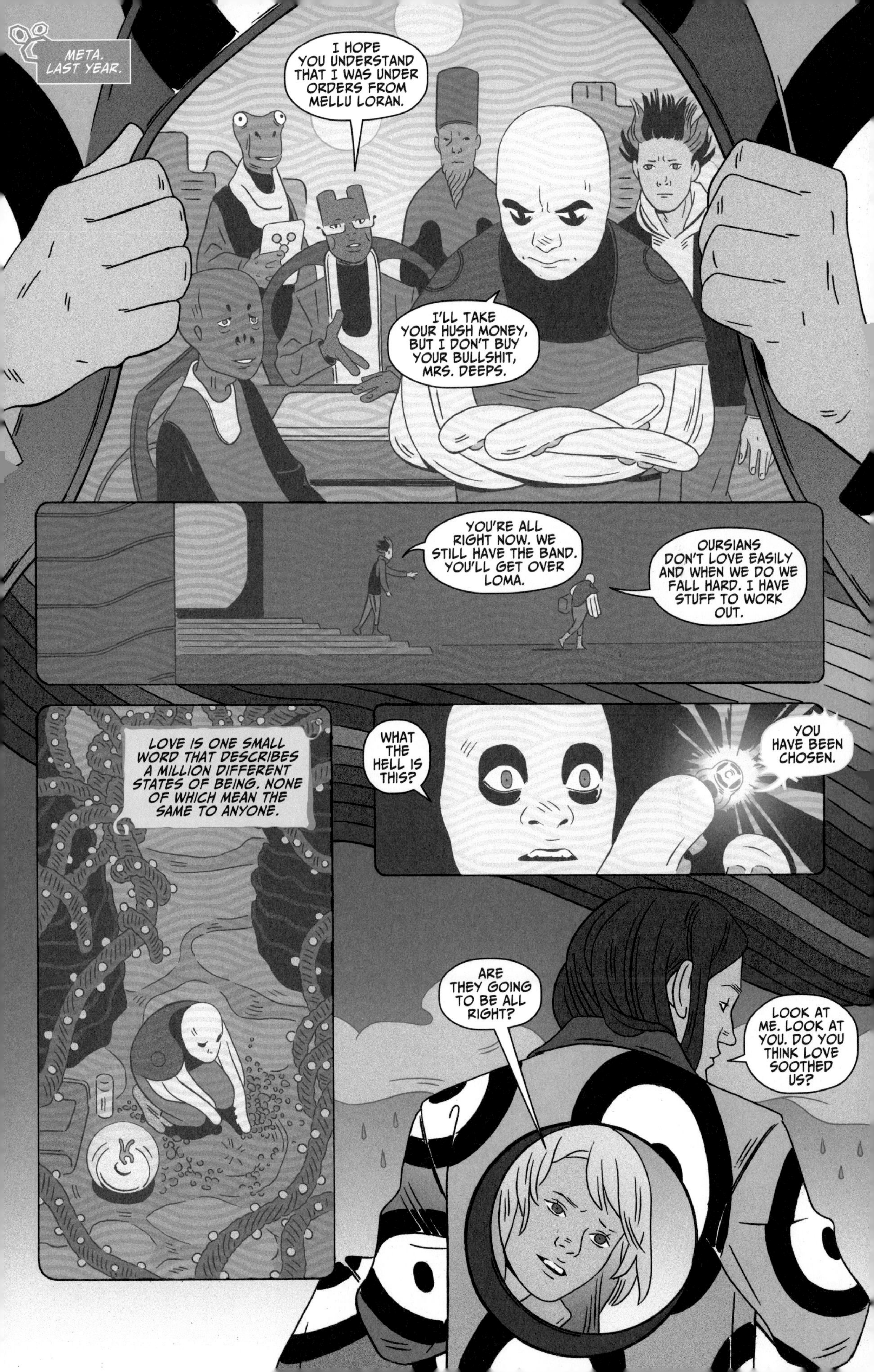
META. LAST YEAR.
I HOPE YOU UNDERSTAND THAT I WAS UNDER ORDERS FROM MELLU LORAN.
I'LL TAKE YOUR HUSH MONEY, BUT I DON'T BUY YOUR BULLSHIT, MRS. DEEPS.
YOU'RE ALL RIGHT NOW. WE STILL HAVE THE BAND. YOU'LL GET OVER LOMA.
OURSIANS DON'T LOVE EASILY AND WHEN WE DO WE FALL HARD. I HAVE STUFF TO WORK OUT.
LOVE IS ONE SMALL WORD THAT DESCRIBES A MILLION DIFFERENT STATES OF BEING. NONE OF WHICH MEAN THE SAME TO ANYONE.
WHAT THE HELL IS THIS?
YOU HAVE BEEN CHOSEN.
ARE THEY GOING TO BE ALL RIGHT?
LOOK AT ME. LOOK AT YOU. DO YOU THINK LOVE SOOTHED US?

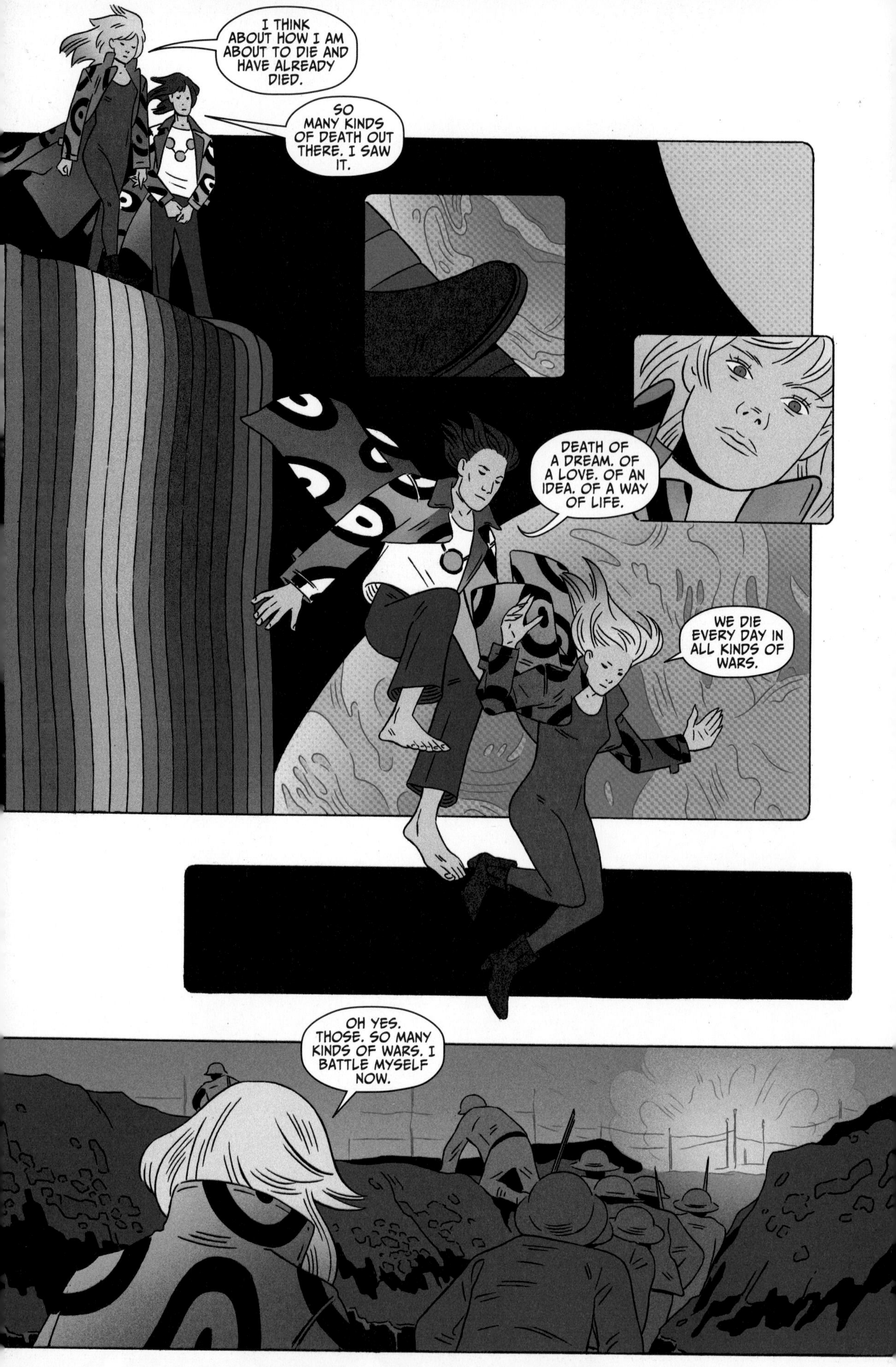
I THINK ABOUT HOW I AM ABOUT TO DIE AND HAVE ALREADY DIED.
SO MANY KINDS OF DEATH OUT THERE. I SAW IT.
DEATH OF A DREAM. OF A LOVE. OF AN IDEA. OF A WAY OF LIFE.
WE DIE EVERY DAY IN ALL KINDS OF WARS.
OH YES. THOSE. SO MANY KINDS OF WARS. I BATTLE MYSELF NOW.

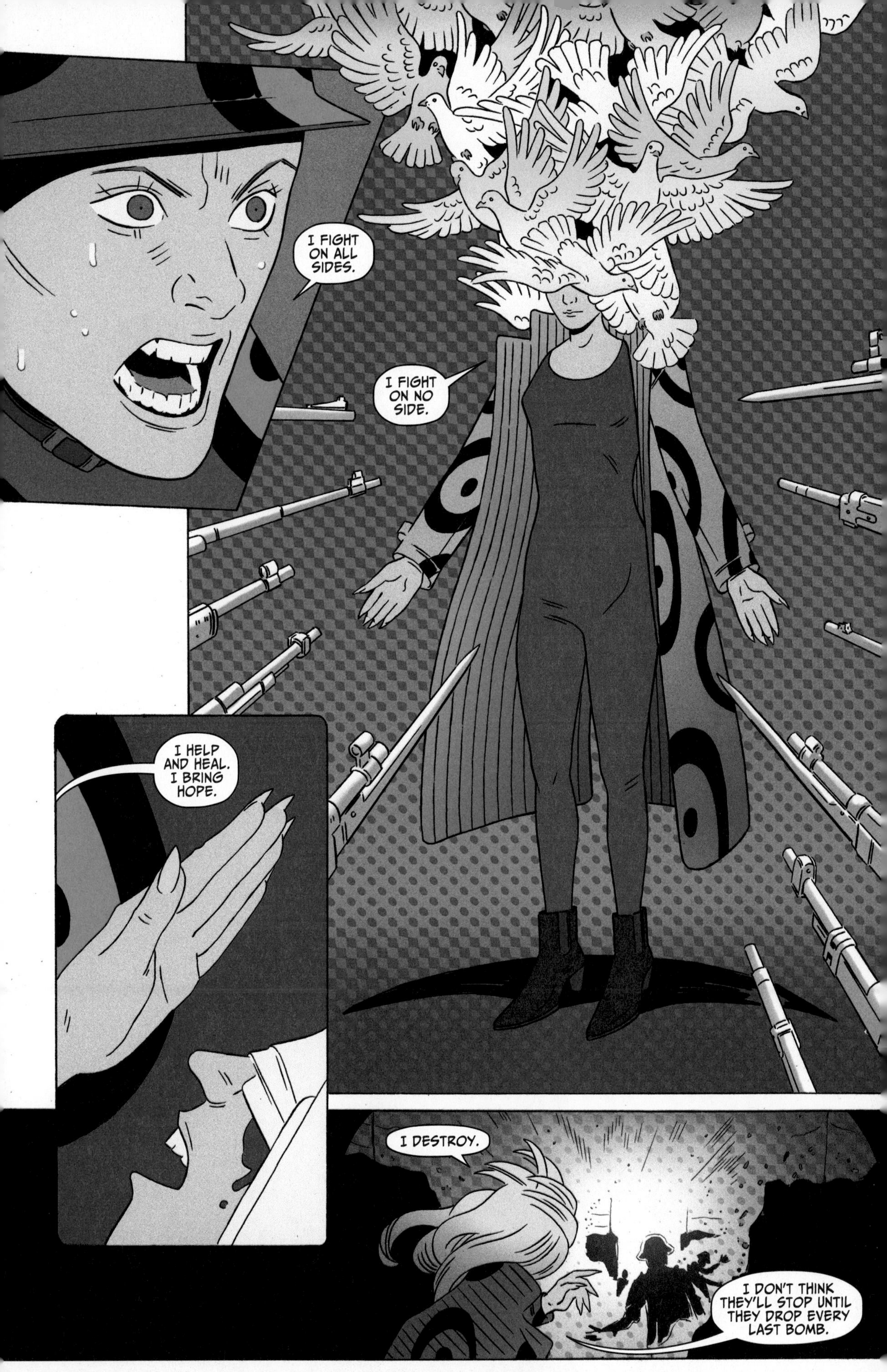
I FIGHT ON ALL SIDES.
I FIGHT ON NO SIDE.
I HELP AND HEAL. I BRING HOPE.
I DESTROY.
I DON'T THINK THEY'LL STOP UNTIL THEY DROP EVERY LAST BOMB.

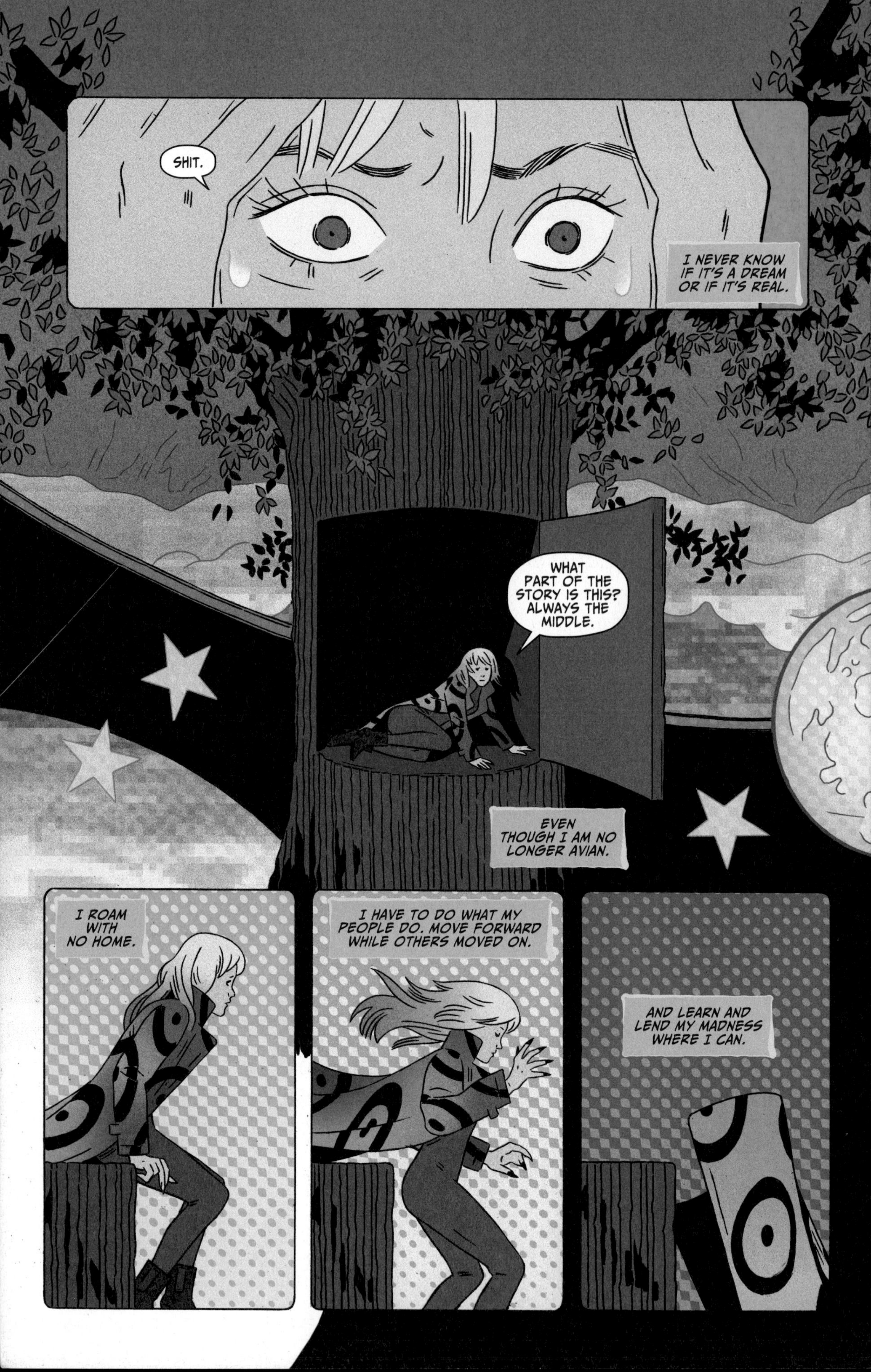
SHIT.
I NEVER KNOW IF IT'S A DREAM OR IF IT'S REAL.
WHAT PART OF THE STORY IS THIS? ALWAYS THE MIDDLE.
EVEN THOUGH I AM NO LONGER AVIAN.
I ROAM WITH NO HOME.
I HAVE TO DO WHAT MY PEOPLE DO. MOVE FORWARD WHILE OTHERS MOVED ON.
AND LEARN AND LEND MY MADNESS WHERE I CAN.

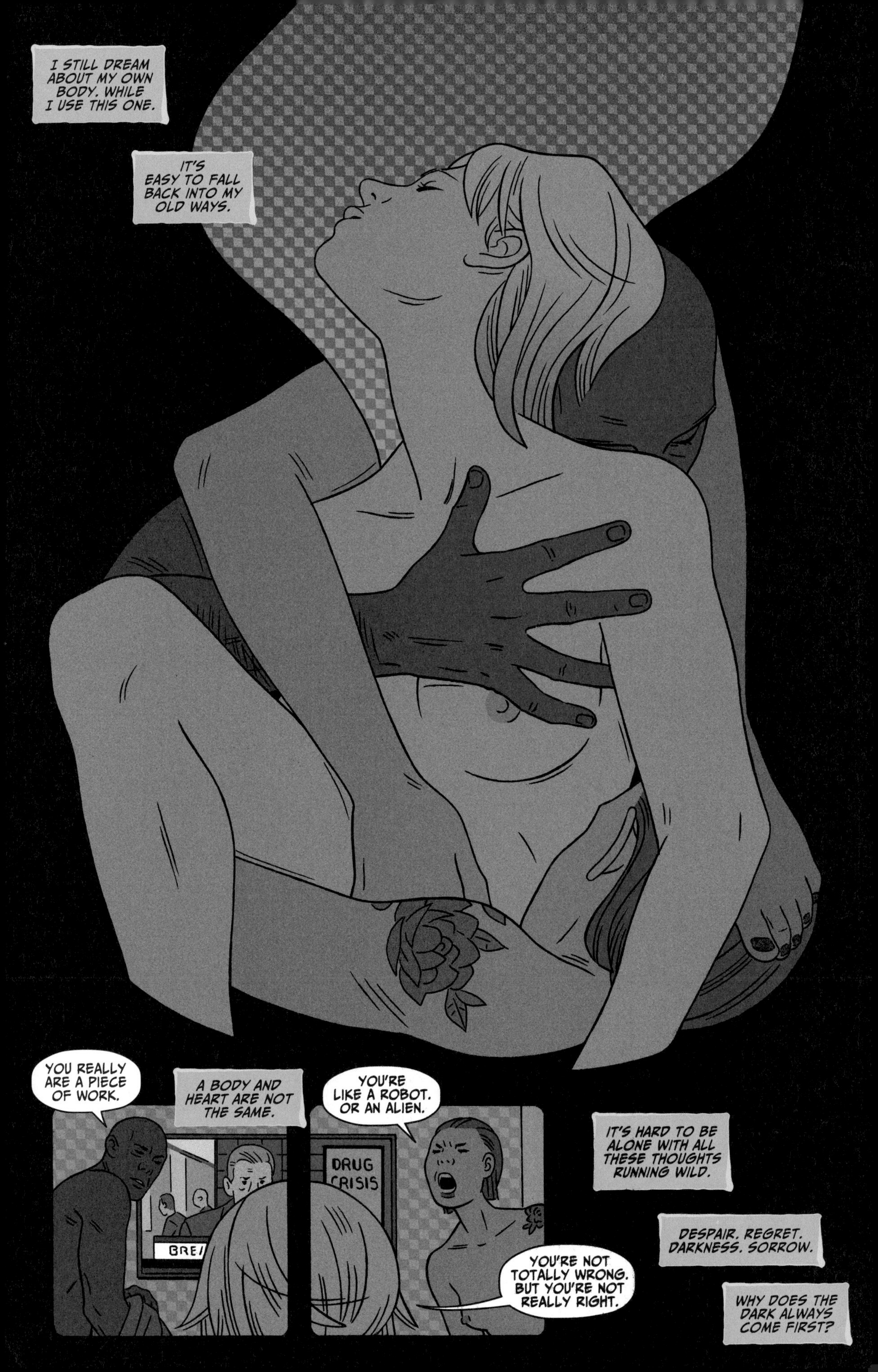
I STILL DREAM ABOUT MY OWN BODY. WHILE I USE THIS ONE.
IT'S EASY TO FALL BACK INTO MY OLD WAYS.
YOU REALLY ARE A PIECE OF WORK.
A BODY AND HEART ARE NOT THE SAME.
BRE
YOU'RE LIKE A ROBOT. OR AN ALIEN.
DRUG CRISIS
YOU'RE NOT TOTALLY WRONG. BUT YOU'RE NOT REALLY RIGHT.
IT'S HARD TO BE ALONE WITH ALL THESE THOUGHTS RUNNING WILD.
DESPAIR. REGRET. DARKNESS. SORROW.
WHY DOES THE DARK ALWAYS COME FIRST?

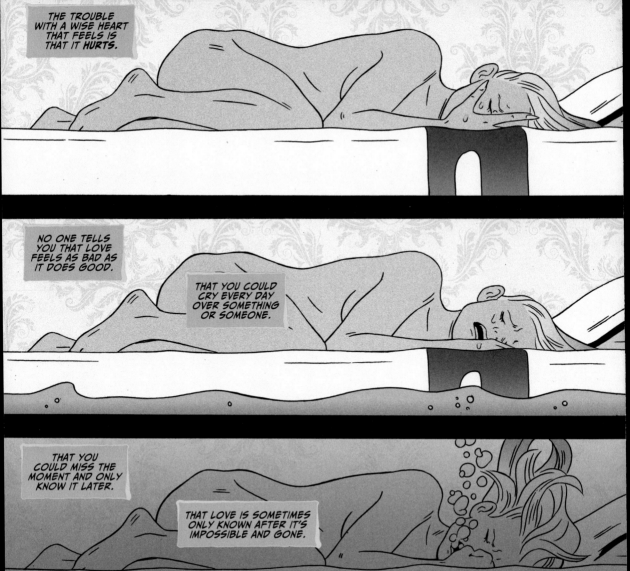

THE TROUBLE WITH A WISE HEART THAT FEELS IS THAT IT HURTS.

NO ONE TELLS YOU THAT LOVE FEELS AS BAD AS IT DOES GOOD.

THAT YOU COULD CRY EVERY DAY OVER SOMETHING OR SOMEONE.

THAT YOU COULD MISS THE MOMENT AND ONLY KNOW IT LATER.

THAT LOVE IS SOMETIMES ONLY KNOWN AFTER IT'S IMPOSSIBLE AND GONE.

I FUCKED UP. TIME TO START AGAIN.

I KNOW WHO TO TURN TO.

REMEMBER. TEACUP AND I ARE ALWAYS HERE IF YOU NEED US.

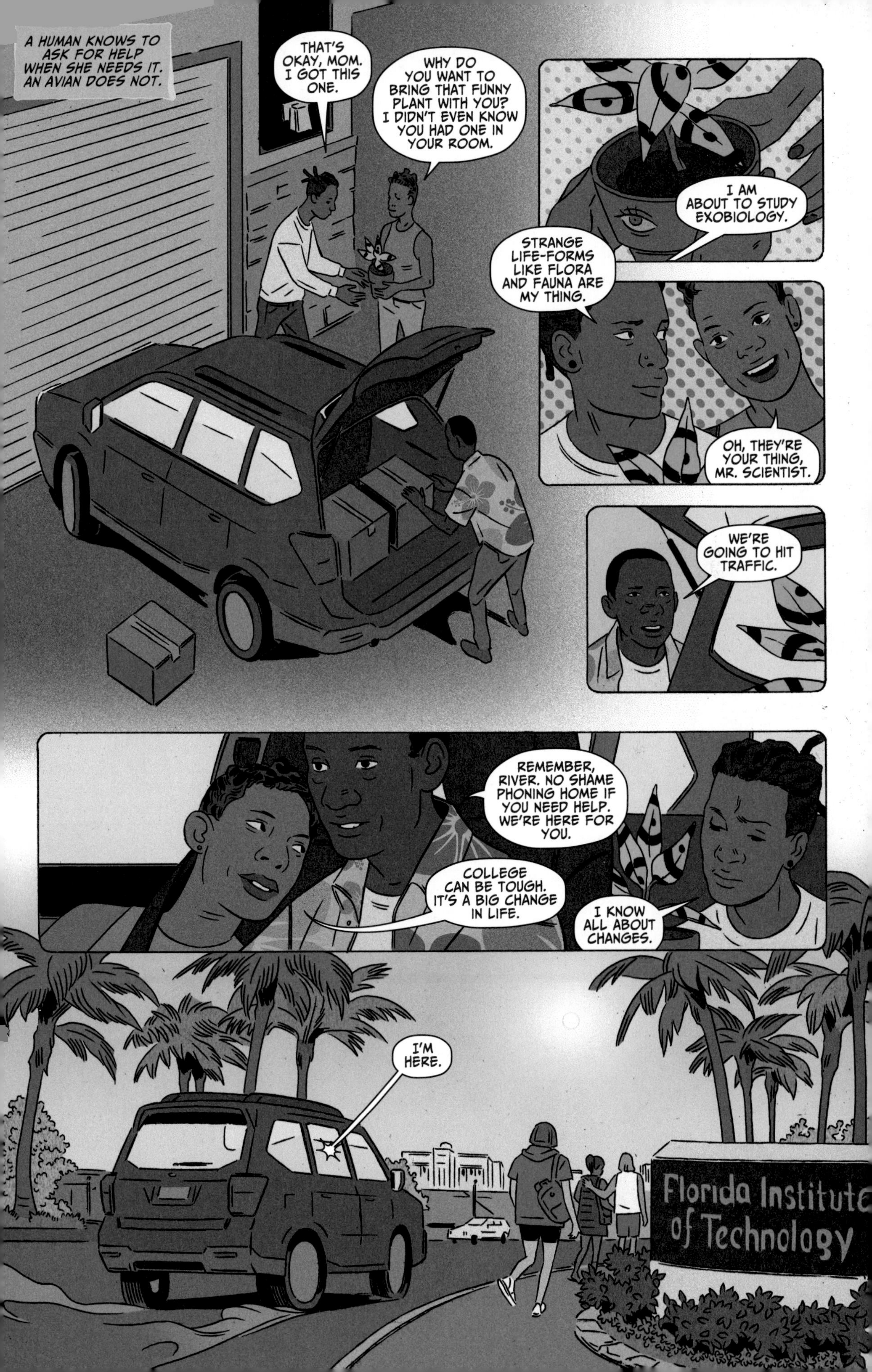
A HUMAN KNOWS TO ASK FOR HELP WHEN SHE NEEDS IT. AN AVIAN DOES NOT.
THAT'S OKAY, MOM. I GOT THIS ONE.
WHY DO YOU WANT TO BRING THAT FUNNY PLANT WITH YOU? I DIDN'T EVEN KNOW YOU HAD ONE IN YOUR ROOM.
I AM ABOUT TO STUDY EXOBIOLOGY.
STRANGE LIFE-FORMS LIKE FLORA AND FAUNA ARE MY THING.
OH, THEY'RE YOUR THING, MR. SCIENTIST.
WE'RE GOING TO HIT TRAFFIC.
REMEMBER, RIVER. NO SHAME PHONING HOME IF YOU NEED HELP. WE'RE HERE FOR YOU.
COLLEGE CAN BE TOUGH. IT'S A BIG CHANGE IN LIFE.
I KNOW ALL ABOUT CHANGES.
I'M HERE.
Florida Institute of Technology

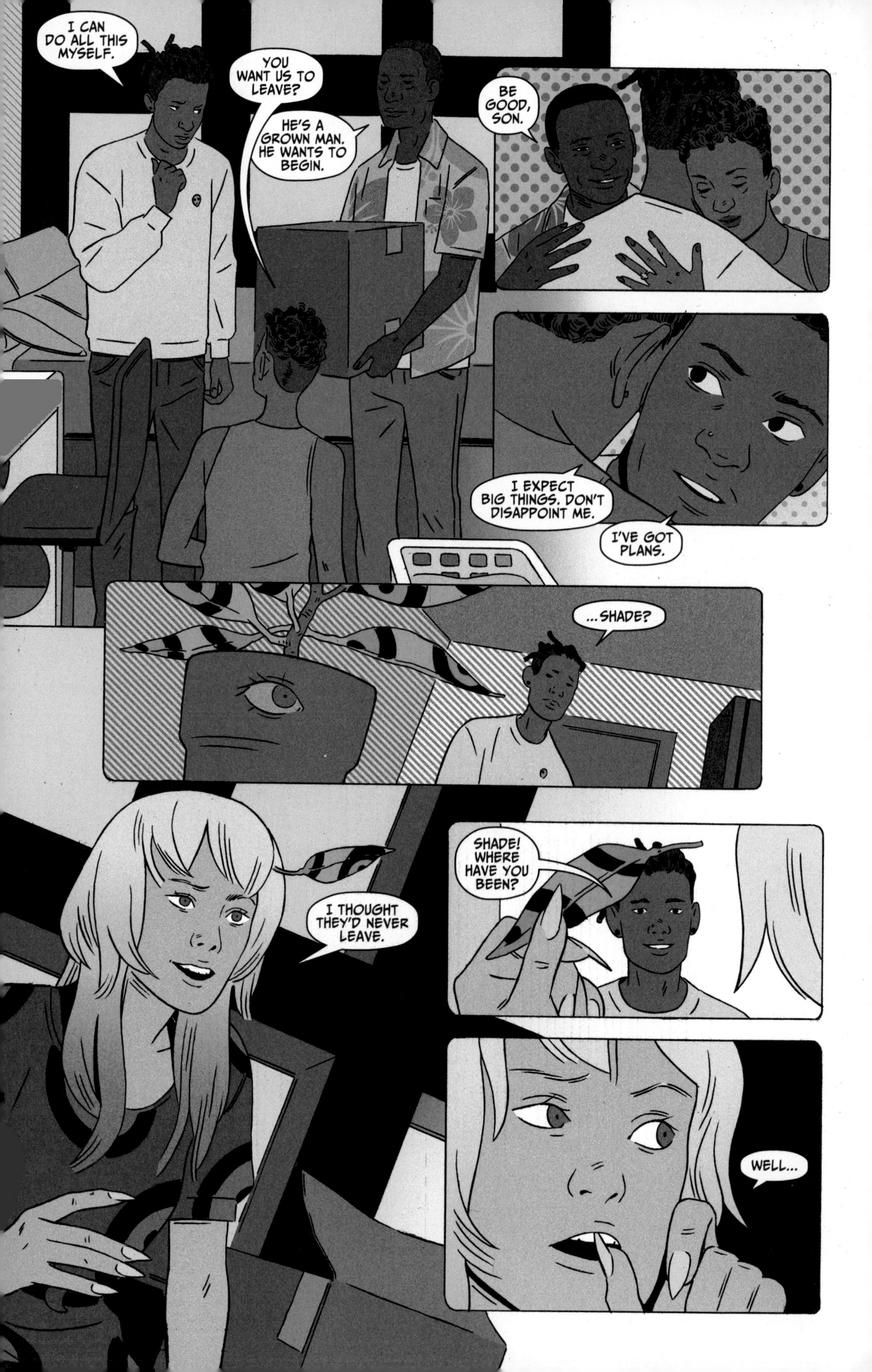
I CAN DO ALL THIS MYSELF.
YOU WANT US TO LEAVE?
HE'S A GROWN MAN. HE WANTS TO BEGIN.
BE GOOD, SON.
I EXPECT BIG THINGS. DON'T DISAPPOINT ME.
I'VE GOT PLANS.
...SHADE?
I THOUGHT THEY'D NEVER LEAVE.
SHADE! WHERE HAVE YOU BEEN?
WELL...

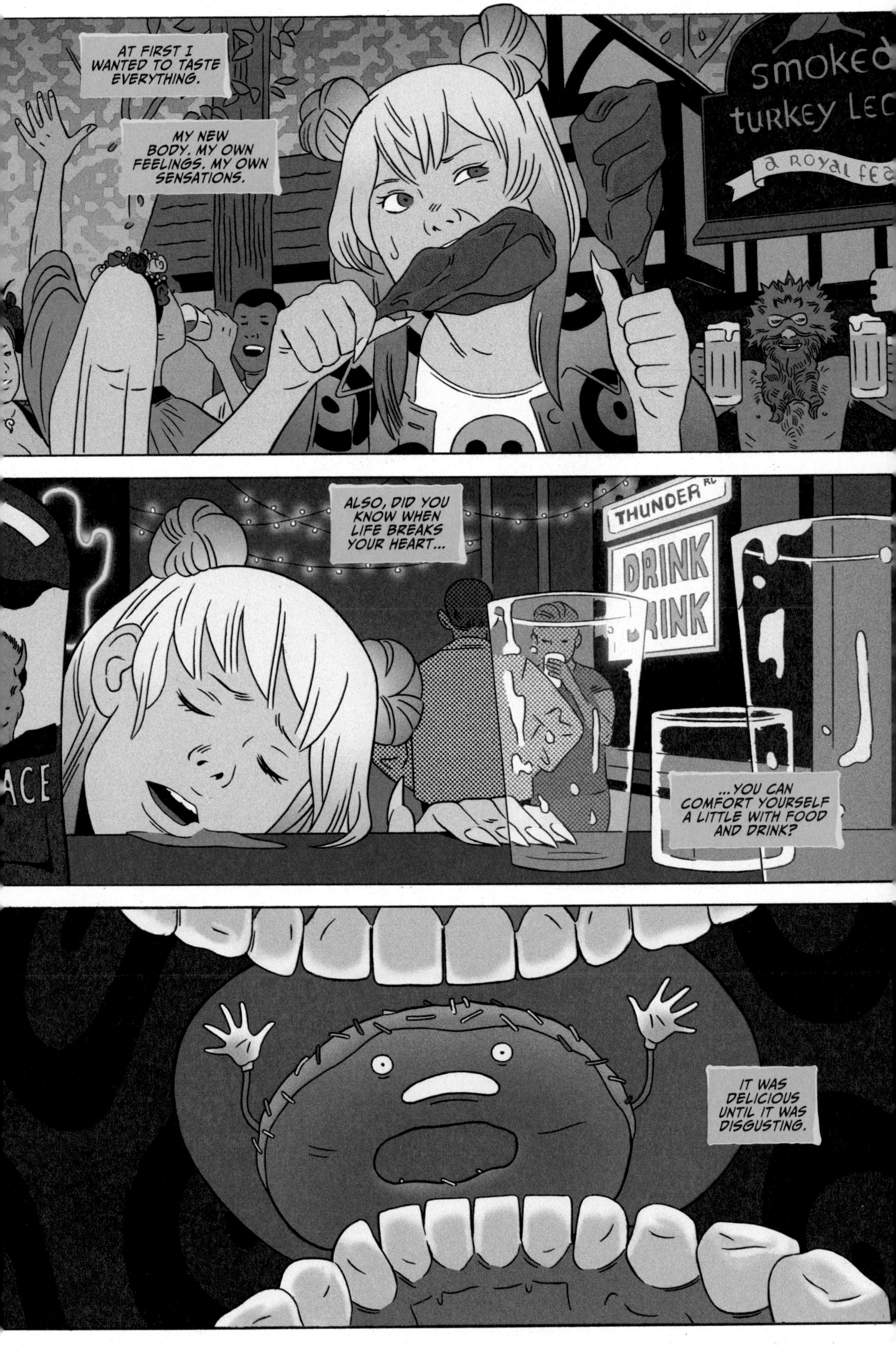
AT FIRST I WANTED TO TASTE EVERYTHING.
MY NEW BODY. MY OWN FEELINGS. MY OWN SENSATIONS.
smoked turkey leg
a royal fea
ALSO, DID YOU KNOW WHEN LIFE BREAKS YOUR HEART...
THUNDER
DRINK
...YOU CAN COMFORT YOURSELF A LITTLE WITH FOOD AND DRINK?
IT WAS DELICIOUS UNTIL IT WAS DISGUSTING.

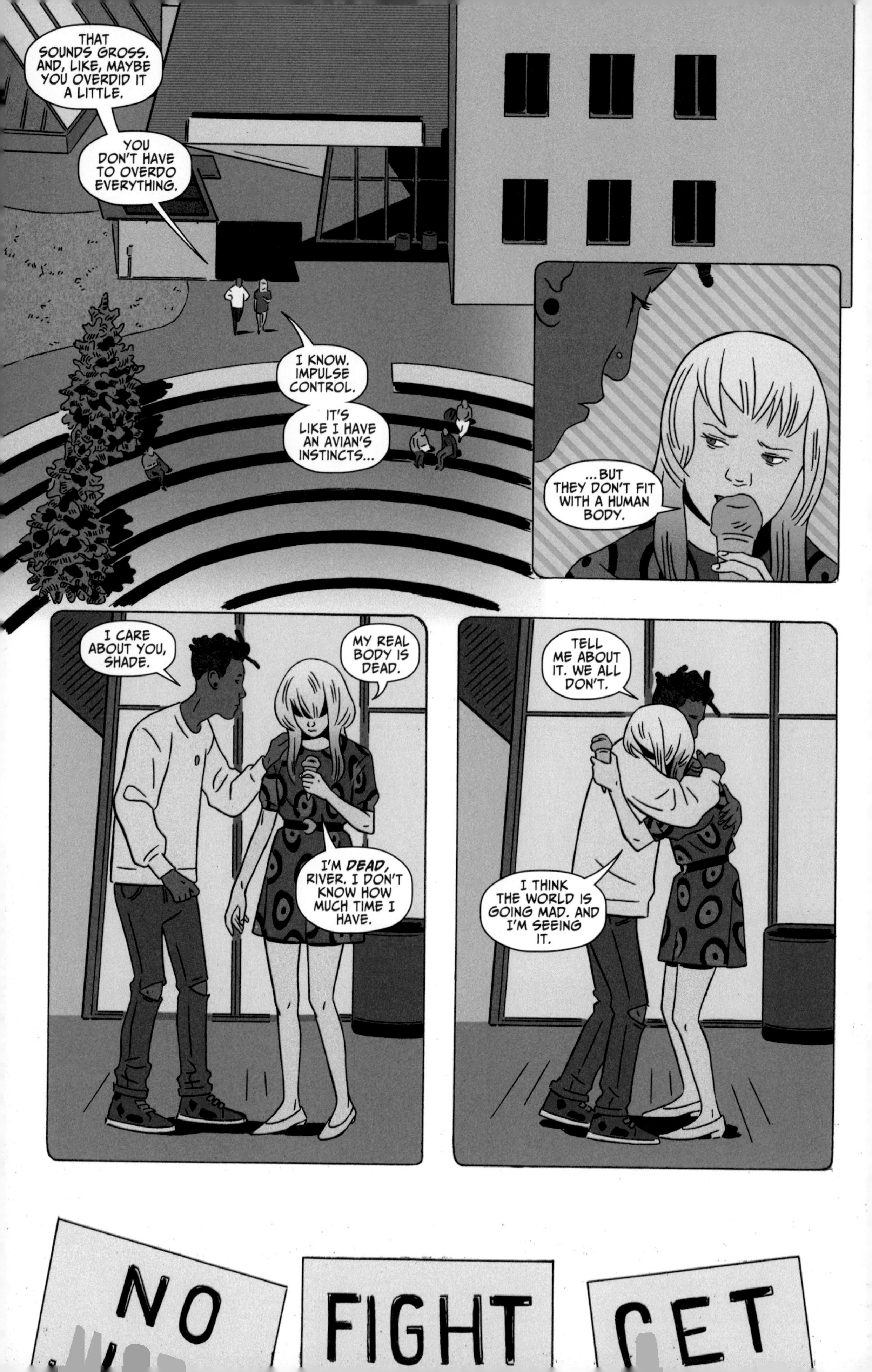
THAT SOUNDS GROSS. AND, LIKE, MAYBE YOU OVERDID IT A LITTLE.
YOU DON'T HAVE TO OVERDO EVERYTHING.
I KNOW. IMPULSE CONTROL.
IT'S LIKE I HAVE AN AVIAN'S INSTINCTS...
...BUT THEY DON'T FIT WITH A HUMAN BODY.
I CARE ABOUT YOU, SHADE.
MY REAL BODY IS DEAD.
I'M *DEAD*, RIVER. I DON'T KNOW HOW MUCH TIME I HAVE.
TELL ME ABOUT IT. WE ALL DON'T.
I THINK THE WORLD IS GOING MAD. AND I'M SEEING IT.
NO
FIGHT
GET

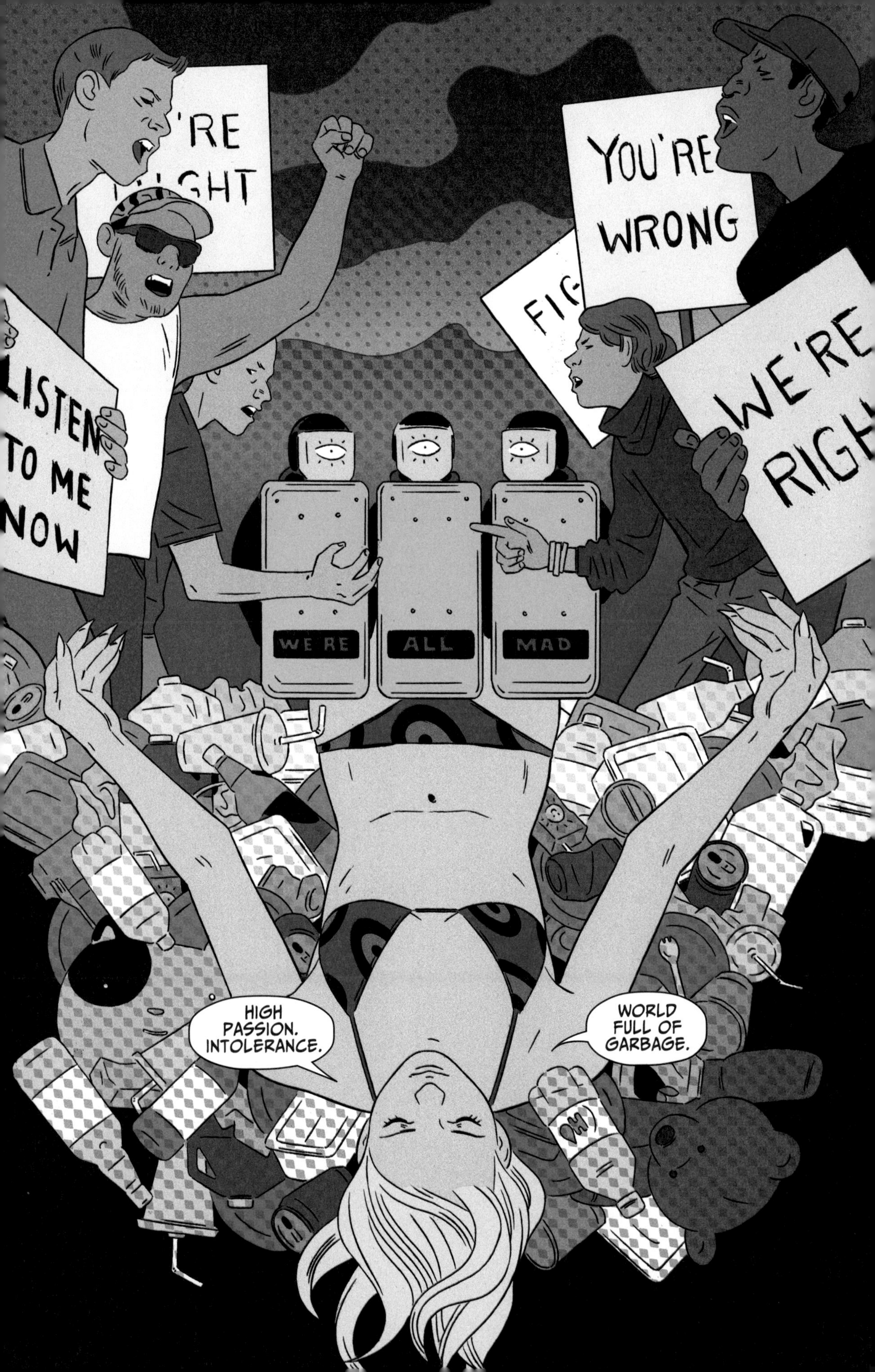
LISTEN TO ME NOW
YOU'RE WRONG
WE'RE
ALL
MAD
HIGH PASSION. INTOLERANCE.
WORLD FULL OF GARBAGE.

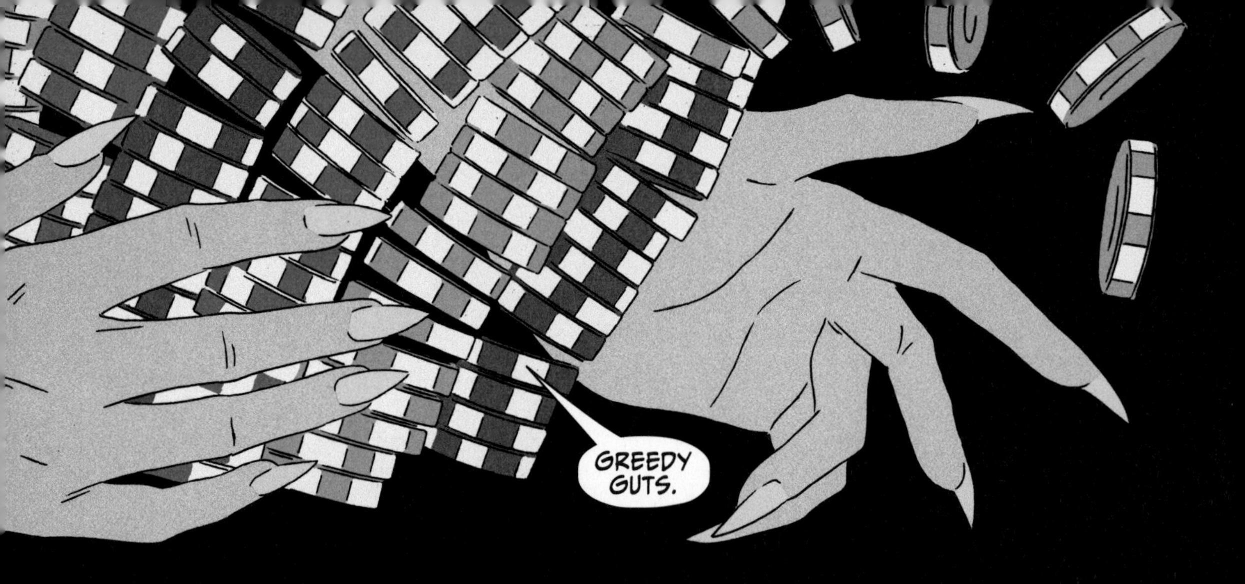
GREEDY GUTS.

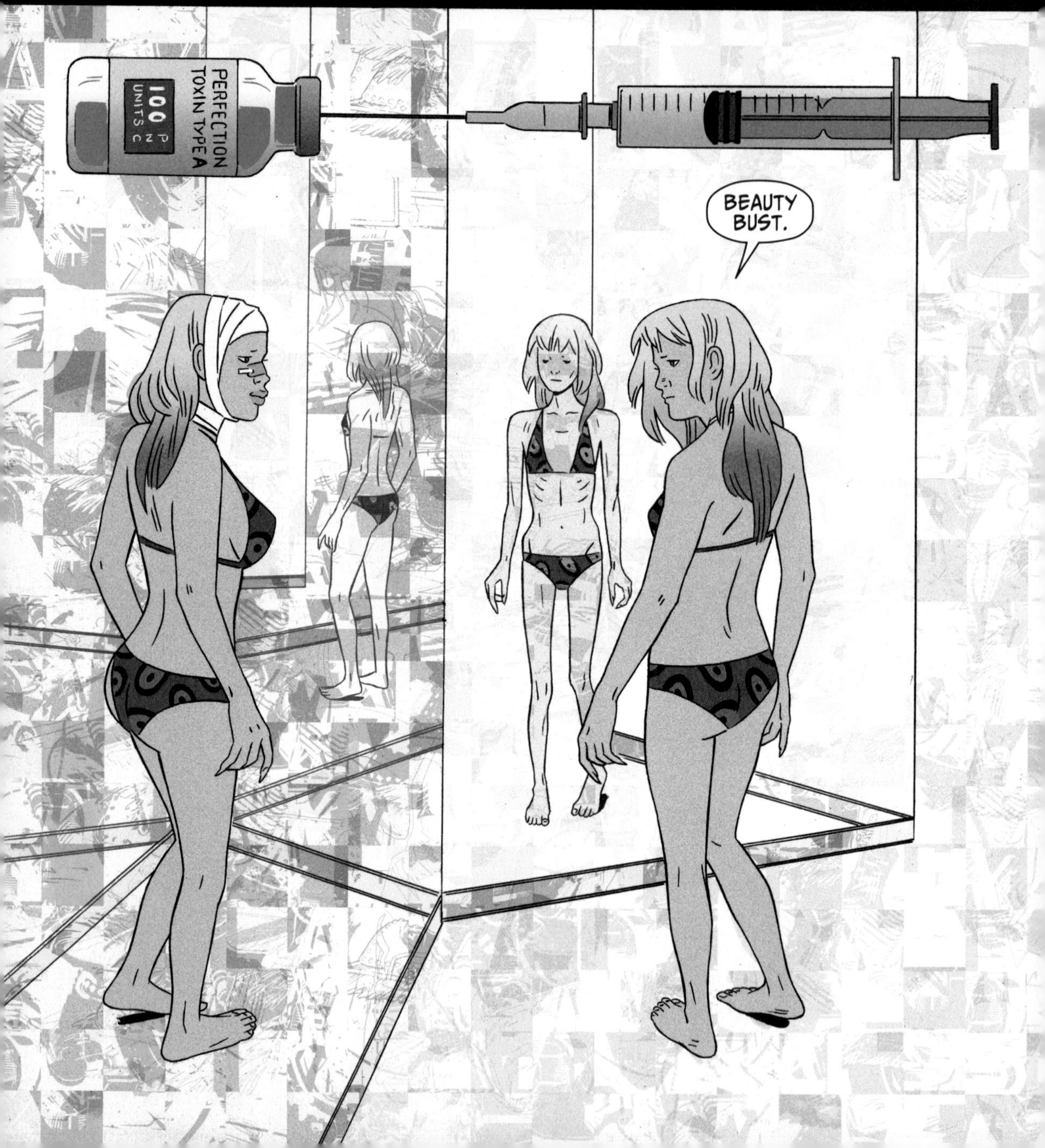
PERFECTION
TOXIN TYPE A
BEAUTY BUST.

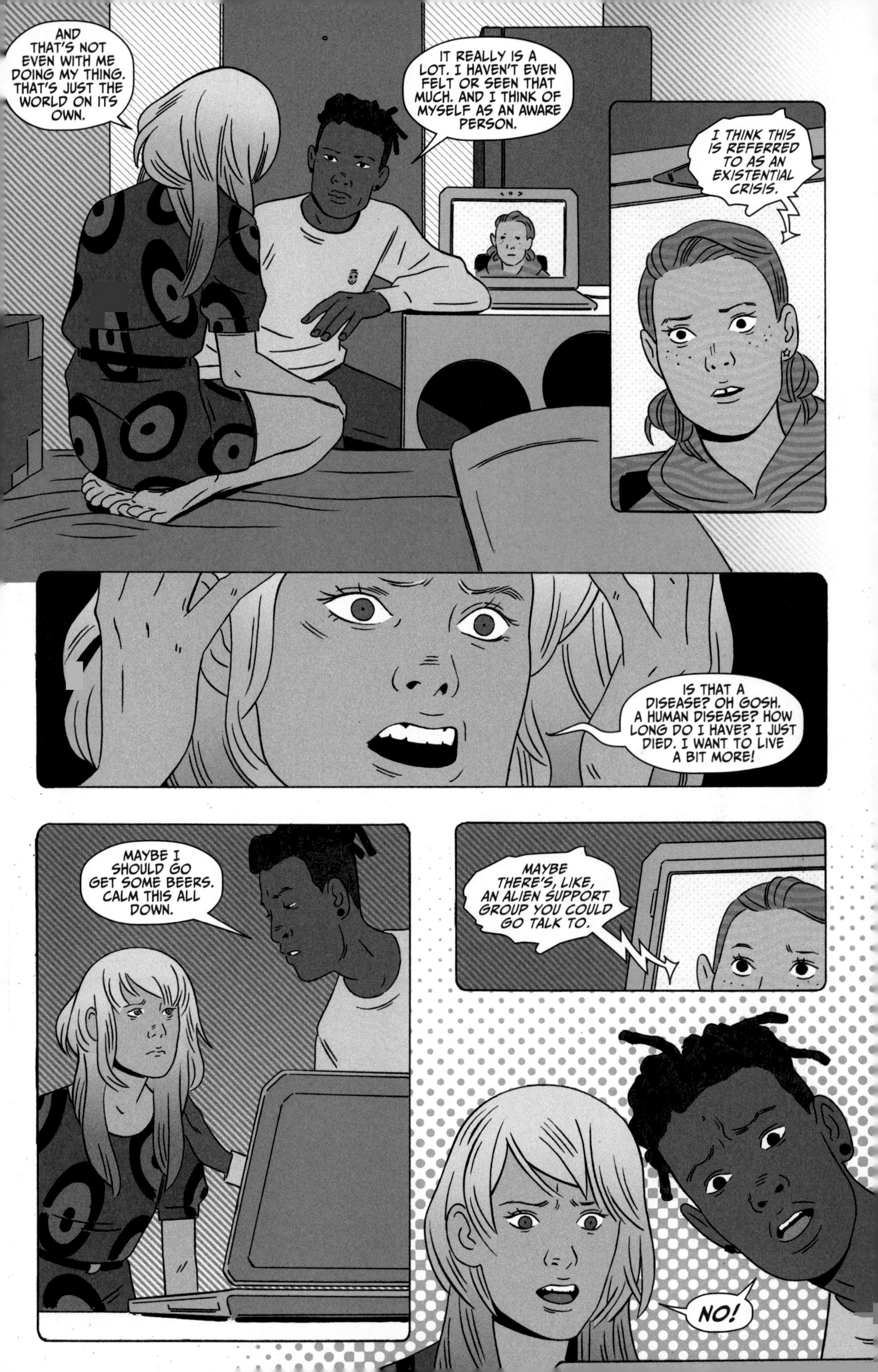
AND THAT'S NOT EVEN WITH ME DOING MY THING. THAT'S JUST THE WORLD ON ITS OWN.
IT REALLY IS A LOT. I HAVEN'T EVEN FELT OR SEEN THAT MUCH. AND I THINK OF MYSELF AS AN AWARE PERSON.
I THINK THIS IS REFERRED TO AS AN EXISTENTIAL CRISIS.
IS THAT A DISEASE? OH GOSH. A HUMAN DISEASE? HOW LONG DO I HAVE? I JUST DIED. I WANT TO LIVE A BIT MORE!
MAYBE I SHOULD GO GET SOME BEERS. CALM THIS ALL DOWN.
MAYBE THERE'S, LIKE, AN ALIEN SUPPORT GROUP YOU COULD GO TALK TO.
NO!

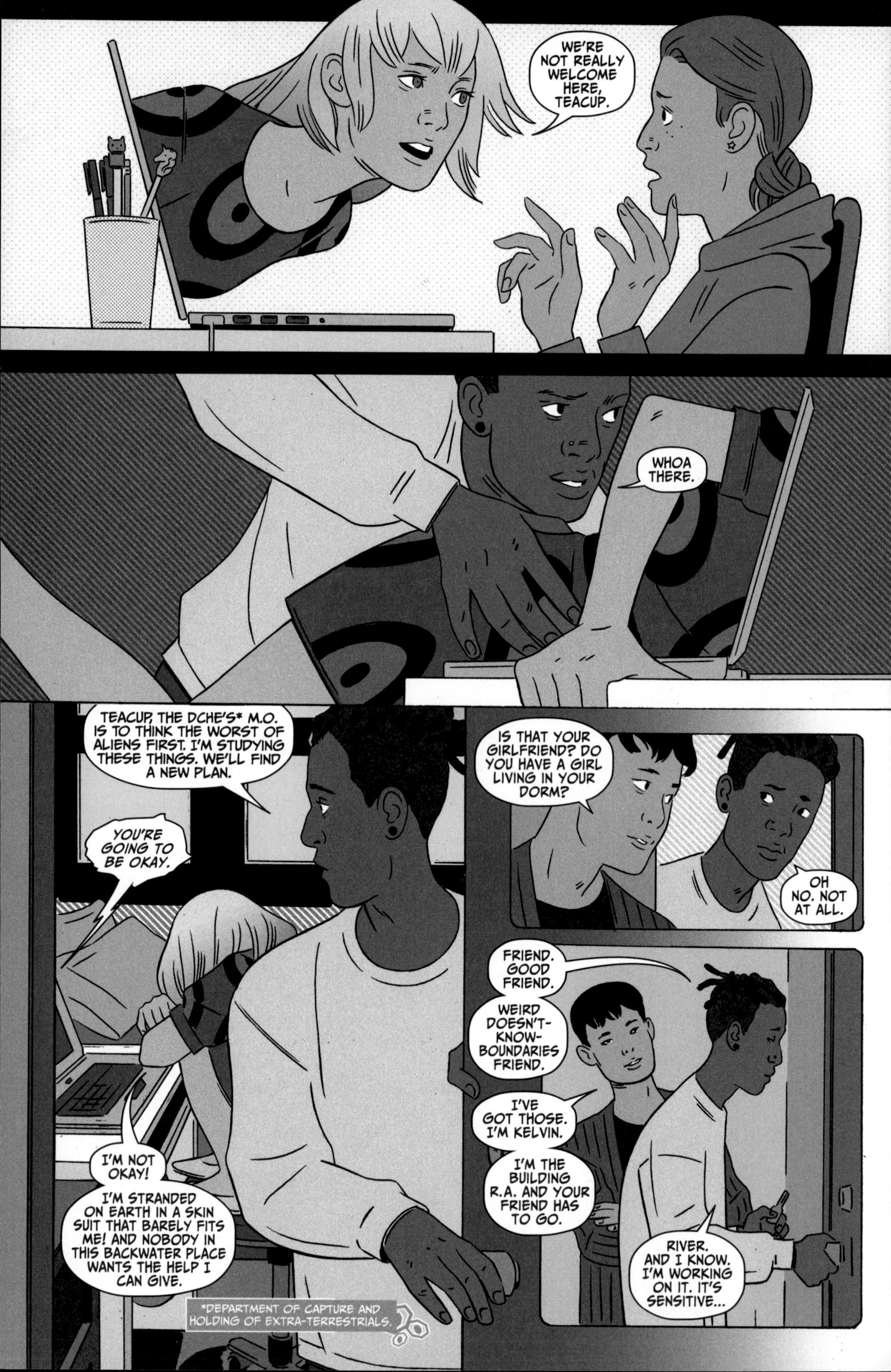
WE'RE NOT REALLY WELCOME HERE, TEACUP.
WHOA THERE.
TEACUP, THE DCHE'S* M.O. IS TO THINK THE WORST OF ALIENS FIRST. I'M STUDYING THESE THINGS. WE'LL FIND A NEW PLAN.
YOU'RE GOING TO BE OKAY.
I'M NOT OKAY!
I'M STRANDED ON EARTH IN A SKIN SUIT THAT BARELY FITS ME! AND NOBODY IN THIS BACKWATER PLACE WANTS THE HELP I CAN GIVE.
*DEPARTMENT OF CAPTURE AND HOLDING OF EXTRA-TERRESTRIALS.
IS THAT YOUR GIRLFRIEND? DO YOU HAVE A GIRL LIVING IN YOUR DORM?
OH NO. NOT AT ALL.
FRIEND. GOOD FRIEND.
WEIRD DOESN'T-KNOW-BOUNDARIES FRIEND.
I'VE GOT THOSE. I'M KELVIN.
I'M THE BUILDING R.A. AND YOUR FRIEND HAS TO GO.
RIVER. AND I KNOW. I'M WORKING ON IT. IT'S SENSITIVE...

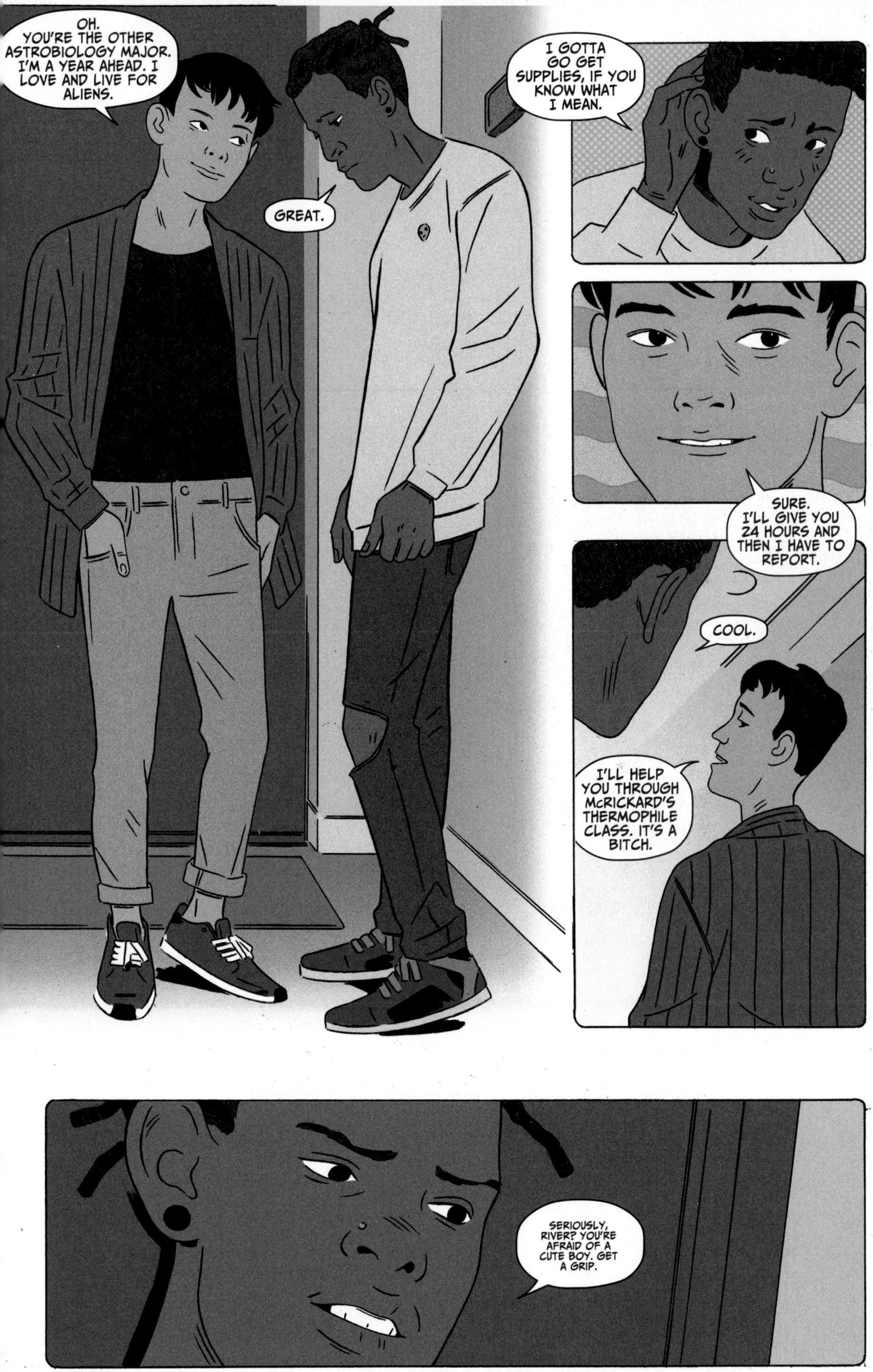
OH. YOU'RE THE OTHER ASTROBIOLOGY MAJOR. I'M A YEAR AHEAD. I LOVE AND LIVE FOR ALIENS.
GREAT.
I GOTTA GO GET SUPPLIES, IF YOU KNOW WHAT I MEAN.
SURE. I'LL GIVE YOU 24 HOURS AND THEN I HAVE TO REPORT.
COOL.
I'LL HELP YOU THROUGH McRICKARD'S THERMOPHILE CLASS. IT'S A BITCH.
SERIOUSLY, RIVER? YOU'RE AFRAID OF A CUTE BOY. GET A GRIP.

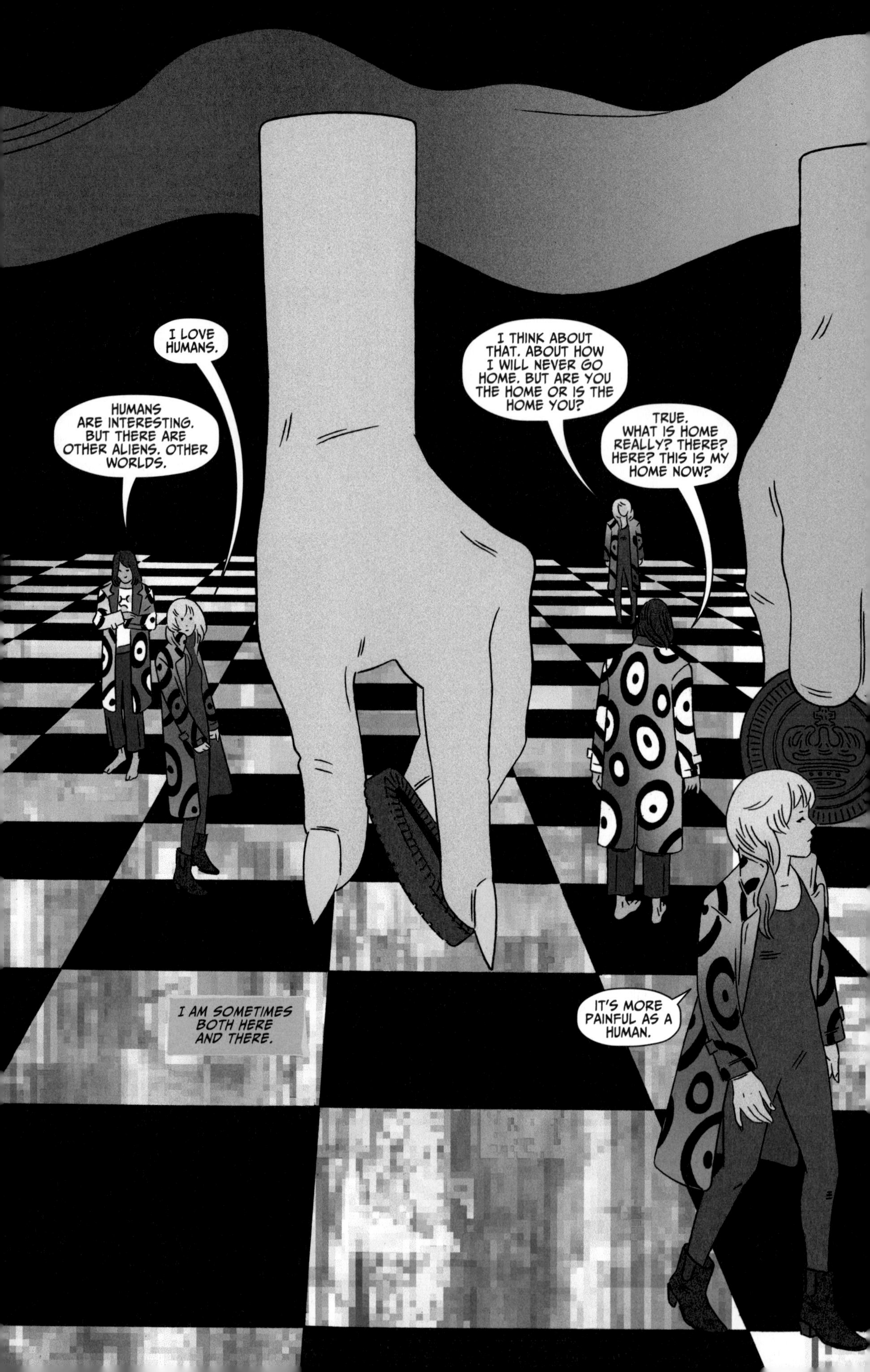
HUMANS ARE INTERESTING. BUT THERE ARE OTHER ALIENS. OTHER WORLDS.
I LOVE HUMANS.
I THINK ABOUT THAT. ABOUT HOW I WILL NEVER GO HOME. BUT ARE YOU THE HOME OR IS THE HOME YOU?
TRUE. WHAT IS HOME REALLY? THERE? HERE? THIS IS MY HOME NOW?
I AM SOMETIMES BOTH HERE AND THERE.
IT'S MORE PAINFUL AS A HUMAN.

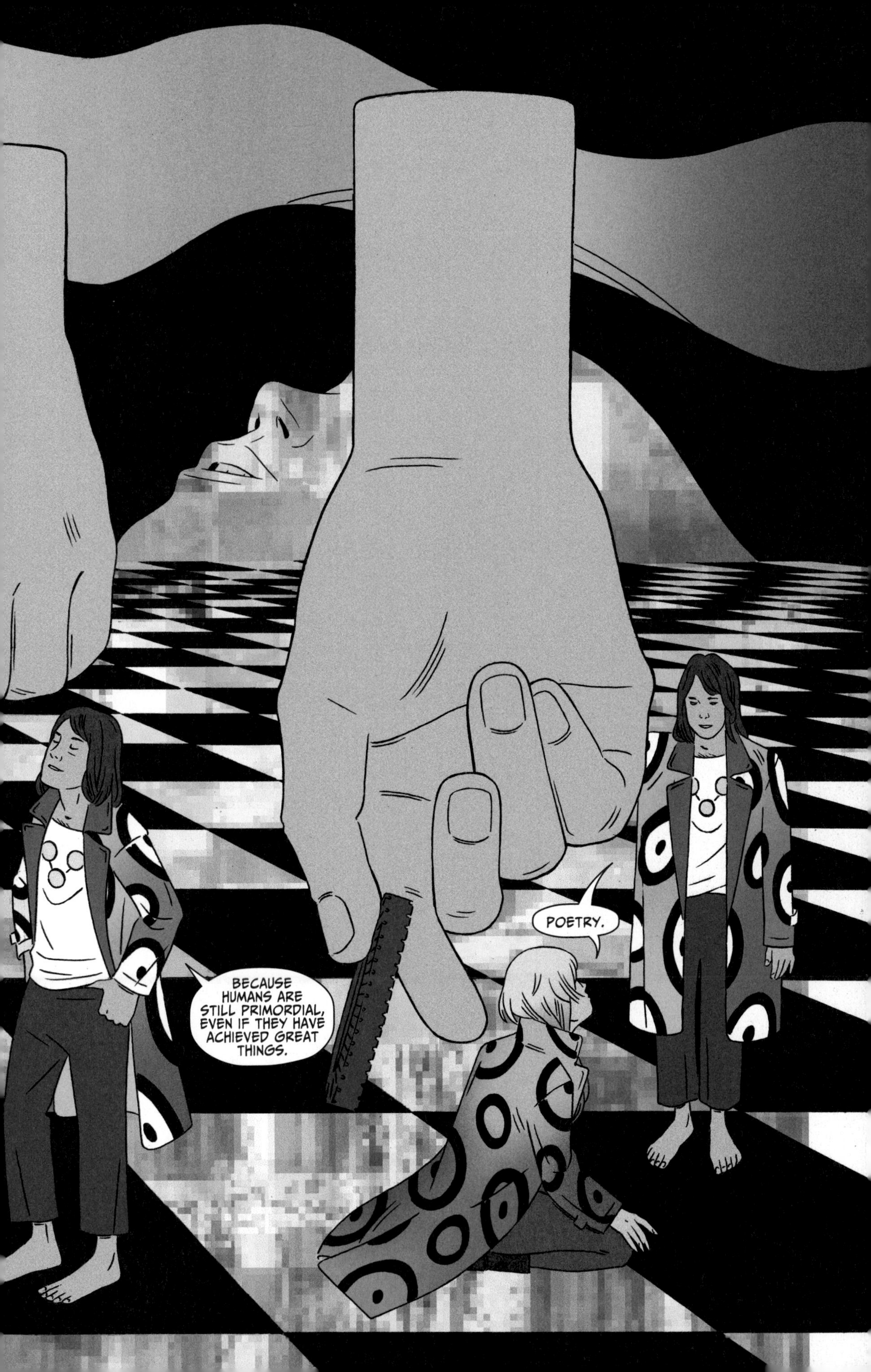
POETRY.
BECAUSE HUMANS ARE STILL PRIMORDIAL, EVEN IF THEY HAVE ACHIEVED GREAT THINGS.

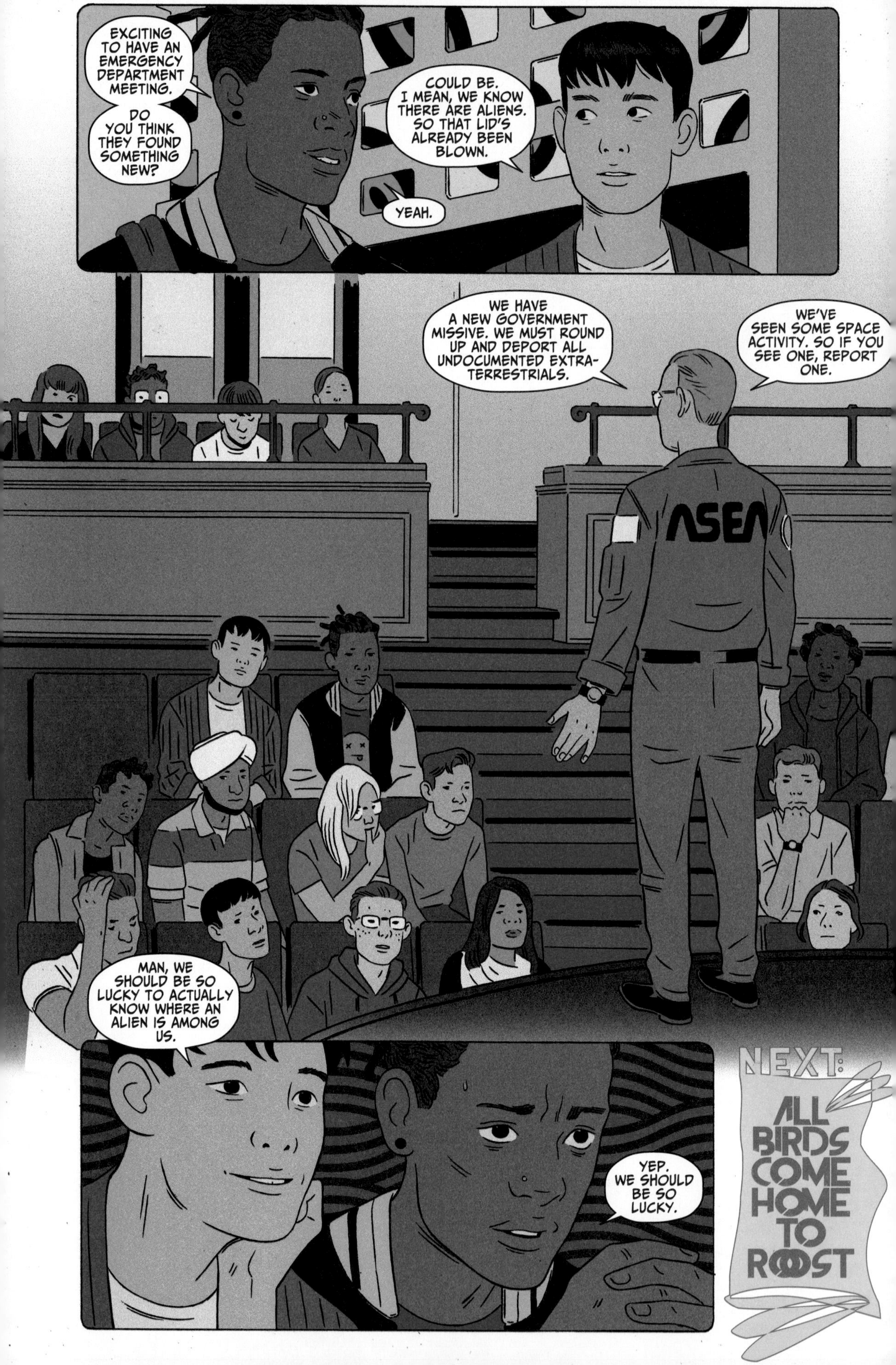
EXCITING TO HAVE AN EMERGENCY DEPARTMENT MEETING.
DO YOU THINK THEY FOUND SOMETHING NEW?
COULD BE. I MEAN, WE KNOW THERE ARE ALIENS. SO THAT LID'S ALREADY BEEN BLOWN.
YEAH.
WE HAVE A NEW GOVERNMENT MISSIVE. WE MUST ROUND UP AND DEPORT ALL UNDOCUMENTED EXTRA-TERRESTRIALS.
WE'VE SEEN SOME SPACE ACTIVITY. SO IF YOU SEE ONE, REPORT ONE.
ASEA
MAN, WE SHOULD BE SO LUCKY TO ACTUALLY KNOW WHERE AN ALIEN IS AMONG US.
YEP. WE SHOULD BE SO LUCKY.
NEXT:
ALL BIRDS COME HOME TO ROOST

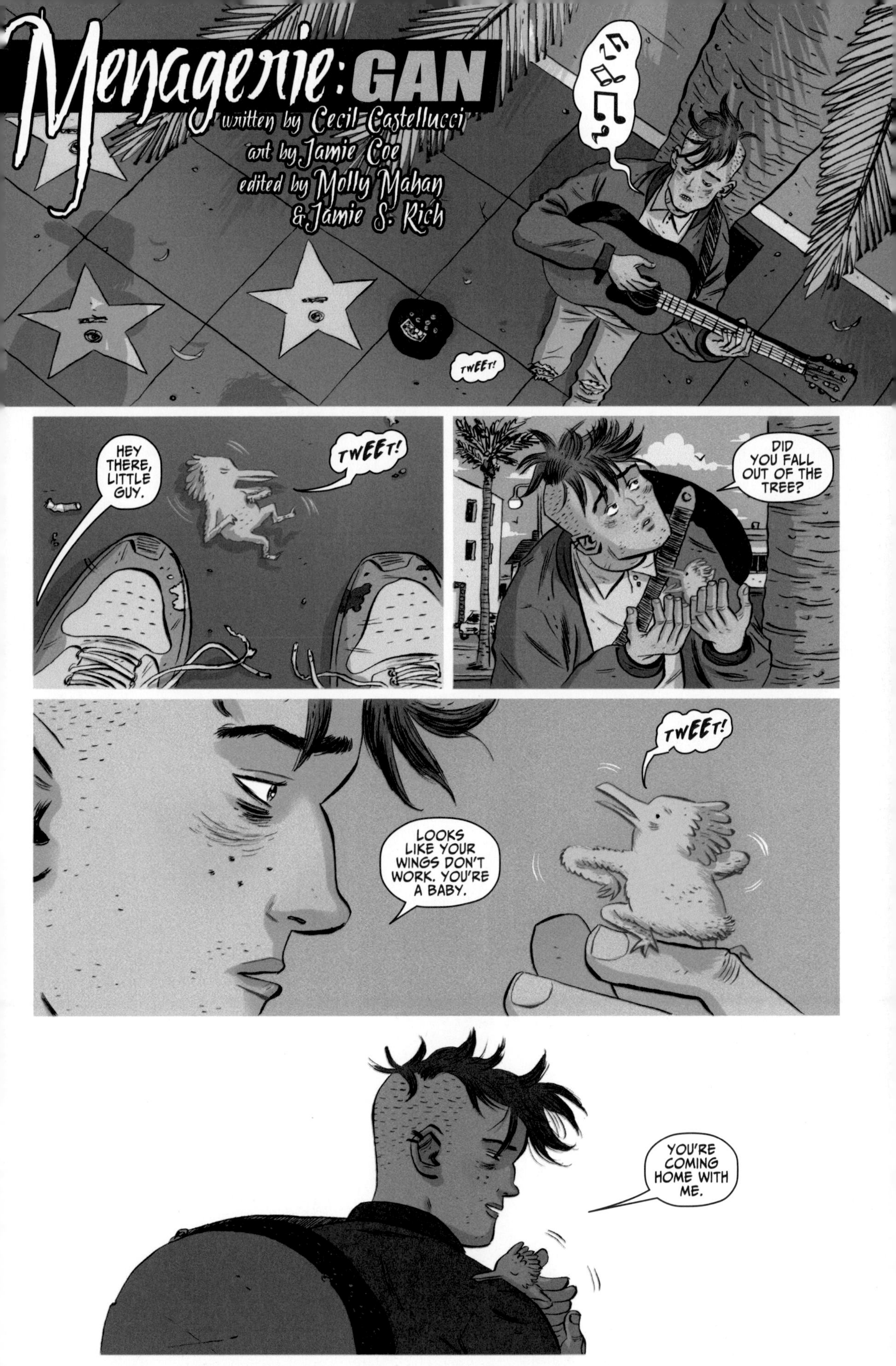
Menagerie: GAN
written by Cecil Castellucci
art by Jamie Coe
edited by Molly Mahan & Jamie S. Rich
TWEET!
HEY THERE, LITTLE GUY.
TWEET!
DID YOU FALL OUT OF THE TREE?
TWEET!
LOOKS LIKE YOUR WINGS DON'T WORK. YOU'RE A BABY.
YOU'RE COMING HOME WITH ME.

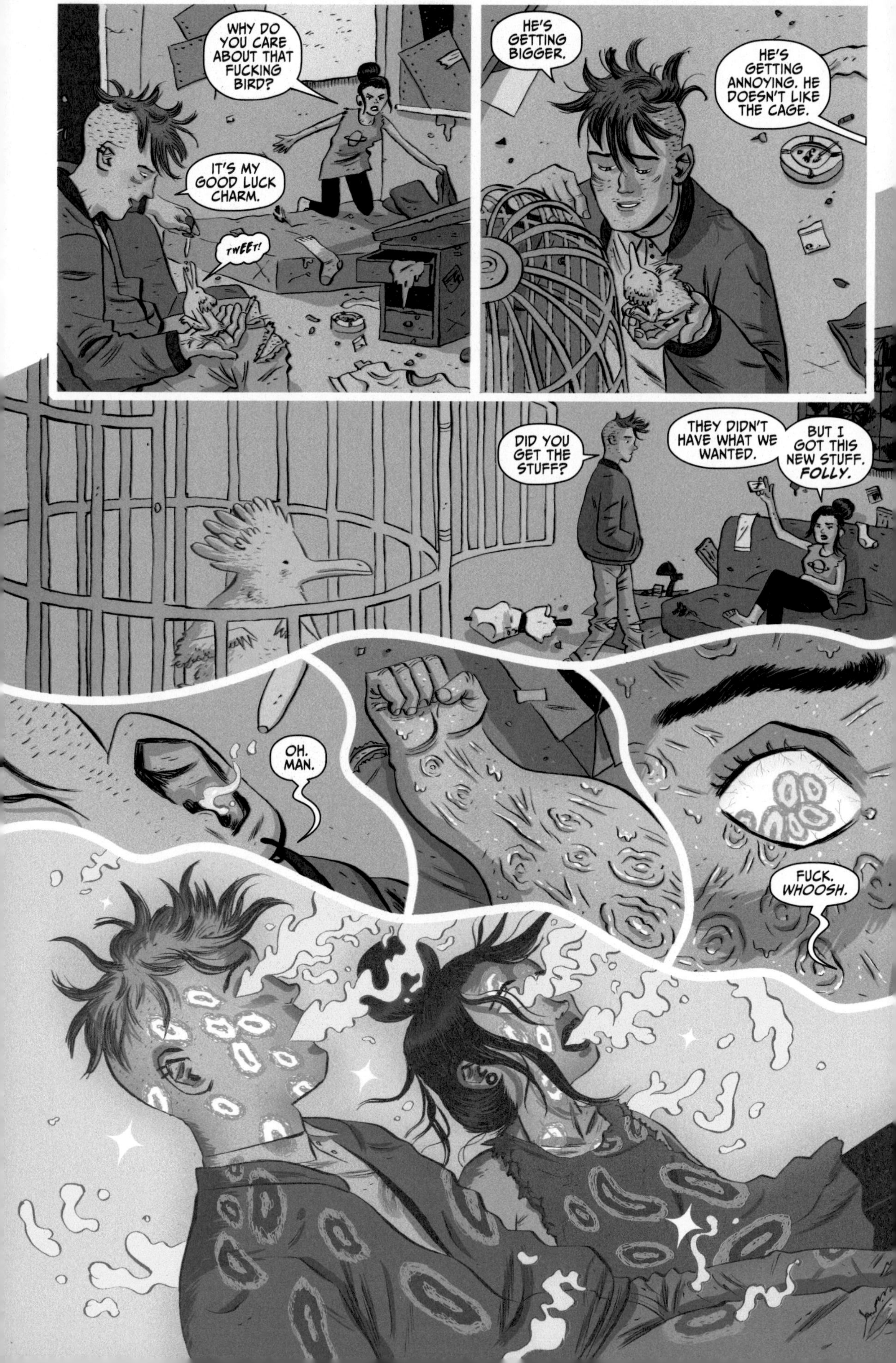
WHY DO YOU CARE ABOUT THAT FUCKING BIRD?
IT'S MY GOOD LUCK CHARM.
TWEET!
HE'S GETTING BIGGER.
HE'S GETTING ANNOYING. HE DOESN'T LIKE THE CAGE.
DID YOU GET THE STUFF?
THEY DIDN'T HAVE WHAT WE WANTED.
BUT I GOT THIS NEW STUFF. *FOLLY.*
OH. MAN.
FUCK. WHOOSH.

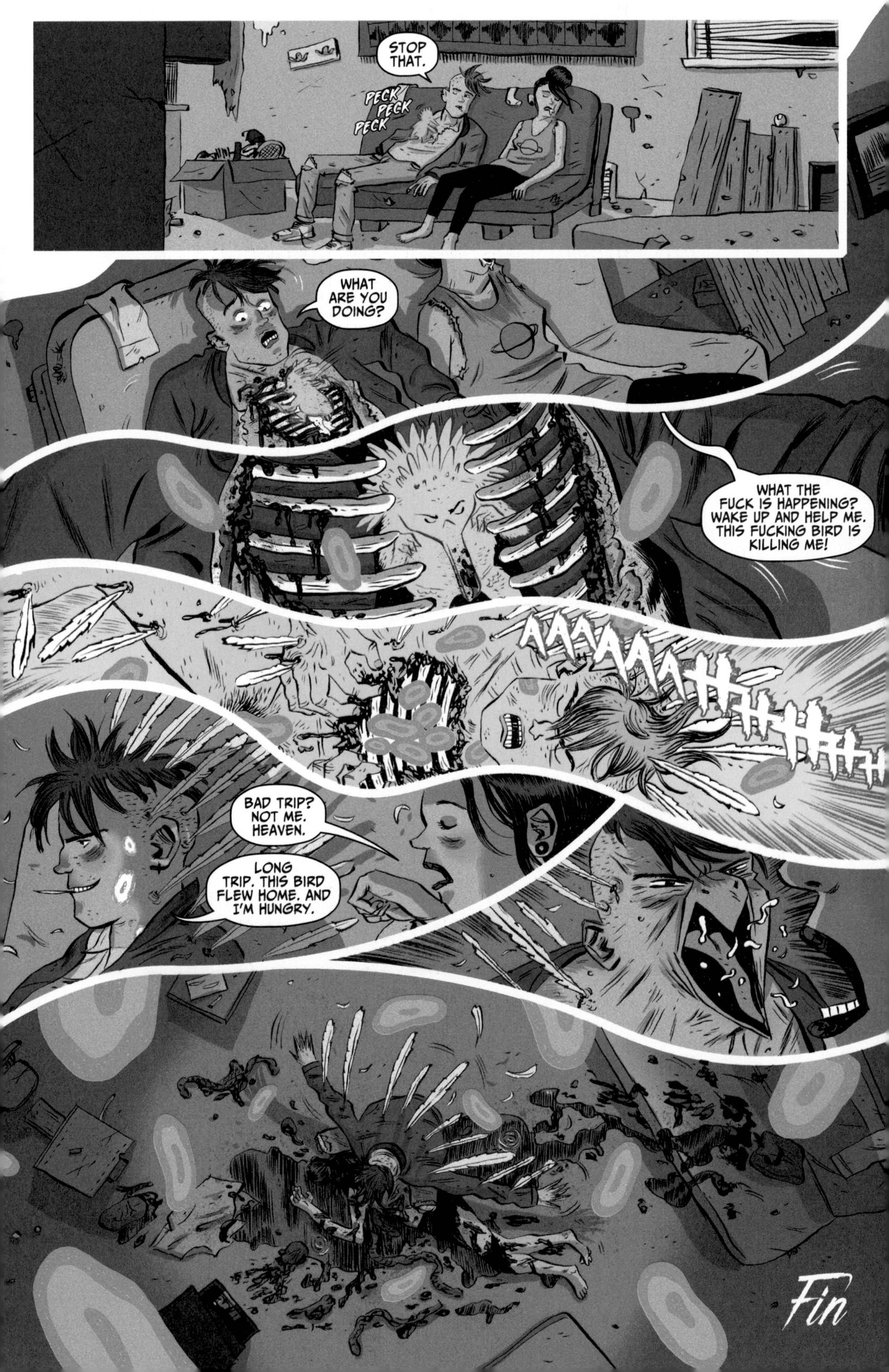
STOP THAT.
PECK PECK PECK
WHAT ARE YOU DOING?
WHAT THE FUCK IS HAPPENING? WAKE UP AND HELP ME. THIS FUCKING BIRD IS KILLING ME!
AAAAAAAHHHHHHH
BAD TRIP? NOT ME. HEAVEN.
LONG TRIP. THIS BIRD FLEW HOME. AND I'M HUNGRY.
Fin

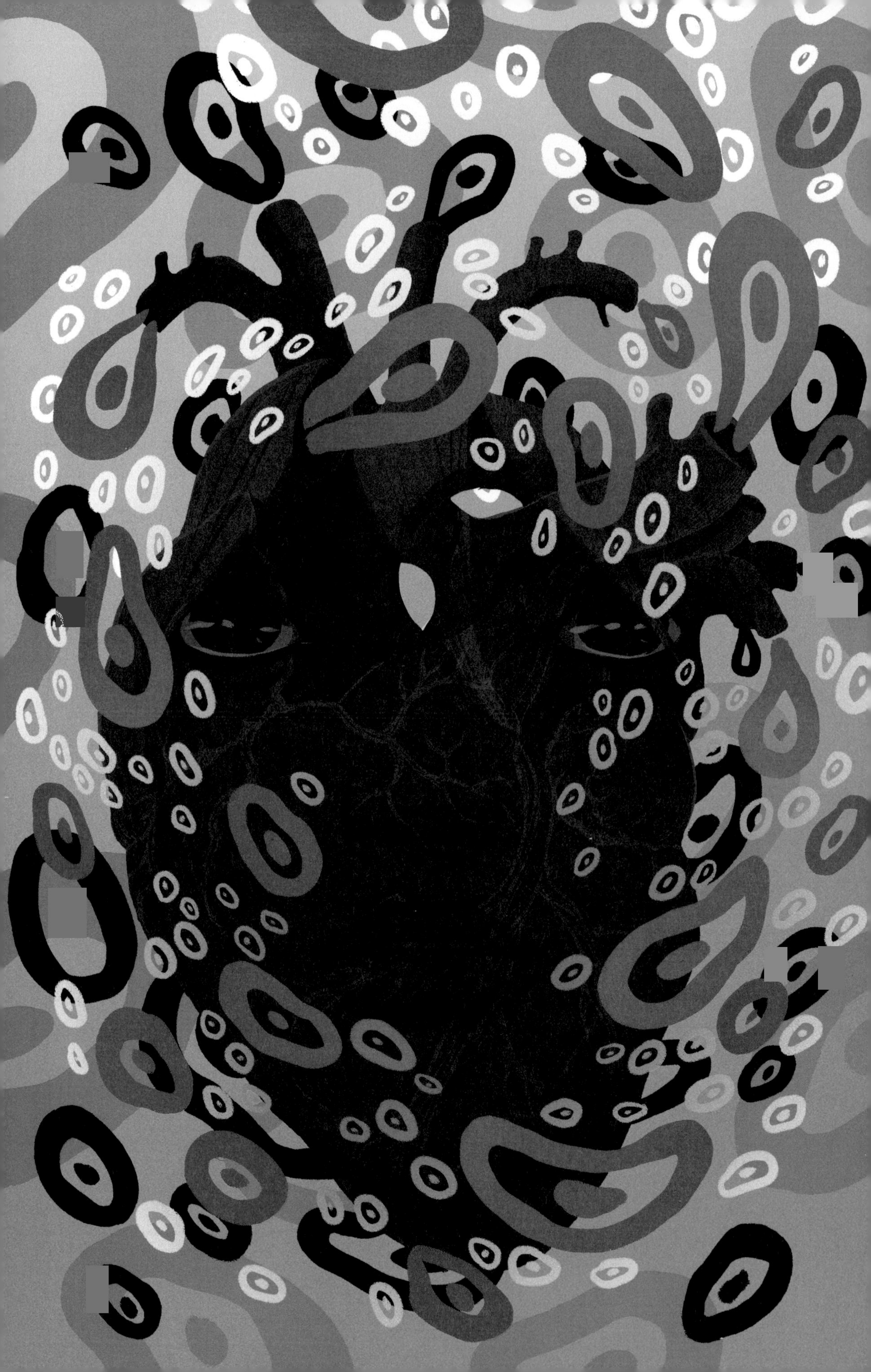

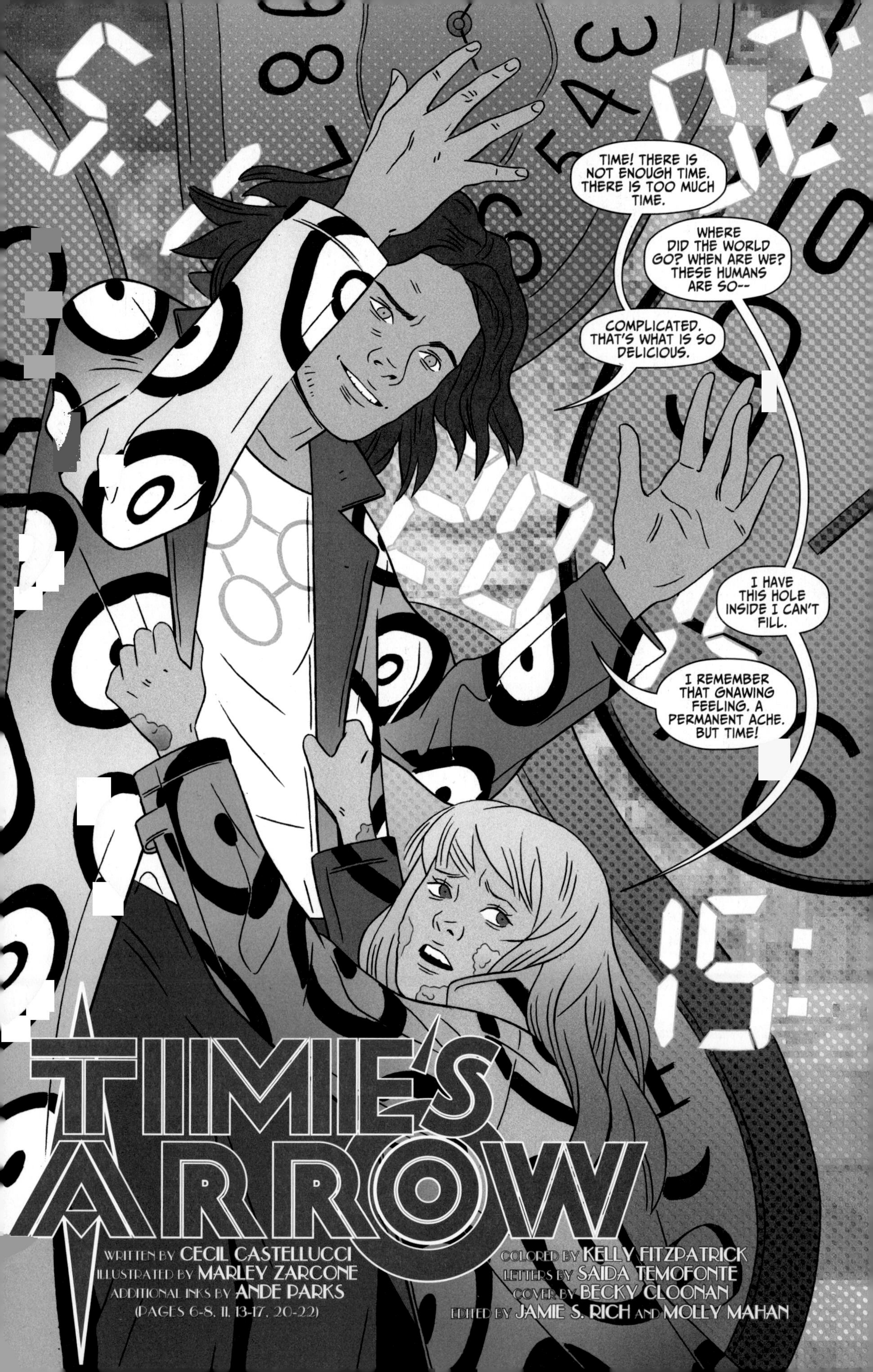

TIME! THERE IS NOT ENOUGH TIME. THERE IS TOO MUCH TIME.
WHERE DID THE WORLD GO? WHEN ARE WE? THESE HUMANS ARE SO--
COMPLICATED. THAT'S WHAT IS SO DELICIOUS.
I HAVE THIS HOLE INSIDE I CAN'T FILL.
I REMEMBER THAT GNAWING FEELING. A PERMANENT ACHE. BUT TIME!
TIME'S ARROW
WRITTEN BY CECIL CASTELLUCCI
ILLUSTRATED BY MARLEY ZARCONE
ADDITIONAL INKS BY ANDE PARKS
(PAGES 6-8, 11, 13-17, 20-22)
COLORED BY KELLY FITZPATRICK
LETTERS BY SAIDA TEMOFONTE
COVER BY BECKY CLOONAN
EDITED BY JAMIE S. RICH AND MOLLY MAHAN

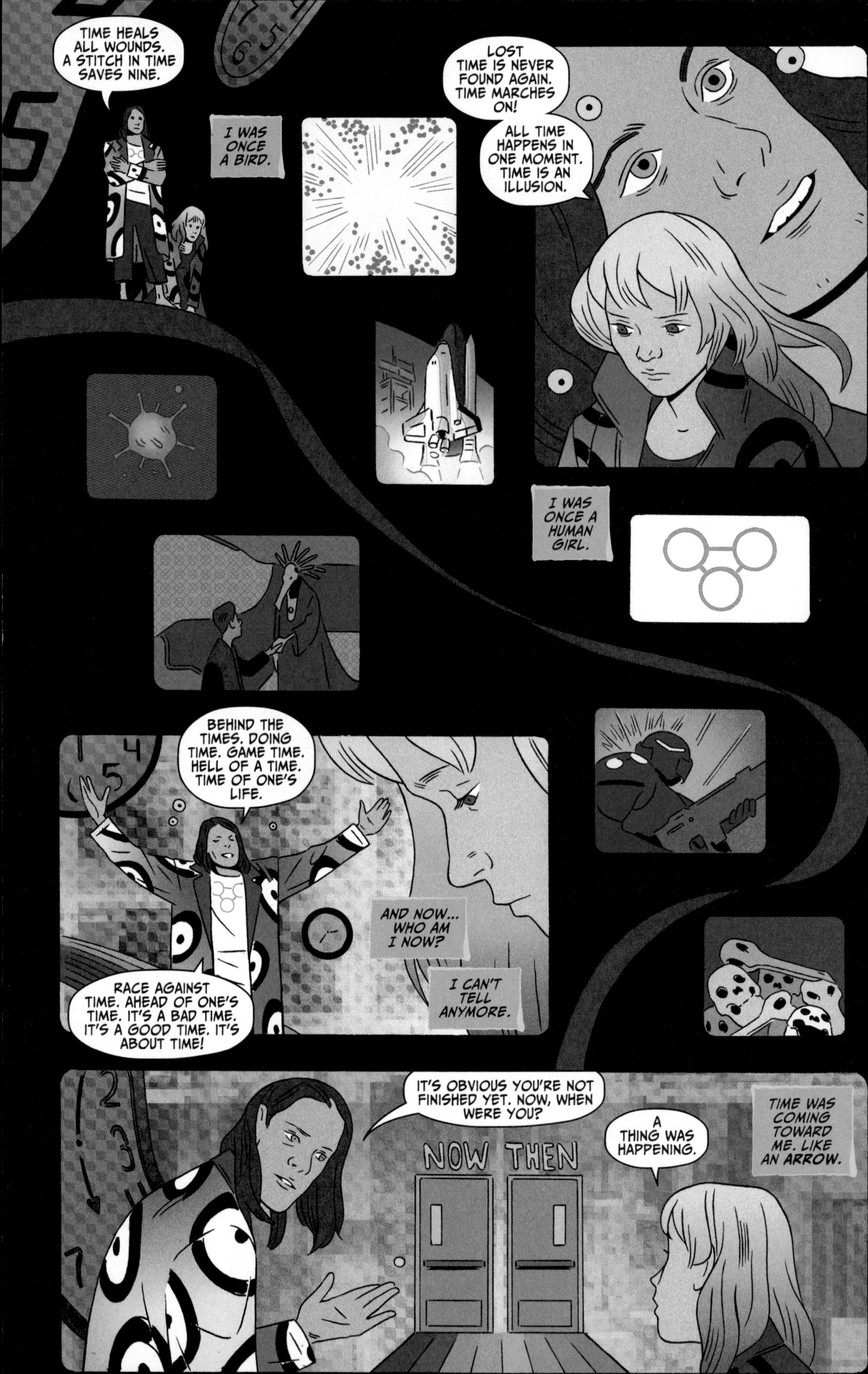
TIME HEALS ALL WOUNDS. A STITCH IN TIME SAVES NINE.
I WAS ONCE A BIRD.
LOST TIME IS NEVER FOUND AGAIN. TIME MARCHES ON!
ALL TIME HAPPENS IN ONE MOMENT. TIME IS AN ILLUSION.
I WAS ONCE A HUMAN GIRL.
BEHIND THE TIMES. DOING TIME. GAME TIME. HELL OF A TIME. TIME OF ONE'S LIFE.
RACE AGAINST TIME. AHEAD OF ONE'S TIME. IT'S A BAD TIME. IT'S A GOOD TIME. IT'S ABOUT TIME!
AND NOW... WHO AM I NOW?
I CAN'T TELL ANYMORE.
IT'S OBVIOUS YOU'RE NOT FINISHED YET. NOW, WHEN WERE YOU?
NOW THEN
A THING WAS HAPPENING.
TIME WAS COMING TOWARD ME. LIKE AN ARROW.

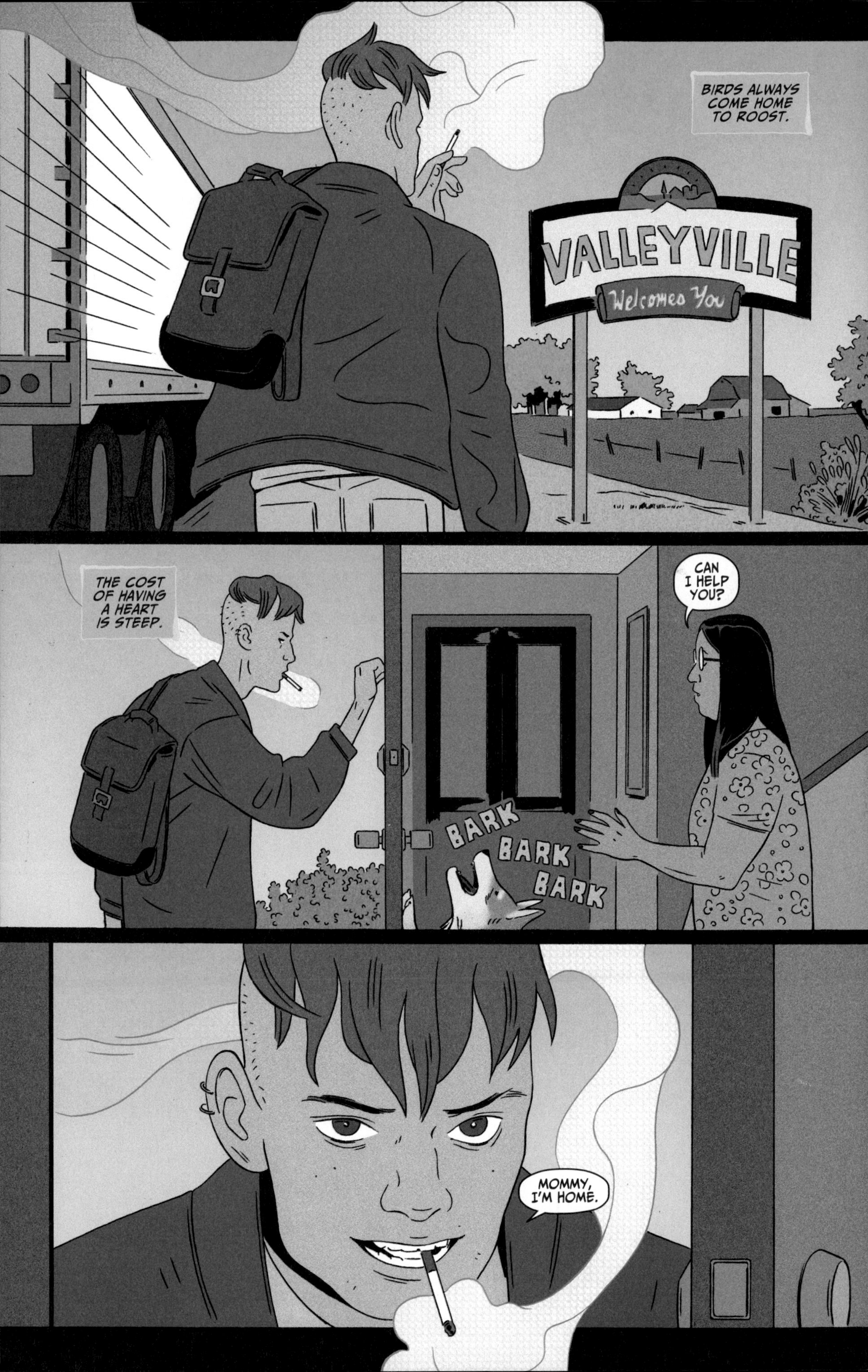
BIRDS ALWAYS COME HOME TO ROOST.
VALLEYVILLE
Welcomes You
THE COST OF HAVING A HEART IS STEEP.
CAN I HELP YOU?
BARK
BARK
BARK
MOMMY, I'M HOME.

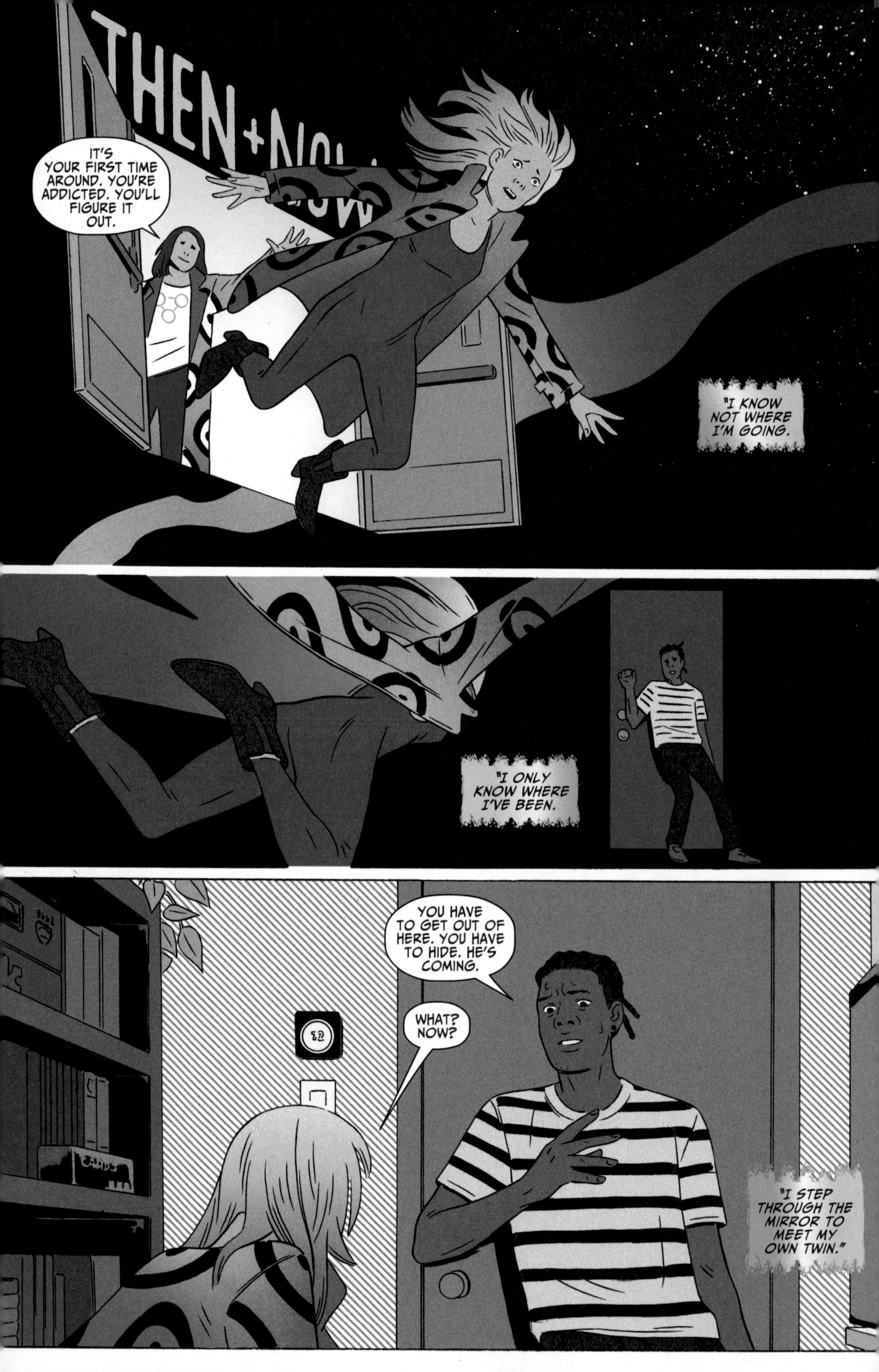
IT'S YOUR FIRST TIME AROUND. YOU'RE ADDICTED. YOU'LL FIGURE IT OUT.
"I KNOW NOT WHERE I'M GOING.
"I ONLY KNOW WHERE I'VE BEEN.
YOU HAVE TO GET OUT OF HERE. YOU HAVE TO HIDE. HE'S COMING.
WHAT? NOW?
"I STEP THROUGH THE MIRROR TO MEET MY OWN TWIN."

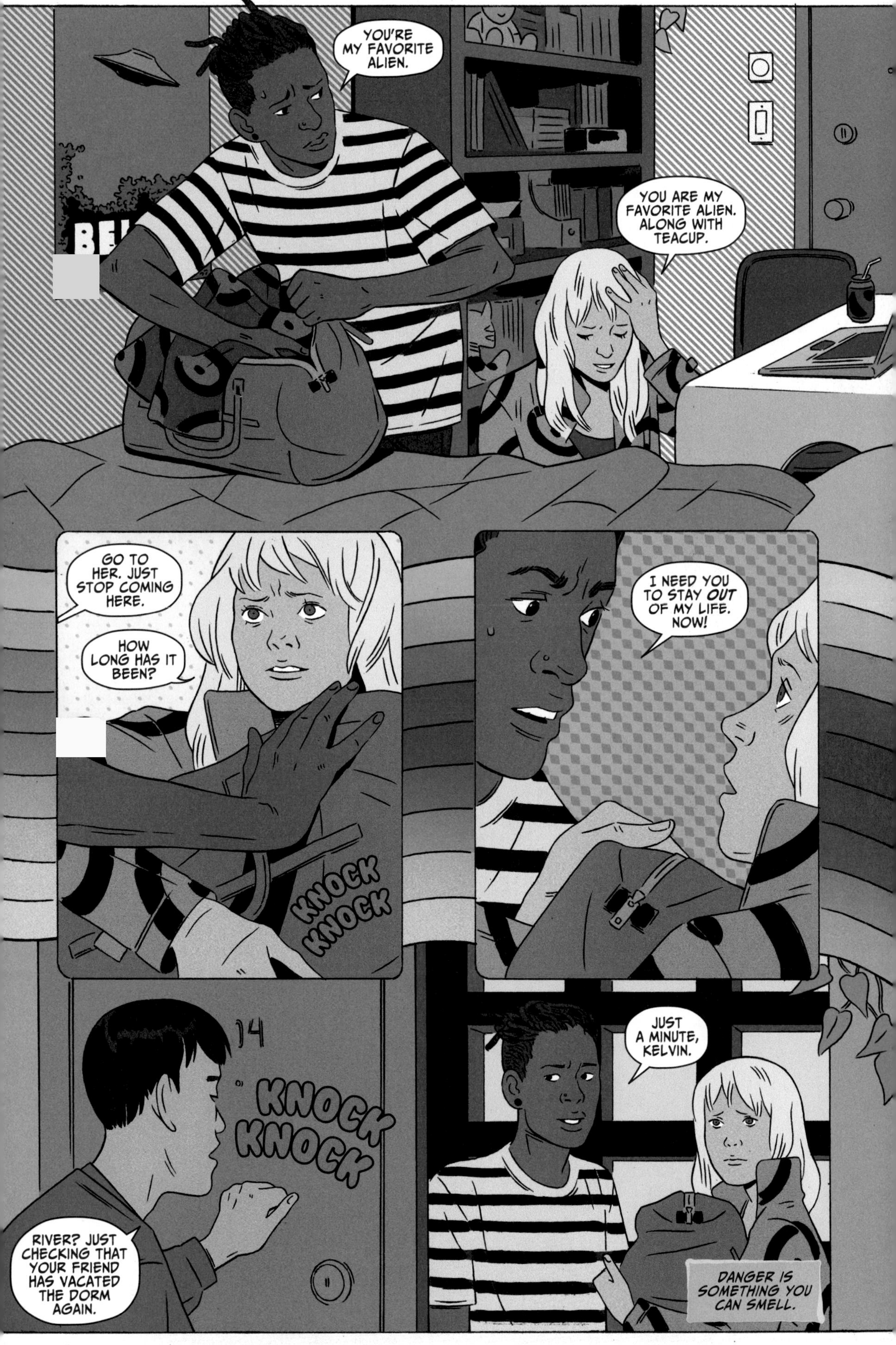

YOU'RE MY FAVORITE ALIEN.
YOU ARE MY FAVORITE ALIEN. ALONG WITH TEACUP.
GO TO HER. JUST STOP COMING HERE.
HOW LONG HAS IT BEEN?
KNOCK KNOCK
I NEED YOU TO STAY OUT OF MY LIFE. NOW!
14
KNOCK KNOCK
RIVER? JUST CHECKING THAT YOUR FRIEND HAS VACATED THE DORM AGAIN.
JUST A MINUTE, KELVIN.
DANGER IS SOMETHING YOU CAN SMELL.

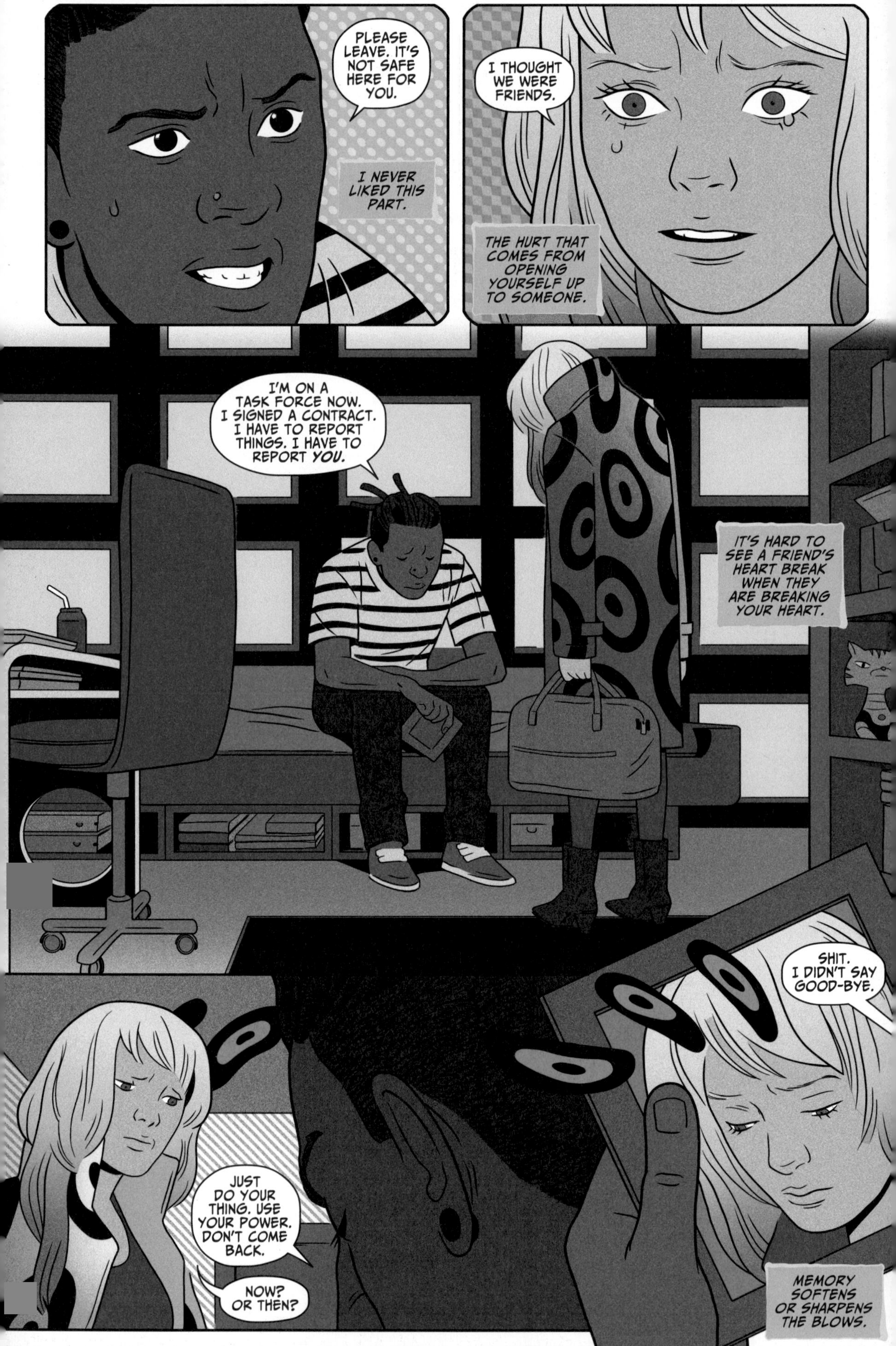
PLEASE LEAVE. IT'S NOT SAFE HERE FOR YOU.
I NEVER LIKED THIS PART.
I THOUGHT WE WERE FRIENDS.
THE HURT THAT COMES FROM OPENING YOURSELF UP TO SOMEONE.
I'M ON A TASK FORCE NOW. I SIGNED A CONTRACT. I HAVE TO REPORT THINGS. I HAVE TO REPORT *YOU.*
IT'S HARD TO SEE A FRIEND'S HEART BREAK WHEN THEY ARE BREAKING YOUR HEART.
JUST DO YOUR THING. USE YOUR POWER. DON'T COME BACK.
NOW? OR THEN?
SHIT. I DIDN'T SAY GOOD-BYE.
MEMORY SOFTENS OR SHARPENS THE BLOWS.

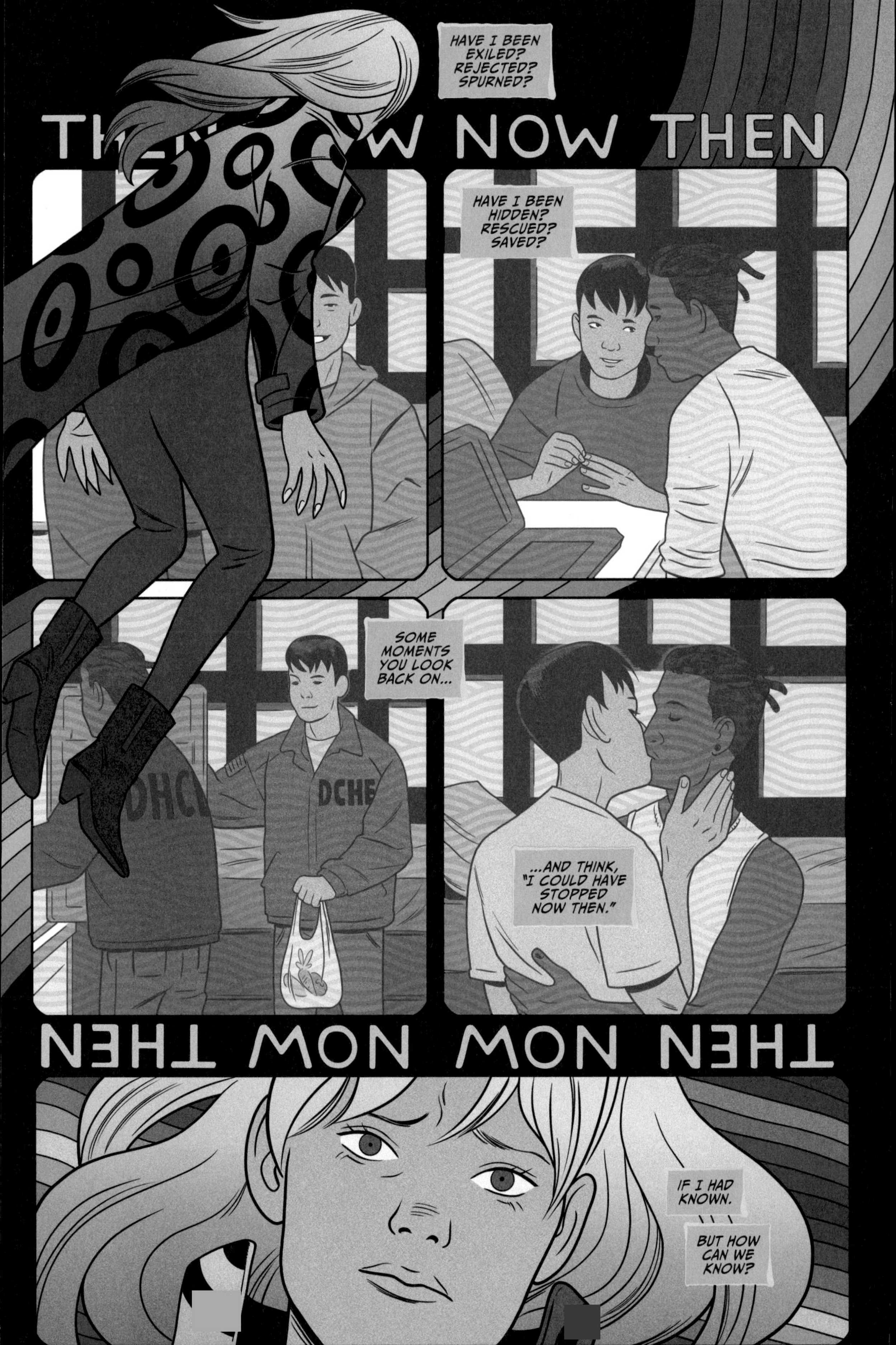
HAVE I BEEN EXILED? REJECTED? SPURNED?
NOW THEN
HAVE I BEEN HIDDEN? RESCUED? SAVED?
SOME MOMENTS YOU LOOK BACK ON...
DHCE
DCHE
...AND THINK, "I COULD HAVE STOPPED NOW THEN."
THEN NOW NOW THEN
IF I HAD KNOWN.
BUT HOW CAN WE KNOW?

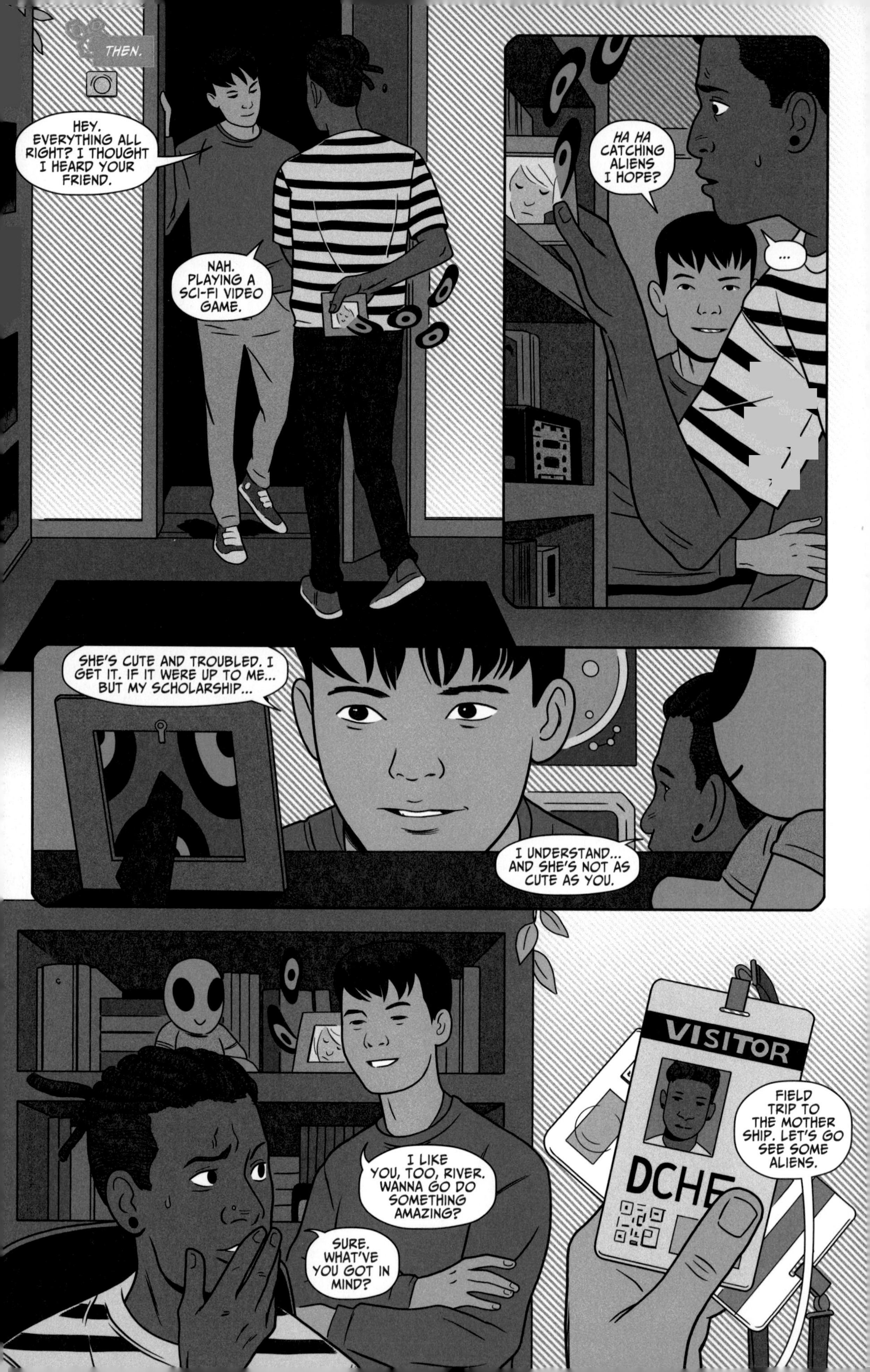
THEN.
HEY. EVERYTHING ALL RIGHT? I THOUGHT I HEARD YOUR FRIEND.
NAH. PLAYING A SCI-FI VIDEO GAME.
HA HA CATCHING ALIENS I HOPE?
...
SHE'S CUTE AND TROUBLED. I GET IT. IF IT WERE UP TO ME... BUT MY SCHOLARSHIP...
I UNDERSTAND... AND SHE'S NOT AS CUTE AS YOU.
I LIKE YOU, TOO, RIVER. WANNA GO DO SOMETHING AMAZING?
SURE. WHAT'VE YOU GOT IN MIND?
VISITOR
DCHE
FIELD TRIP TO THE MOTHER SHIP. LET'S GO SEE SOME ALIENS.

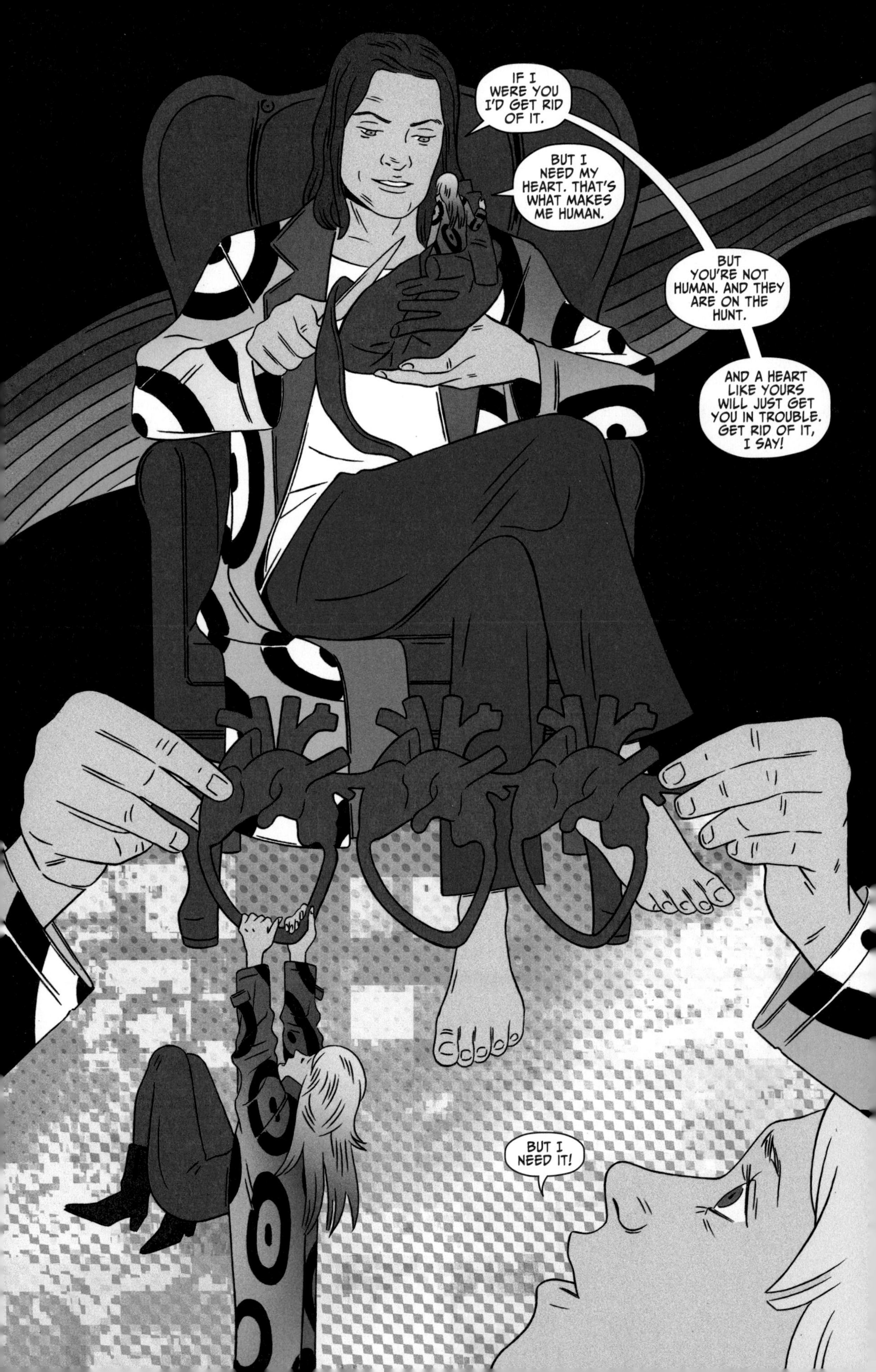
IF I WERE YOU I'D GET RID OF IT.
BUT I NEED MY HEART. THAT'S WHAT MAKES ME HUMAN.
BUT YOU'RE NOT HUMAN. AND THEY ARE ON THE HUNT.
AND A HEART LIKE YOURS WILL JUST GET YOU IN TROUBLE. GET RID OF IT, I SAY!
BUT I NEED IT!

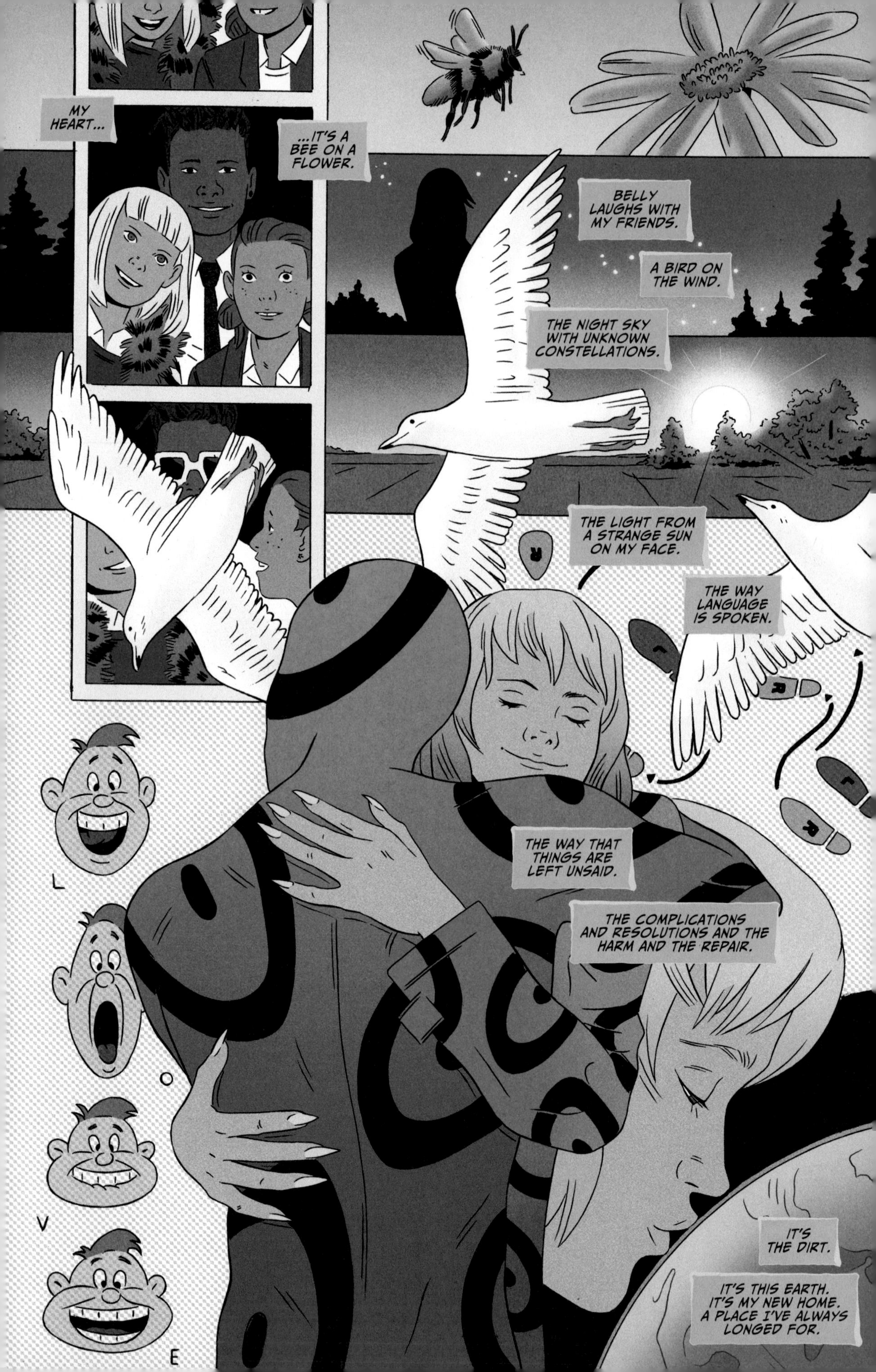
MY HEART...
...IT'S A BEE ON A FLOWER.
BELLY LAUGHS WITH MY FRIENDS.
A BIRD ON THE WIND.
THE NIGHT SKY WITH UNKNOWN CONSTELLATIONS.
THE LIGHT FROM A STRANGE SUN ON MY FACE.
THE WAY LANGUAGE IS SPOKEN.
THE WAY THAT THINGS ARE LEFT UNSAID.
THE COMPLICATIONS AND RESOLUTIONS AND THE HARM AND THE REPAIR.
L
V
E
IT'S THE DIRT.
IT'S THIS EARTH. IT'S MY NEW HOME. A PLACE I'VE ALWAYS LONGED FOR.

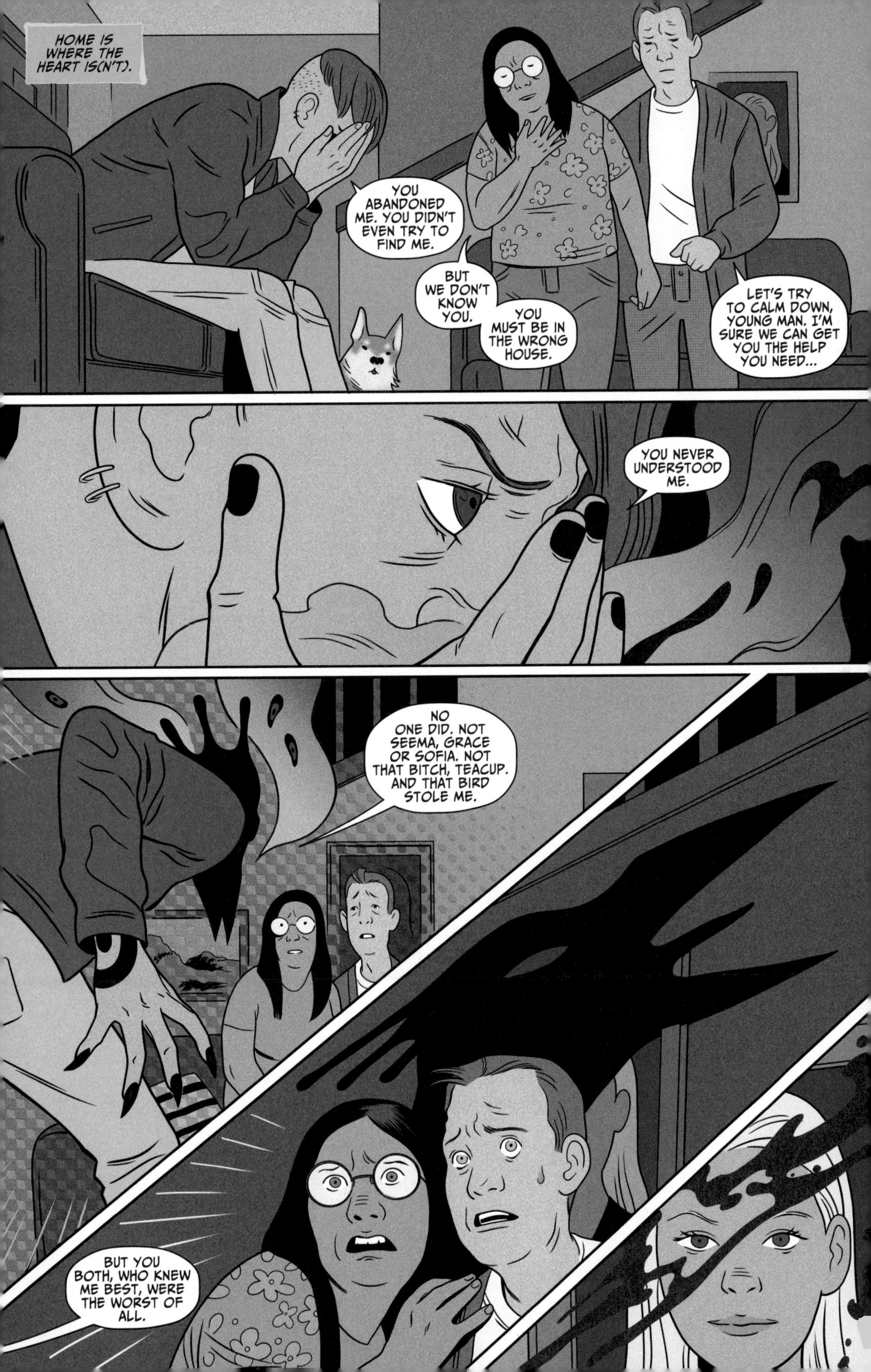
HOME IS WHERE THE HEART IS(N'T).
YOU ABANDONED ME. YOU DIDN'T EVEN TRY TO FIND ME.
BUT WE DON'T KNOW YOU.
YOU MUST BE IN THE WRONG HOUSE.
LET'S TRY TO CALM DOWN, YOUNG MAN. I'M SURE WE CAN GET YOU THE HELP YOU NEED...
YOU NEVER UNDERSTOOD ME.
NO ONE DID. NOT SEEMA, GRACE OR SOFIA. NOT THAT BITCH, TEACUP. AND THAT BIRD STOLE ME.
BUT YOU BOTH, WHO KNEW ME BEST, WERE THE WORST OF ALL.

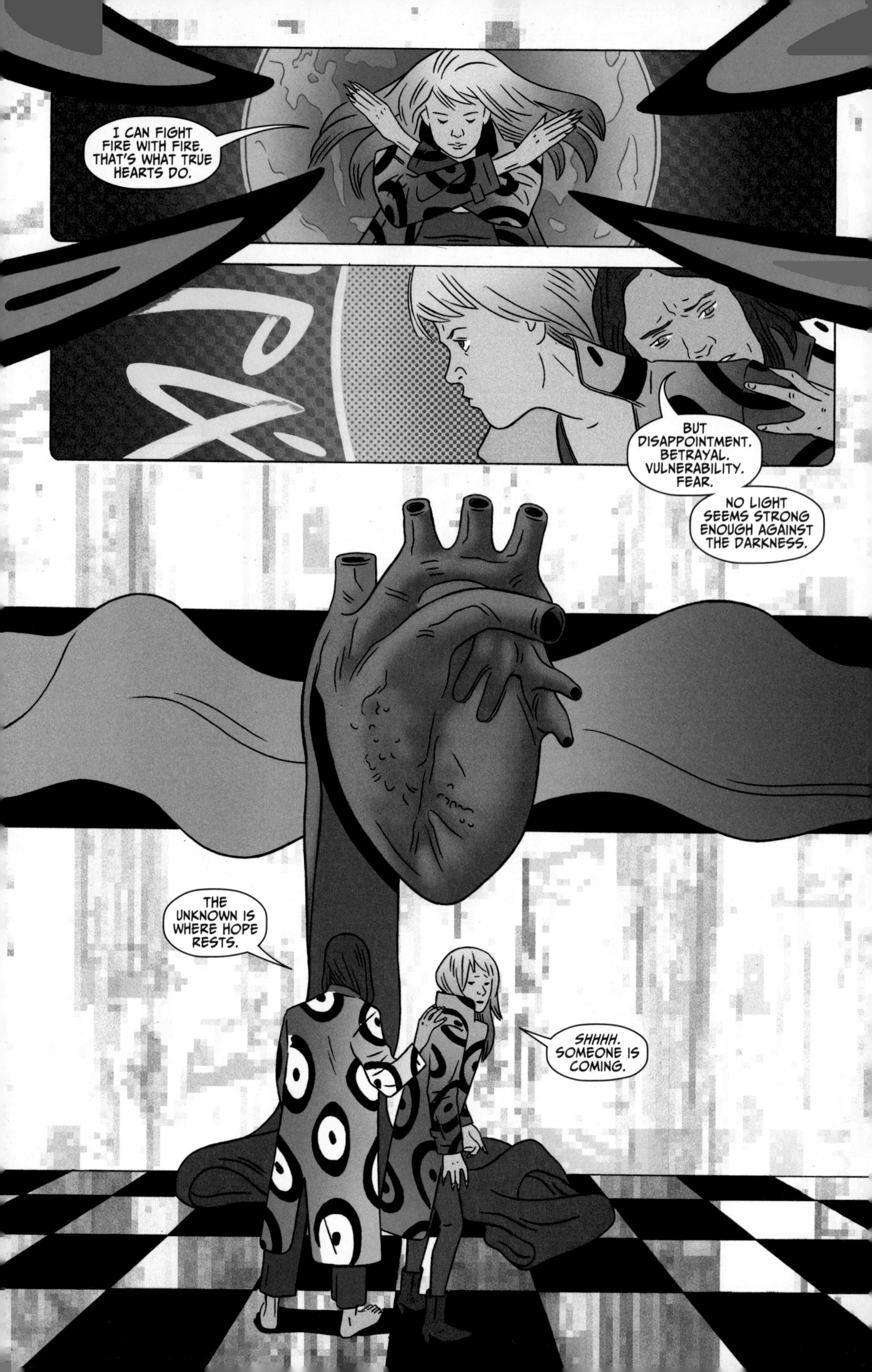
I CAN FIGHT FIRE WITH FIRE. THAT'S WHAT TRUE HEARTS DO.
BUT DISAPPOINTMENT. BETRAYAL. VULNERABILITY. FEAR.
NO LIGHT SEEMS STRONG ENOUGH AGAINST THE DARKNESS.
THE UNKNOWN IS WHERE HOPE RESTS.
SHHHH. SOMEONE IS COMING.

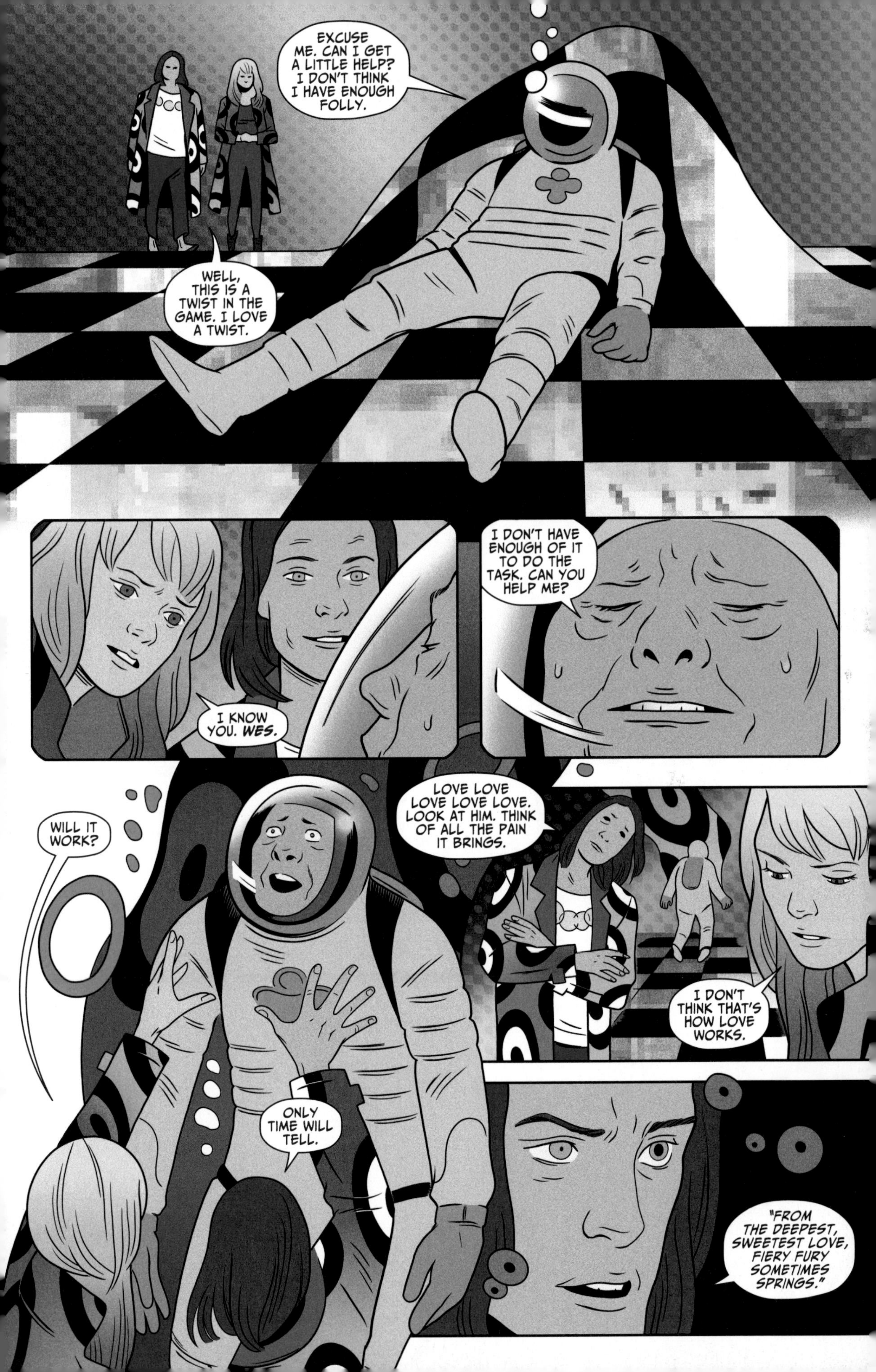
EXCUSE ME. CAN I GET A LITTLE HELP? I DON'T THINK I HAVE ENOUGH FOLLY.
WELL, THIS IS A TWIST IN THE GAME. I LOVE A TWIST.
I KNOW YOU. WES.
I DON'T HAVE ENOUGH OF IT TO DO THE TASK. CAN YOU HELP ME?
WILL IT WORK?
LOVE LOVE LOVE LOVE LOVE. LOOK AT HIM. THINK OF ALL THE PAIN IT BRINGS.
I DON'T THINK THAT'S HOW LOVE WORKS.
ONLY TIME WILL TELL.
"FROM THE DEEPEST, SWEETEST LOVE, FIERY FURY SOMETIMES SPRINGS."

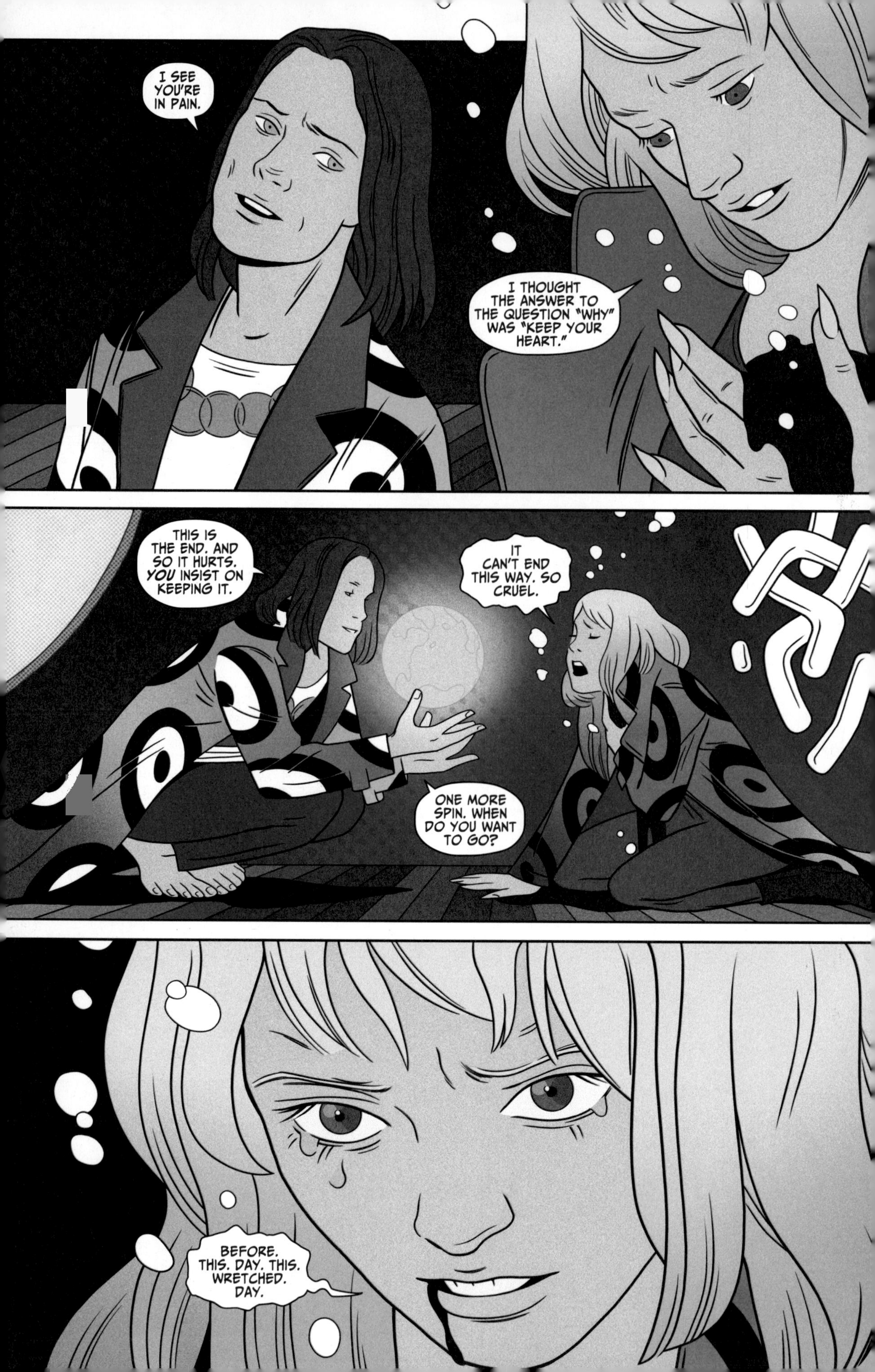
I SEE YOU'RE IN PAIN.
I THOUGHT THE ANSWER TO THE QUESTION "WHY" WAS "KEEP YOUR HEART."
THIS IS THE END. AND SO IT HURTS. *YOU* INSIST ON KEEPING IT.
IT CAN'T END THIS WAY. SO CRUEL.
ONE MORE SPIN. WHEN DO YOU WANT TO GO?
BEFORE. THIS. DAY. THIS. WRETCHED. DAY.

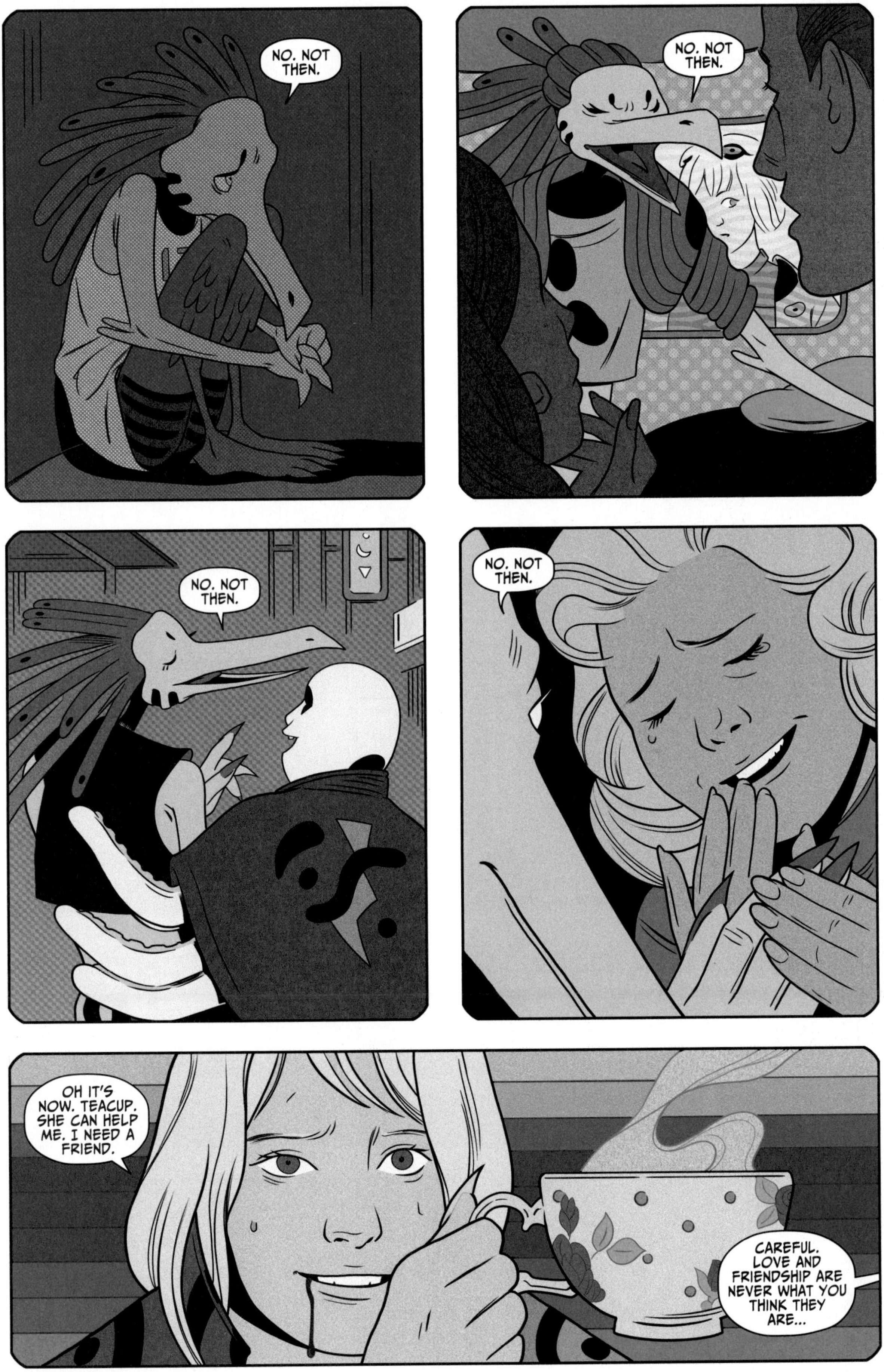
NO. NOT THEN.
NO. NOT THEN.
NO. NOT THEN.
NO. NOT THEN.
OH IT'S NOW. TEACUP. SHE CAN HELP ME. I NEED A FRIEND.
CAREFUL. LOVE AND FRIENDSHIP ARE NEVER WHAT YOU THINK THEY ARE...

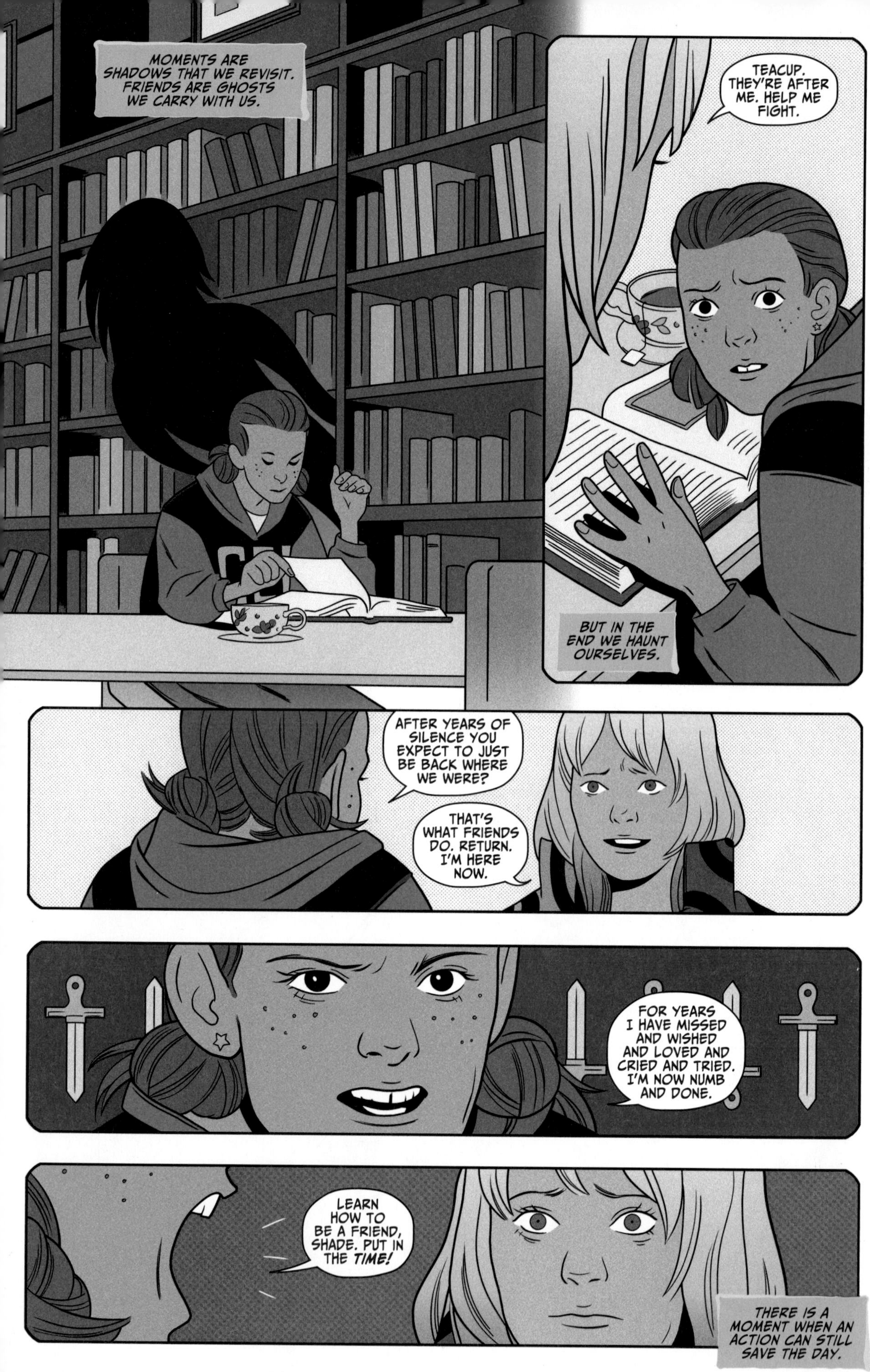
MOMENTS ARE SHADOWS THAT WE REVISIT. FRIENDS ARE GHOSTS WE CARRY WITH US.
TEACUP. THEY'RE AFTER ME. HELP ME FIGHT.
BUT IN THE END WE HAUNT OURSELVES.
AFTER YEARS OF SILENCE YOU EXPECT TO JUST BE BACK WHERE WE WERE?
THAT'S WHAT FRIENDS DO. RETURN. I'M HERE NOW.
FOR YEARS I HAVE MISSED AND WISHED AND LOVED AND CRIED AND TRIED. I'M NOW NUMB AND DONE.
LEARN HOW TO BE A FRIEND, SHADE. PUT IN THE TIME!
THERE IS A MOMENT WHEN AN ACTION CAN STILL SAVE THE DAY.

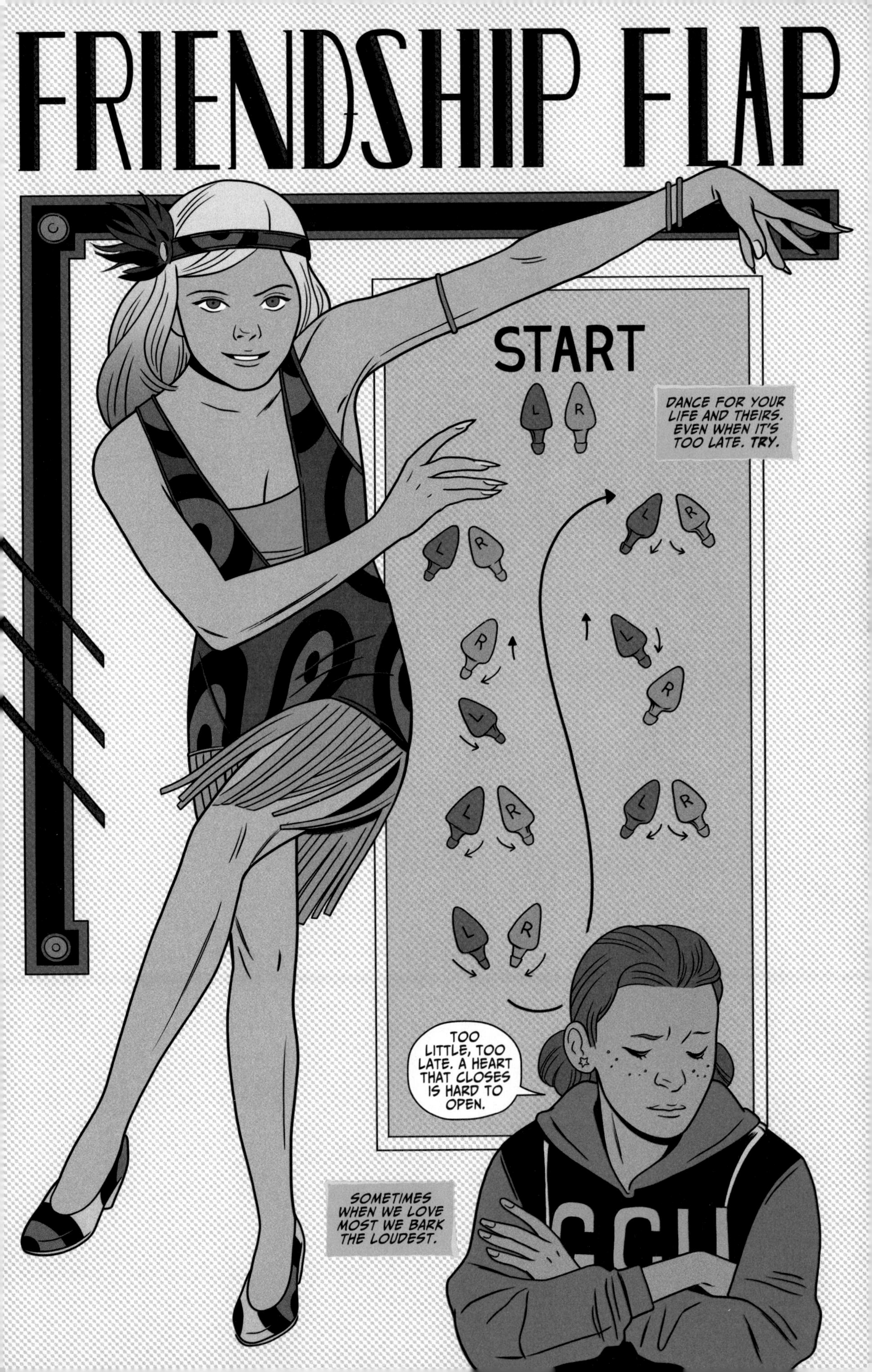
FRIENDSHIP FLAP
START
L
R
DANCE FOR YOUR LIFE AND THEIRS. EVEN WHEN IT'S TOO LATE. TRY.
TOO LITTLE, TOO LATE. A HEART THAT CLOSES IS HARD TO OPEN.
SOMETIMES WHEN WE LOVE MOST WE BARK THE LOUDEST.
CCU

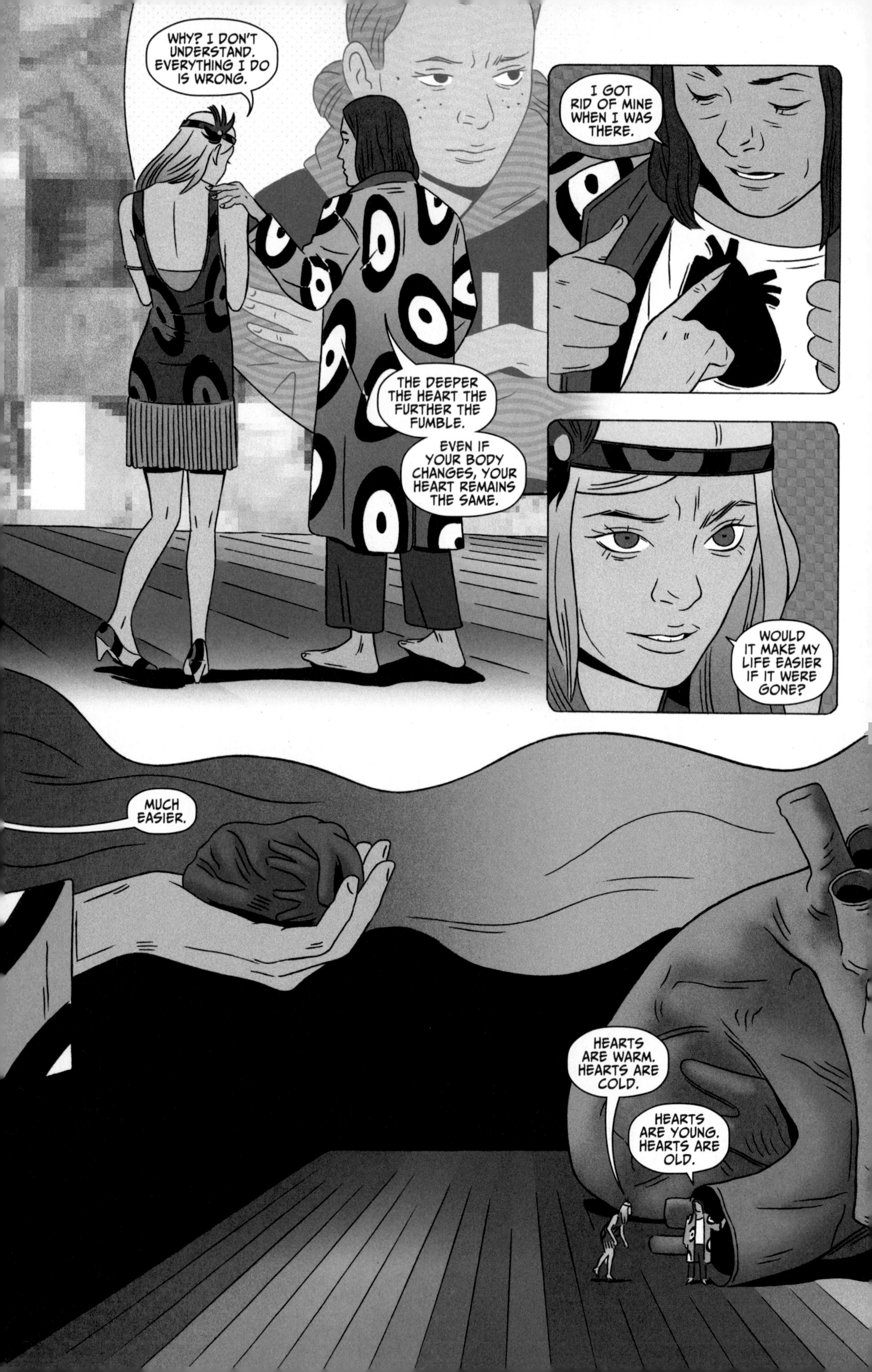
WHY? I DON'T UNDERSTAND. EVERYTHING I DO IS WRONG.
I GOT RID OF MINE WHEN I WAS THERE.
THE DEEPER THE HEART THE FURTHER THE FUMBLE.
EVEN IF YOUR BODY CHANGES, YOUR HEART REMAINS THE SAME.
WOULD IT MAKE MY LIFE EASIER IF IT WERE GONE?
MUCH EASIER.
HEARTS ARE WARM. HEARTS ARE COLD.
HEARTS ARE YOUNG. HEARTS ARE OLD.

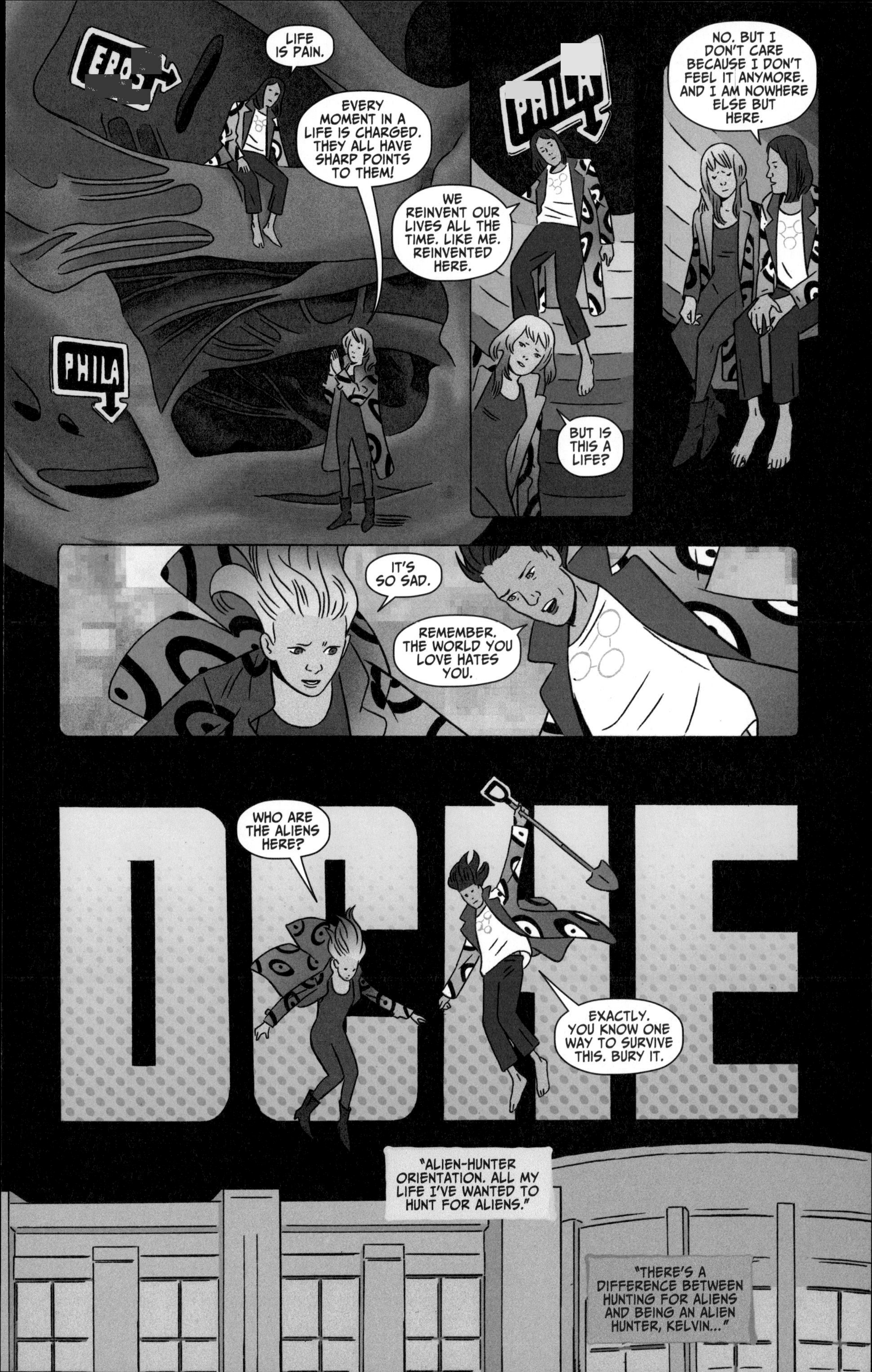

LIFE IS PAIN.
EVERY MOMENT IN A LIFE IS CHARGED. THEY ALL HAVE SHARP POINTS TO THEM!
WE REINVENT OUR LIVES ALL THE TIME. LIKE ME. REINVENTED HERE.
PHILA
BUT IS THIS A LIFE?
NO. BUT I DON'T CARE BECAUSE I DON'T FEEL IT ANYMORE. AND I AM NOWHERE ELSE BUT HERE.
IT'S SO SAD.
REMEMBER. THE WORLD YOU LOVE HATES YOU.
WHO ARE THE ALIENS HERE?
EXACTLY. YOU KNOW ONE WAY TO SURVIVE THIS. BURY IT.
"ALIEN-HUNTER ORIENTATION. ALL MY LIFE I'VE WANTED TO HUNT FOR ALIENS."
"THERE'S A DIFFERENCE BETWEEN HUNTING FOR ALIENS AND BEING AN ALIEN HUNTER, KELVIN..."

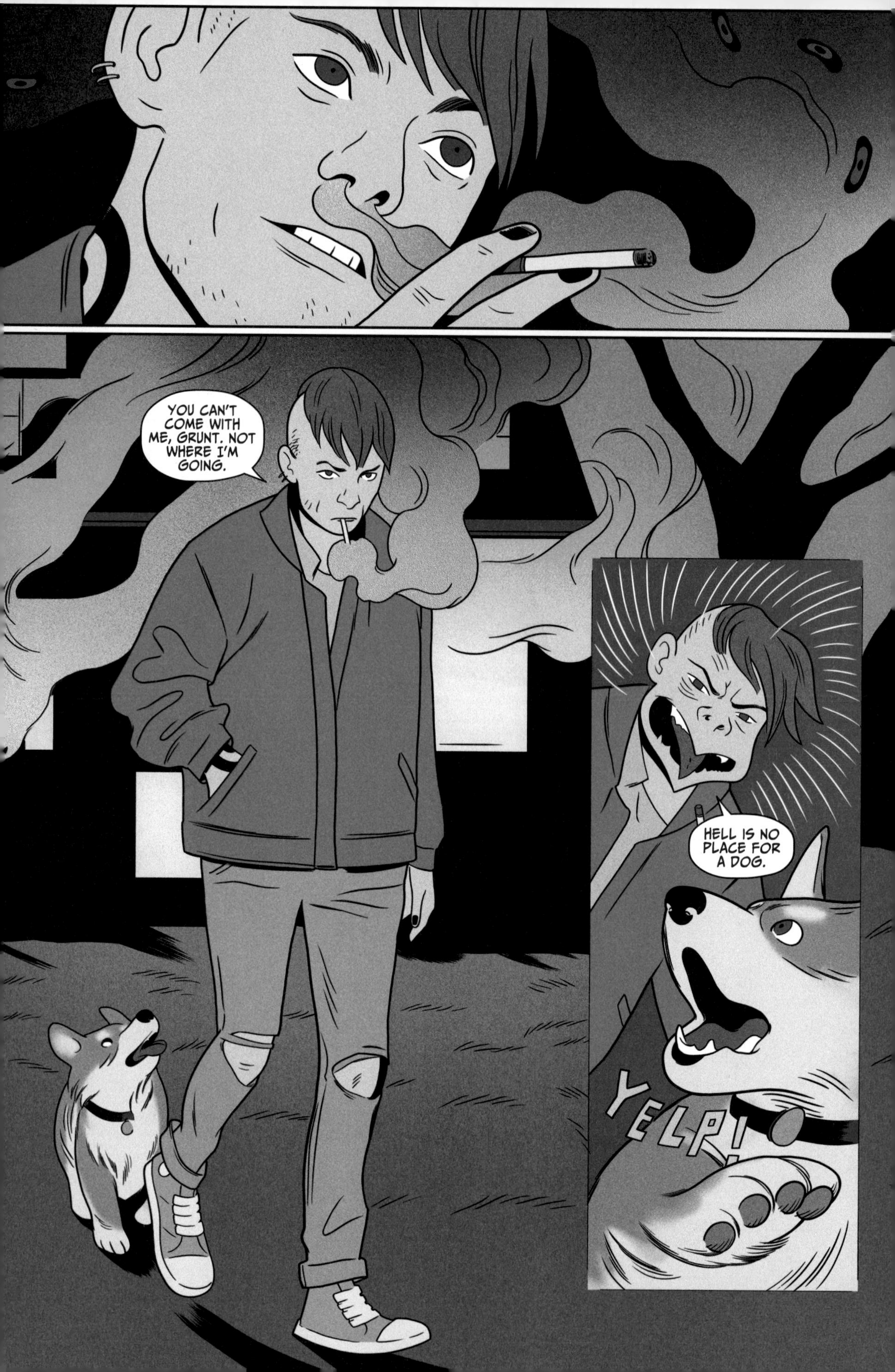
YOU CAN'T COME WITH ME, GRUNT. NOT WHERE I'M GOING.
HELL IS NO PLACE FOR A DOG.
YELP!

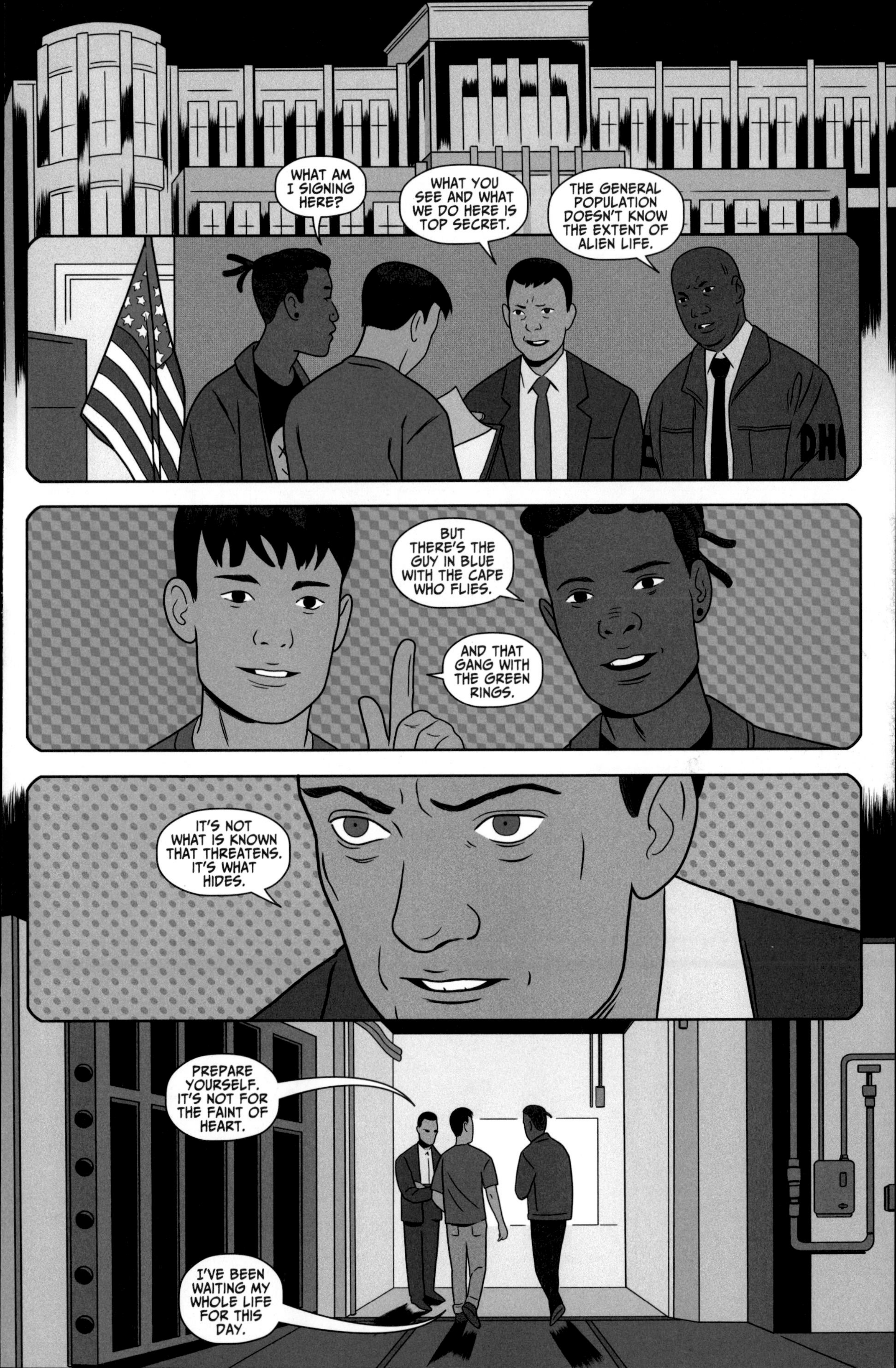
WHAT AM I SIGNING HERE?
WHAT YOU SEE AND WHAT WE DO HERE IS TOP SECRET.
THE GENERAL POPULATION DOESN'T KNOW THE EXTENT OF ALIEN LIFE.
DHS
BUT THERE'S THE GUY IN BLUE WITH THE CAPE WHO FLIES.
AND THAT GANG WITH THE GREEN RINGS.
IT'S NOT WHAT IS KNOWN THAT THREATENS. IT'S WHAT HIDES.
PREPARE YOURSELF. IT'S NOT FOR THE FAINT OF HEART.
I'VE BEEN WAITING MY WHOLE LIFE FOR THIS DAY.

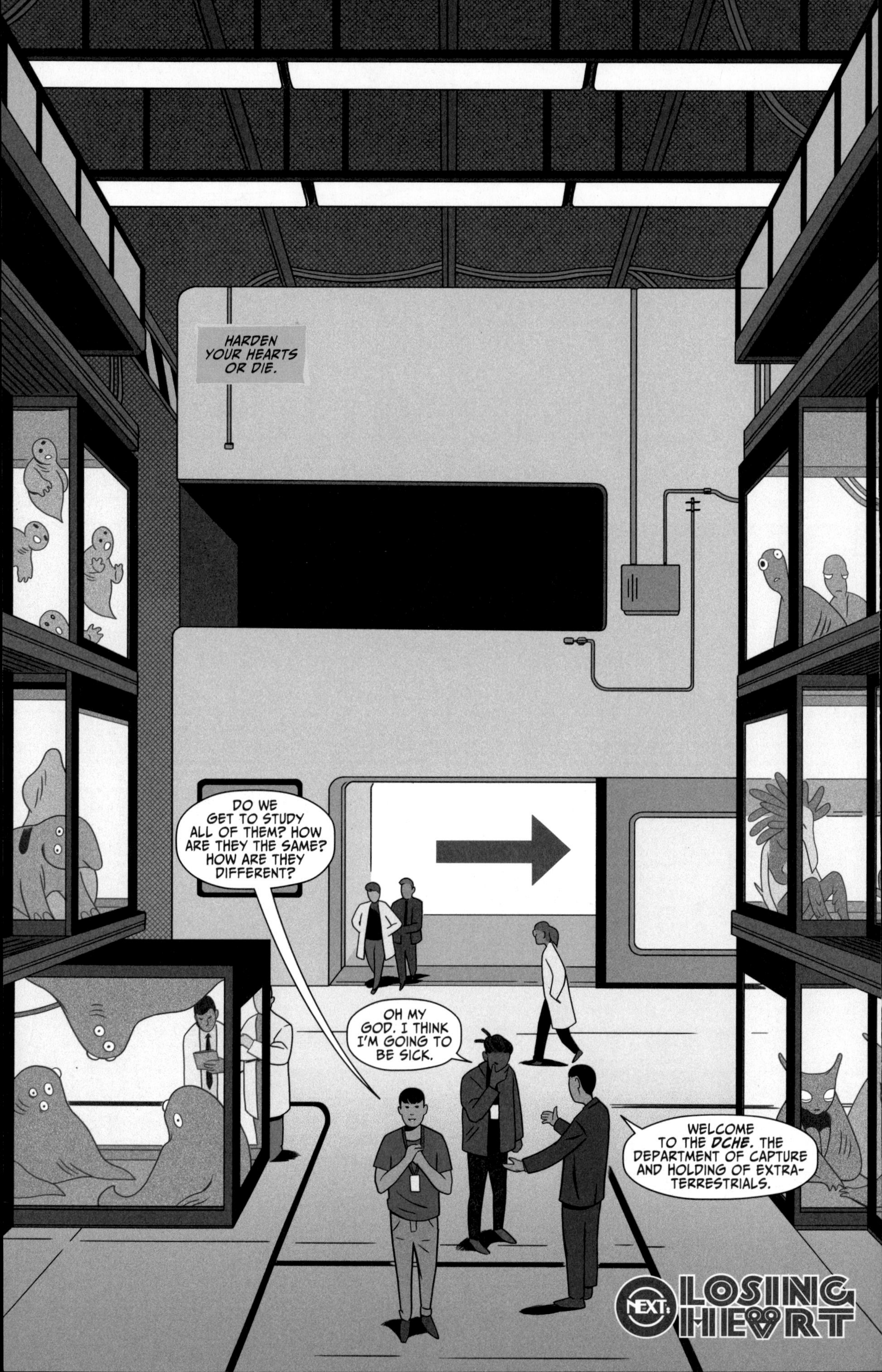
HARDEN YOUR HEARTS OR DIE.
DO WE GET TO STUDY ALL OF THEM? HOW ARE THEY THE SAME? HOW ARE THEY DIFFERENT?
OH MY GOD. I THINK I'M GOING TO BE SICK.
WELCOME TO THE DCHE. THE DEPARTMENT OF CAPTURE AND HOLDING OF EXTRA-TERRESTRIALS.
NEXT: LOSING HEART

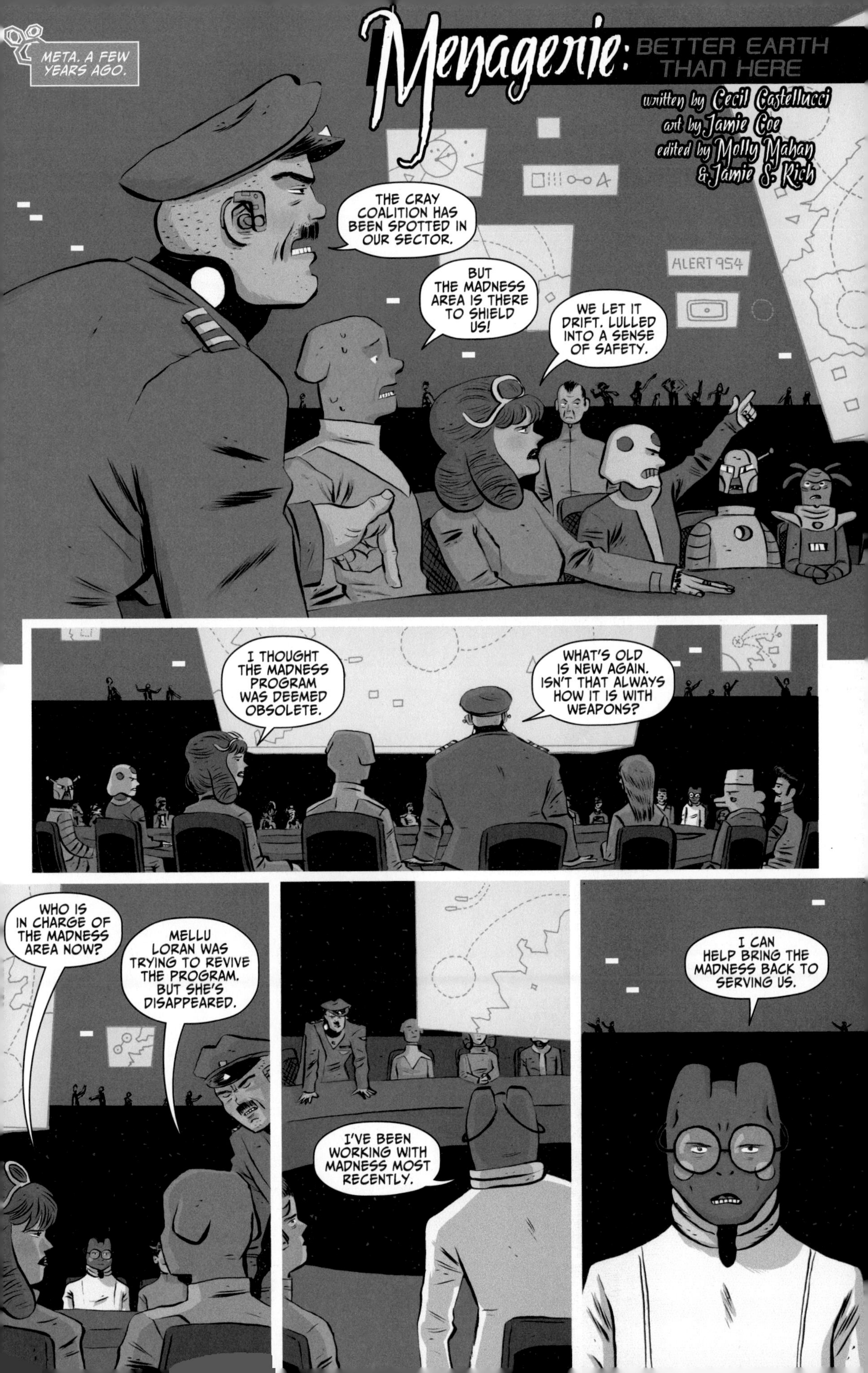
META. A FEW YEARS AGO.
Menagerie: BETTER EARTH THAN HERE
written by Cecil Castellucci
art by Jamie Coe
edited by Molly Mahan & Jamie S. Rich
THE CRAY COALITION HAS BEEN SPOTTED IN OUR SECTOR.
BUT THE MADNESS AREA IS THERE TO SHIELD US!
WE LET IT DRIFT. LULLED INTO A SENSE OF SAFETY.
ALERT 954
I THOUGHT THE MADNESS PROGRAM WAS DEEMED OBSOLETE.
WHAT'S OLD IS NEW AGAIN. ISN'T THAT ALWAYS HOW IT IS WITH WEAPONS?
WHO IS IN CHARGE OF THE MADNESS AREA NOW?
MELLU LORAN WAS TRYING TO REVIVE THE PROGRAM. BUT SHE'S DISAPPEARED.
I'VE BEEN WORKING WITH MADNESS MOST RECENTLY.
I CAN HELP BRING THE MADNESS BACK TO SERVING US.

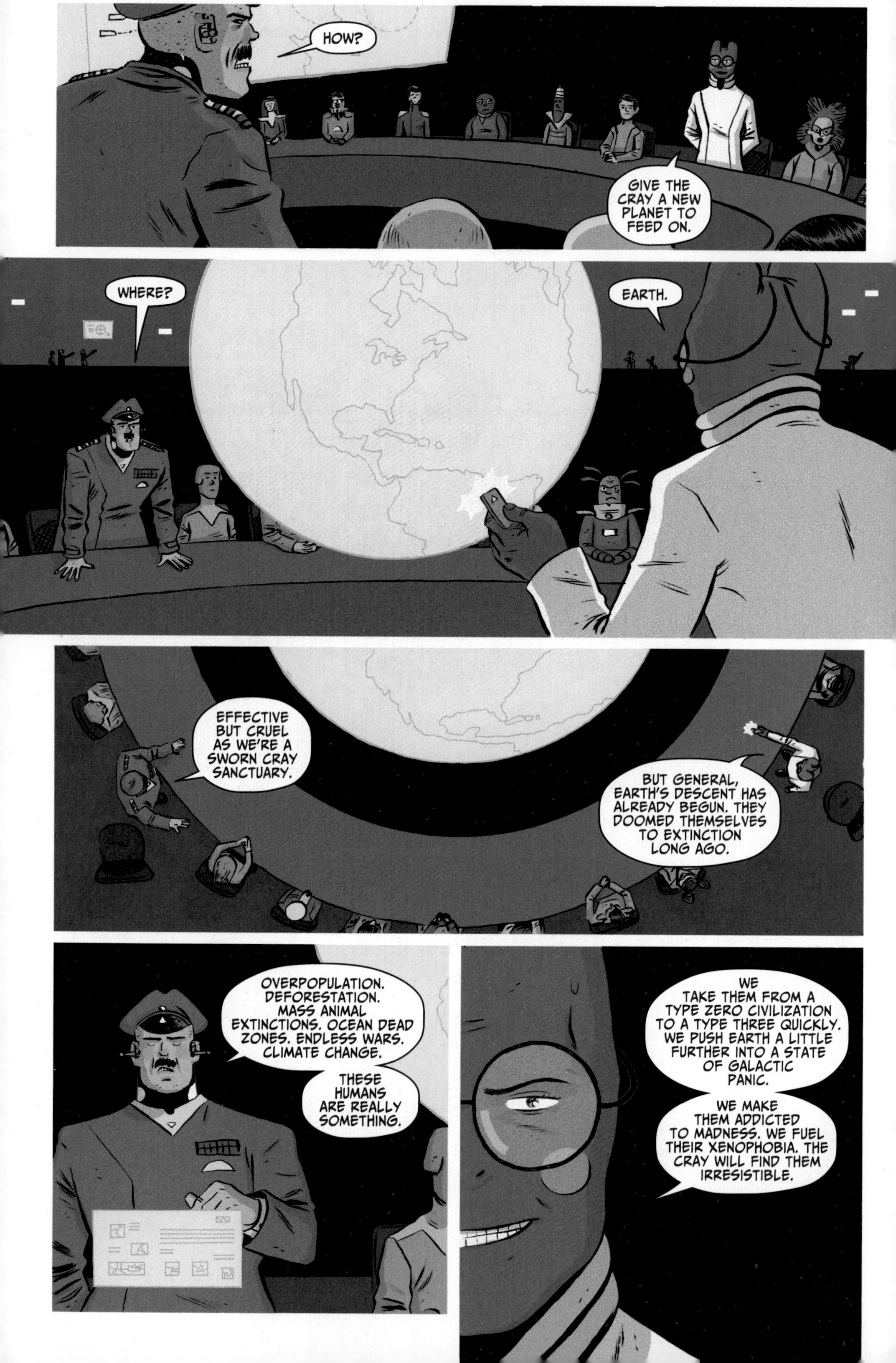
HOW?
GIVE THE CRAY A NEW PLANET TO FEED ON.
WHERE?
EARTH.
EFFECTIVE BUT CRUEL AS WE'RE A SWORN CRAY SANCTUARY.
BUT GENERAL, EARTH'S DESCENT HAS ALREADY BEGUN. THEY DOOMED THEMSELVES TO EXTINCTION LONG AGO.
OVERPOPULATION. DEFORESTATION. MASS ANIMAL EXTINCTIONS. OCEAN DEAD ZONES. ENDLESS WARS. CLIMATE CHANGE.
THESE HUMANS ARE REALLY SOMETHING.
WE TAKE THEM FROM A TYPE ZERO CIVILIZATION TO A TYPE THREE QUICKLY. WE PUSH EARTH A LITTLE FURTHER INTO A STATE OF GALACTIC PANIC.
WE MAKE THEM ADDICTED TO MADNESS. WE FUEL THEIR XENOPHOBIA. THE CRAY WILL FIND THEM IRRESISTIBLE.

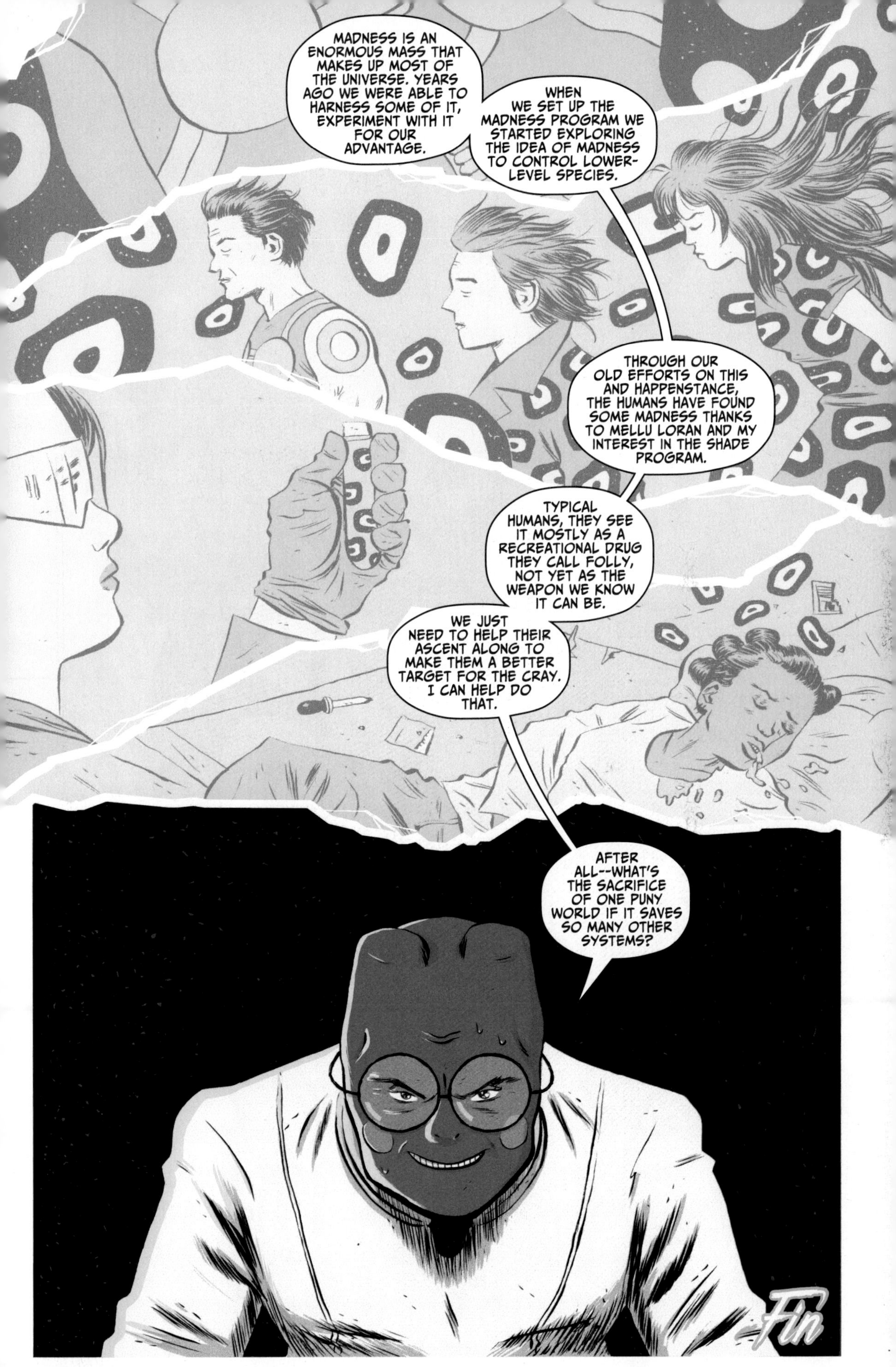
MADNESS IS AN ENORMOUS MASS THAT MAKES UP MOST OF THE UNIVERSE. YEARS AGO WE WERE ABLE TO HARNESS SOME OF IT, EXPERIMENT WITH IT FOR OUR ADVANTAGE.
WHEN WE SET UP THE MADNESS PROGRAM WE STARTED EXPLORING THE IDEA OF MADNESS TO CONTROL LOWER-LEVEL SPECIES.
THROUGH OUR OLD EFFORTS ON THIS AND HAPPENSTANCE, THE HUMANS HAVE FOUND SOME MADNESS THANKS TO MELLU LORAN AND MY INTEREST IN THE SHADE PROGRAM.
TYPICAL HUMANS, THEY SEE IT MOSTLY AS A RECREATIONAL DRUG THEY CALL FOLLY, NOT YET AS THE WEAPON WE KNOW IT CAN BE.
WE JUST NEED TO HELP THEIR ASCENT ALONG TO MAKE THEM A BETTER TARGET FOR THE CRAY. I CAN HELP DO THAT.
AFTER ALL--WHAT'S THE SACRIFICE OF ONE PUNY WORLD IF IT SAVES SO MANY OTHER SYSTEMS?
Fin

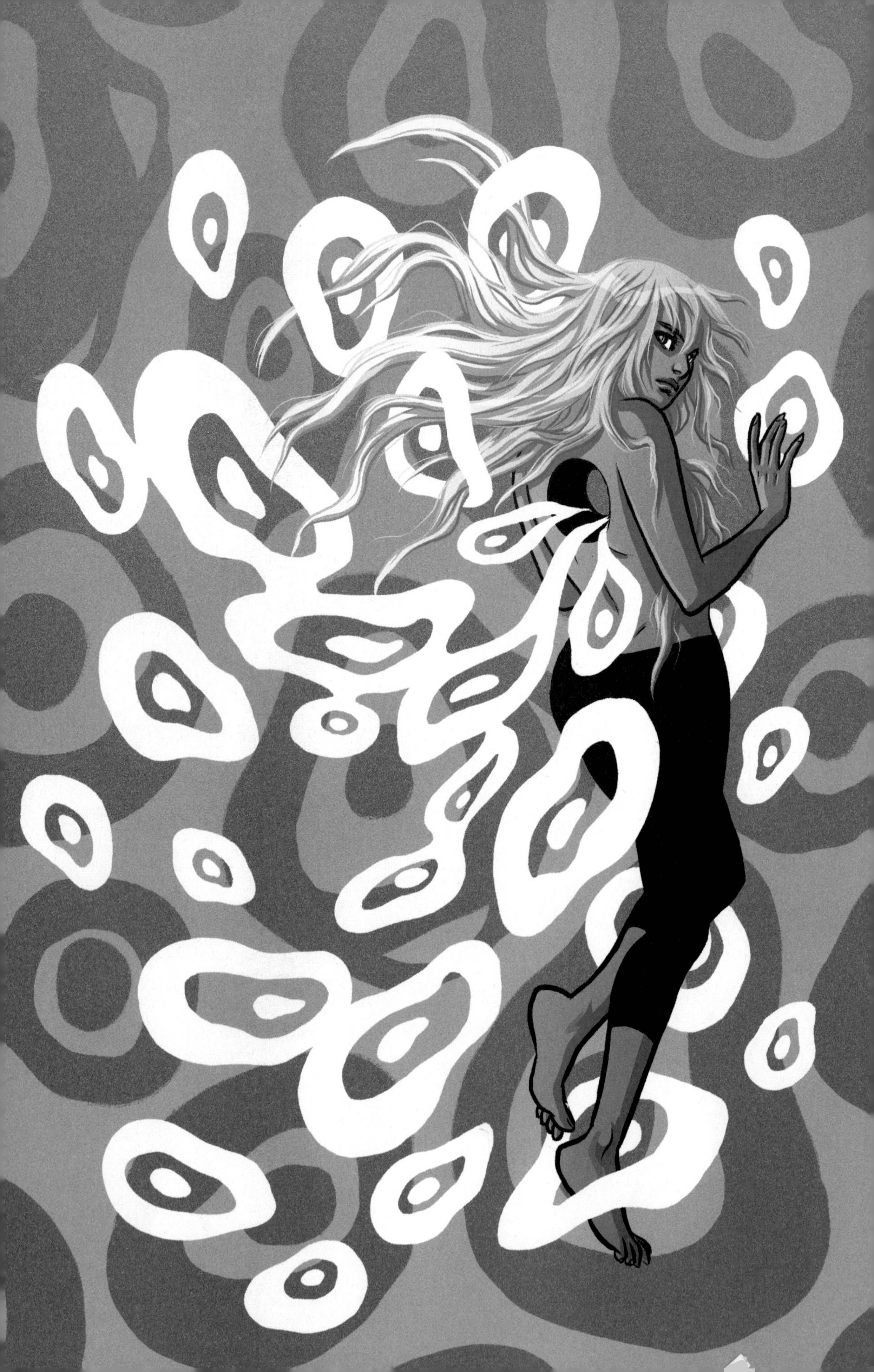

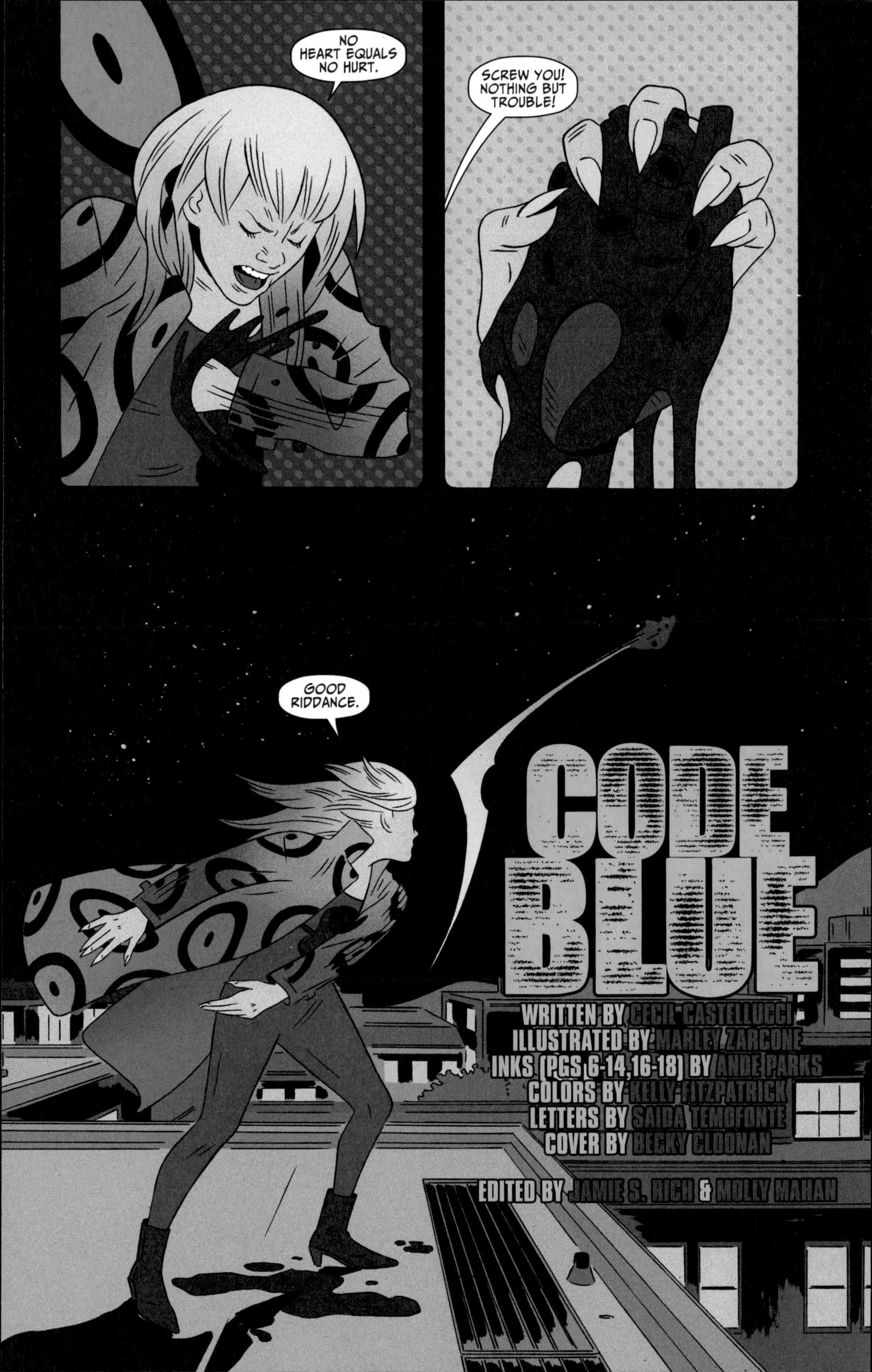
NO HEART EQUALS NO HURT.
SCREW YOU! NOTHING BUT TROUBLE!
GOOD RIDDANCE.
CODE BLUE
WRITTEN BY CECIL CASTELLUCCI
ILLUSTRATED BY MARLEY ZARCONE
INKS (PGS 6-14,16-18) BY ANDE PARKS
COLORS BY KELLY FITZPATRICK
LETTERS BY SAIDA TEMOFONTE
COVER BY BECKY CLOONAN
EDITED BY JAMIE S. RICH & MOLLY MAHAN

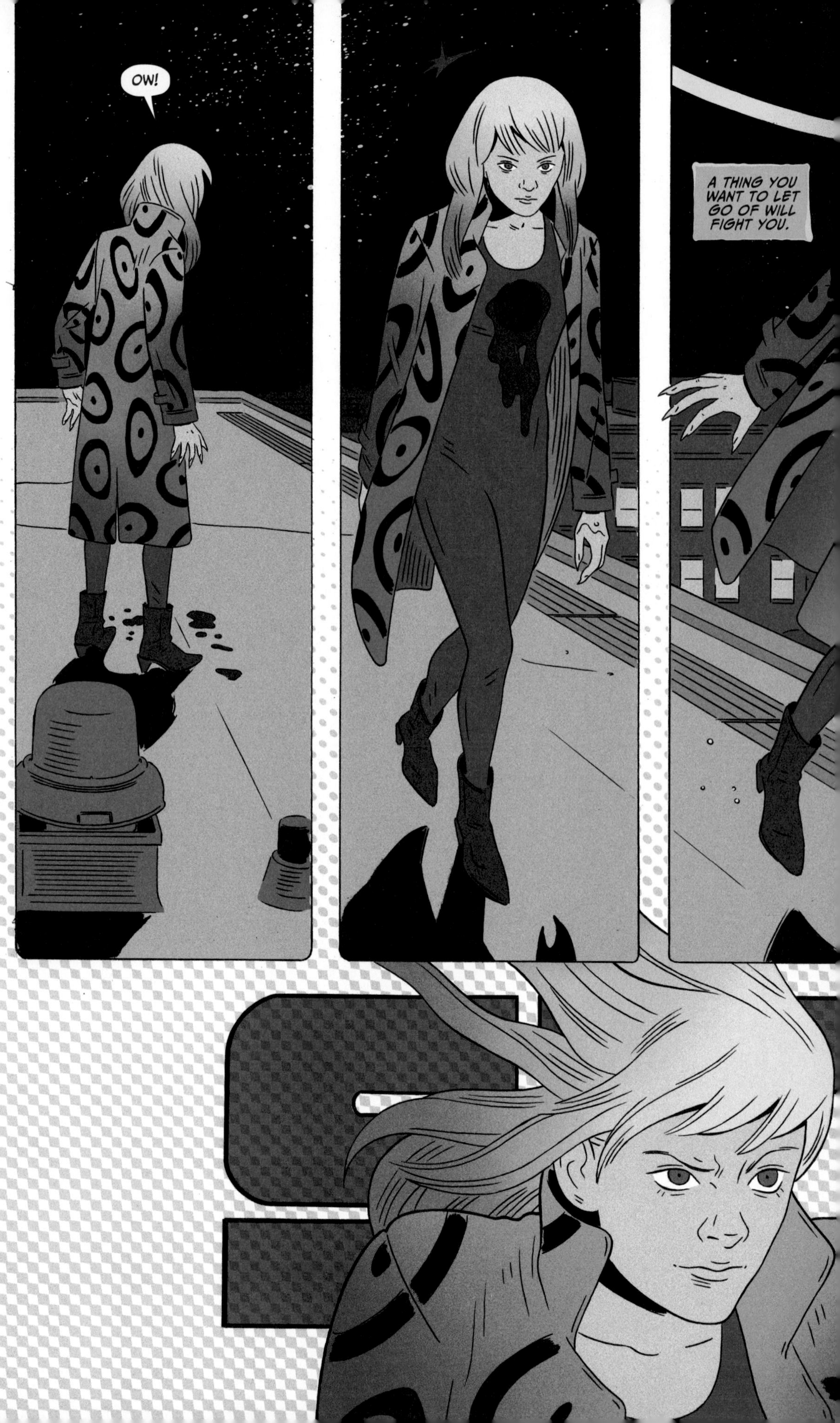
OW!
A THING YOU WANT TO LET GO OF WILL FIGHT YOU.

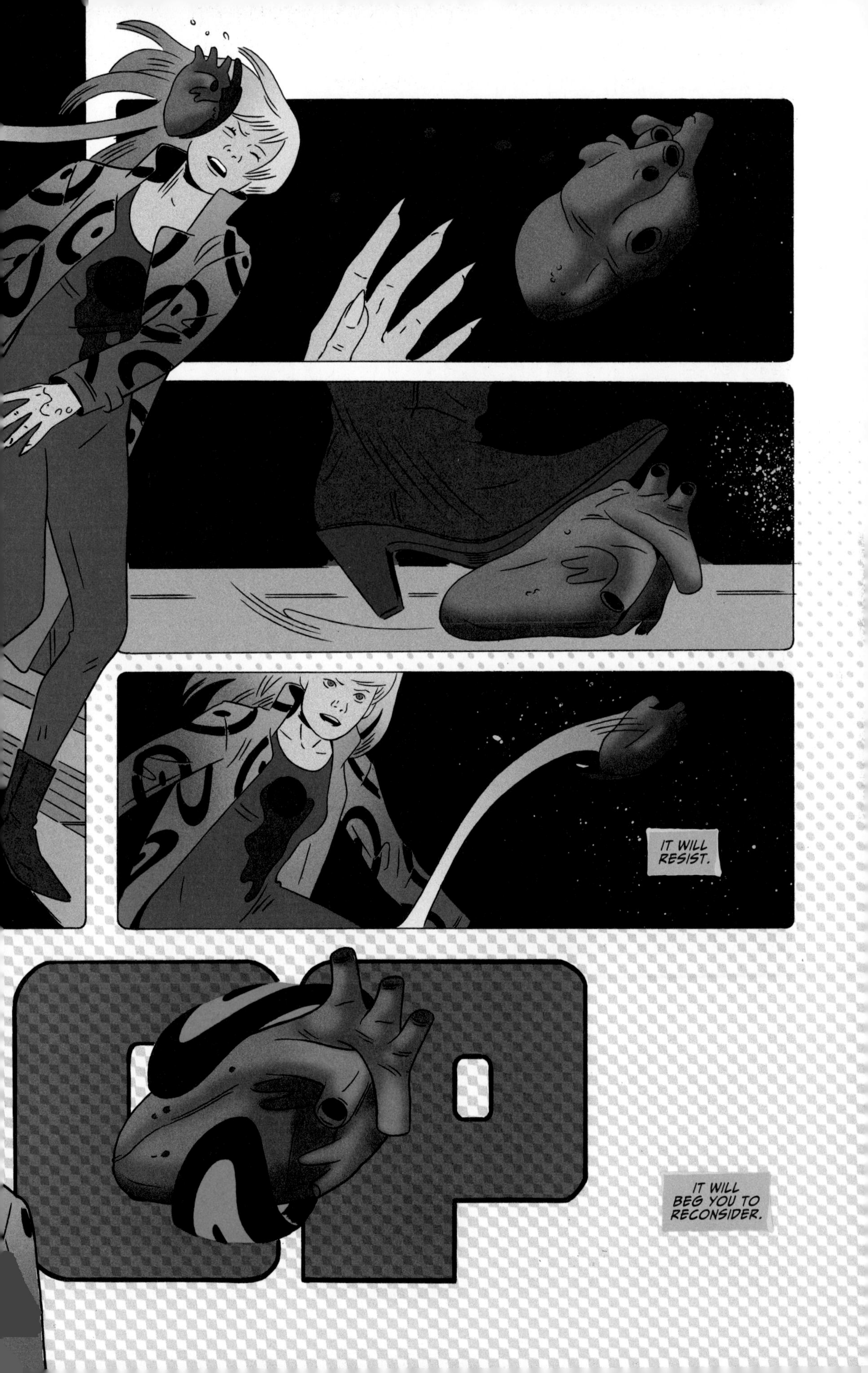
IT WILL RESIST.
IT WILL BEG YOU TO RECONSIDER.

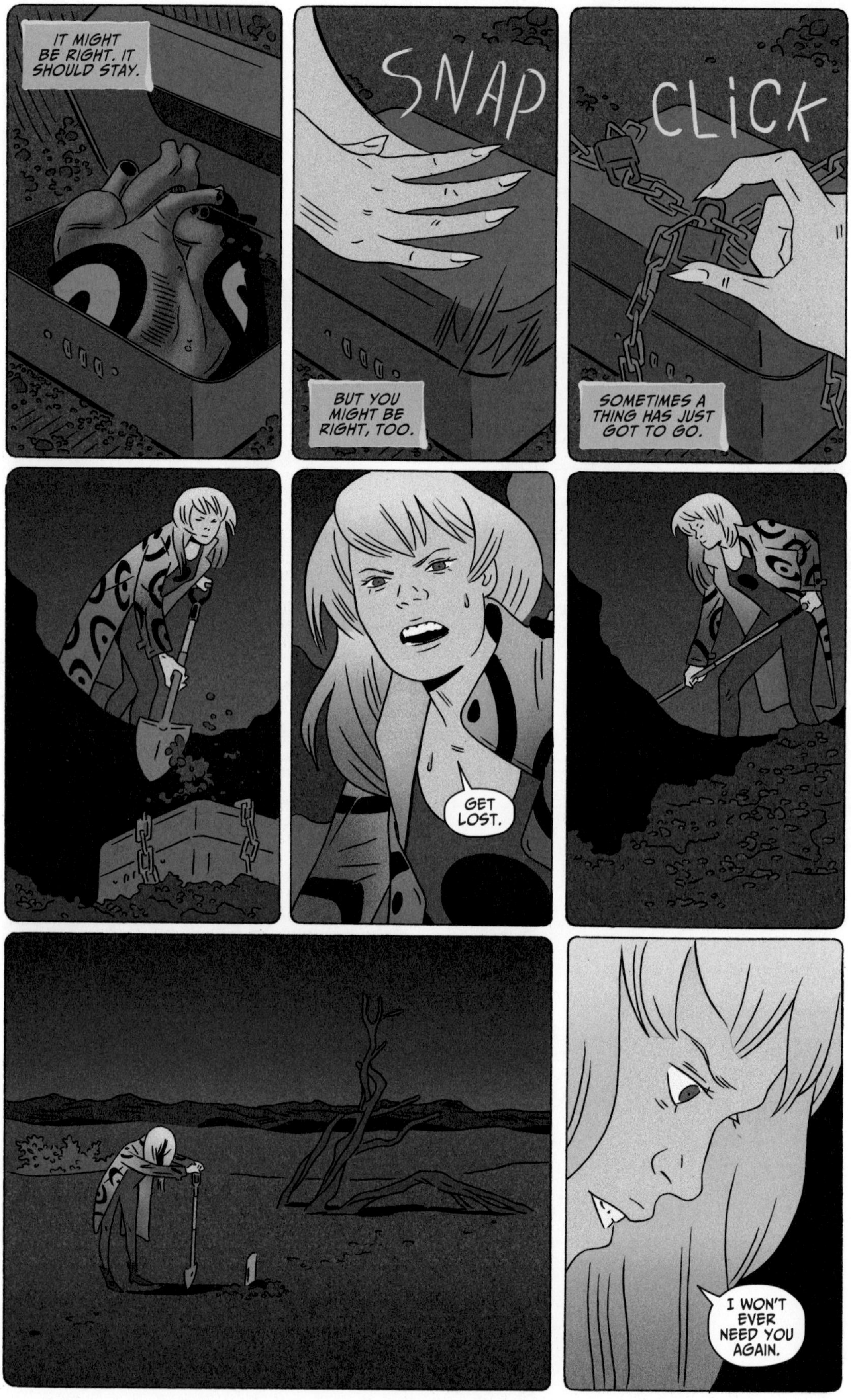
IT MIGHT BE RIGHT. IT SHOULD STAY.
SNAP
BUT YOU MIGHT BE RIGHT, TOO.
CLICK
SOMETIMES A THING HAS JUST GOT TO GO.
GET LOST.
I WON'T EVER NEED YOU AGAIN.

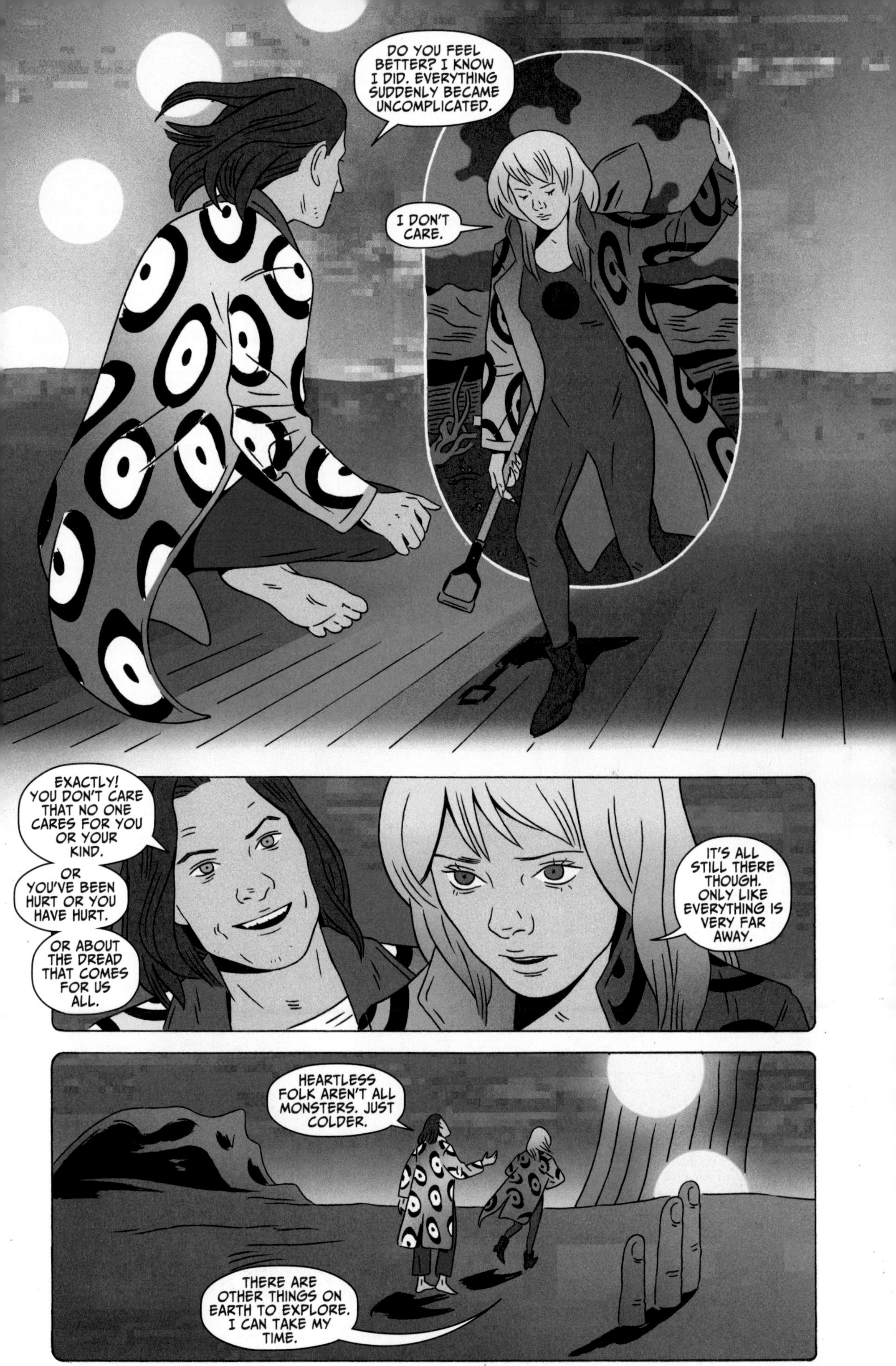
DO YOU FEEL BETTER? I KNOW I DID. EVERYTHING SUDDENLY BECAME UNCOMPLICATED.
I DON'T CARE.
EXACTLY! YOU DON'T CARE THAT NO ONE CARES FOR YOU OR YOUR KIND.
OR YOU'VE BEEN HURT OR YOU HAVE HURT.
OR ABOUT THE DREAD THAT COMES FOR US ALL.
IT'S ALL STILL THERE THOUGH. ONLY LIKE EVERYTHING IS VERY FAR AWAY.
HEARTLESS FOLK AREN'T ALL MONSTERS. JUST COLDER.
THERE ARE OTHER THINGS ON EARTH TO EXPLORE. I CAN TAKE MY TIME.

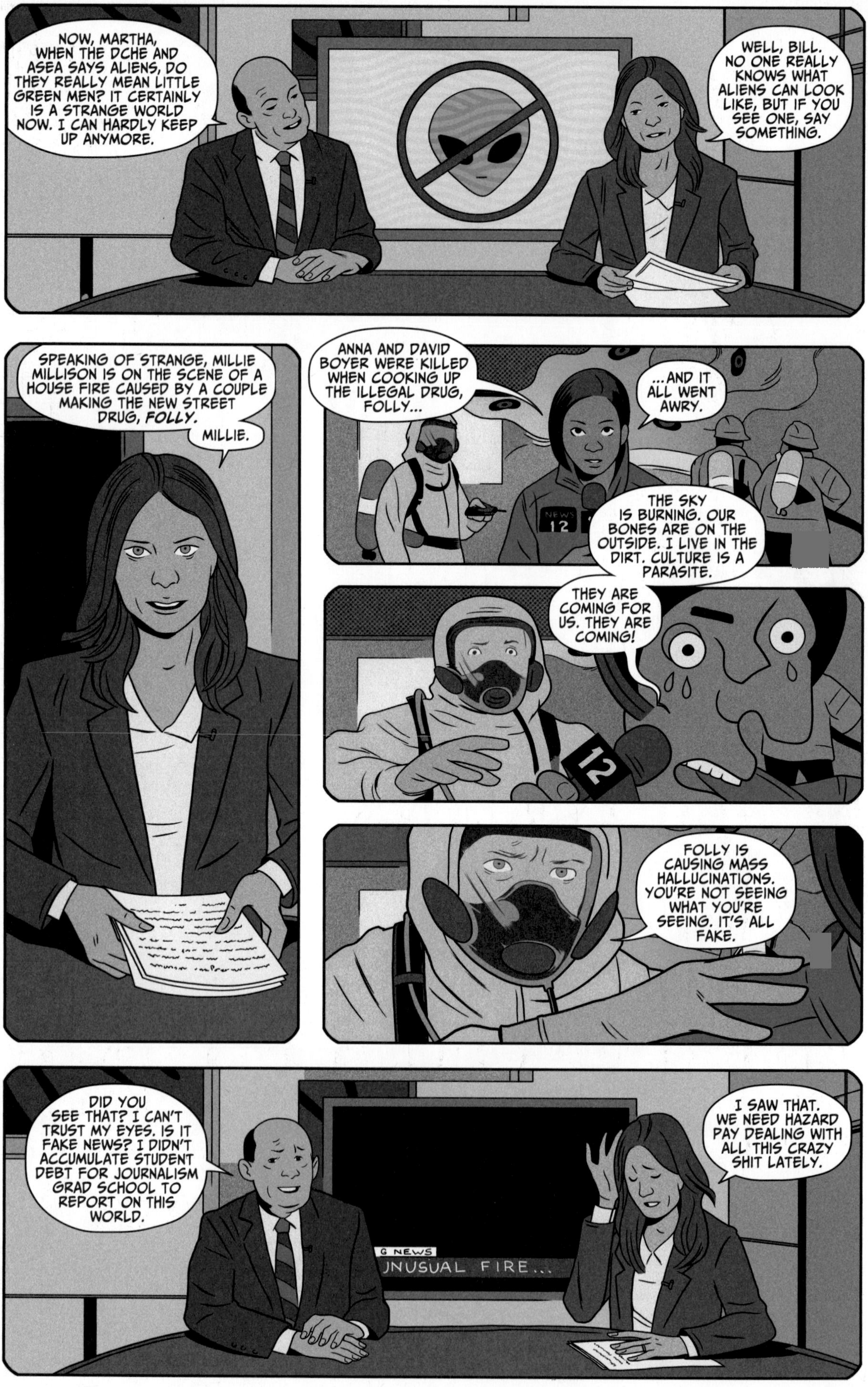
NOW, MARTHA, WHEN THE DCHE AND ASEA SAYS ALIENS, DO THEY REALLY MEAN LITTLE GREEN MEN? IT CERTAINLY IS A STRANGE WORLD NOW. I CAN HARDLY KEEP UP ANYMORE.
WELL, BILL. NO ONE REALLY KNOWS WHAT ALIENS CAN LOOK LIKE, BUT IF YOU SEE ONE, SAY SOMETHING.
SPEAKING OF STRANGE, MILLIE MILLISON IS ON THE SCENE OF A HOUSE FIRE CAUSED BY A COUPLE MAKING THE NEW STREET DRUG, *FOLLY*.
MILLIE.
ANNA AND DAVID BOYER WERE KILLED WHEN COOKING UP THE ILLEGAL DRUG, FOLLY...
...AND IT ALL WENT AWRY.
NEWS 12
THE SKY IS BURNING. OUR BONES ARE ON THE OUTSIDE. I LIVE IN THE DIRT. CULTURE IS A PARASITE.
THEY ARE COMING FOR US. THEY ARE COMING!
12
FOLLY IS CAUSING MASS HALLUCINATIONS. YOU'RE NOT SEEING WHAT YOU'RE SEEING. IT'S ALL FAKE.
DID YOU SEE THAT? I CAN'T TRUST MY EYES. IS IT FAKE NEWS? I DIDN'T ACCUMULATE STUDENT DEBT FOR JOURNALISM GRAD SCHOOL TO REPORT ON THIS WORLD.
G NEWS
JNUSUAL FIRE...
I SAW THAT. WE NEED HAZARD PAY DEALING WITH ALL THIS CRAZY SHIT LATELY.

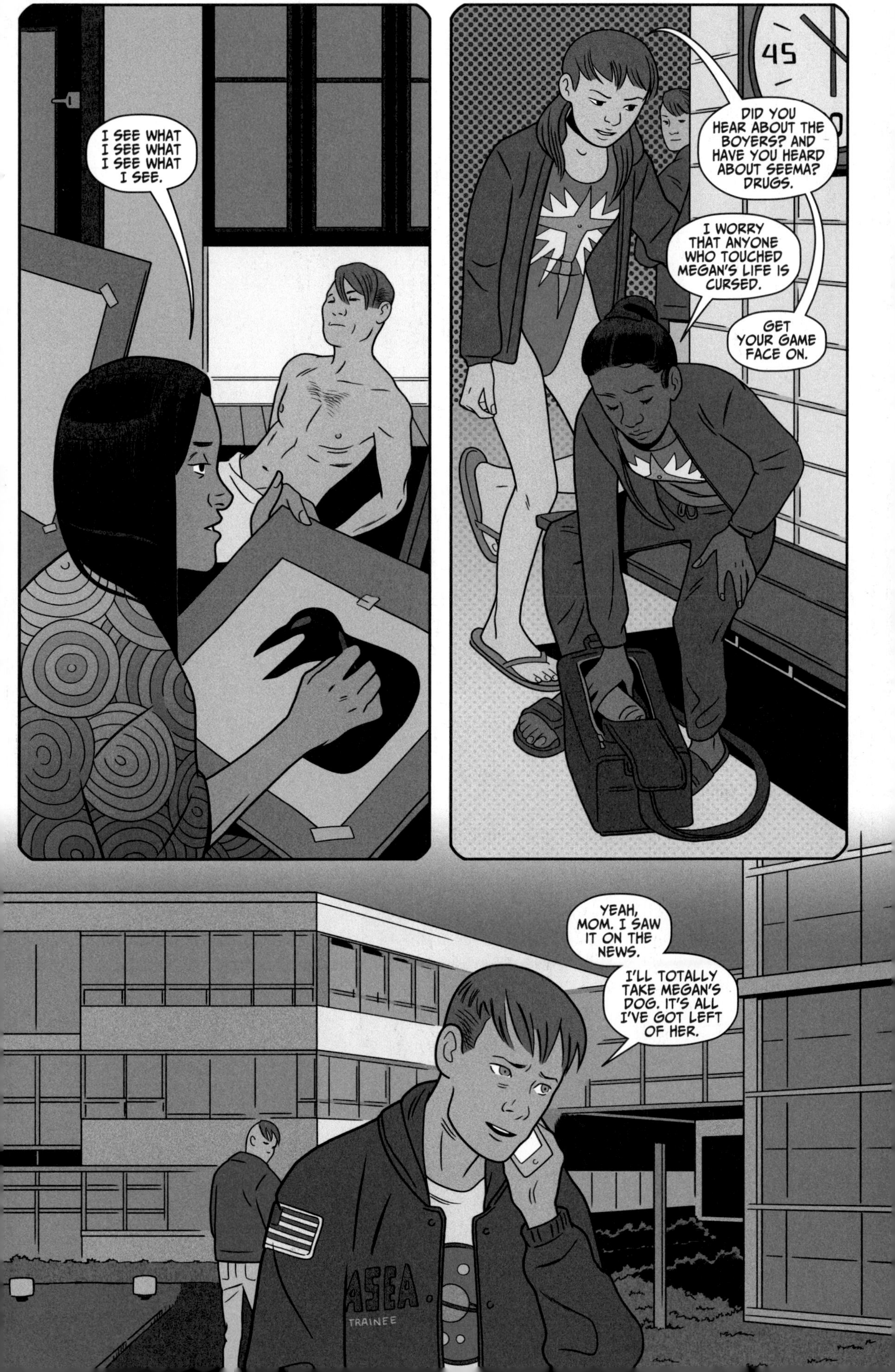
I SEE WHAT I SEE WHAT I SEE WHAT I SEE.
DID YOU HEAR ABOUT THE BOYERS? AND HAVE YOU HEARD ABOUT SEEMA? DRUGS.
I WORRY THAT ANYONE WHO TOUCHED MEGAN'S LIFE IS CURSED.
GET YOUR GAME FACE ON.
YEAH, MOM. I SAW IT ON THE NEWS.
I'LL TOTALLY TAKE MEGAN'S DOG. IT'S ALL I'VE GOT LEFT OF HER.
ASEA
TRAINEE

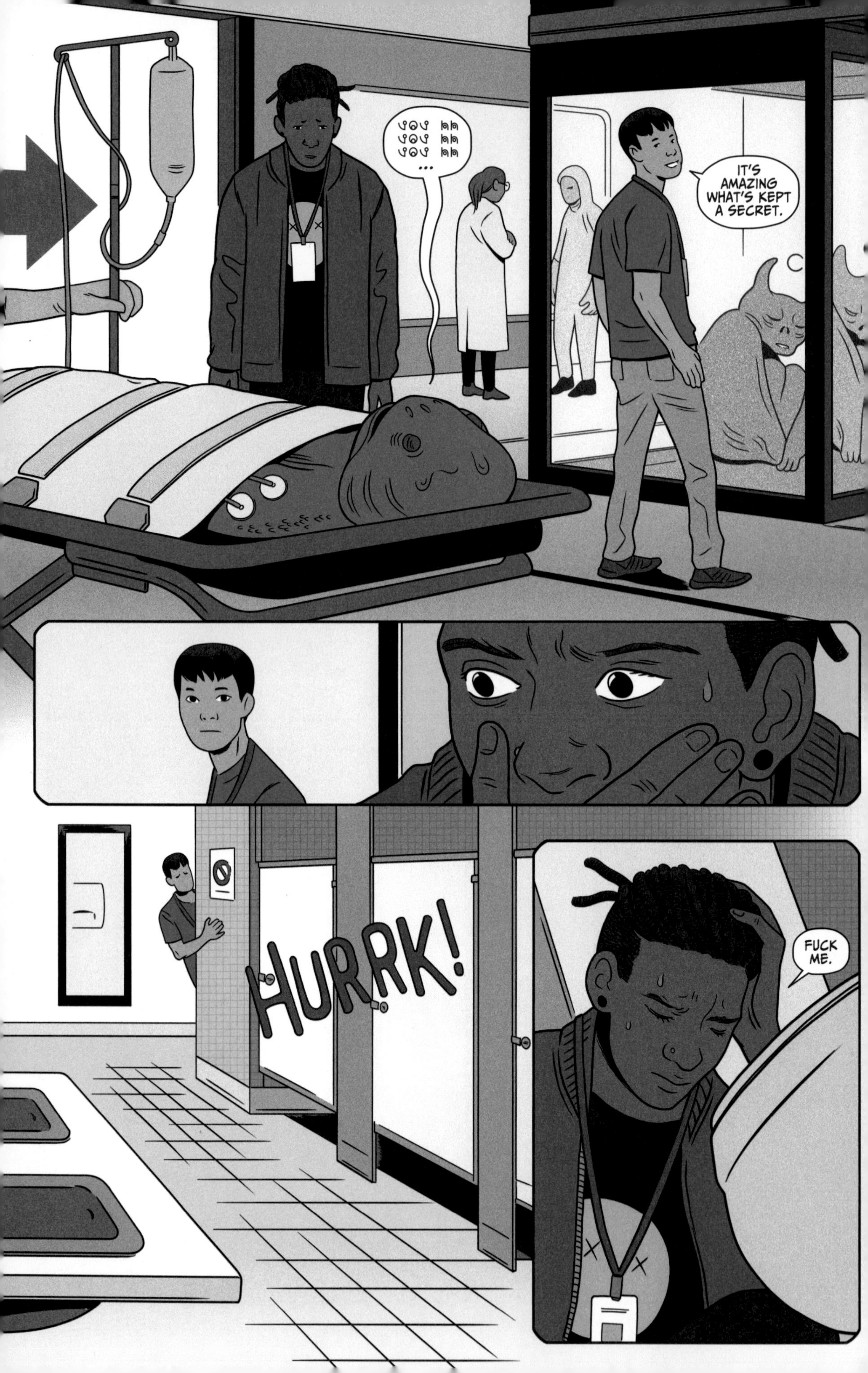
IT'S AMAZING WHAT'S KEPT A SECRET.
HURRK!
FUCK ME.

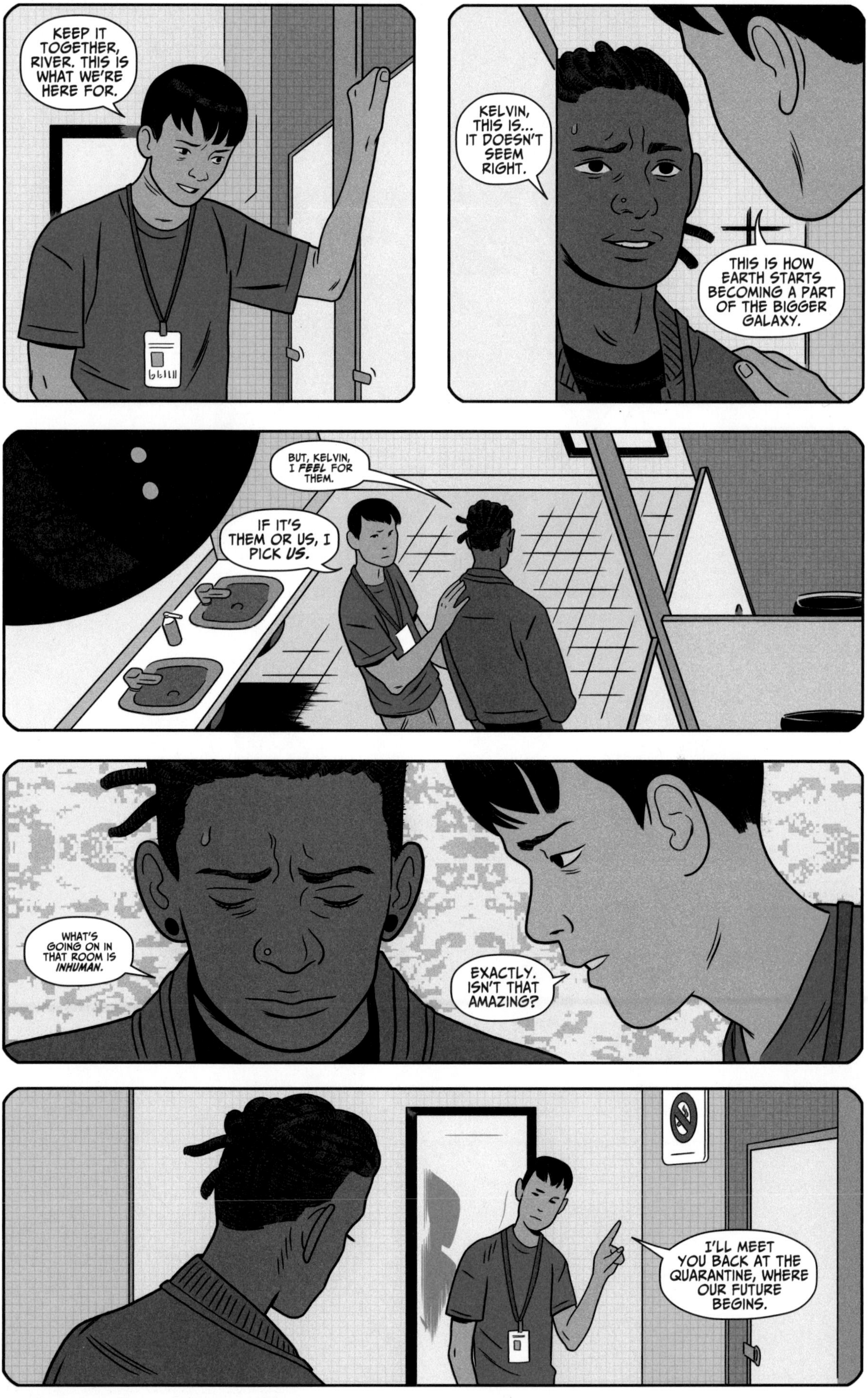
KEEP IT TOGETHER, RIVER. THIS IS WHAT WE'RE HERE FOR.
KELVIN, THIS IS... IT DOESN'T SEEM RIGHT.
THIS IS HOW EARTH STARTS BECOMING A PART OF THE BIGGER GALAXY.
BUT, KELVIN, I *FEEL* FOR THEM.
IF IT'S THEM OR US, I PICK *US*.
WHAT'S GOING ON IN THAT ROOM IS *INHUMAN*.
EXACTLY. ISN'T THAT AMAZING?
I'LL MEET YOU BACK AT THE QUARANTINE, WHERE OUR FUTURE BEGINS.

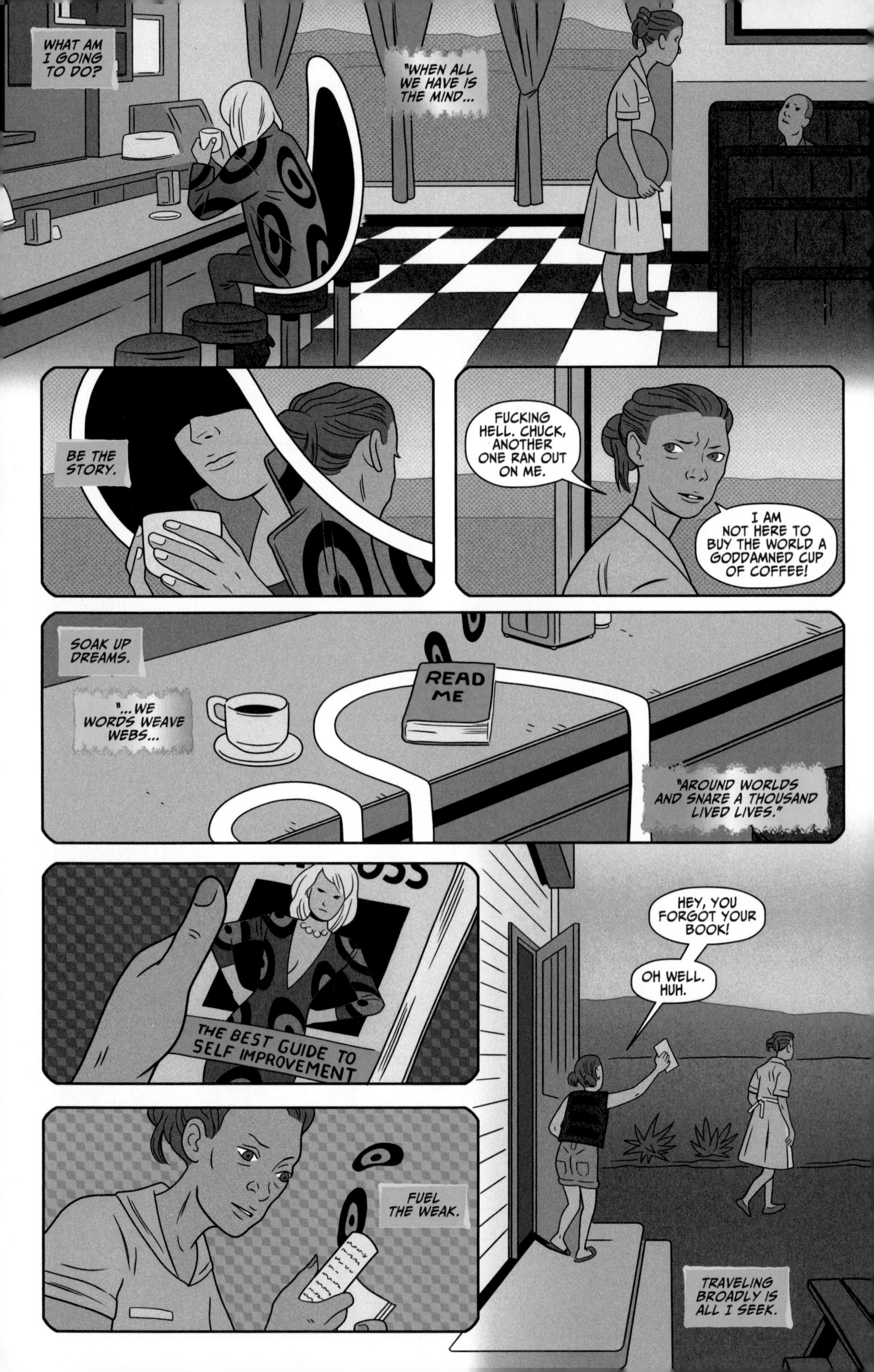

WHAT AM I GOING TO DO?
"WHEN ALL WE HAVE IS THE MIND...
BE THE STORY.
FUCKING HELL. CHUCK, ANOTHER ONE RAN OUT ON ME.
I AM NOT HERE TO BUY THE WORLD A GODDAMNED CUP OF COFFEE!
SOAK UP DREAMS.
"...WE WORDS WEAVE WEBS...
READ ME
"AROUND WORLDS AND SNARE A THOUSAND LIVED LIVES."
THE BEST GUIDE TO SELF IMPROVEMENT
HEY, YOU FORGOT YOUR BOOK!
OH WELL. HUH.
FUEL THE WEAK.
TRAVELING BROADLY IS ALL I SEEK.

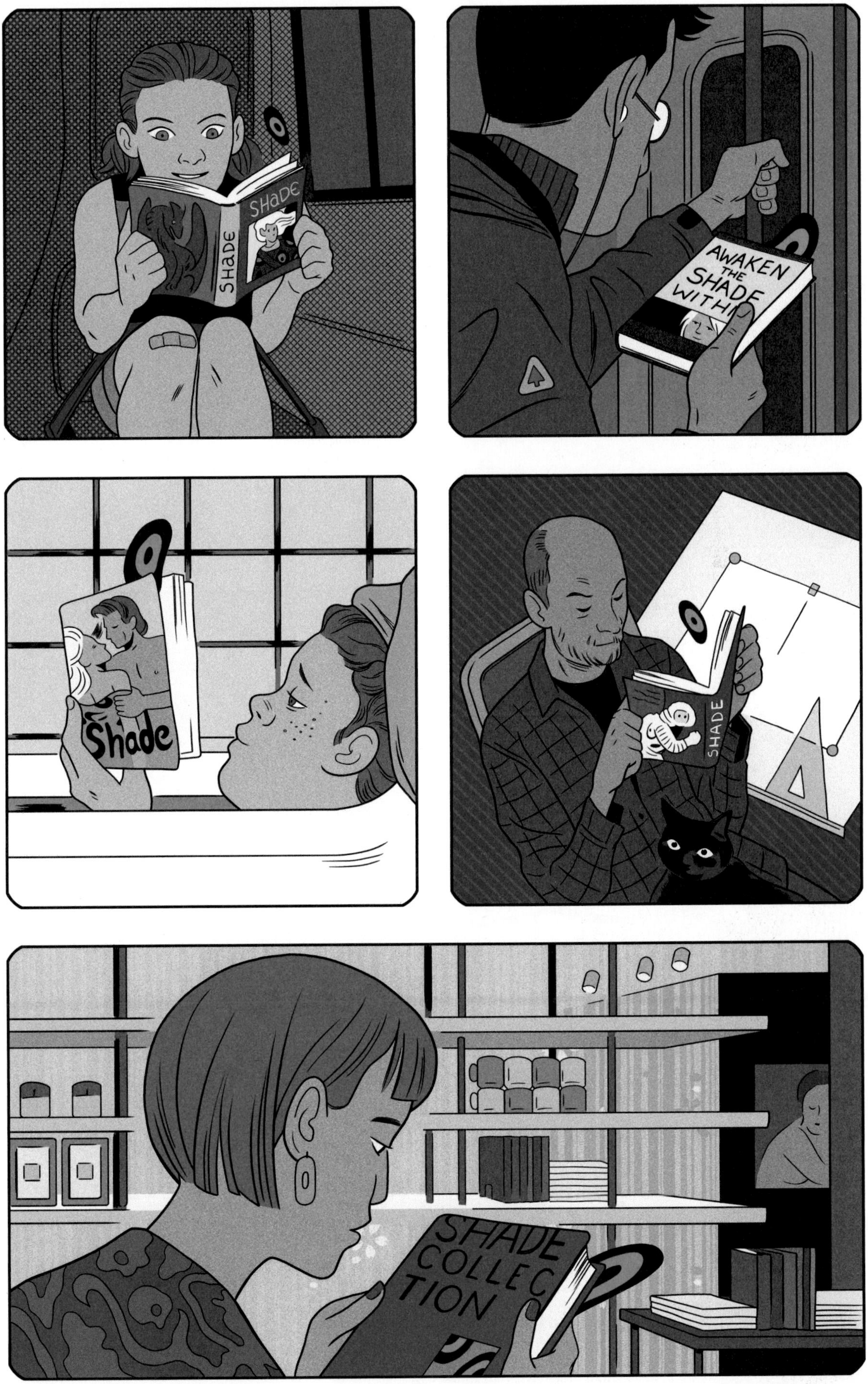
SHADE
SHADE
SHADE
AWAKEN THE SHADE WITHI
Shade
SHADE
SHADE COLLEC TION

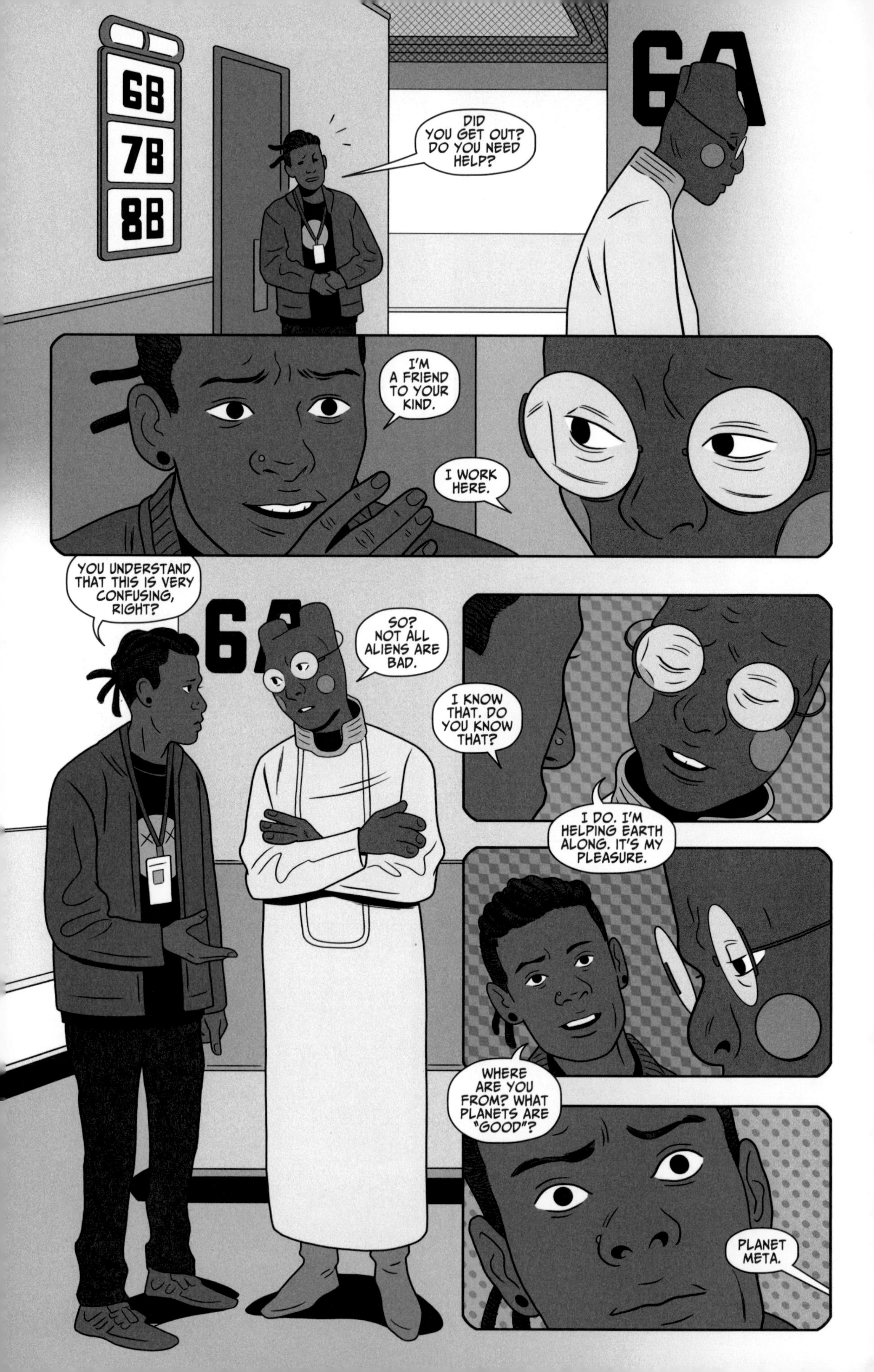
6B
7B
8B
DID YOU GET OUT? DO YOU NEED HELP?
I'M A FRIEND TO YOUR KIND.
I WORK HERE.
YOU UNDERSTAND THAT THIS IS VERY CONFUSING, RIGHT?
SO? NOT ALL ALIENS ARE BAD.
I KNOW THAT. DO YOU KNOW THAT?
I DO. I'M HELPING EARTH ALONG. IT'S MY PLEASURE.
WHERE ARE YOU FROM? WHAT PLANETS ARE "GOOD"?
PLANET META.

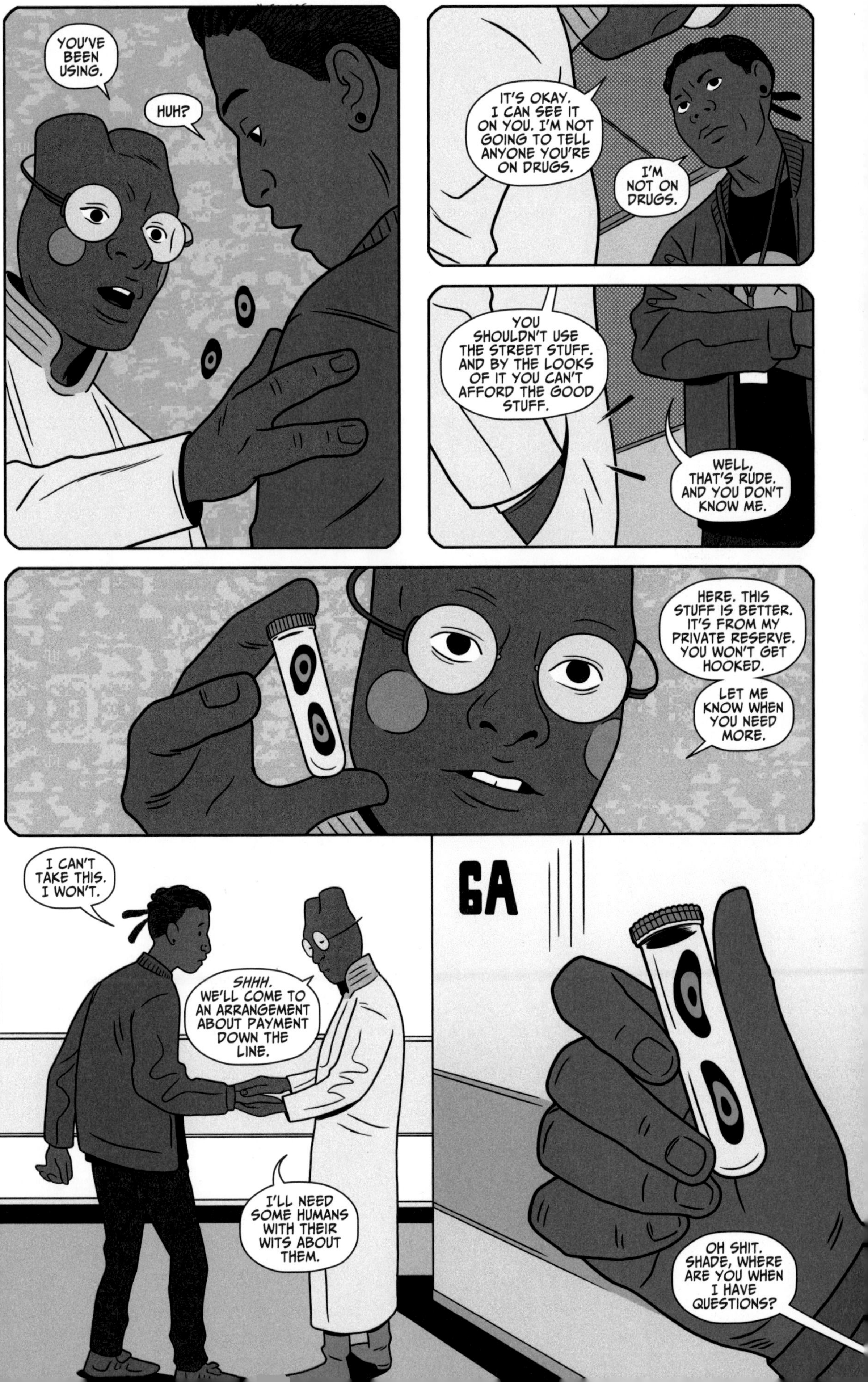
YOU'VE BEEN USING.
HUH?
IT'S OKAY. I CAN SEE IT ON YOU. I'M NOT GOING TO TELL ANYONE YOU'RE ON DRUGS.
I'M NOT ON DRUGS.
YOU SHOULDN'T USE THE STREET STUFF. AND BY THE LOOKS OF IT YOU CAN'T AFFORD THE GOOD STUFF.
WELL, THAT'S RUDE. AND YOU DON'T KNOW ME.
HERE. THIS STUFF IS BETTER. IT'S FROM MY PRIVATE RESERVE. YOU WON'T GET HOOKED.
LET ME KNOW WHEN YOU NEED MORE.
I CAN'T TAKE THIS. I WON'T.
SHHH. WE'LL COME TO AN ARRANGEMENT ABOUT PAYMENT DOWN THE LINE.
I'LL NEED SOME HUMANS WITH THEIR WITS ABOUT THEM.
6A
OH SHIT. SHADE, WHERE ARE YOU WHEN I HAVE QUESTIONS?

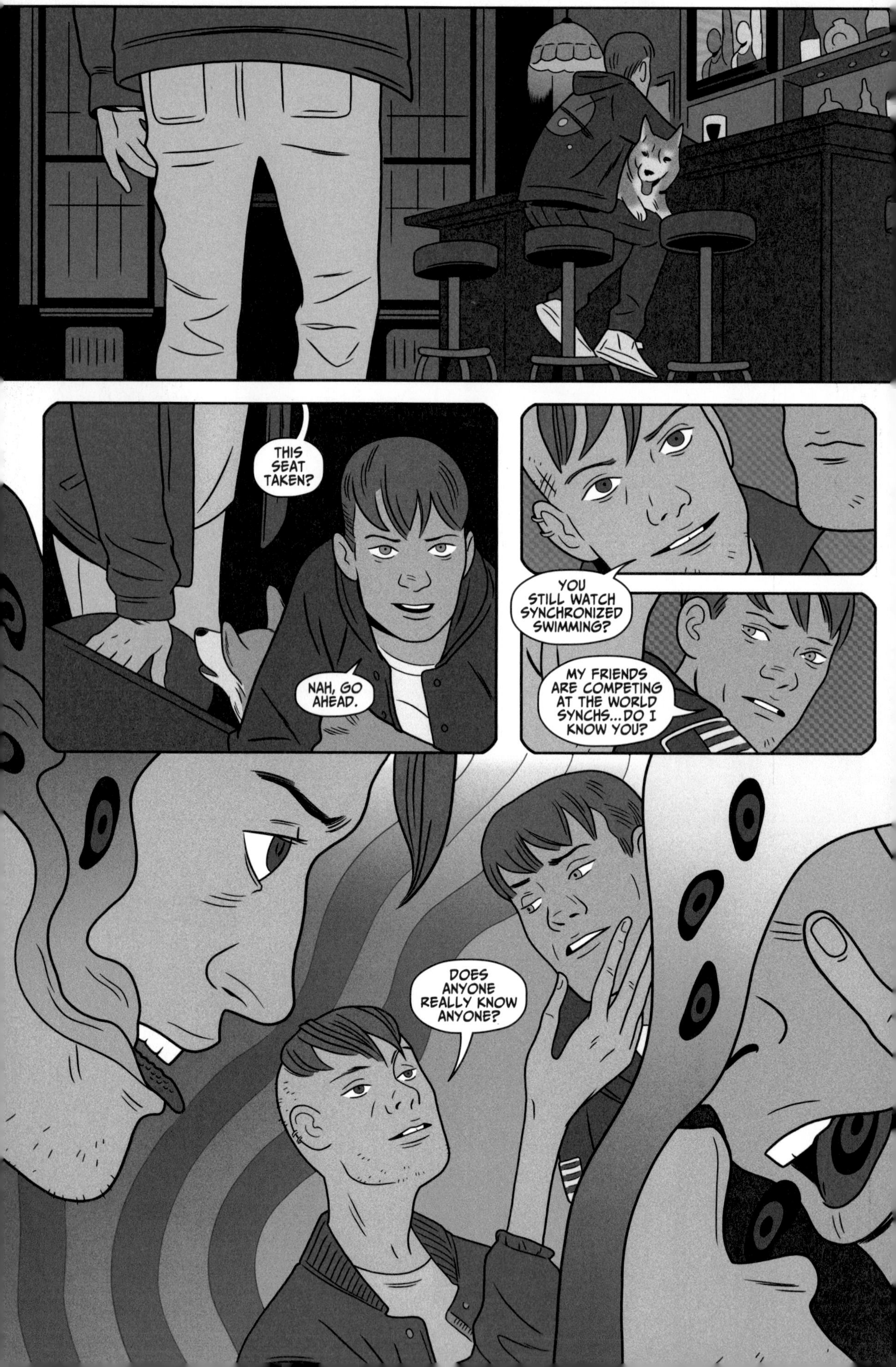
THIS SEAT TAKEN?
NAH, GO AHEAD.
YOU STILL WATCH SYNCHRONIZED SWIMMING?
MY FRIENDS ARE COMPETING AT THE WORLD SYNCHS...DO I KNOW YOU?
DOES ANYONE REALLY KNOW ANYONE?

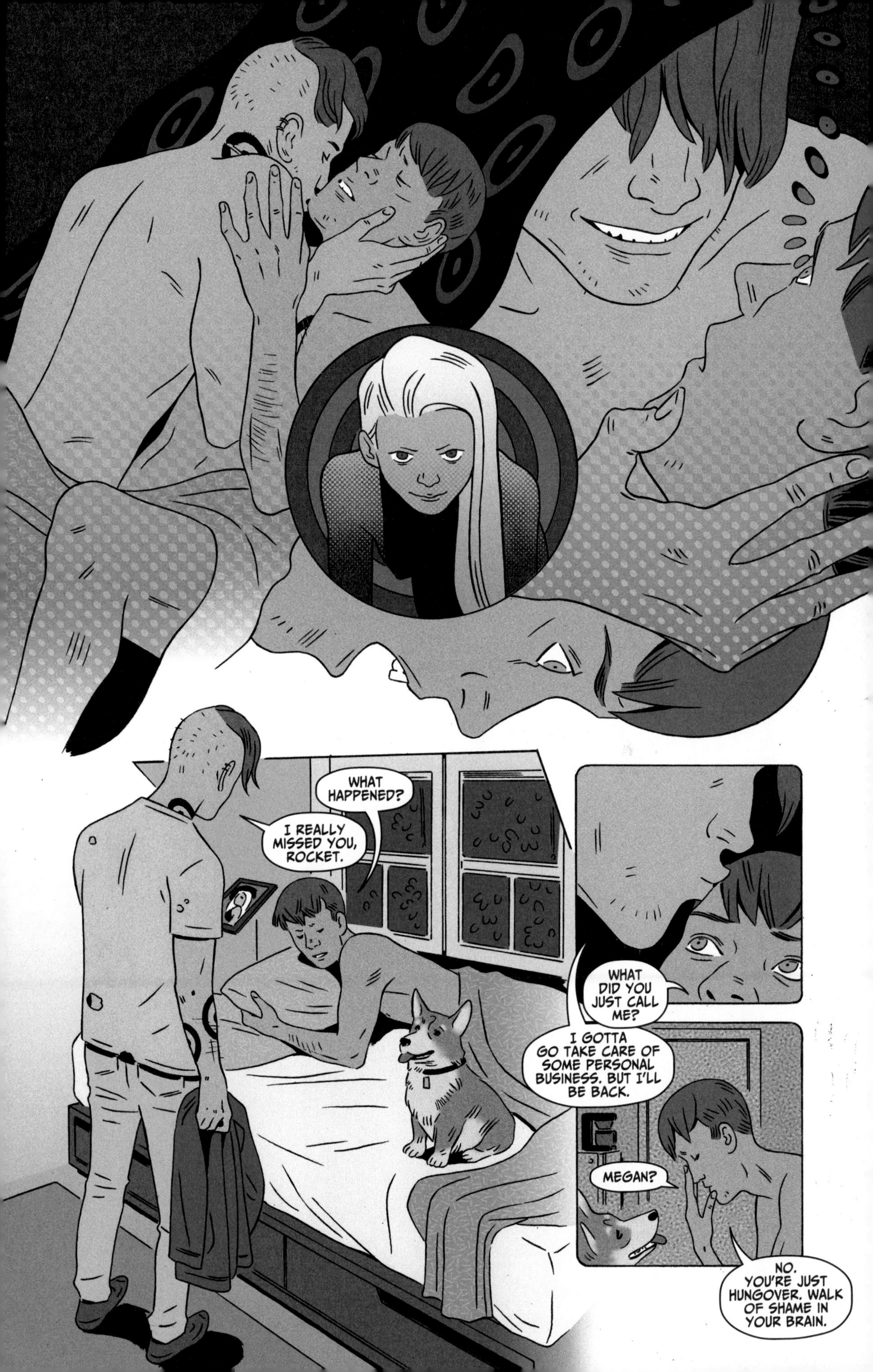
WHAT HAPPENED?
I REALLY MISSED YOU, ROCKET.
WHAT DID YOU JUST CALL ME?
I GOTTA GO TAKE CARE OF SOME PERSONAL BUSINESS. BUT I'LL BE BACK.
MEGAN?
NO. YOU'RE JUST HUNGOVER. WALK OF SHAME IN YOUR BRAIN.

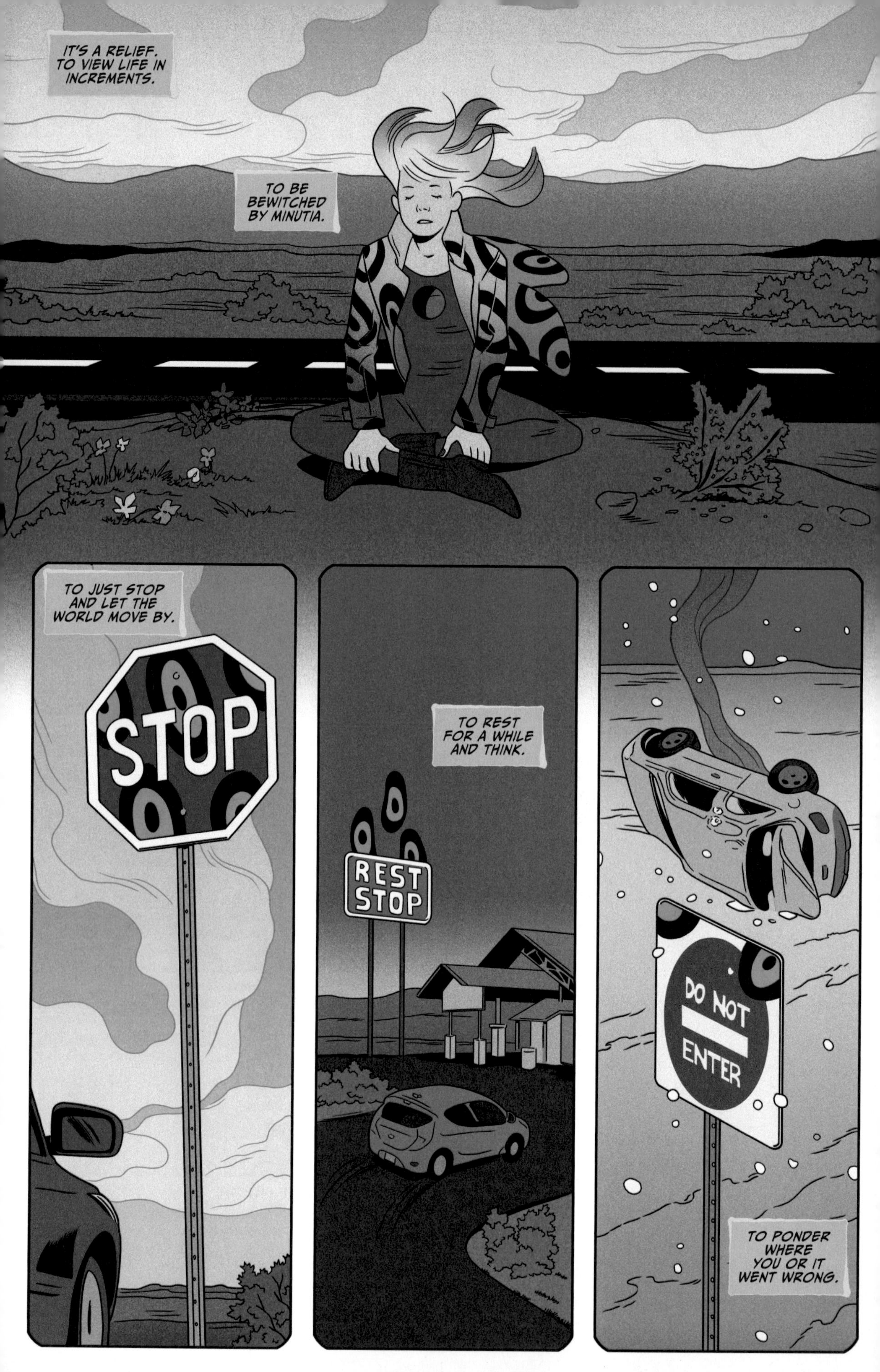
IT'S A RELIEF. TO VIEW LIFE IN INCREMENTS.
TO BE BEWITCHED BY MINUTIA.
TO JUST STOP AND LET THE WORLD MOVE BY.
STOP
TO REST FOR A WHILE AND THINK.
REST STOP
DO NOT ENTER
TO PONDER WHERE YOU OR IT WENT WRONG.

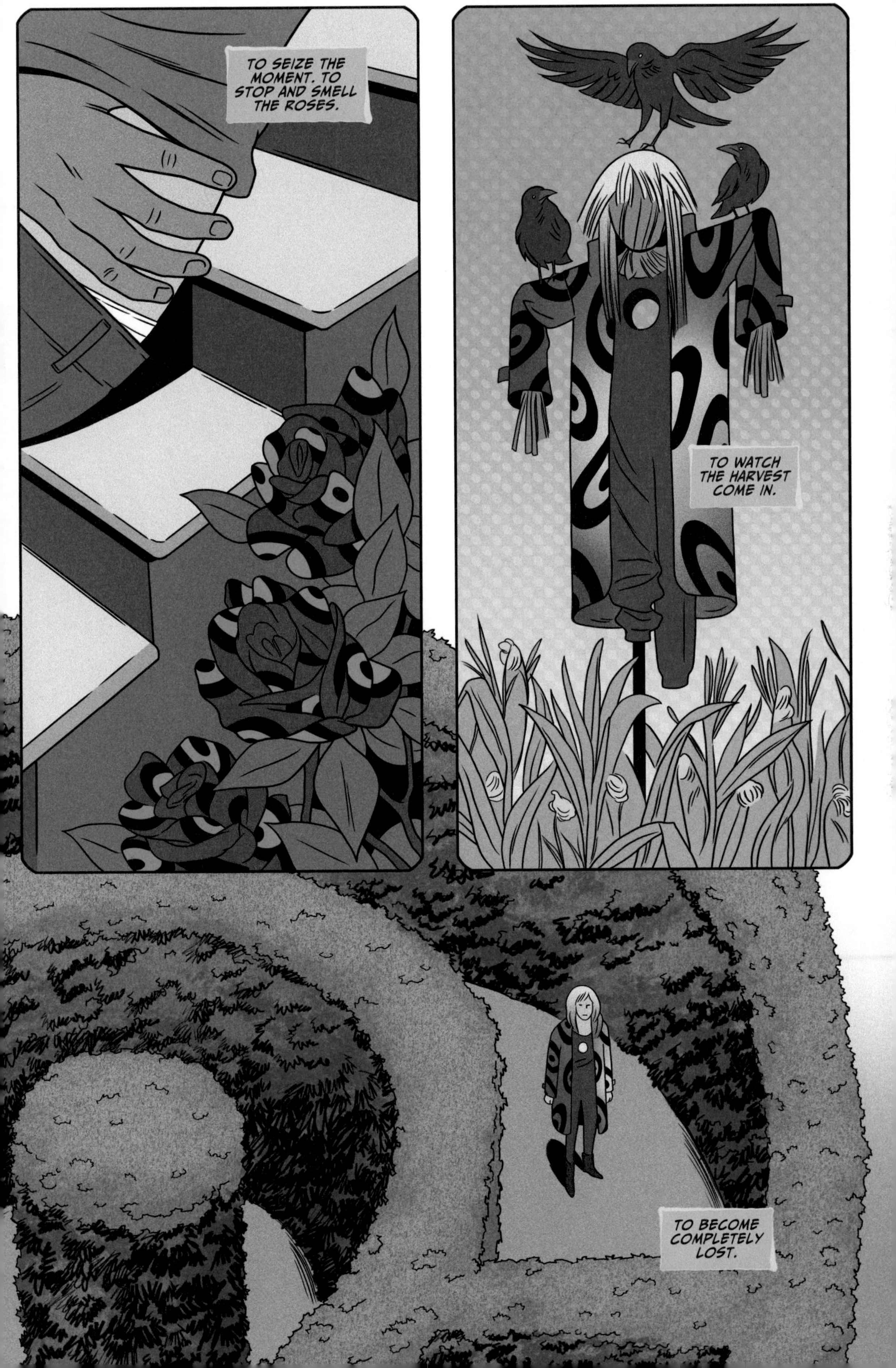
TO SEIZE THE MOMENT. TO STOP AND SMELL THE ROSES.
TO WATCH THE HARVEST COME IN.
TO BECOME COMPLETELY LOST.

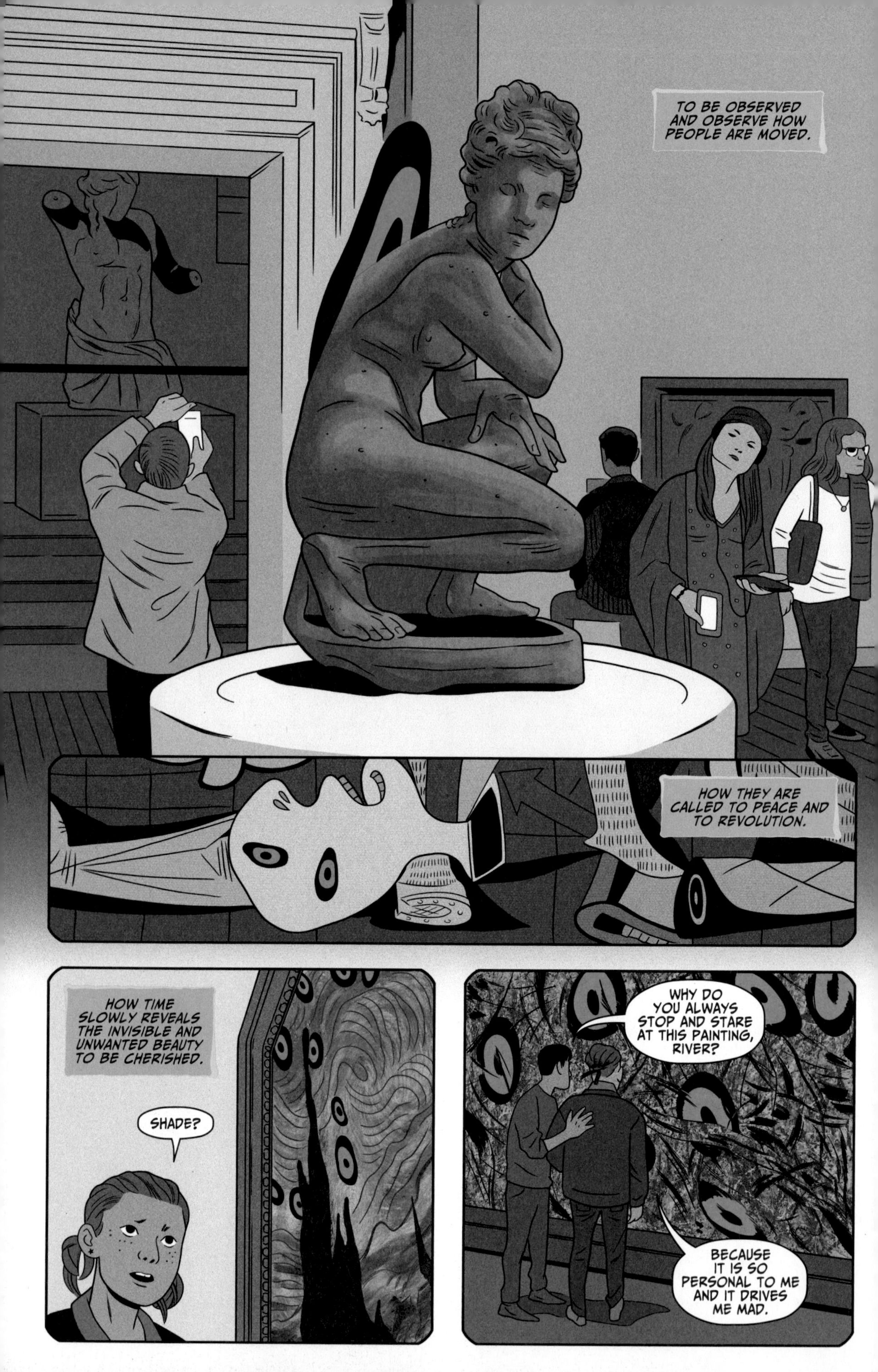
TO BE OBSERVED AND OBSERVE HOW PEOPLE ARE MOVED.
HOW THEY ARE CALLED TO PEACE AND TO REVOLUTION.
HOW TIME SLOWLY REVEALS THE INVISIBLE AND UNWANTED BEAUTY TO BE CHERISHED.
SHADE?
WHY DO YOU ALWAYS STOP AND STARE AT THIS PAINTING, RIVER?
BECAUSE IT IS SO PERSONAL TO ME AND IT DRIVES ME MAD.

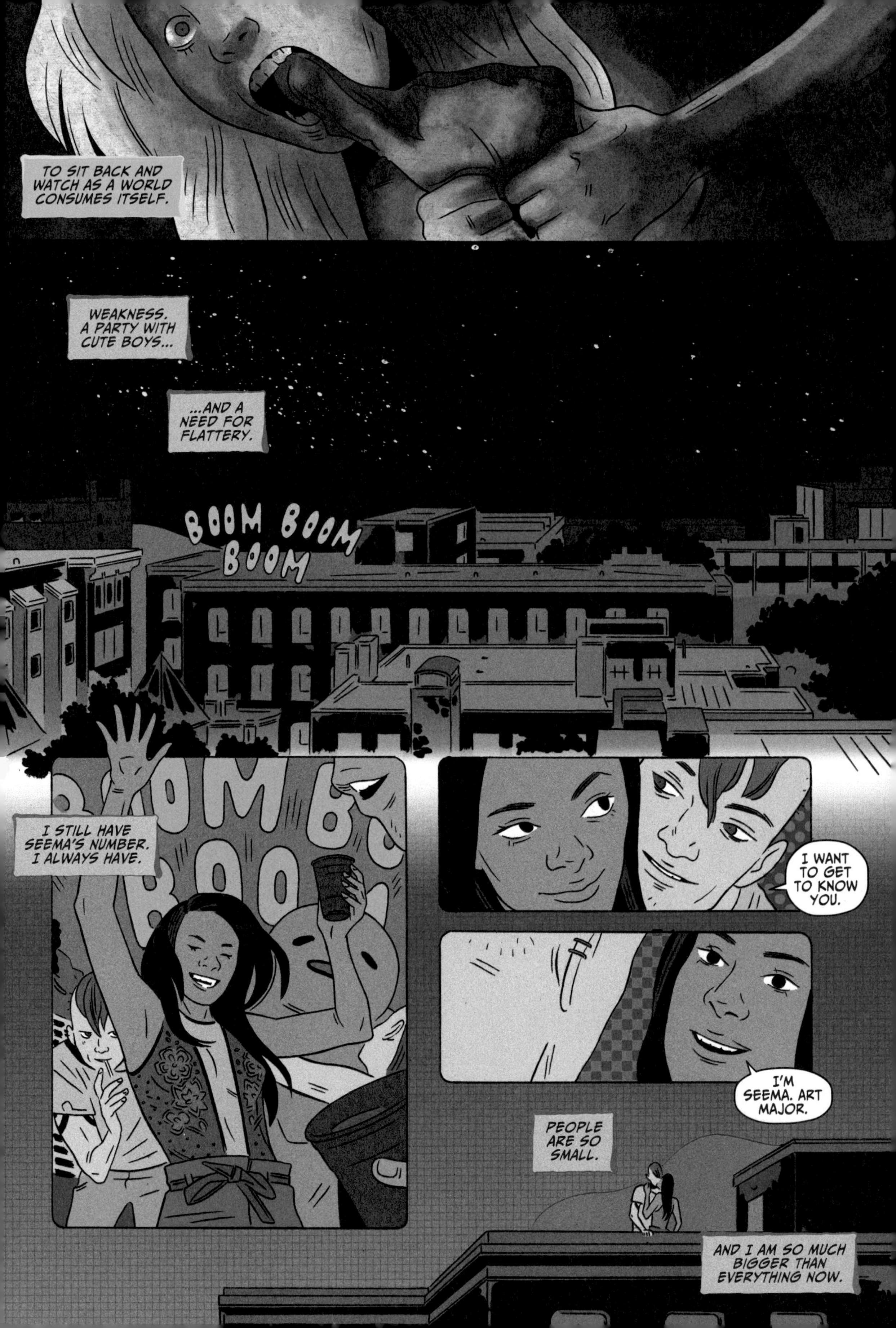
TO SIT BACK AND WATCH AS A WORLD CONSUMES ITSELF.
WEAKNESS. A PARTY WITH CUTE BOYS...
...AND A NEED FOR FLATTERY.
BOOM BOOM BOOM
I STILL HAVE SEEMA'S NUMBER. I ALWAYS HAVE.
I WANT TO GET TO KNOW YOU.
I'M SEEMA. ART MAJOR.
PEOPLE ARE SO SMALL.
AND I AM SO MUCH BIGGER THAN EVERYTHING NOW.

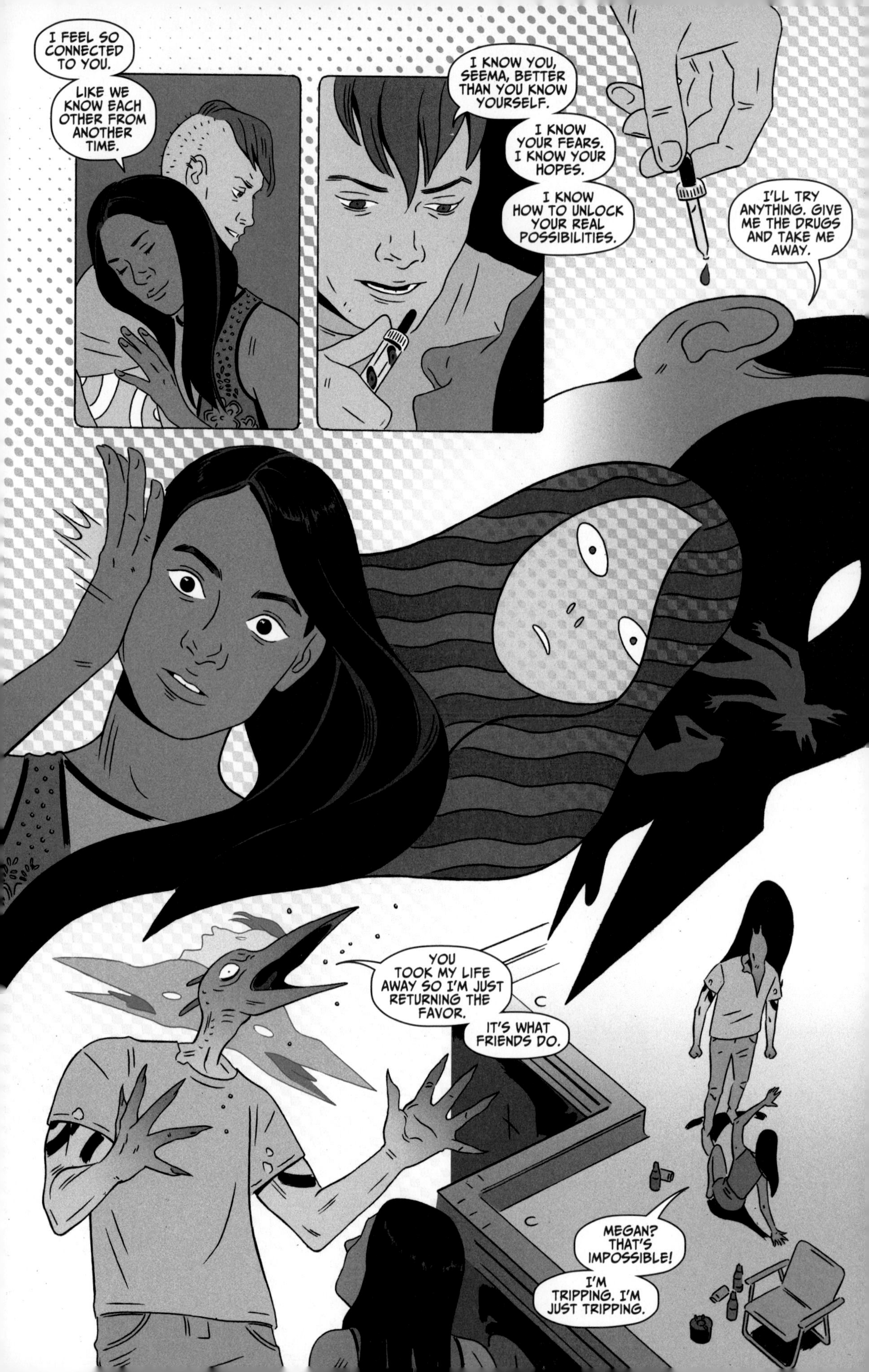
I FEEL SO CONNECTED TO YOU.
LIKE WE KNOW EACH OTHER FROM ANOTHER TIME.
I KNOW YOU, SEEMA, BETTER THAN YOU KNOW YOURSELF.
I KNOW YOUR FEARS. I KNOW YOUR HOPES.
I KNOW HOW TO UNLOCK YOUR REAL POSSIBILITIES.
I'LL TRY ANYTHING. GIVE ME THE DRUGS AND TAKE ME AWAY.
YOU TOOK MY LIFE AWAY SO I'M JUST RETURNING THE FAVOR.
IT'S WHAT FRIENDS DO.
MEGAN? THAT'S IMPOSSIBLE!
I'M TRIPPING. I'M JUST TRIPPING.

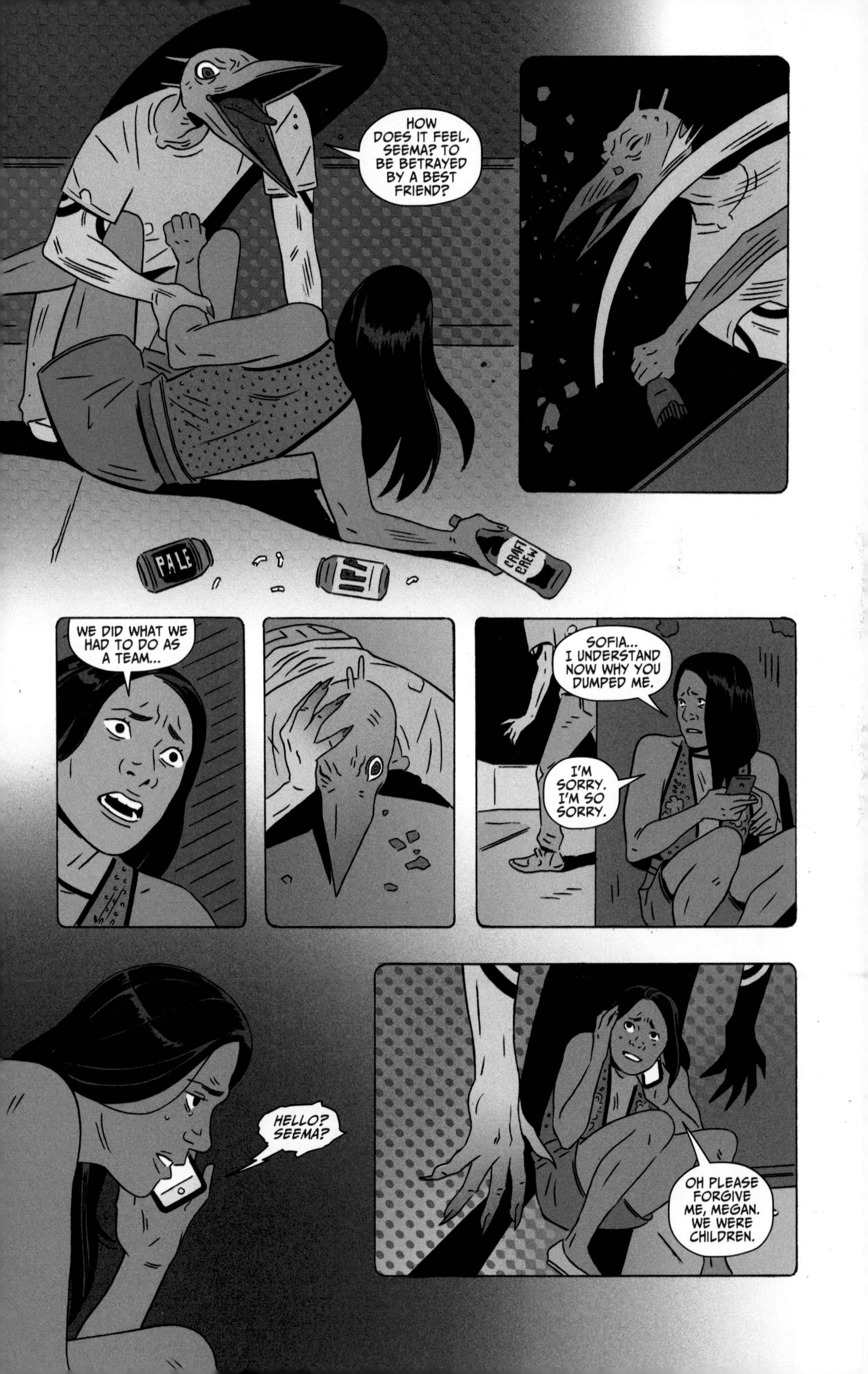
HOW DOES IT FEEL, SEEMA? TO BE BETRAYED BY A BEST FRIEND?
PALE
IPA
CRAFT CREW
WE DID WHAT WE HAD TO DO AS A TEAM...
SOFIA... I UNDERSTAND NOW WHY YOU DUMPED ME.
I'M SORRY. I'M SO SORRY.
HELLO? SEEMA?
OH PLEASE FORGIVE ME, MEGAN. WE WERE CHILDREN.

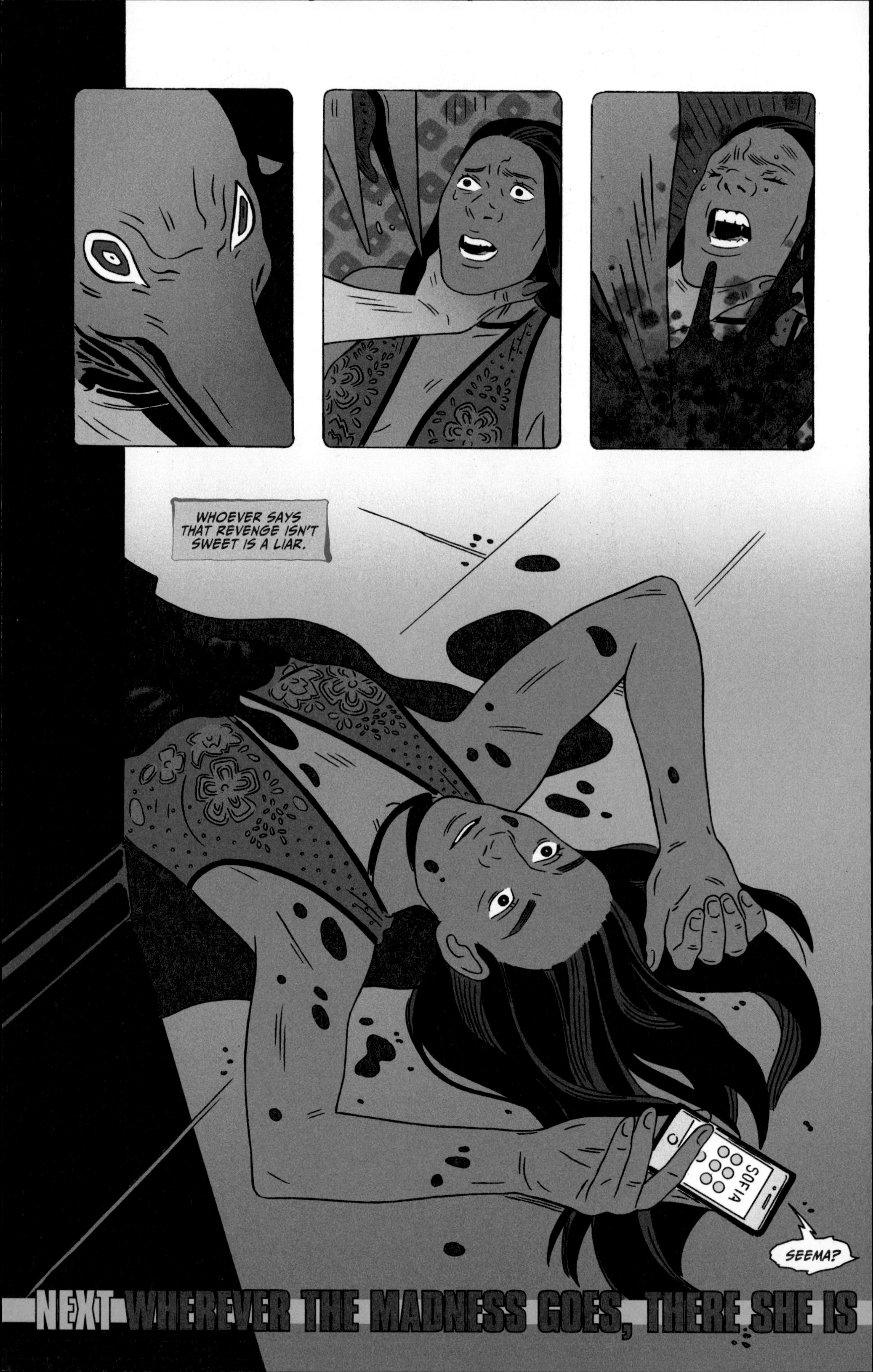
WHOEVER SAYS THAT REVENGE ISN'T SWEET IS A LIAR.
SOFIA
SEEMA?
NEXT WHEREVER THE MADNESS GOES, THERE SHE IS

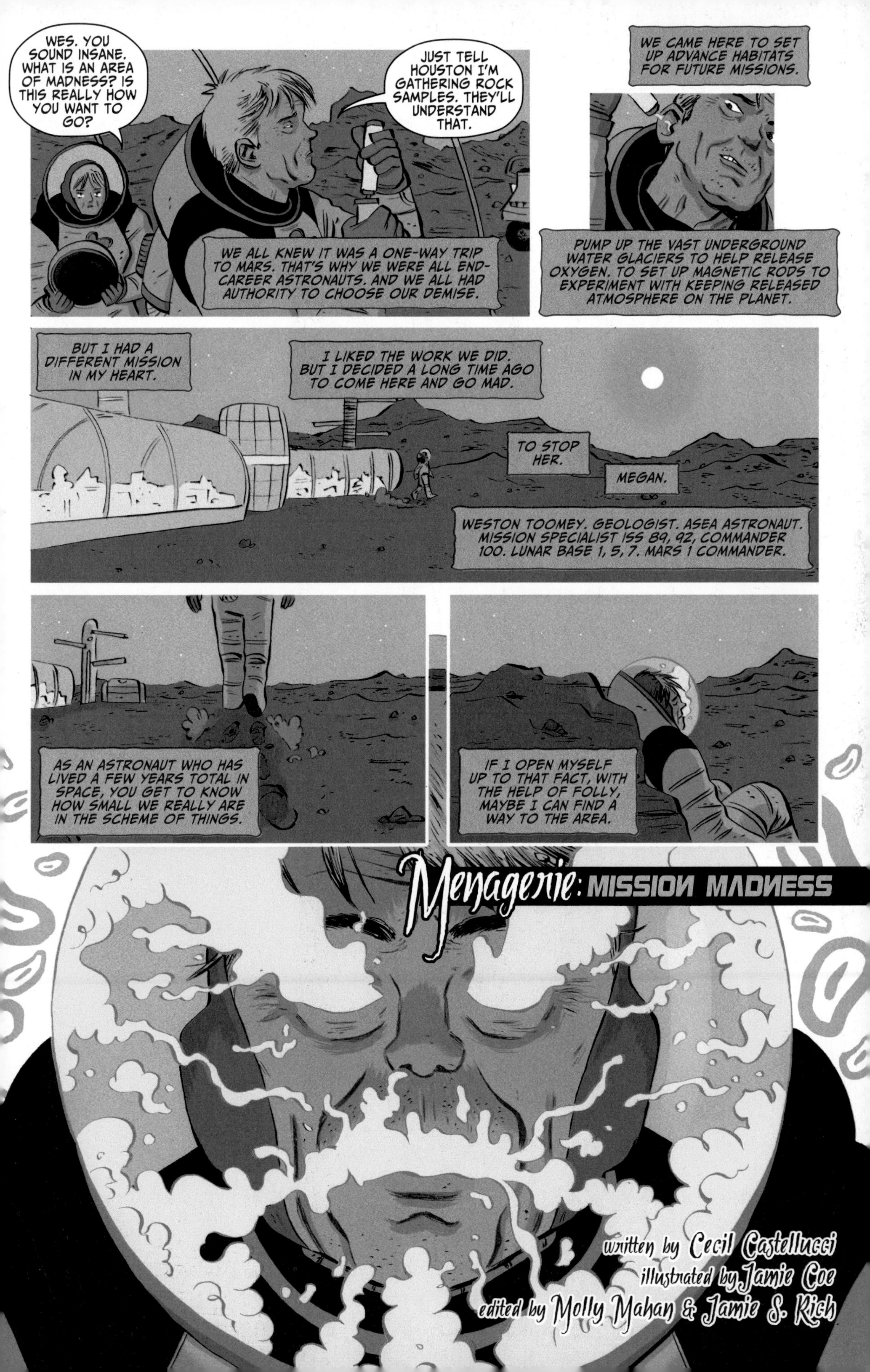
WES. YOU SOUND INSANE. WHAT IS AN AREA OF MADNESS? IS THIS REALLY HOW YOU WANT TO GO?
JUST TELL HOUSTON I'M GATHERING ROCK SAMPLES. THEY'LL UNDERSTAND THAT.
WE ALL KNEW IT WAS A ONE-WAY TRIP TO MARS. THAT'S WHY WE WERE ALL END-CAREER ASTRONAUTS. AND WE ALL HAD AUTHORITY TO CHOOSE OUR DEMISE.
WE CAME HERE TO SET UP ADVANCE HABITATS FOR FUTURE MISSIONS.
PUMP UP THE VAST UNDERGROUND WATER GLACIERS TO HELP RELEASE OXYGEN. TO SET UP MAGNETIC RODS TO EXPERIMENT WITH KEEPING RELEASED ATMOSPHERE ON THE PLANET.
BUT I HAD A DIFFERENT MISSION IN MY HEART.
I LIKED THE WORK WE DID. BUT I DECIDED A LONG TIME AGO TO COME HERE AND GO MAD.
TO STOP HER.
MEGAN.
WESTON TOOMEY. GEOLOGIST. ASEA ASTRONAUT. MISSION SPECIALIST ISS 89, 92, COMMANDER 100. LUNAR BASE 1, 5, 7. MARS 1 COMMANDER.
AS AN ASTRONAUT WHO HAS LIVED A FEW YEARS TOTAL IN SPACE, YOU GET TO KNOW HOW SMALL WE REALLY ARE IN THE SCHEME OF THINGS.
IF I OPEN MYSELF UP TO THAT FACT, WITH THE HELP OF FOLLY, MAYBE I CAN FIND A WAY TO THE AREA.
Menagerie: MISSION MADNESS
written by Cecil Castellucci
illustrated by Jamie Coe
edited by Molly Mahan & Jamie S. Rich

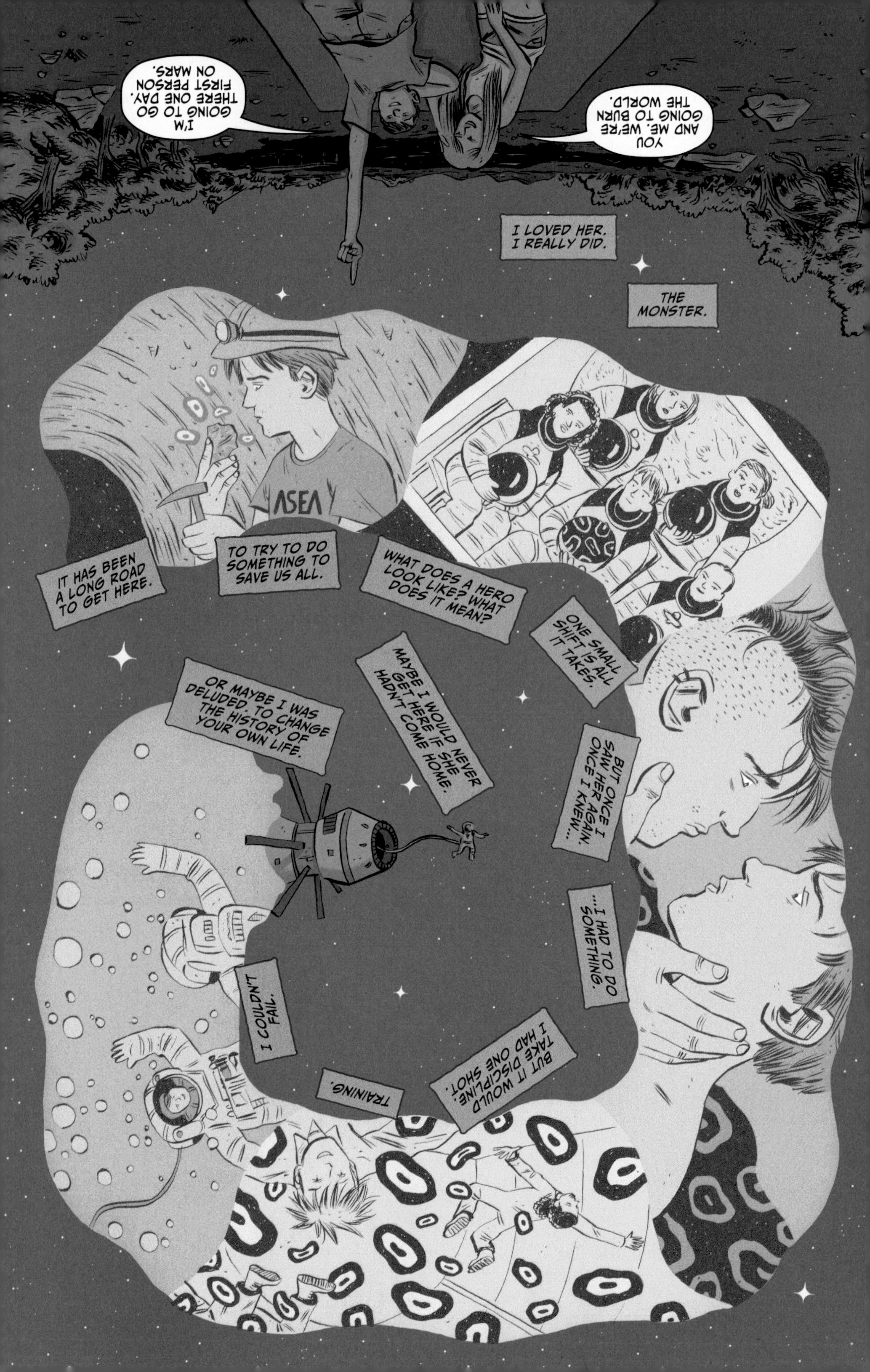
YOU AND ME. WE'RE GOING TO BURN THE WORLD.
I'M GOING TO GO THERE ONE DAY. FIRST PERSON ON MARS.
I LOVED HER. I REALLY DID.
THE MONSTER.
ASEA
IT HAS BEEN A LONG ROAD TO GET HERE.
TO TRY TO DO SOMETHING TO SAVE US ALL.
WHAT DOES A HERO LOOK LIKE? WHAT DOES IT MEAN?
ONE SMALL SHIFT IS ALL IT TAKES.
BUT ONCE I SAW HER AGAIN. ONCE I KNEW...
...I HAD TO DO SOMETHING.
BUT IT WOULD TAKE DISCIPLINE. I HAD ONE SHOT.
TRAINING.
I COULDN'T FAIL.
OR MAYBE I WAS DELUDED. TO CHANGE THE HISTORY OF YOUR OWN LIFE.
MAYBE I WOULD NEVER GET HERE IF SHE HADN'T COME HOME.

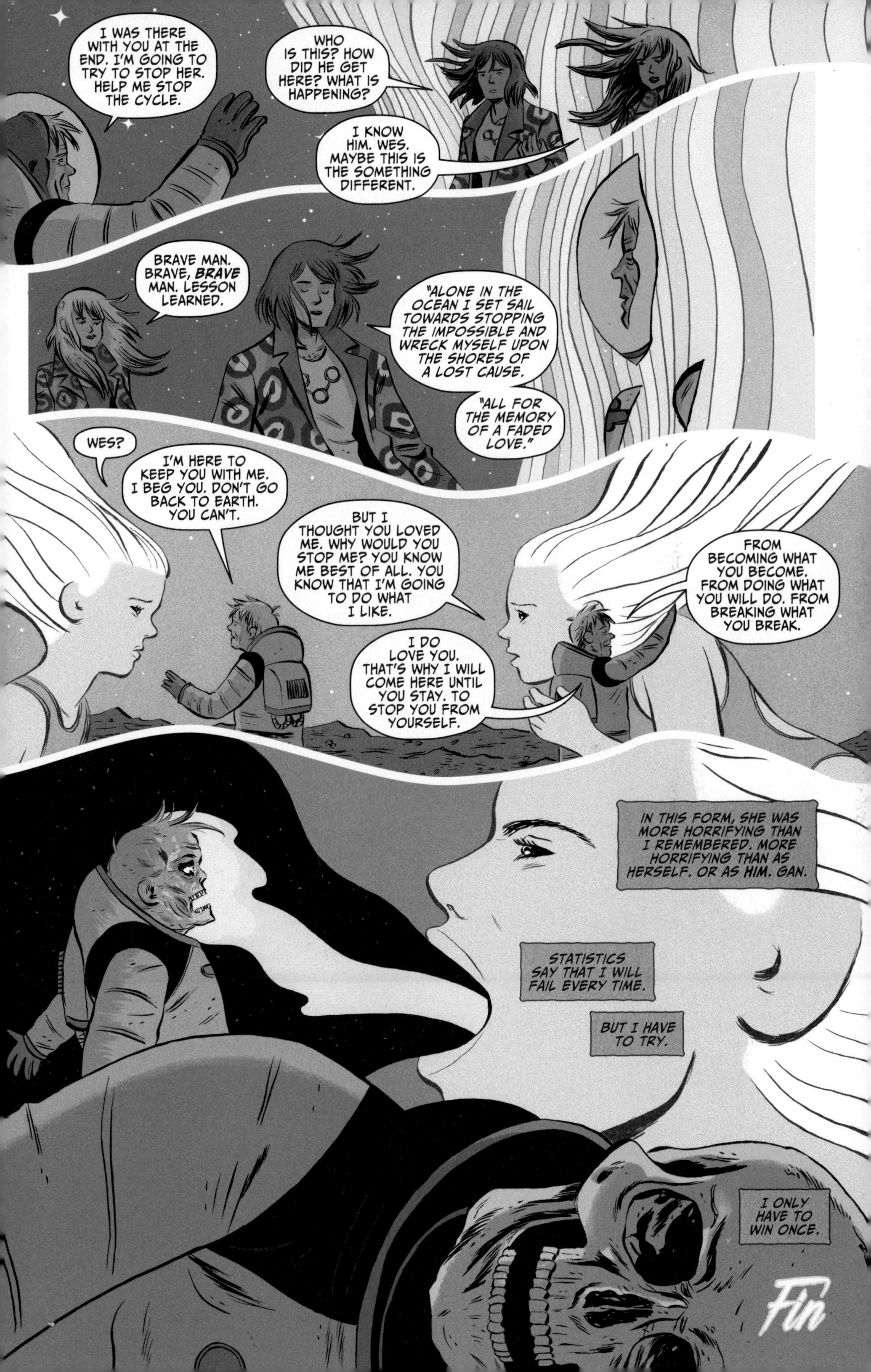
I WAS THERE WITH YOU AT THE END. I'M GOING TO TRY TO STOP HER. HELP ME STOP THE CYCLE.
WHO IS THIS? HOW DID HE GET HERE? WHAT IS HAPPENING?
I KNOW HIM. WES. MAYBE THIS IS THE SOMETHING DIFFERENT.
BRAVE MAN. BRAVE, BRAVE MAN. LESSON LEARNED.
"ALONE IN THE OCEAN I SET SAIL TOWARDS STOPPING THE IMPOSSIBLE AND WRECK MYSELF UPON THE SHORES OF A LOST CAUSE.
"ALL FOR THE MEMORY OF A FADED LOVE."
WES?
I'M HERE TO KEEP YOU WITH ME. I BEG YOU. DON'T GO BACK TO EARTH. YOU CAN'T.
BUT I THOUGHT YOU LOVED ME. WHY WOULD YOU STOP ME? YOU KNOW ME BEST OF ALL. YOU KNOW THAT I'M GOING TO DO WHAT I LIKE.
FROM BECOMING WHAT YOU BECOME. FROM DOING WHAT YOU WILL DO. FROM BREAKING WHAT YOU BREAK.
I DO LOVE YOU. THAT'S WHY I WILL COME HERE UNTIL YOU STAY. TO STOP YOU FROM YOURSELF.
IN THIS FORM, SHE WAS MORE HORRIFYING THAN I REMEMBERED. MORE HORRIFYING THAN AS HERSELF. OR AS HIM. GAN.
STATISTICS SAY THAT I WILL FAIL EVERY TIME.
BUT I HAVE TO TRY.
I ONLY HAVE TO WIN ONCE.
Fin

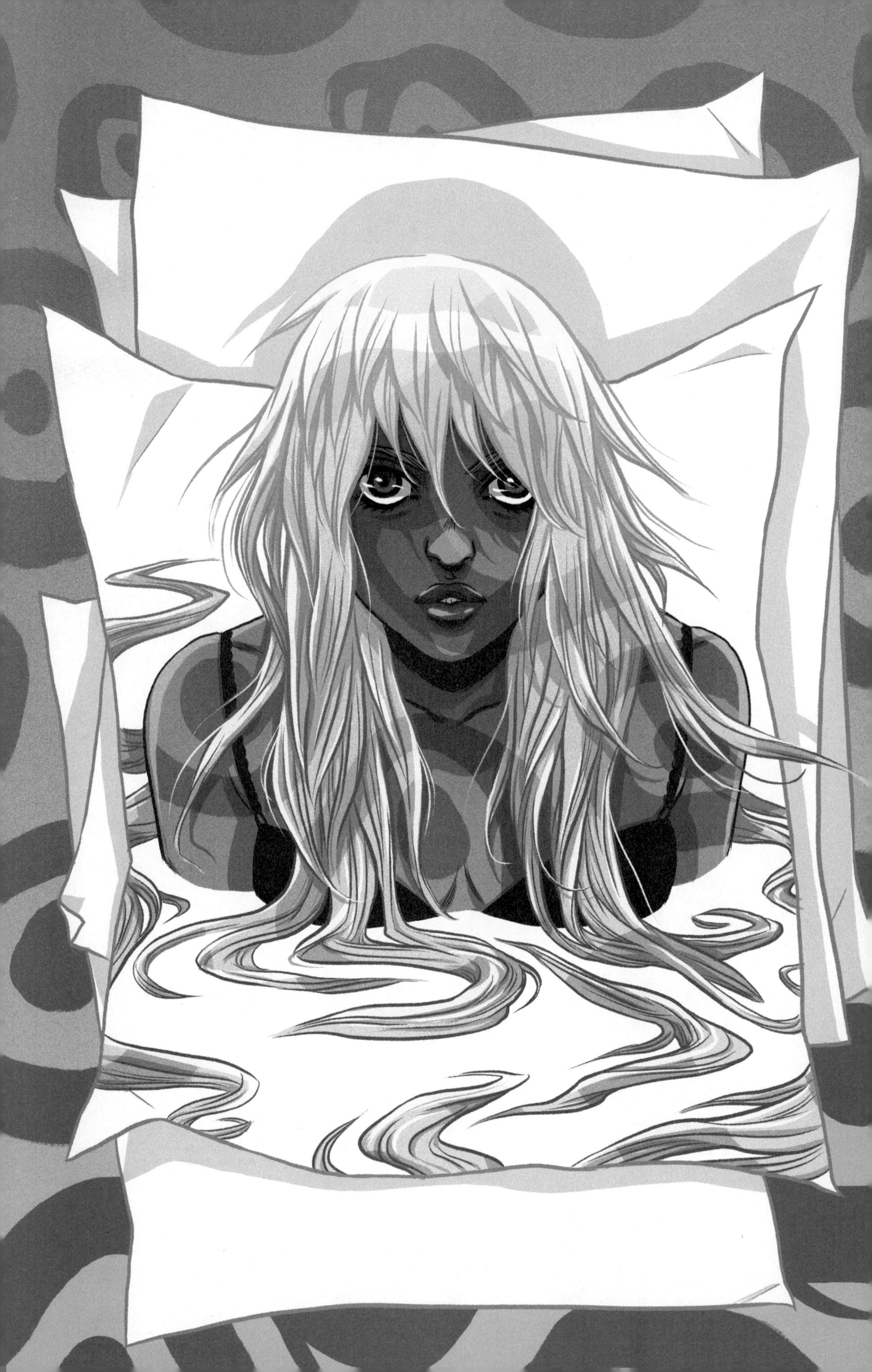

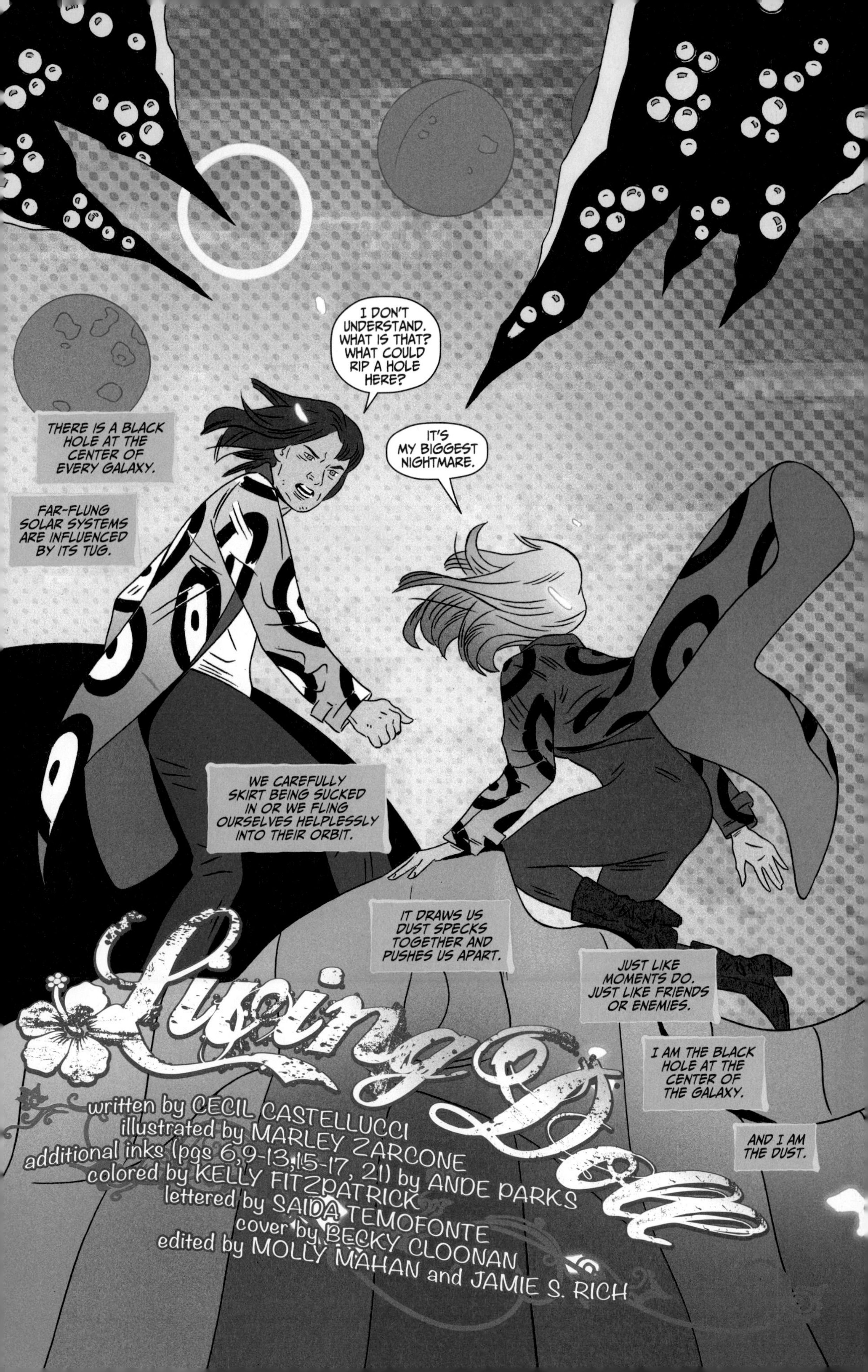
I DON'T UNDERSTAND. WHAT IS THAT? WHAT COULD RIP A HOLE HERE?
THERE IS A BLACK HOLE AT THE CENTER OF EVERY GALAXY.
IT'S MY BIGGEST NIGHTMARE.
FAR-FLUNG SOLAR SYSTEMS ARE INFLUENCED BY ITS TUG.
WE CAREFULLY SKIRT BEING SUCKED IN OR WE FLING OURSELVES HELPLESSLY INTO THEIR ORBIT.
IT DRAWS US DUST SPECKS TOGETHER AND PUSHES US APART.
JUST LIKE MOMENTS DO. JUST LIKE FRIENDS OR ENEMIES.
I AM THE BLACK HOLE AT THE CENTER OF THE GALAXY.
AND I AM THE DUST.
written by CECIL CASTELLUCCI
illustrated by MARLEY ZARCONE
additional inks (pgs 6,9-13,15-17, 21) by ANDE PARKS
colored by KELLY FITZPATRICK
lettered by SAIDA TEMOFONTE
cover by BECKY CLOONAN
edited by MOLLY MAHAN and JAMIE S. RICH

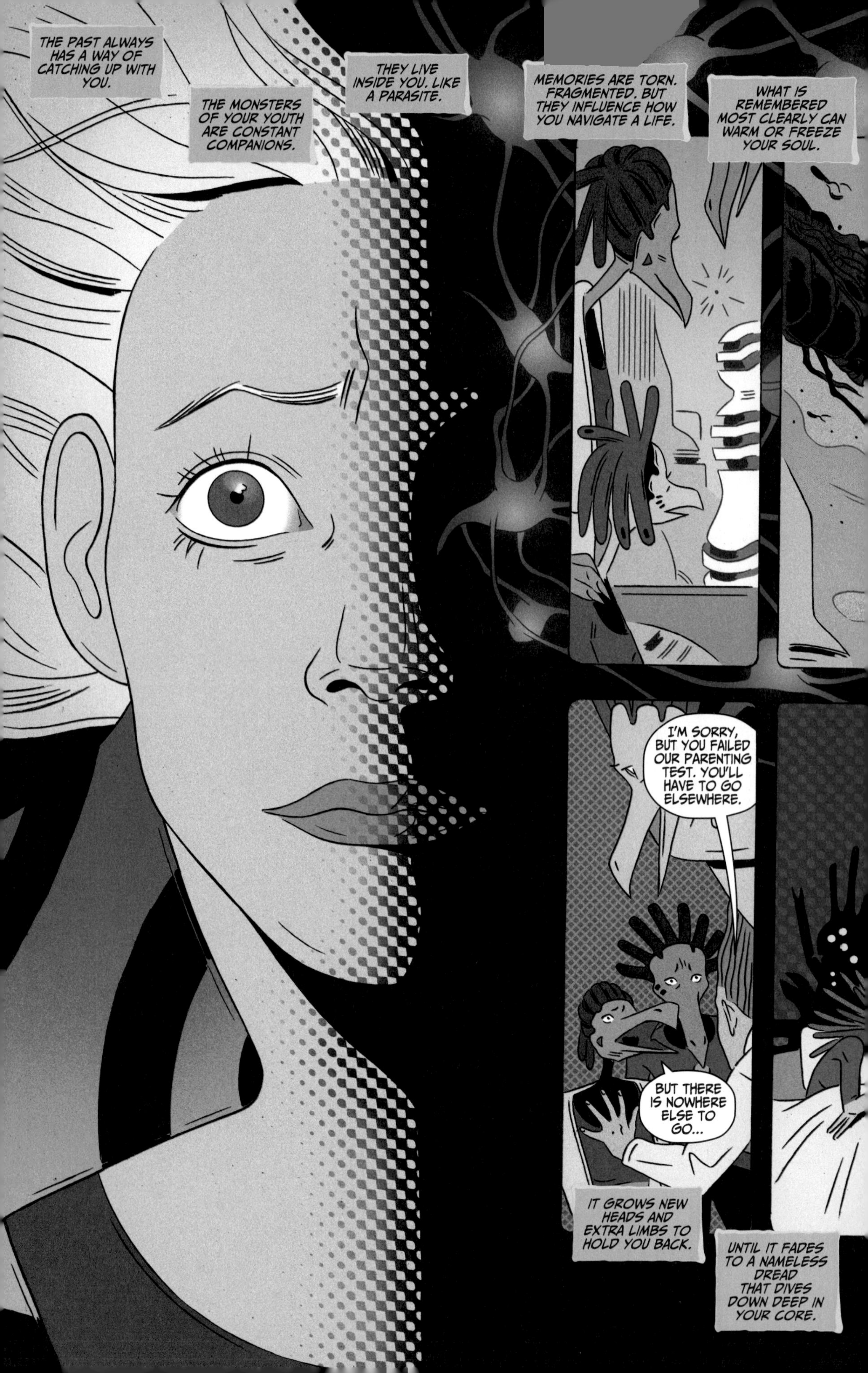
THE PAST ALWAYS HAS A WAY OF CATCHING UP WITH YOU.
THE MONSTERS OF YOUR YOUTH ARE CONSTANT COMPANIONS.
THEY LIVE INSIDE YOU. LIKE A PARASITE.
MEMORIES ARE TORN. FRAGMENTED. BUT THEY INFLUENCE HOW YOU NAVIGATE A LIFE.
WHAT IS REMEMBERED MOST CLEARLY CAN WARM OR FREEZE YOUR SOUL.
I'M SORRY, BUT YOU FAILED OUR PARENTING TEST. YOU'LL HAVE TO GO ELSEWHERE.
BUT THERE IS NOWHERE ELSE TO GO...
IT GROWS NEW HEADS AND EXTRA LIMBS TO HOLD YOU BACK.
UNTIL IT FADES TO A NAMELESS DREAD THAT DIVES DOWN DEEP IN YOUR CORE.

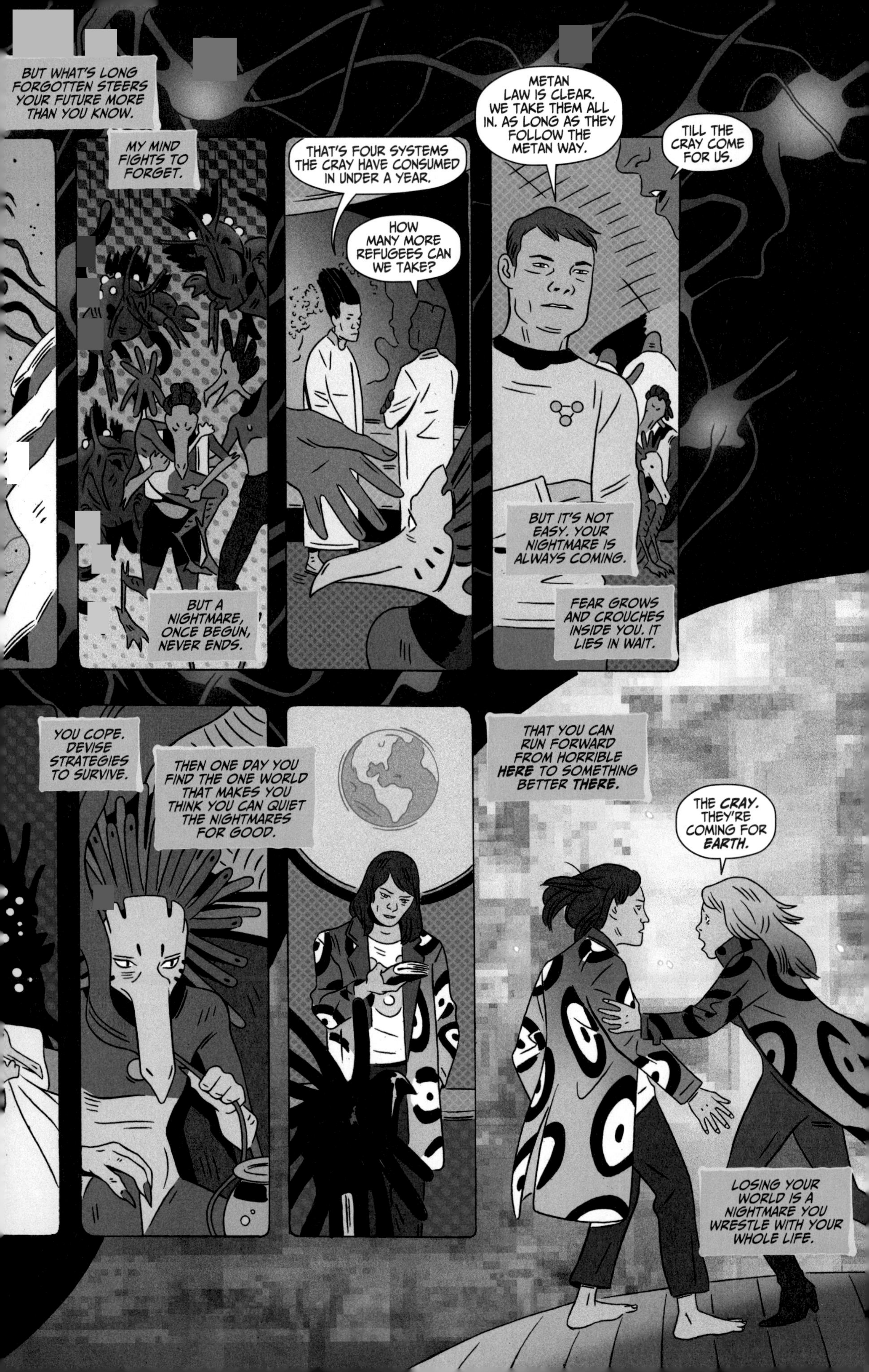

BUT WHAT'S LONG FORGOTTEN STEERS YOUR FUTURE MORE THAN YOU KNOW.
MY MIND FIGHTS TO FORGET.
BUT A NIGHTMARE, ONCE BEGUN, NEVER ENDS.
THAT'S FOUR SYSTEMS THE CRAY HAVE CONSUMED IN UNDER A YEAR.
HOW MANY MORE REFUGEES CAN WE TAKE?
METAN LAW IS CLEAR. WE TAKE THEM ALL IN. AS LONG AS THEY FOLLOW THE METAN WAY.
TILL THE CRAY COME FOR US.
BUT IT'S NOT EASY. YOUR NIGHTMARE IS ALWAYS COMING.
FEAR GROWS AND CROUCHES INSIDE YOU. IT LIES IN WAIT.
YOU COPE. DEVISE STRATEGIES TO SURVIVE.
THEN ONE DAY YOU FIND THE ONE WORLD THAT MAKES YOU THINK YOU CAN QUIET THE NIGHTMARES FOR GOOD.
THAT YOU CAN RUN FORWARD FROM HORRIBLE **HERE** TO SOMETHING BETTER **THERE.**
THE ***CRAY.*** THEY'RE COMING FOR ***EARTH.***
LOSING YOUR WORLD IS A NIGHTMARE YOU WRESTLE WITH YOUR WHOLE LIFE.

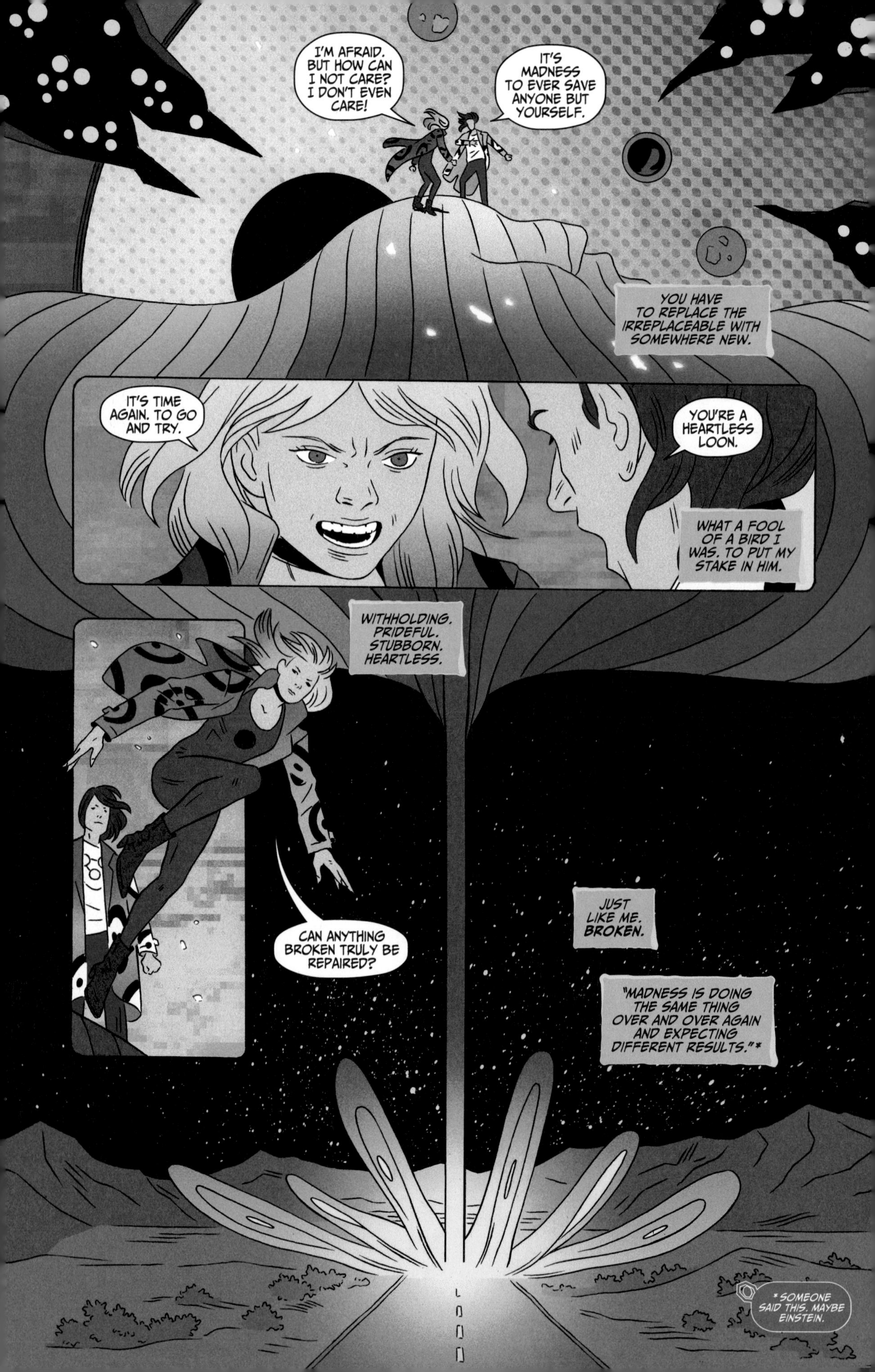
I'M AFRAID. BUT HOW CAN I NOT CARE? I DON'T EVEN CARE!
IT'S MADNESS TO EVER SAVE ANYONE BUT YOURSELF.
YOU HAVE TO REPLACE THE IRREPLACEABLE WITH SOMEWHERE NEW.
IT'S TIME AGAIN. TO GO AND TRY.
YOU'RE A HEARTLESS LOON.
WHAT A FOOL OF A BIRD I WAS. TO PUT MY STAKE IN HIM.
WITHHOLDING. PRIDEFUL. STUBBORN. HEARTLESS.
CAN ANYTHING BROKEN TRULY BE REPAIRED?
JUST LIKE ME. BROKEN.
"MADNESS IS DOING THE SAME THING OVER AND OVER AGAIN AND EXPECTING DIFFERENT RESULTS."*
* SOMEONE SAID THIS. MAYBE EINSTEIN.

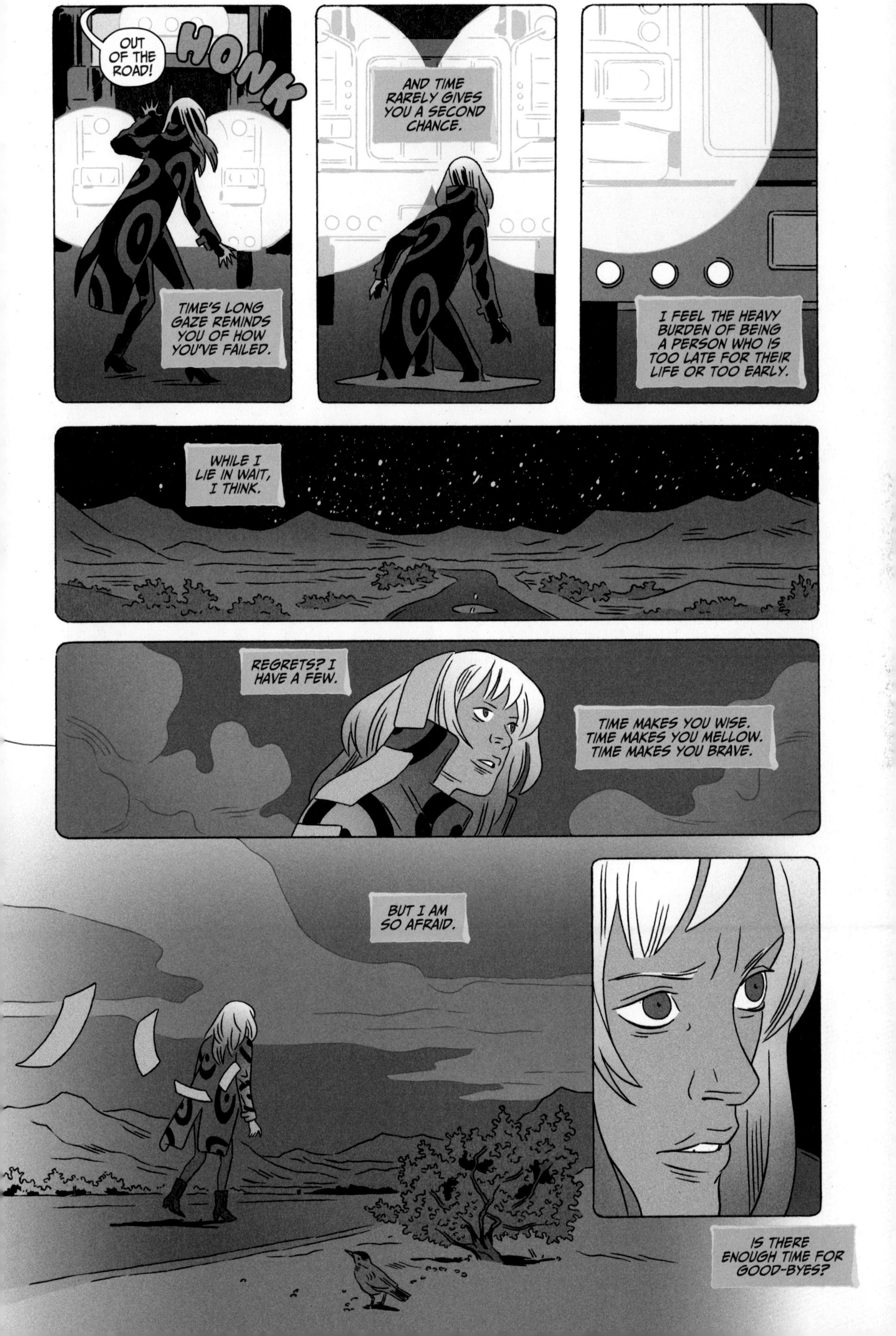
OUT OF THE ROAD!
HONK
TIME'S LONG GAZE REMINDS YOU OF HOW YOU'VE FAILED.
AND TIME RARELY GIVES YOU A SECOND CHANCE.
I FEEL THE HEAVY BURDEN OF BEING A PERSON WHO IS TOO LATE FOR THEIR LIFE OR TOO EARLY.
WHILE I LIE IN WAIT, I THINK.
REGRETS? I HAVE A FEW.
TIME MAKES YOU WISE. TIME MAKES YOU MELLOW. TIME MAKES YOU BRAVE.
BUT I AM SO AFRAID.
IS THERE ENOUGH TIME FOR GOOD-BYES?

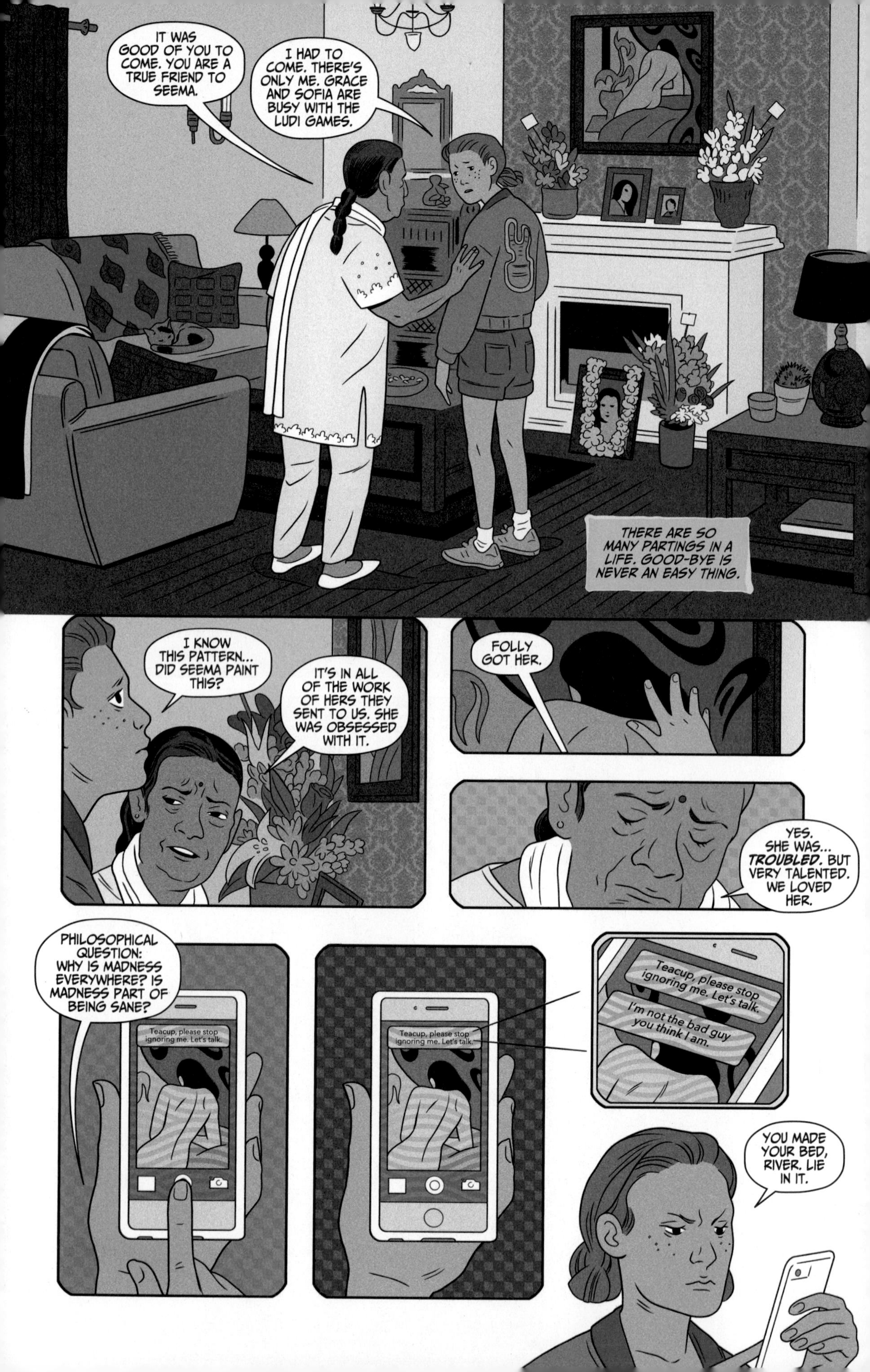
IT WAS GOOD OF YOU TO COME. YOU ARE A TRUE FRIEND TO SEEMA.
I HAD TO COME. THERE'S ONLY ME. GRACE AND SOFIA ARE BUSY WITH THE LUDI GAMES.
THERE ARE SO MANY PARTINGS IN A LIFE. GOOD-BYE IS NEVER AN EASY THING.
I KNOW THIS PATTERN... DID SEEMA PAINT THIS?
IT'S IN ALL OF THE WORK OF HERS THEY SENT TO US. SHE WAS OBSESSED WITH IT.
FOLLY GOT HER.
YES. SHE WAS... ***TROUBLED***. BUT VERY TALENTED. WE LOVED HER.
PHILOSOPHICAL QUESTION: WHY IS MADNESS EVERYWHERE? IS MADNESS PART OF BEING SANE?
Teacup, please stop ignoring me. Let's talk.
Teacup, please stop ignoring me. Let's talk.
Teacup, please stop ignoring me. Let's talk.
I'm not the bad guy you think I am.
YOU MADE YOUR BED, RIVER. LIE IN IT.

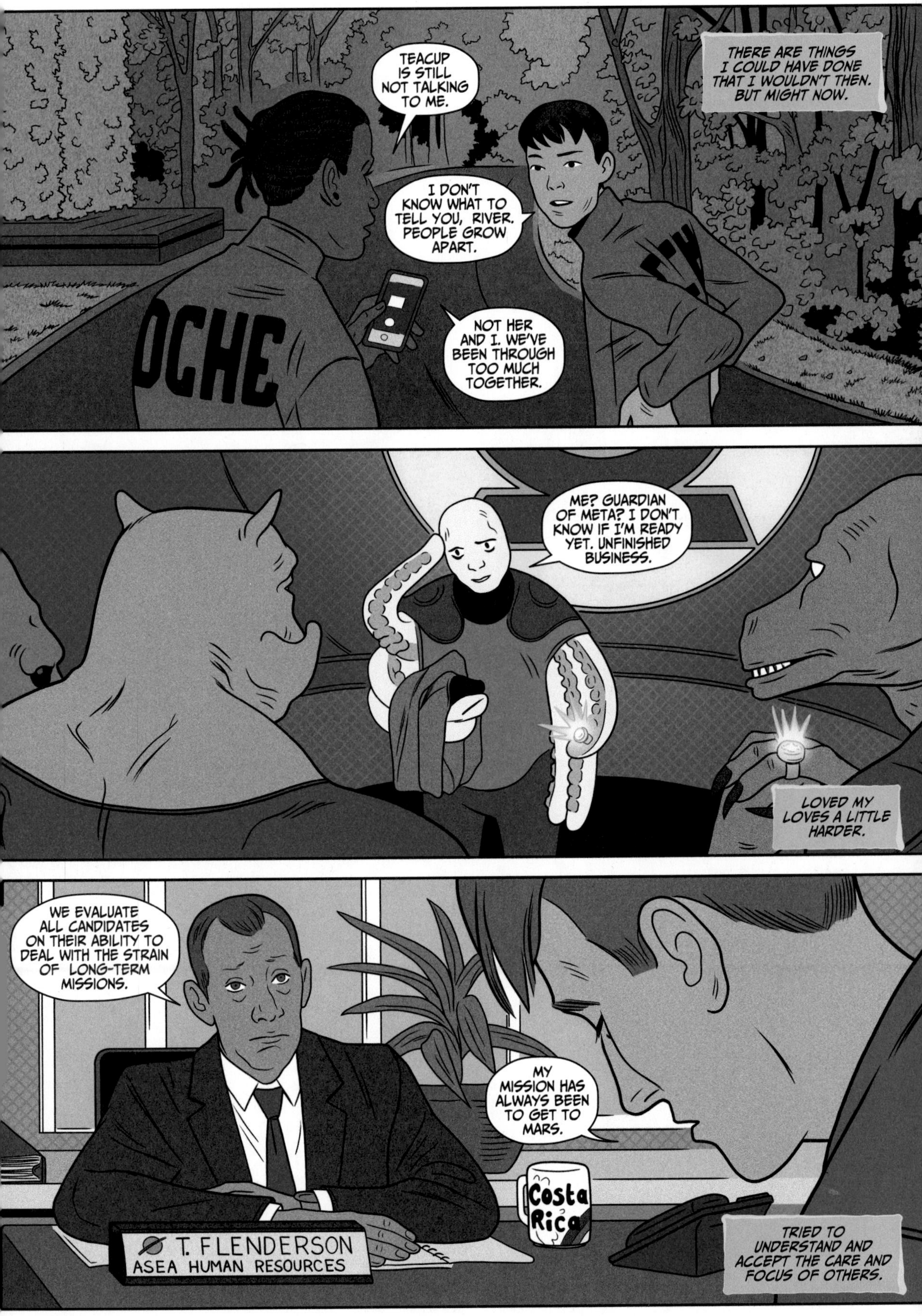
TEACUP IS STILL NOT TALKING TO ME.
THERE ARE THINGS I COULD HAVE DONE THAT I WOULDN'T THEN. BUT MIGHT NOW.
I DON'T KNOW WHAT TO TELL YOU, RIVER. PEOPLE GROW APART.
NOT HER AND I. WE'VE BEEN THROUGH TOO MUCH TOGETHER.
OCHE
ME? GUARDIAN OF META? I DON'T KNOW IF I'M READY YET. UNFINISHED BUSINESS.
LOVED MY LOVES A LITTLE HARDER.
WE EVALUATE ALL CANDIDATES ON THEIR ABILITY TO DEAL WITH THE STRAIN OF LONG-TERM MISSIONS.
MY MISSION HAS ALWAYS BEEN TO GET TO MARS.
Costa Rica
T. FLENDERSON
ASEA HUMAN RESOURCES
TRIED TO UNDERSTAND AND ACCEPT THE CARE AND FOCUS OF OTHERS.

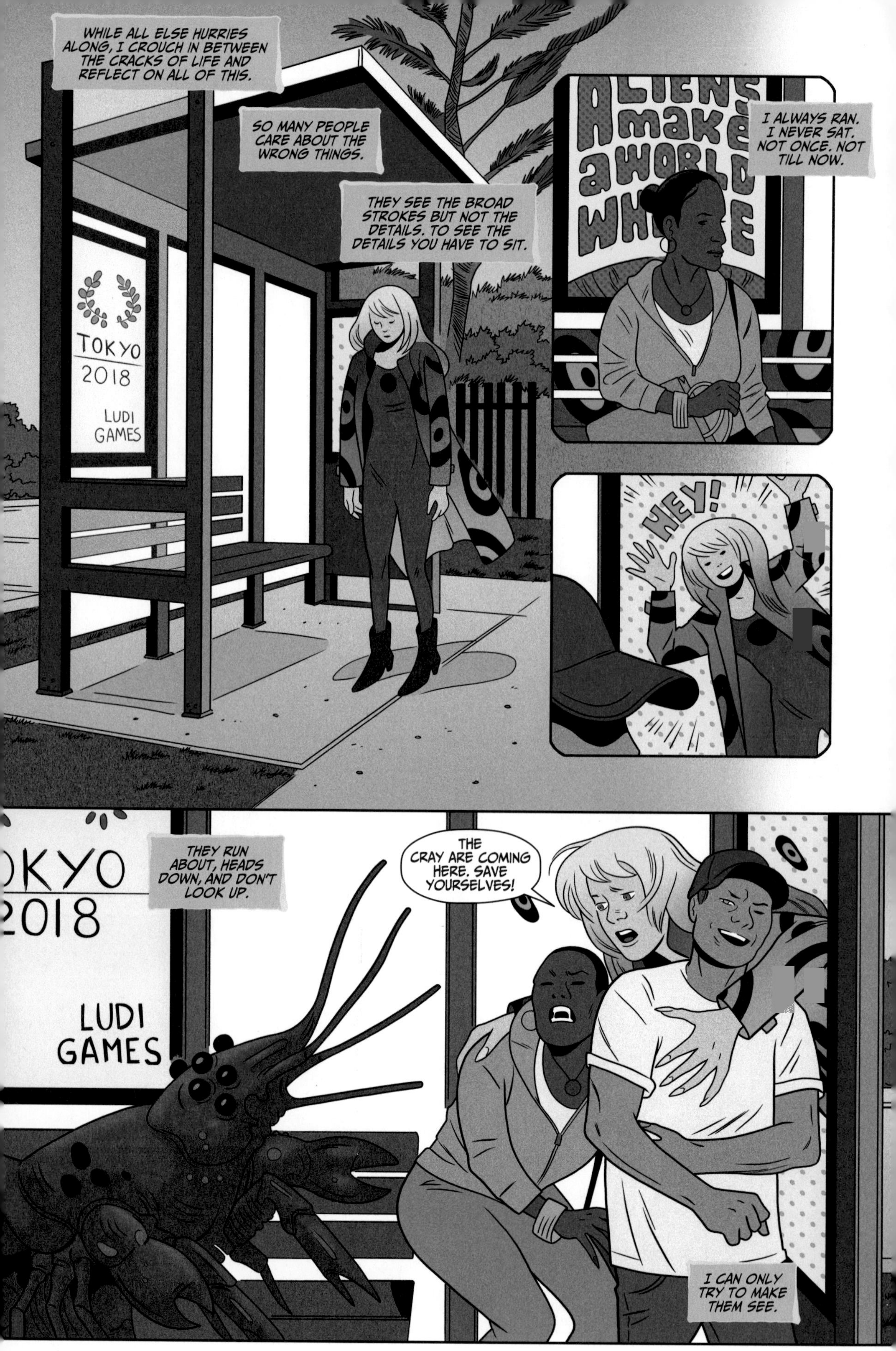
WHILE ALL ELSE HURRIES ALONG, I CROUCH IN BETWEEN THE CRACKS OF LIFE AND REFLECT ON ALL OF THIS.
SO MANY PEOPLE CARE ABOUT THE WRONG THINGS.
THEY SEE THE BROAD STROKES BUT NOT THE DETAILS. TO SEE THE DETAILS YOU HAVE TO SIT.
TOKYO 2018
LUDI GAMES
I ALWAYS RAN. I NEVER SAT. NOT ONCE. NOT TILL NOW.
HEY!
THEY RUN ABOUT, HEADS DOWN, AND DON'T LOOK UP.
THE CRAY ARE COMING HERE. SAVE YOURSELVES!
I CAN ONLY TRY TO MAKE THEM SEE.

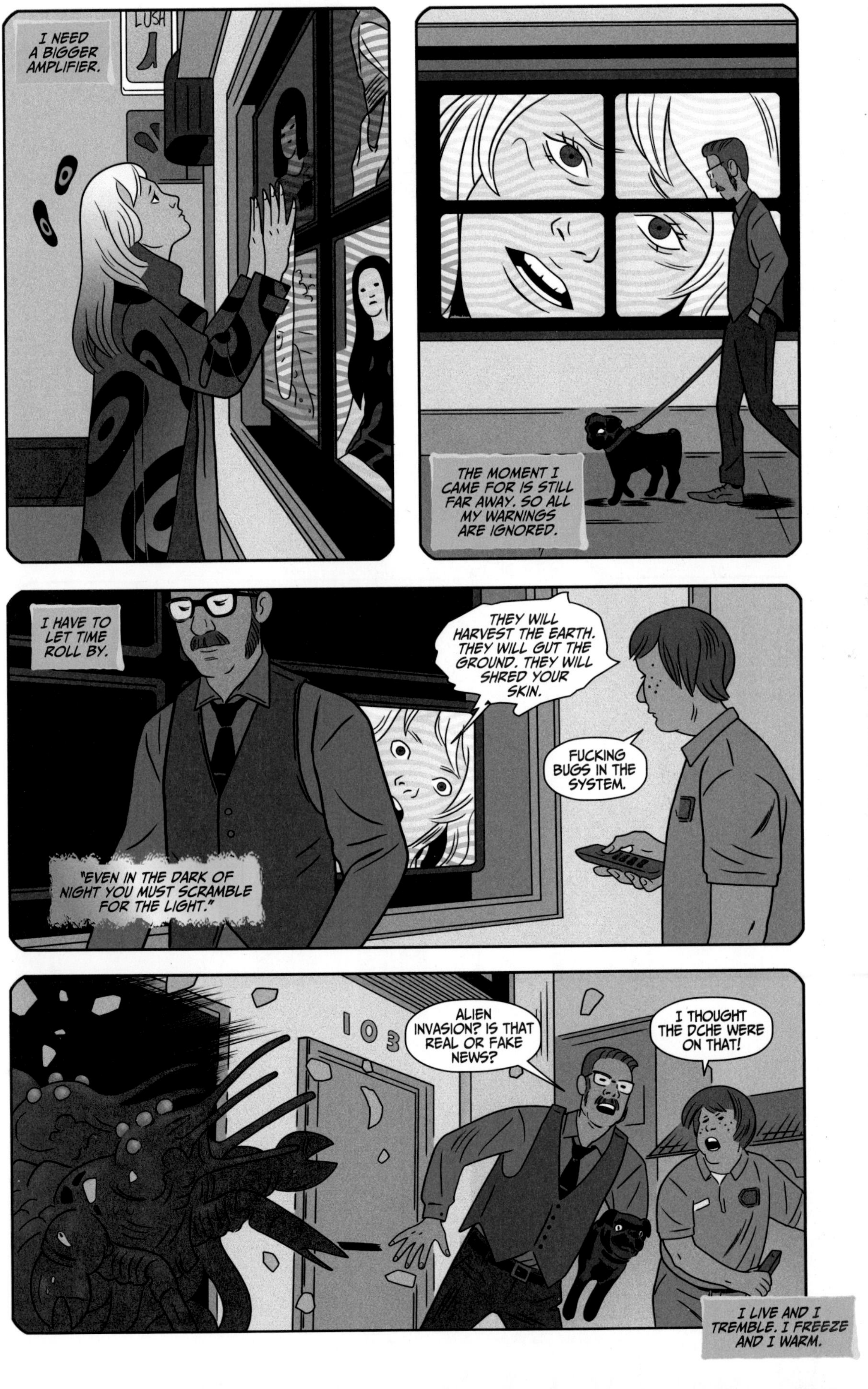
I NEED A BIGGER AMPLIFIER.
LUSH
THE MOMENT I CAME FOR IS STILL FAR AWAY. SO ALL MY WARNINGS ARE IGNORED.
I HAVE TO LET TIME ROLL BY.
THEY WILL HARVEST THE EARTH. THEY WILL GUT THE GROUND. THEY WILL SHRED YOUR SKIN.
FUCKING BUGS IN THE SYSTEM.
"EVEN IN THE DARK OF NIGHT YOU MUST SCRAMBLE FOR THE LIGHT."
103
ALIEN INVASION? IS THAT REAL OR FAKE NEWS?
I THOUGHT THE DCHE WERE ON THAT!
I LIVE AND I TREMBLE. I FREEZE AND I WARM.

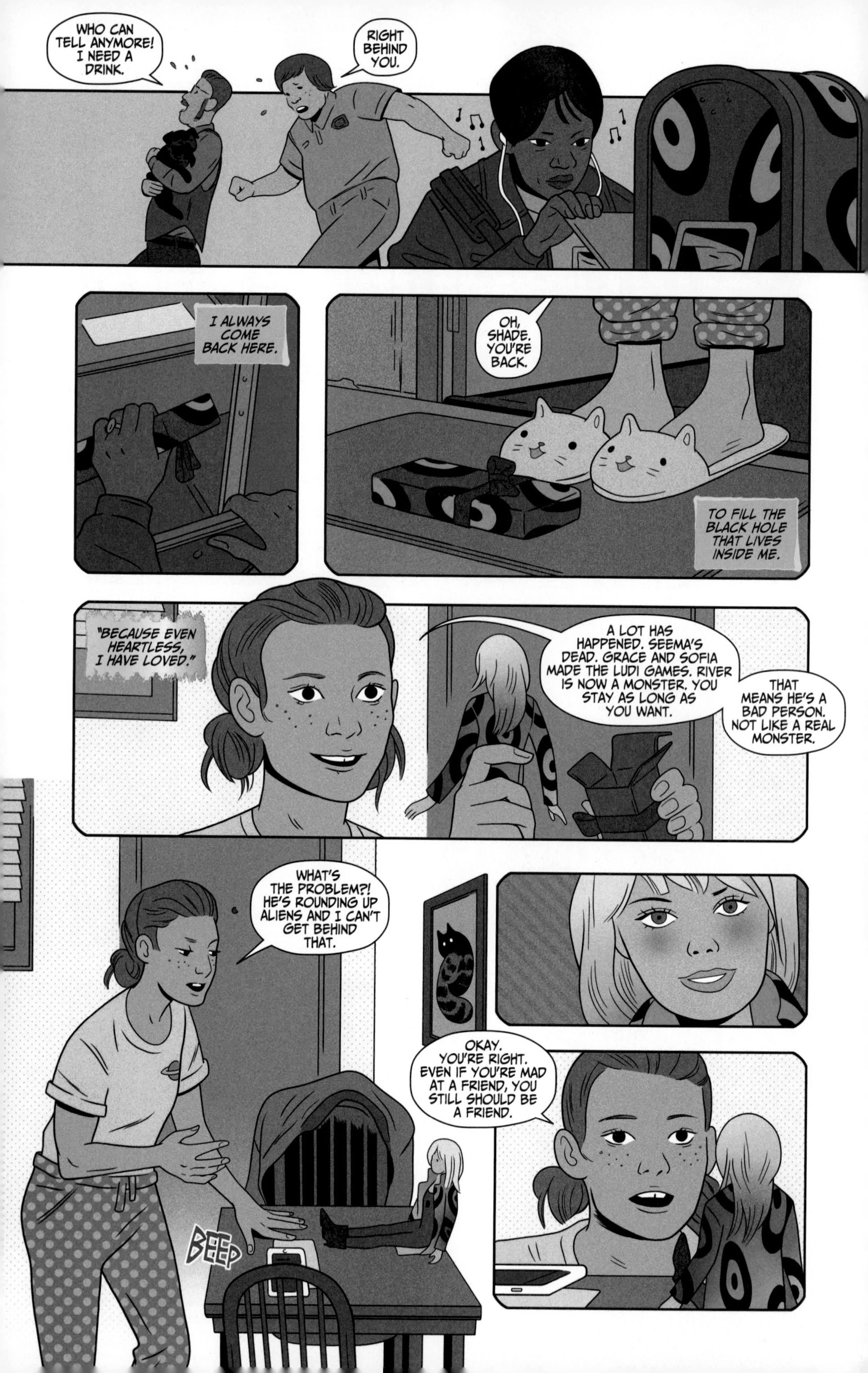
WHO CAN TELL ANYMORE! I NEED A DRINK.
RIGHT BEHIND YOU.
I ALWAYS COME BACK HERE.
OH, SHADE. YOU'RE BACK.
TO FILL THE BLACK HOLE THAT LIVES INSIDE ME.
"BECAUSE EVEN HEARTLESS, I HAVE LOVED."
A LOT HAS HAPPENED. SEEMA'S DEAD. GRACE AND SOFIA MADE THE LUDI GAMES. RIVER IS NOW A MONSTER. YOU STAY AS LONG AS YOU WANT.
THAT MEANS HE'S A BAD PERSON. NOT LIKE A REAL MONSTER.
WHAT'S THE PROBLEM?! HE'S ROUNDING UP ALIENS AND I CAN'T GET BEHIND THAT.
OKAY. YOU'RE RIGHT. EVEN IF YOU'RE MAD AT A FRIEND, YOU STILL SHOULD BE A FRIEND.
BEEP

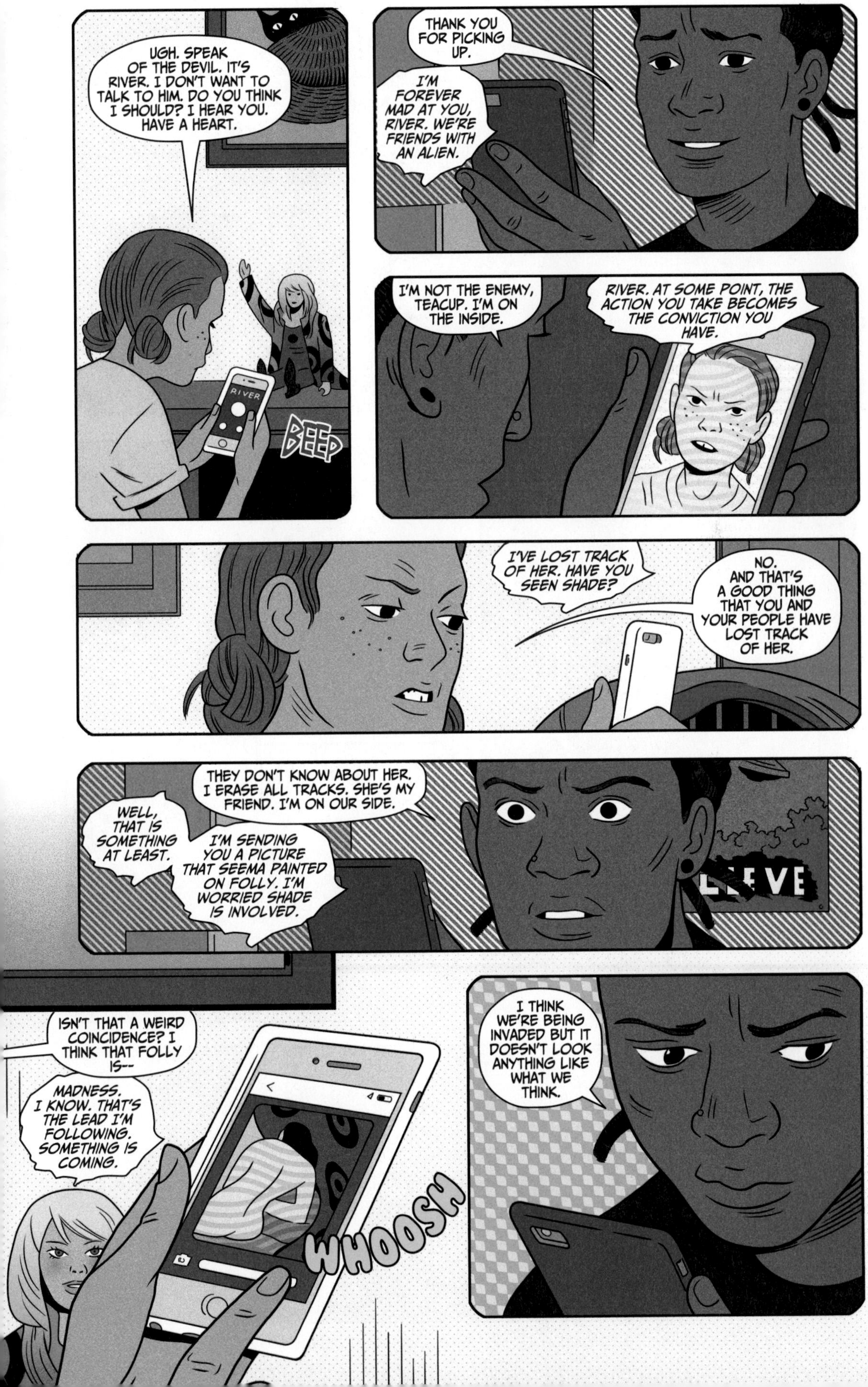
UGH. SPEAK OF THE DEVIL. IT'S RIVER. I DON'T WANT TO TALK TO HIM. DO YOU THINK I SHOULD? I HEAR YOU. HAVE A HEART.
RIVER
BEEP
THANK YOU FOR PICKING UP.
I'M FOREVER MAD AT YOU, RIVER. WE'RE FRIENDS WITH AN ALIEN.
I'M NOT THE ENEMY, TEACUP. I'M ON THE INSIDE.
RIVER. AT SOME POINT, THE ACTION YOU TAKE BECOMES THE CONVICTION YOU HAVE.
I'VE LOST TRACK OF HER. HAVE YOU SEEN SHADE?
NO. AND THAT'S A GOOD THING THAT YOU AND YOUR PEOPLE HAVE LOST TRACK OF HER.
THEY DON'T KNOW ABOUT HER. I ERASE ALL TRACKS. SHE'S MY FRIEND. I'M ON OUR SIDE.
WELL, THAT IS SOMETHING AT LEAST.
I'M SENDING YOU A PICTURE THAT SEEMA PAINTED ON FOLLY. I'M WORRIED SHADE IS INVOLVED.
ISN'T THAT A WEIRD COINCIDENCE? I THINK THAT FOLLY IS--
MADNESS. I KNOW. THAT'S THE LEAD I'M FOLLOWING. SOMETHING IS COMING.
WHOOSH
I THINK WE'RE BEING INVADED BUT IT DOESN'T LOOK ANYTHING LIKE WHAT WE THINK.

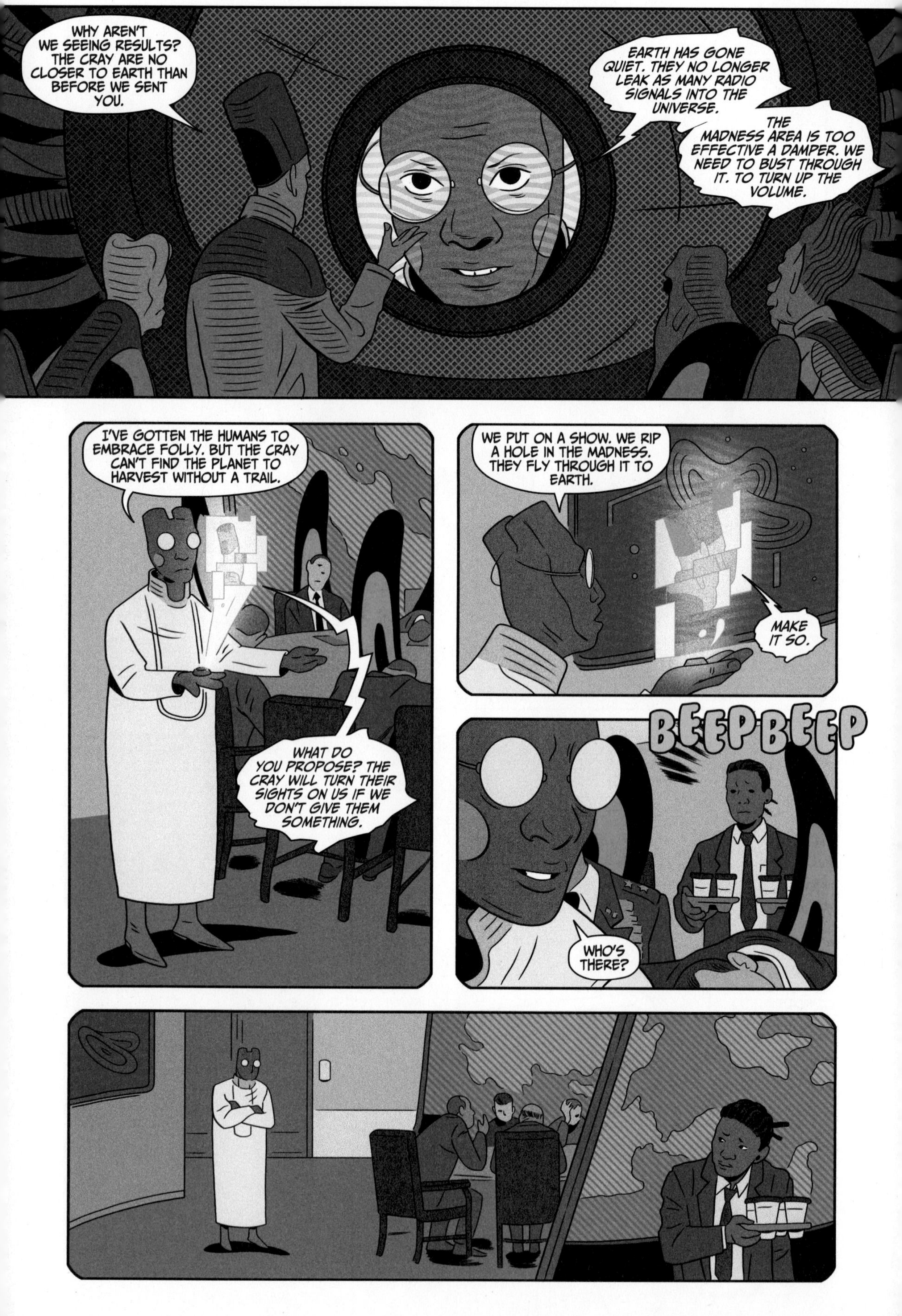
WHY AREN'T WE SEEING RESULTS? THE CRAY ARE NO CLOSER TO EARTH THAN BEFORE WE SENT YOU.
EARTH HAS GONE QUIET. THEY NO LONGER LEAK AS MANY RADIO SIGNALS INTO THE UNIVERSE.
THE MADNESS AREA IS TOO EFFECTIVE A DAMPER. WE NEED TO BUST THROUGH IT. TO TURN UP THE VOLUME.
I'VE GOTTEN THE HUMANS TO EMBRACE FOLLY. BUT THE CRAY CAN'T FIND THE PLANET TO HARVEST WITHOUT A TRAIL.
WHAT DO YOU PROPOSE? THE CRAY WILL TURN THEIR SIGHTS ON US IF WE DON'T GIVE THEM SOMETHING.
WE PUT ON A SHOW. WE RIP A HOLE IN THE MADNESS. THEY FLY THROUGH IT TO EARTH.
MAKE IT SO.
BEEPBEEP
WHO'S THERE?

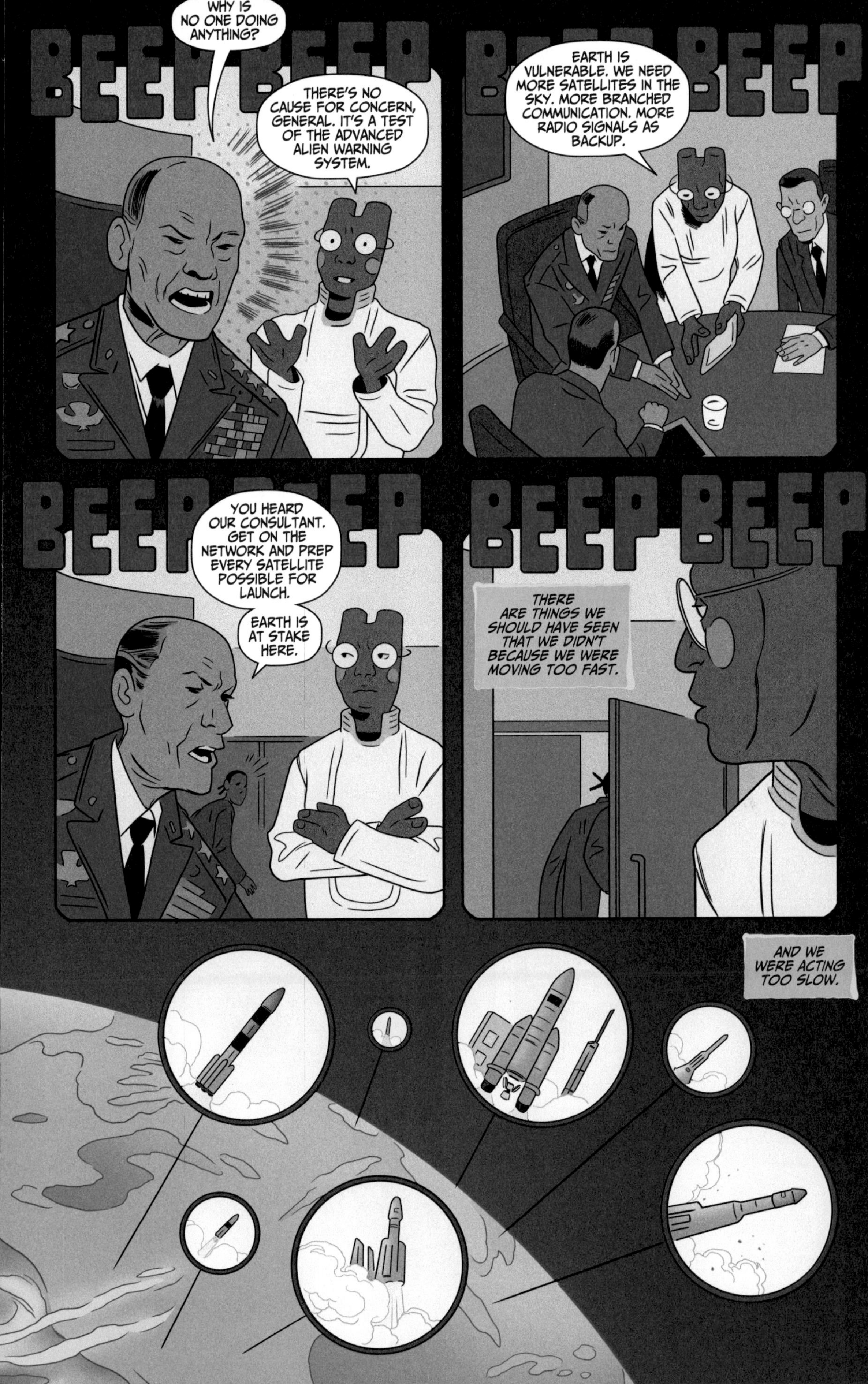
BEEP BEEP
WHY IS NO ONE DOING ANYTHING?
THERE'S NO CAUSE FOR CONCERN, GENERAL. IT'S A TEST OF THE ADVANCED ALIEN WARNING SYSTEM.
BEEP BEEP
EARTH IS VULNERABLE. WE NEED MORE SATELLITES IN THE SKY. MORE BRANCHED COMMUNICATION. MORE RADIO SIGNALS AS BACKUP.
BEEP BEEP
YOU HEARD OUR CONSULTANT. GET ON THE NETWORK AND PREP EVERY SATELLITE POSSIBLE FOR LAUNCH.
EARTH IS AT STAKE HERE.
BEEP BEEP
THERE ARE THINGS WE SHOULD HAVE SEEN THAT WE DIDN'T BECAUSE WE WERE MOVING TOO FAST.
AND WE WERE ACTING TOO SLOW.

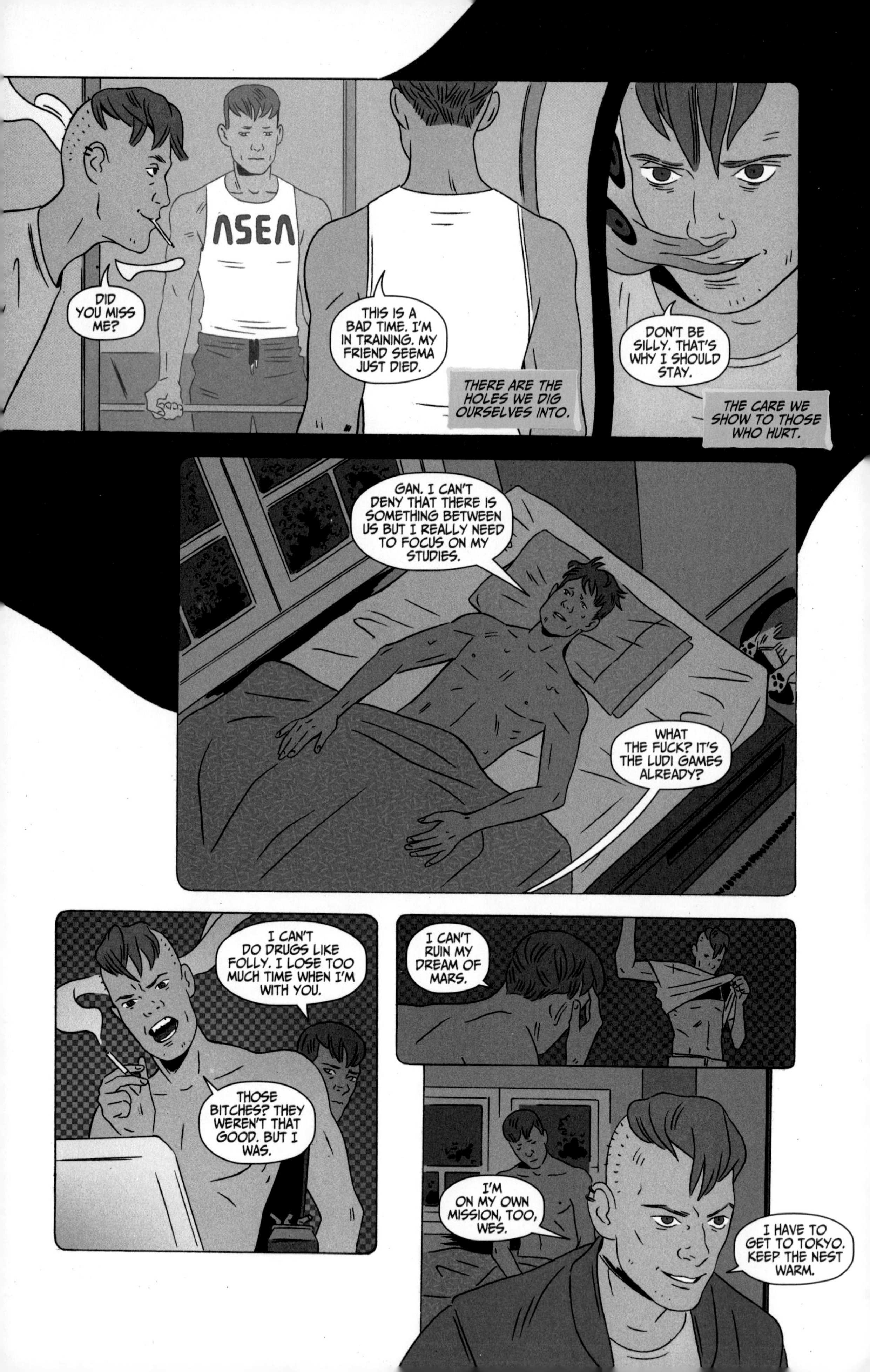
DID YOU MISS ME?
THIS IS A BAD TIME. I'M IN TRAINING. MY FRIEND SEEMA JUST DIED.
THERE ARE THE HOLES WE DIG OURSELVES INTO.
DON'T BE SILLY. THAT'S WHY I SHOULD STAY.
THE CARE WE SHOW TO THOSE WHO HURT.
GAN. I CAN'T DENY THAT THERE IS SOMETHING BETWEEN US BUT I REALLY NEED TO FOCUS ON MY STUDIES.
WHAT THE FUCK? IT'S THE LUDI GAMES ALREADY?
I CAN'T DO DRUGS LIKE FOLLY. I LOSE TOO MUCH TIME WHEN I'M WITH YOU.
THOSE BITCHES? THEY WEREN'T THAT GOOD. BUT I WAS.
I CAN'T RUIN MY DREAM OF MARS.
I'M ON MY OWN MISSION, TOO, WES.
I HAVE TO GET TO TOKYO. KEEP THE NEST WARM.

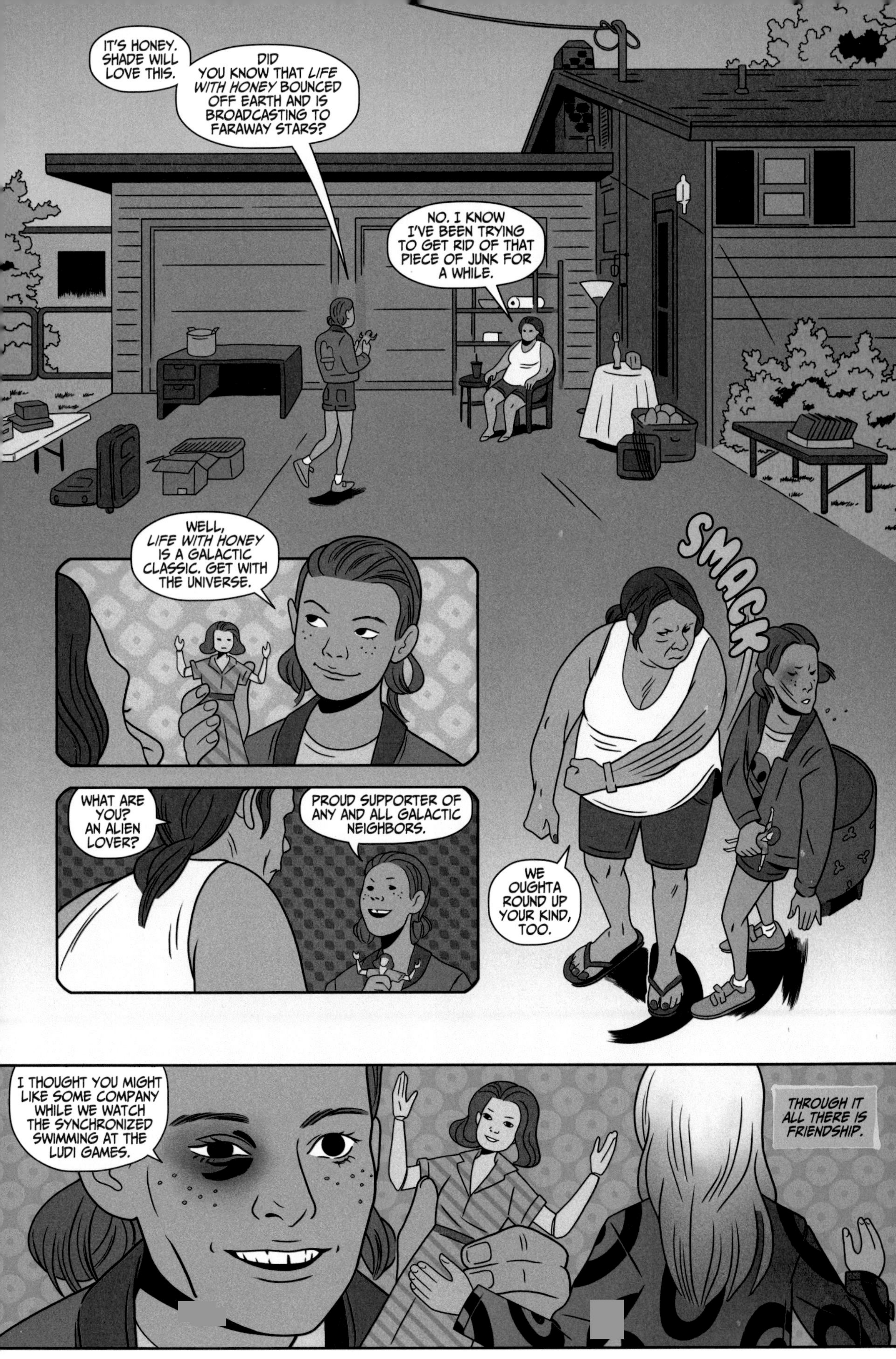
IT'S HONEY. SHADE WILL LOVE THIS.
DID YOU KNOW THAT *LIFE WITH HONEY* BOUNCED OFF EARTH AND IS BROADCASTING TO FARAWAY STARS?
NO. I KNOW I'VE BEEN TRYING TO GET RID OF THAT PIECE OF JUNK FOR A WHILE.
WELL, *LIFE WITH HONEY* IS A GALACTIC CLASSIC. GET WITH THE UNIVERSE.
WHAT ARE YOU? AN ALIEN LOVER?
PROUD SUPPORTER OF ANY AND ALL GALACTIC NEIGHBORS.
SMACK
WE OUGHTA ROUND UP YOUR KIND, TOO.
I THOUGHT YOU MIGHT LIKE SOME COMPANY WHILE WE WATCH THE SYNCHRONIZED SWIMMING AT THE LUDI GAMES.
THROUGH IT ALL THERE IS FRIENDSHIP.

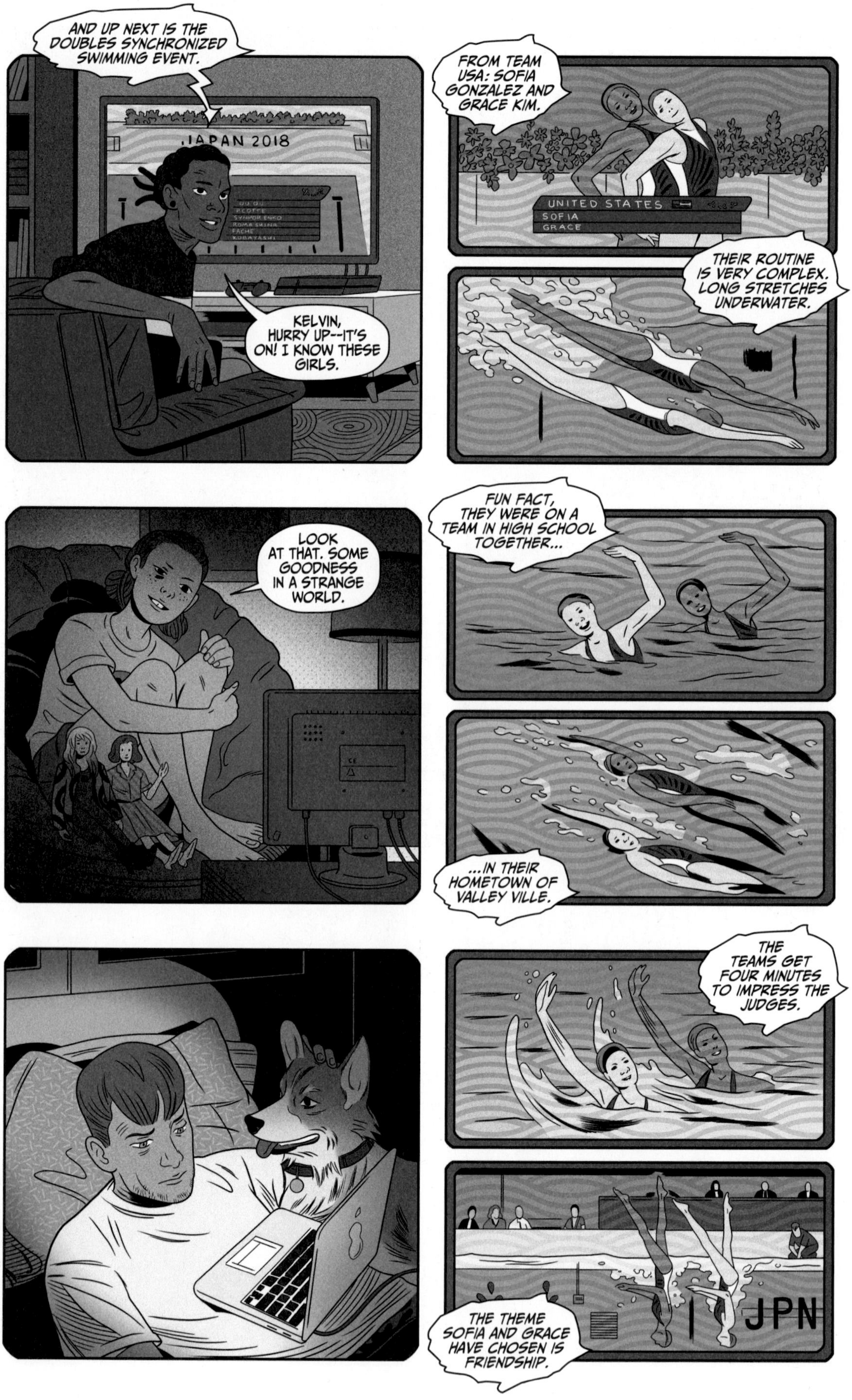

AND UP NEXT IS THE DOUBLES SYNCHRONIZED SWIMMING EVENT.
JAPAN 2018
KELVIN, HURRY UP--IT'S ON! I KNOW THESE GIRLS.
FROM TEAM USA: SOFIA GONZALEZ AND GRACE KIM.
UNITED STATES
SOFIA
GRACE
THEIR ROUTINE IS VERY COMPLEX. LONG STRETCHES UNDERWATER.
LOOK AT THAT. SOME GOODNESS IN A STRANGE WORLD.
FUN FACT, THEY WERE ON A TEAM IN HIGH SCHOOL TOGETHER...
...IN THEIR HOMETOWN OF VALLEY VILLE.
THE TEAMS GET FOUR MINUTES TO IMPRESS THE JUDGES.
JPN
THE THEME SOFIA AND GRACE HAVE CHOSEN IS FRIENDSHIP.

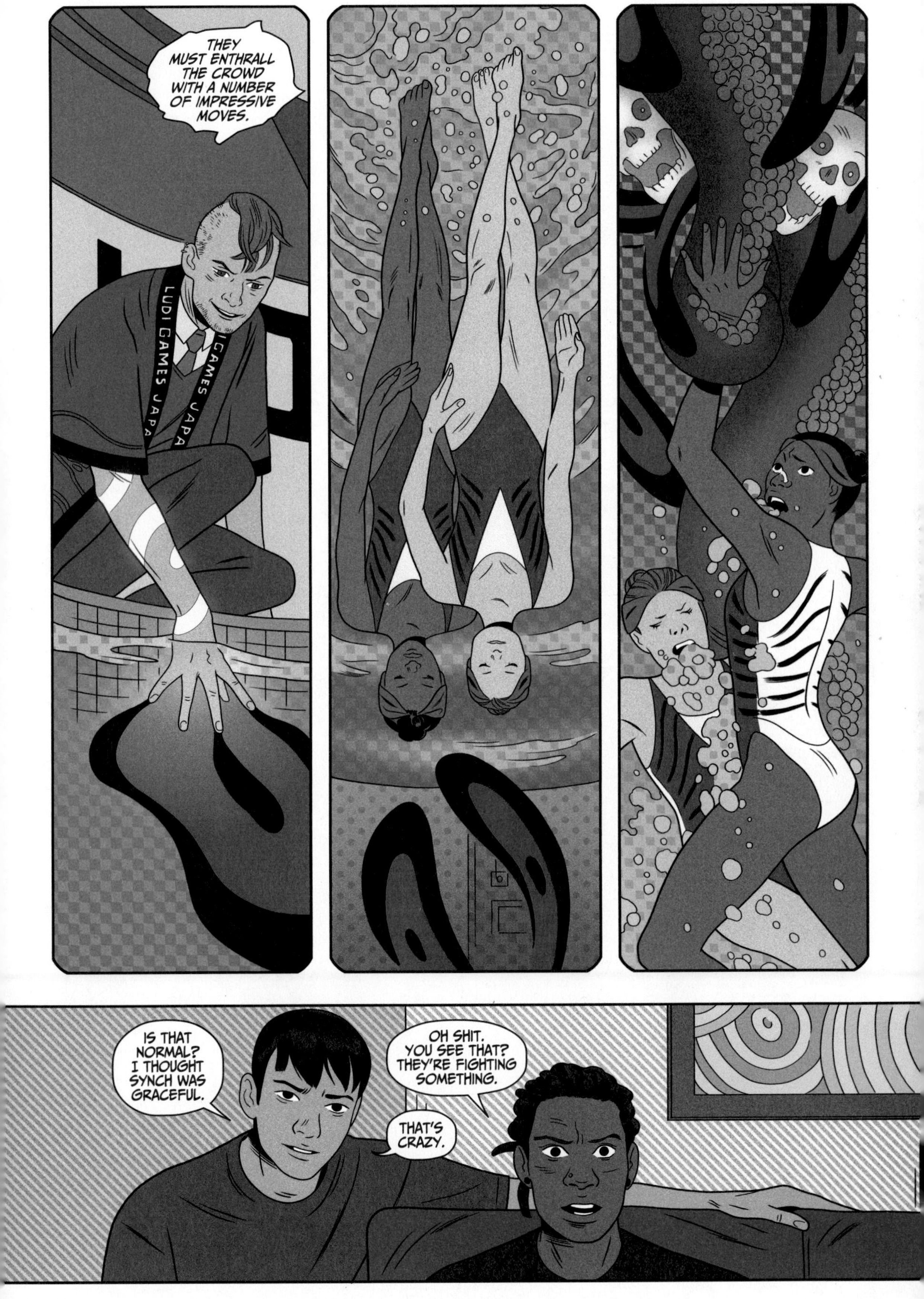
THEY MUST ENTHRALL THE CROWD WITH A NUMBER OF IMPRESSIVE MOVES.
IS THAT NORMAL? I THOUGHT SYNCH WAS GRACEFUL.
OH SHIT. YOU SEE THAT? THEY'RE FIGHTING SOMETHING.
THAT'S CRAZY.

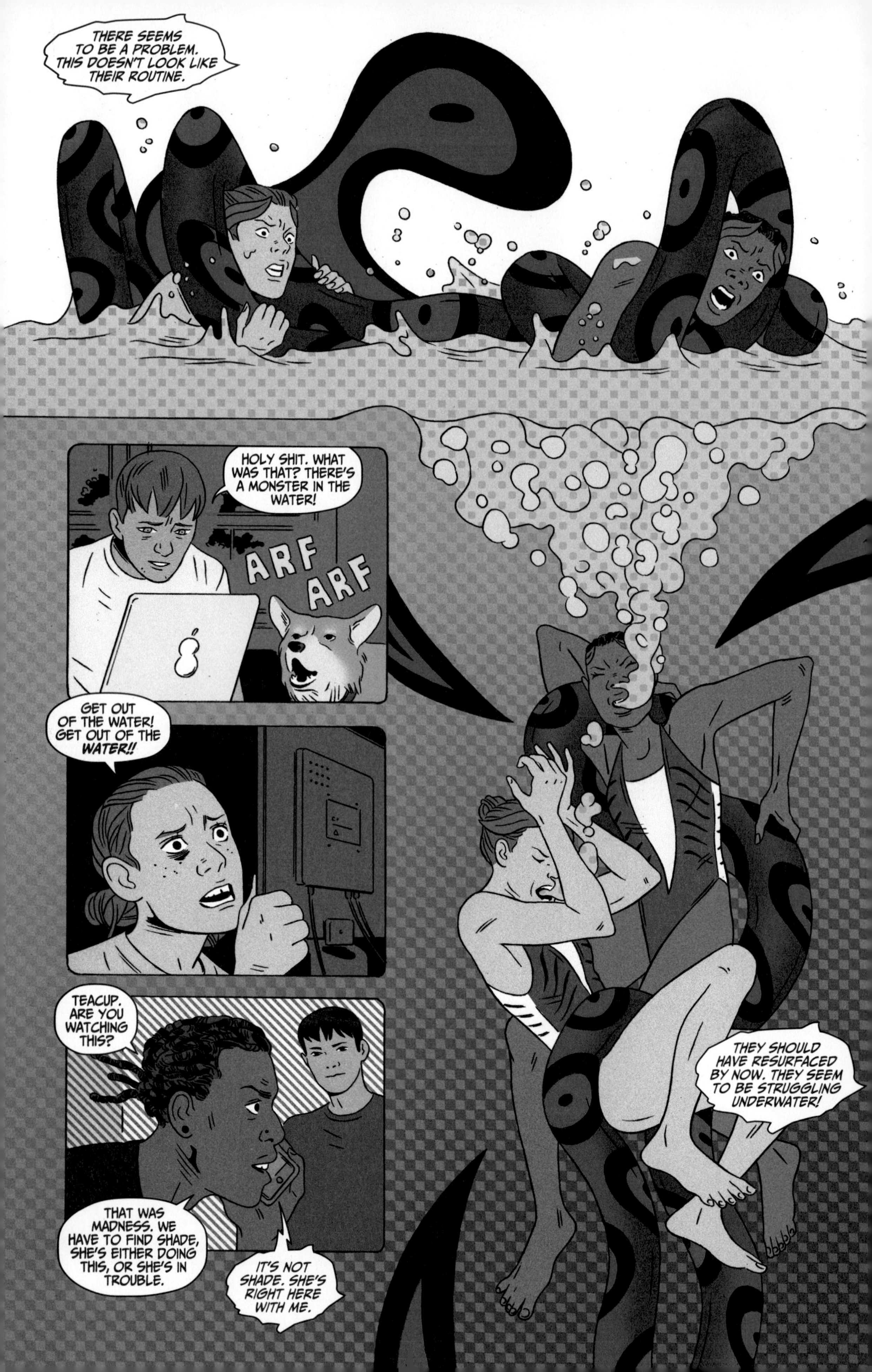
THERE SEEMS TO BE A PROBLEM. THIS DOESN'T LOOK LIKE THEIR ROUTINE.
HOLY SHIT. WHAT WAS THAT? THERE'S A MONSTER IN THE WATER!
ARF ARF
GET OUT OF THE WATER! GET OUT OF THE WATER!!
TEACUP. ARE YOU WATCHING THIS?
THAT WAS MADNESS. WE HAVE TO FIND SHADE, SHE'S EITHER DOING THIS, OR SHE'S IN TROUBLE.
IT'S NOT SHADE. SHE'S RIGHT HERE WITH ME.
THEY SHOULD HAVE RESURFACED BY NOW. THEY SEEM TO BE STRUGGLING UNDERWATER!

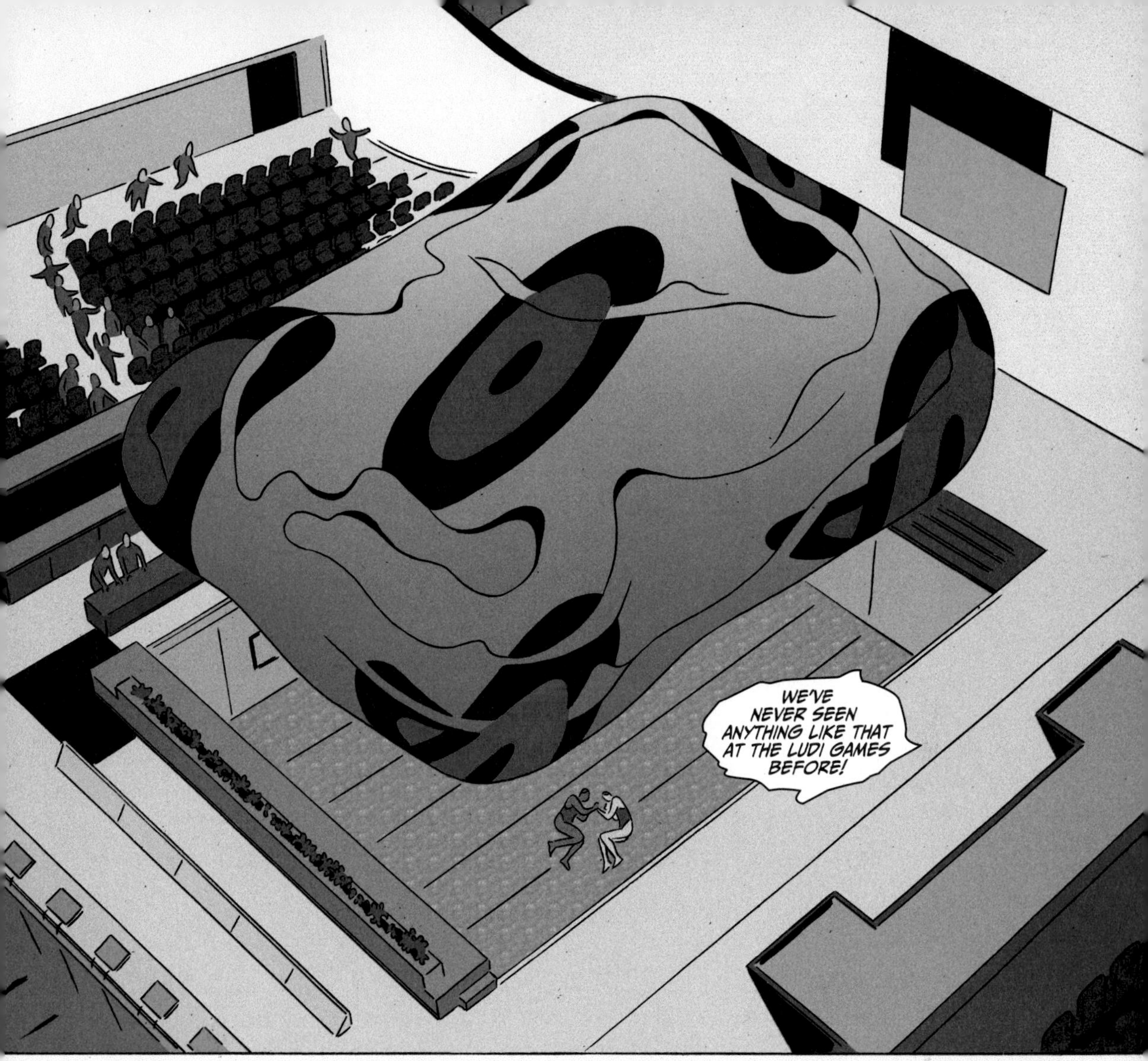
WE'VE NEVER SEEN ANYTHING LIKE THAT AT THE LUDI GAMES BEFORE!

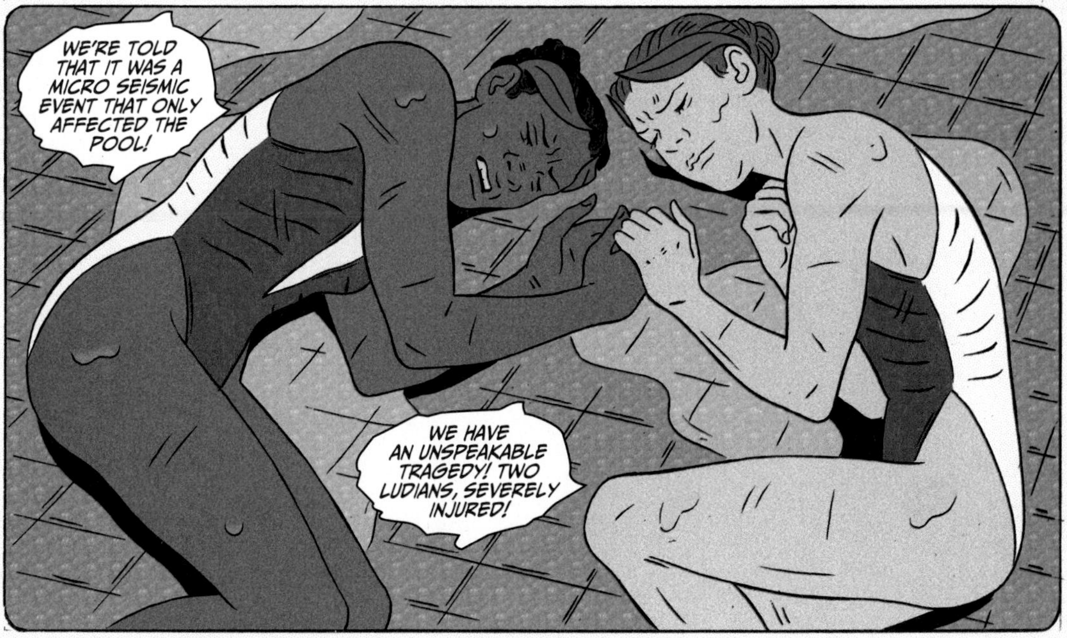
WE'RE TOLD THAT IT WAS A MICRO SEISMIC EVENT THAT ONLY AFFECTED THE POOL!
WE HAVE AN UNSPEAKABLE TRAGEDY! TWO LUDIANS, SEVERELY INJURED!

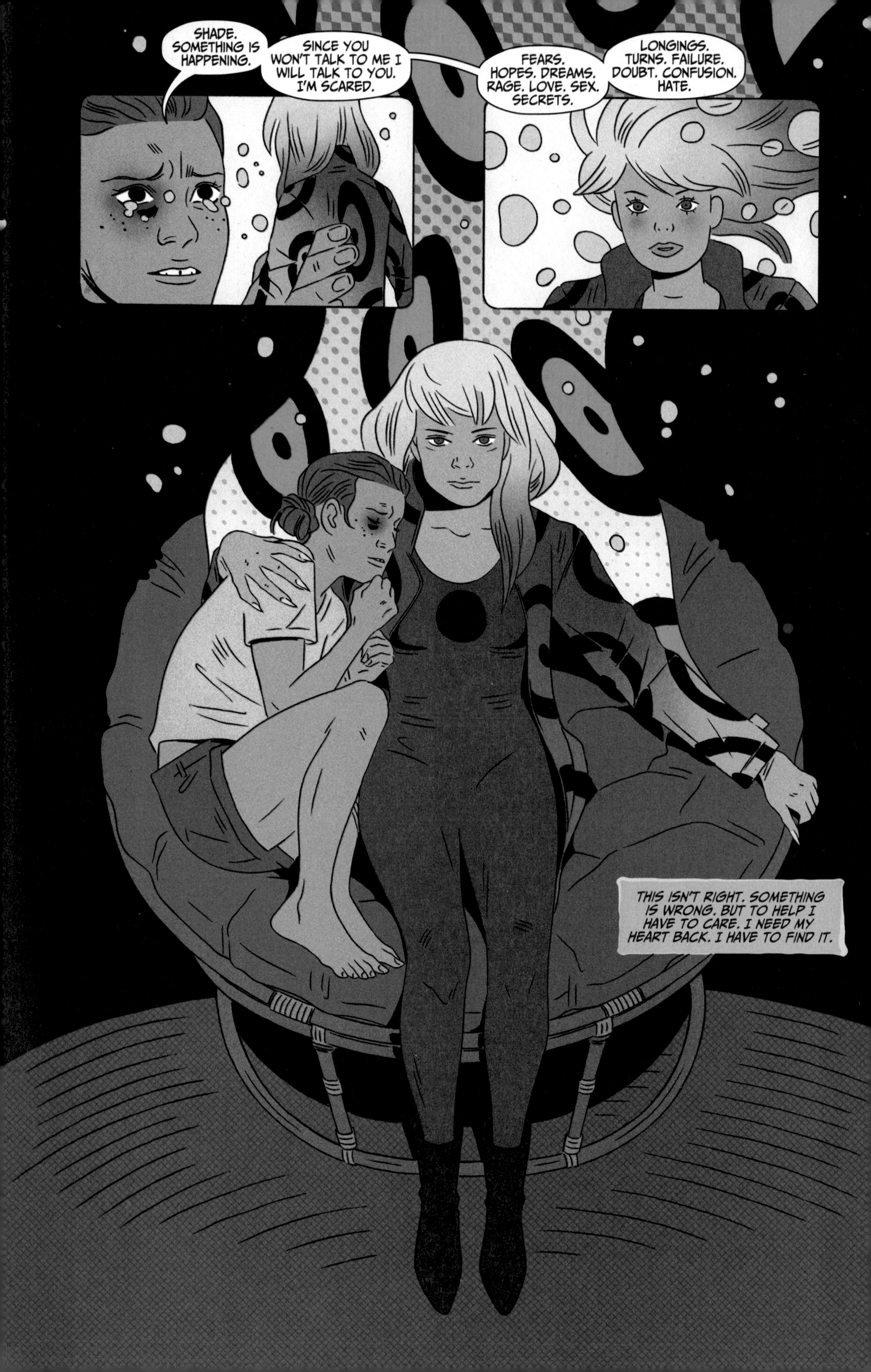
SHADE. SOMETHING IS HAPPENING.
SINCE YOU WON'T TALK TO ME I WILL TALK TO YOU. I'M SCARED.
FEARS. HOPES. DREAMS. RAGE. LOVE. SEX. SECRETS.
LONGINGS. TURNS. FAILURE. DOUBT. CONFUSION. HATE.
THIS ISN'T RIGHT. SOMETHING IS WRONG. BUT TO HELP I HAVE TO CARE. I NEED MY HEART BACK. I HAVE TO FIND IT.

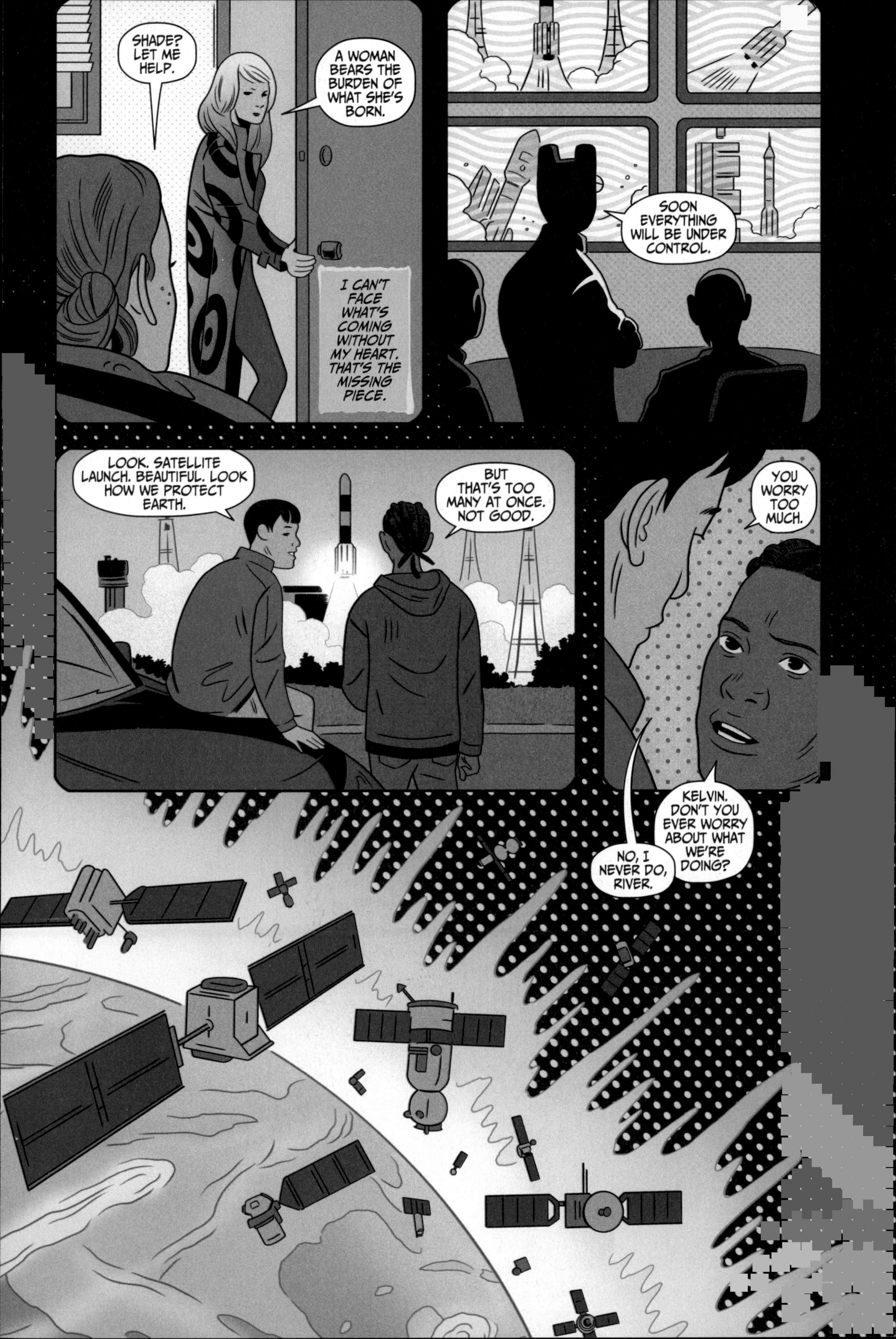
SHADE? LET ME HELP.
A WOMAN BEARS THE BURDEN OF WHAT SHE'S BORN.
I CAN'T FACE WHAT'S COMING WITHOUT MY HEART. THAT'S THE MISSING PIECE.
SOON EVERYTHING WILL BE UNDER CONTROL.
LOOK. SATELLITE LAUNCH. BEAUTIFUL. LOOK HOW WE PROTECT EARTH.
BUT THAT'S TOO MANY AT ONCE. NOT GOOD.
YOU WORRY TOO MUCH.
KELVIN. DON'T YOU EVER WORRY ABOUT WHAT WE'RE DOING?
NO, I NEVER DO, RIVER.

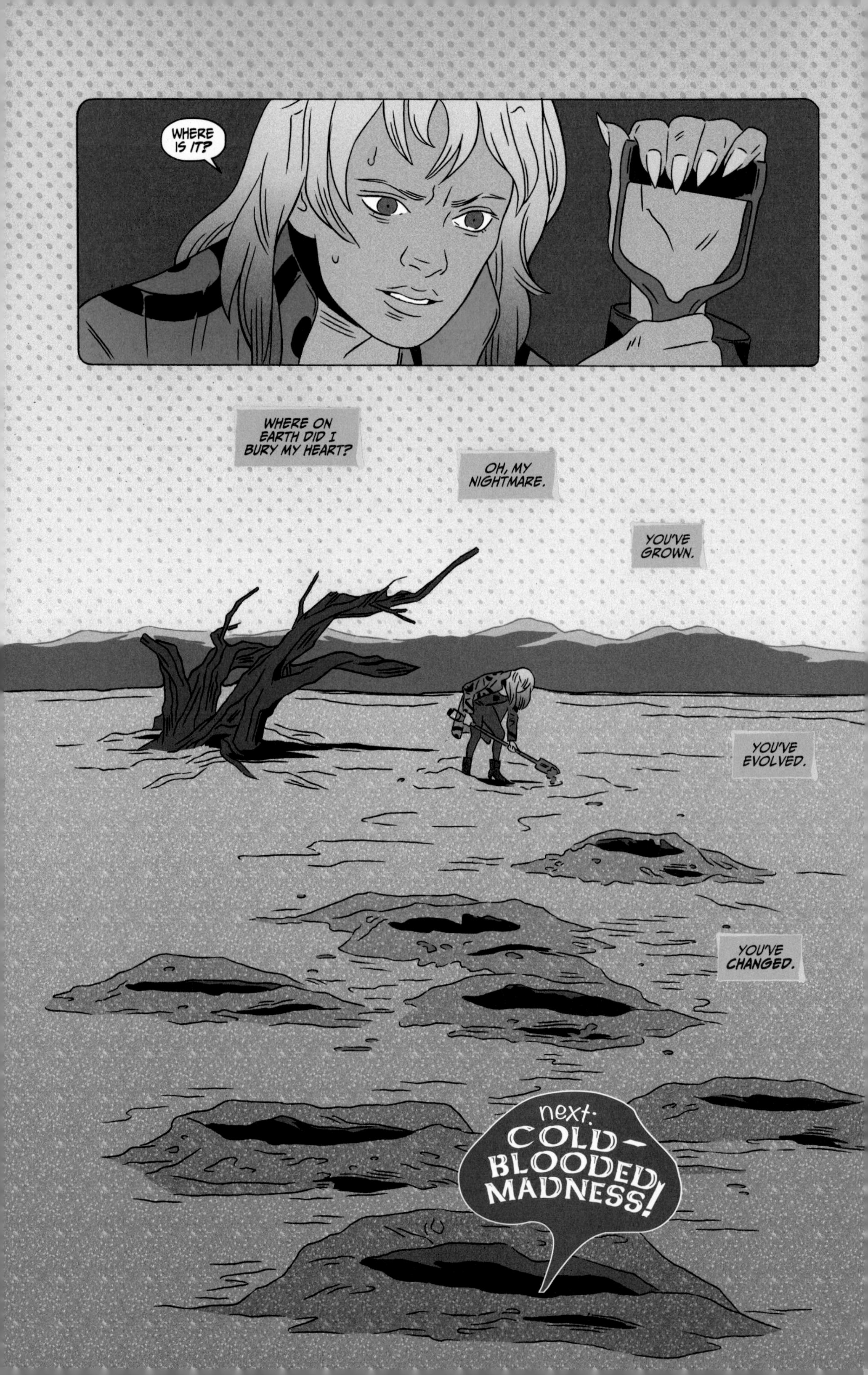
WHERE IS IT?
WHERE ON EARTH DID I BURY MY HEART?
OH, MY NIGHTMARE.
YOU'VE GROWN.
YOU'VE EVOLVED.
YOU'VE CHANGED.
next: COLD-BLOODED MADNESS!

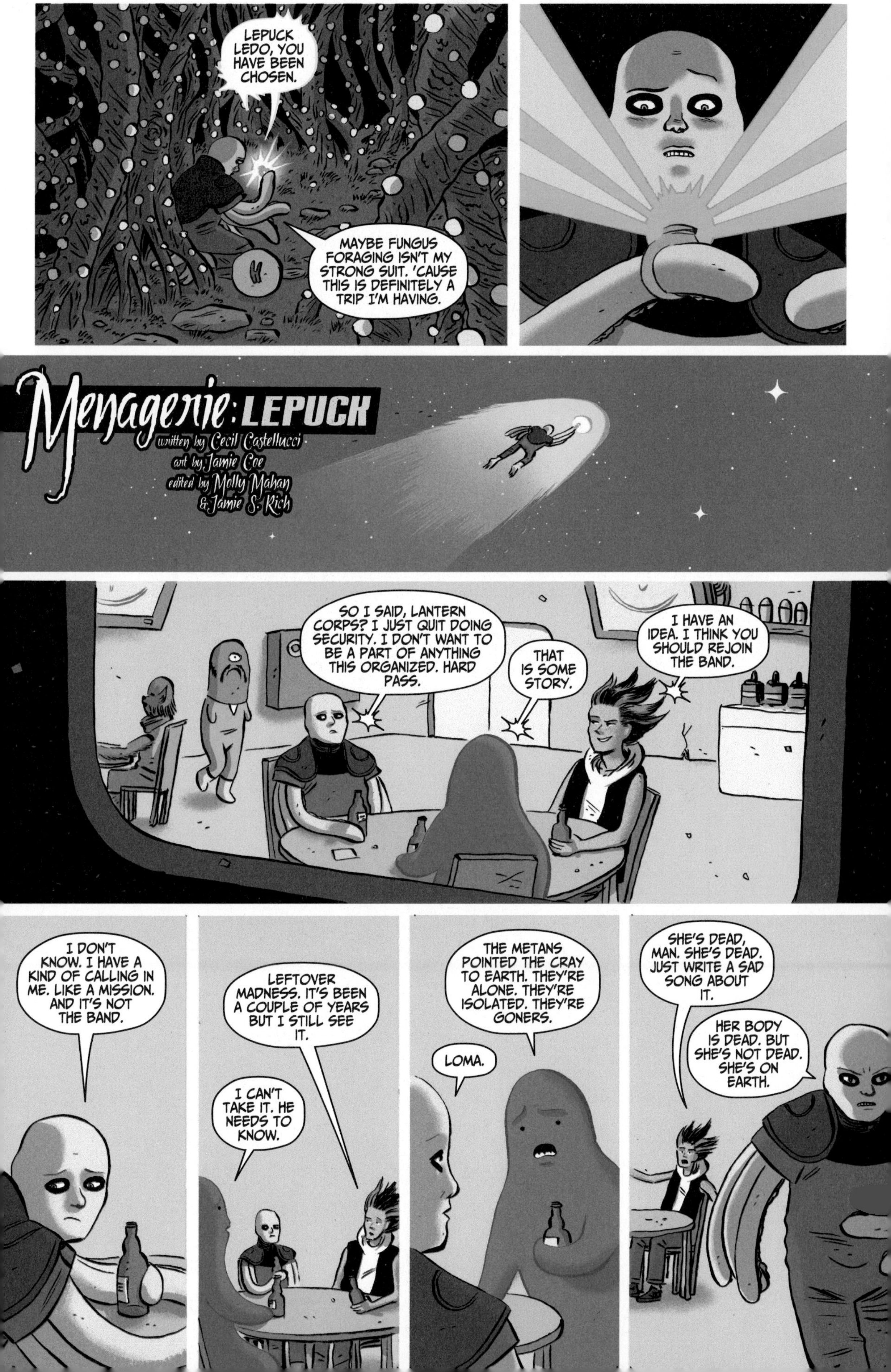
LEPUCK LEDO, YOU HAVE BEEN CHOSEN.
MAYBE FUNGUS FORAGING ISN'T MY STRONG SUIT. 'CAUSE THIS IS DEFINITELY A TRIP I'M HAVING.
Menagerie: LEPUCK
written by Cecil Castellucci
art by Jamie Coe
edited by Molly Mahan & Jamie S. Rich
SO I SAID, LANTERN CORPS? I JUST QUIT DOING SECURITY. I DON'T WANT TO BE A PART OF ANYTHING THIS ORGANIZED. HARD PASS.
THAT IS SOME STORY.
I HAVE AN IDEA. I THINK YOU SHOULD REJOIN THE BAND.
I DON'T KNOW. I HAVE A KIND OF CALLING IN ME. LIKE A MISSION. AND IT'S NOT THE BAND.
LEFTOVER MADNESS. IT'S BEEN A COUPLE OF YEARS BUT I STILL SEE IT.
I CAN'T TAKE IT. HE NEEDS TO KNOW.
THE METANS POINTED THE CRAY TO EARTH. THEY'RE ALONE. THEY'RE ISOLATED. THEY'RE GONERS.
LOMA.
SHE'S DEAD, MAN. SHE'S DEAD. JUST WRITE A SAD SONG ABOUT IT.
HER BODY IS DEAD. BUT SHE'S NOT DEAD. SHE'S ON EARTH.

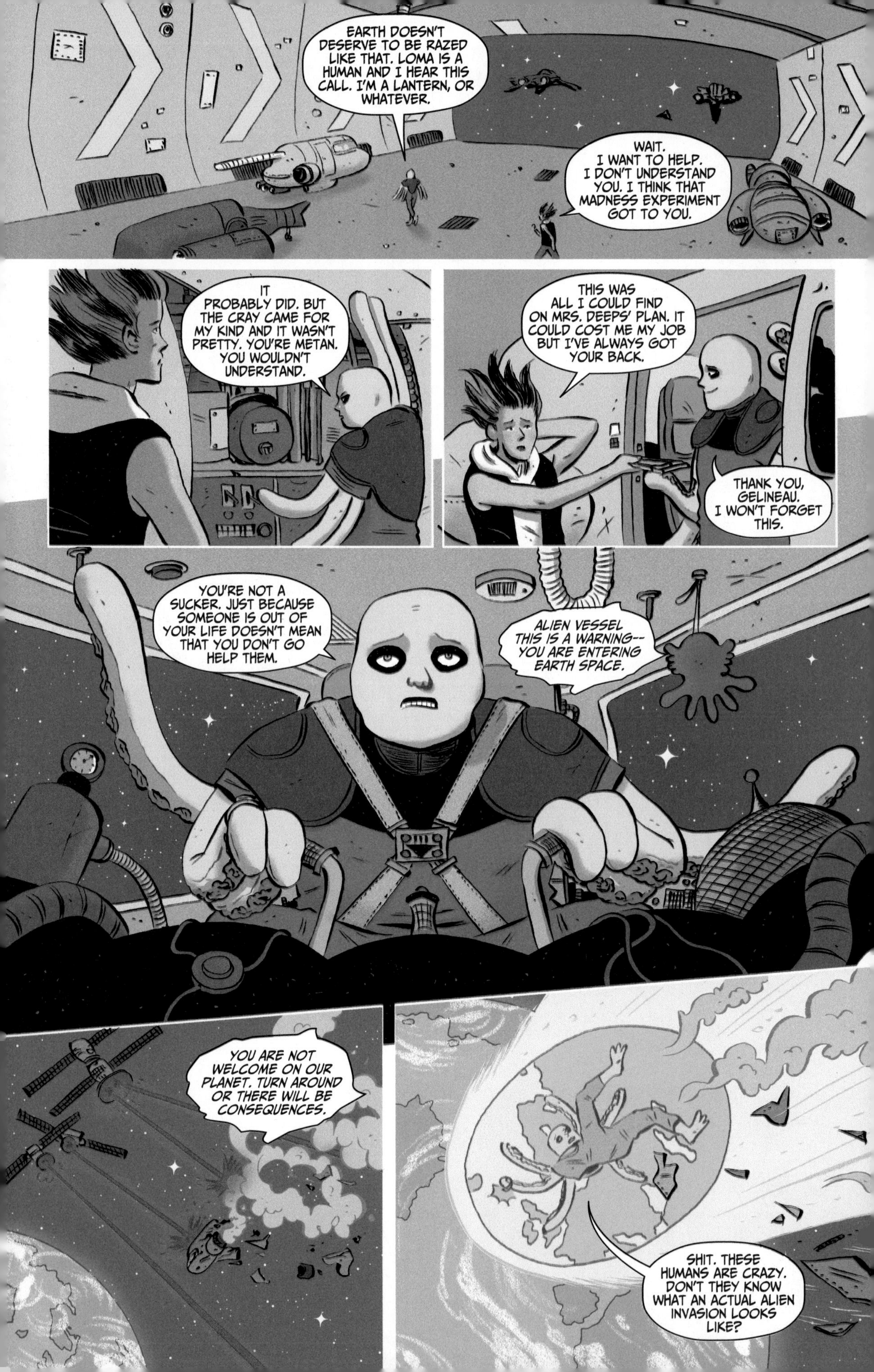
EARTH DOESN'T DESERVE TO BE RAZED LIKE THAT. LOMA IS A HUMAN AND I HEAR THIS CALL. I'M A LANTERN, OR WHATEVER.
WAIT. I WANT TO HELP. I DON'T UNDERSTAND YOU. I THINK THAT MADNESS EXPERIMENT GOT TO YOU.
IT PROBABLY DID. BUT THE CRAY CAME FOR MY KIND AND IT WASN'T PRETTY. YOU'RE METAN. YOU WOULDN'T UNDERSTAND.
THIS WAS ALL I COULD FIND ON MRS. DEEPS' PLAN. IT COULD COST ME MY JOB BUT I'VE ALWAYS GOT YOUR BACK.
THANK YOU, GELINEAU. I WON'T FORGET THIS.
YOU'RE NOT A SUCKER. JUST BECAUSE SOMEONE IS OUT OF YOUR LIFE DOESN'T MEAN THAT YOU DON'T GO HELP THEM.
ALIEN VESSEL THIS IS A WARNING-- YOU ARE ENTERING EARTH SPACE.
YOU ARE NOT WELCOME ON OUR PLANET. TURN AROUND OR THERE WILL BE CONSEQUENCES.
SHIT. THESE HUMANS ARE CRAZY. DON'T THEY KNOW WHAT AN ACTUAL ALIEN INVASION LOOKS LIKE?

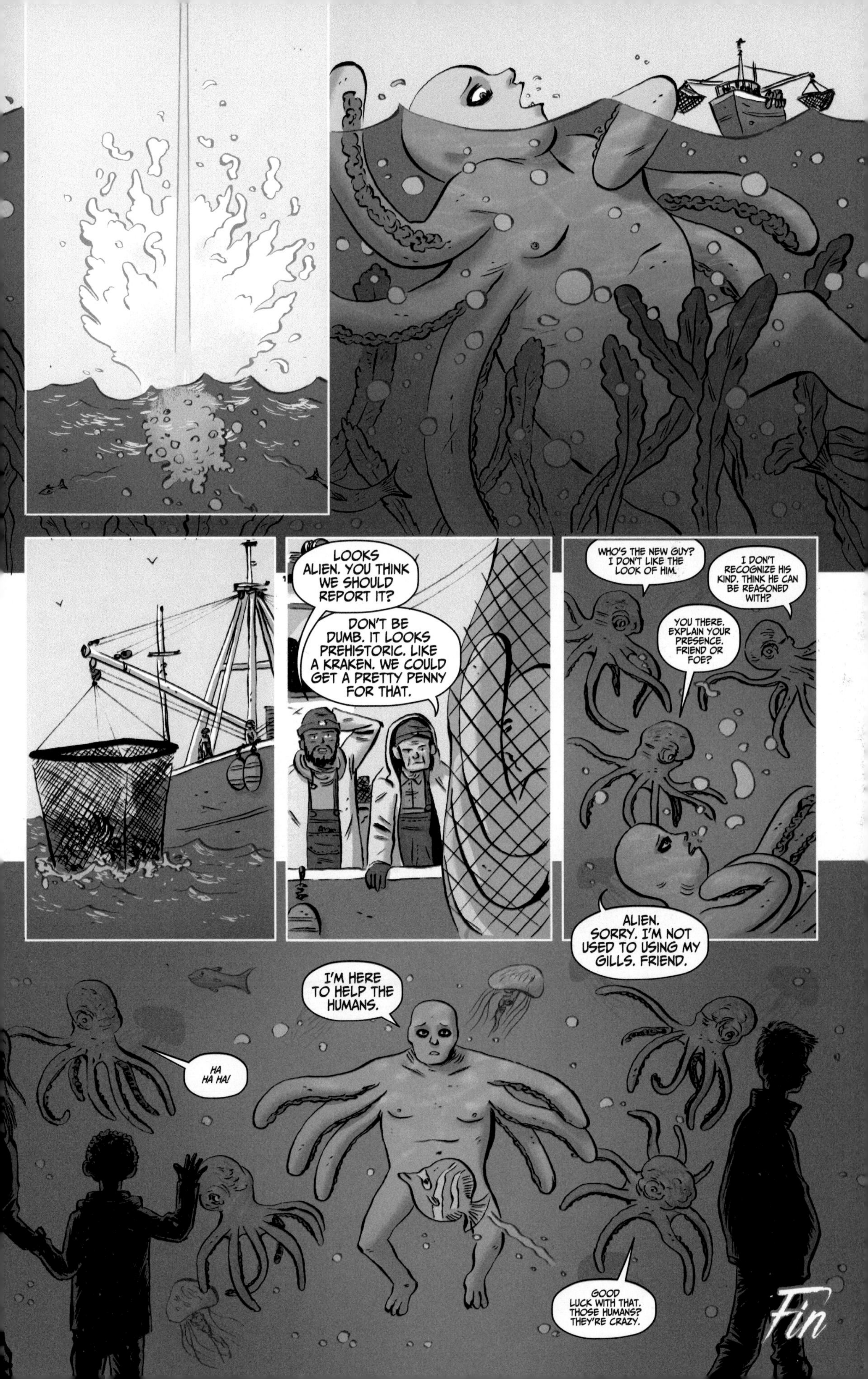

LOOKS ALIEN. YOU THINK WE SHOULD REPORT IT?
DON'T BE DUMB. IT LOOKS PREHISTORIC. LIKE A KRAKEN. WE COULD GET A PRETTY PENNY FOR THAT.
WHO'S THE NEW GUY? I DON'T LIKE THE LOOK OF HIM.
I DON'T RECOGNIZE HIS KIND. THINK HE CAN BE REASONED WITH?
YOU THERE. EXPLAIN YOUR PRESENCE. FRIEND OR FOE?
ALIEN. SORRY. I'M NOT USED TO USING MY GILLS. FRIEND.
I'M HERE TO HELP THE HUMANS.
HA HA HA!
GOOD LUCK WITH THAT. THOSE HUMANS? THEY'RE CRAZY.
Fin

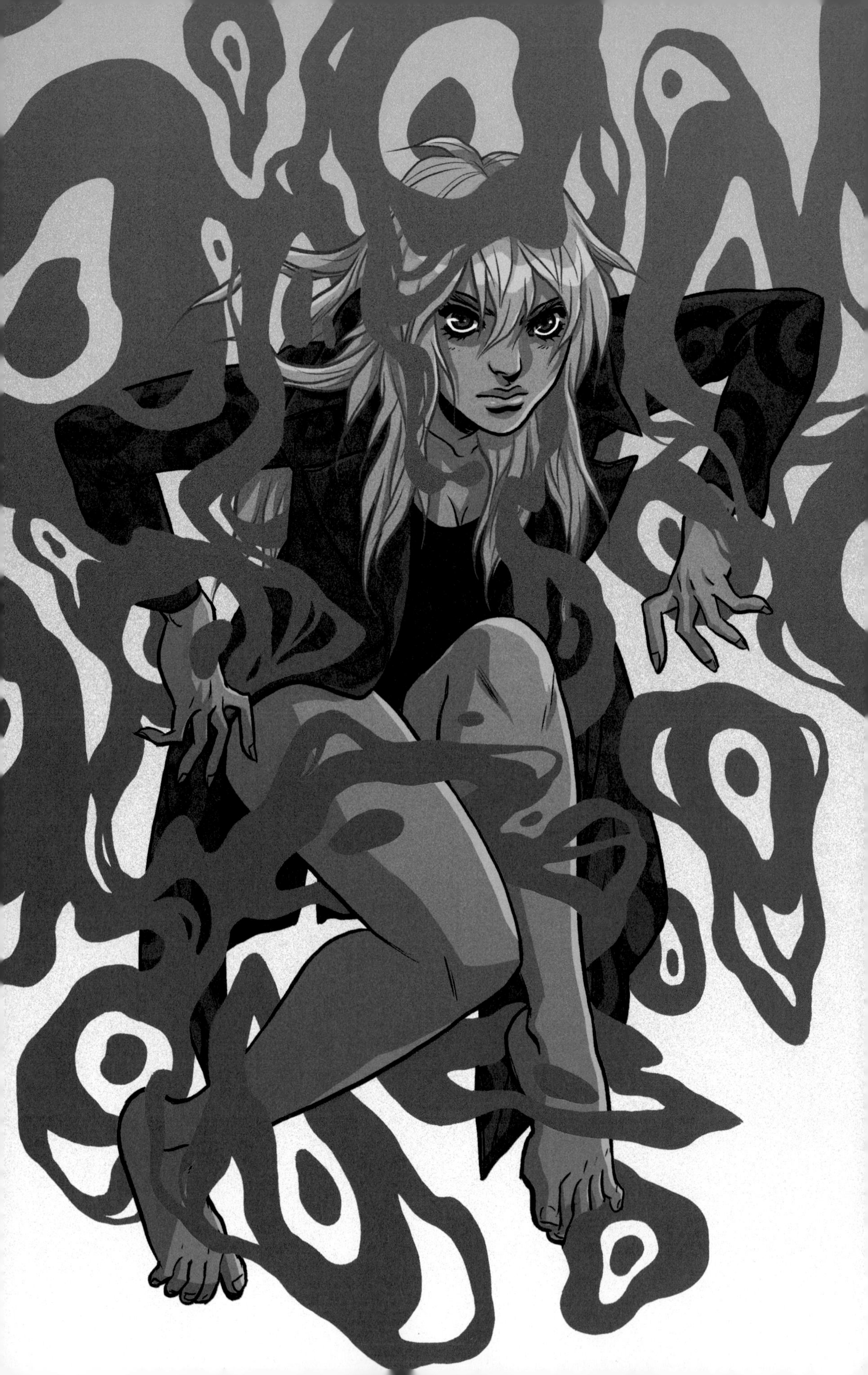

THE WEIGHT OF THE WORLD
WRITTEN BY CECIL CASTELLUCCI
ILLUSTRATED BY MARLEY ZARCONE
ADDITIONAL INKS (4, 7-16, 21) BY ANDE PARKS
COLORS BY KELLY FITZPATRICK
LETTERS BY SAIDA TEMOFONTE
COVER BY BECKY CLOONAN
EDITED BY JAMIE S. RICH
AND MOLLY MAHAN
WELCOME TO THE HEARTLAND
I CAN SEE THE CHANGE IN A DAY. THE SUNLIGHT AND CLOUDS IN FLUX FROM MOMENT TO MOMENT.
NEVER THE SAME LIGHT. NEVER THE SAME.
I NEVER FEEL THE CHANGE IN ME.
I FEEL THE SAME AS ALWAYS. AS THOUGH I'M CARRYING THE WEIGHT OF THE WORLD.
IT'S HARD TO KEEP IT TOGETHER.
I JUST FALL TO PIECES.

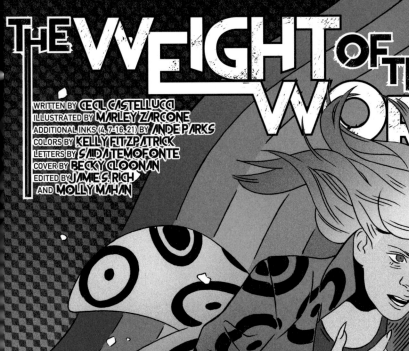

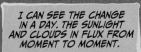

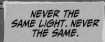

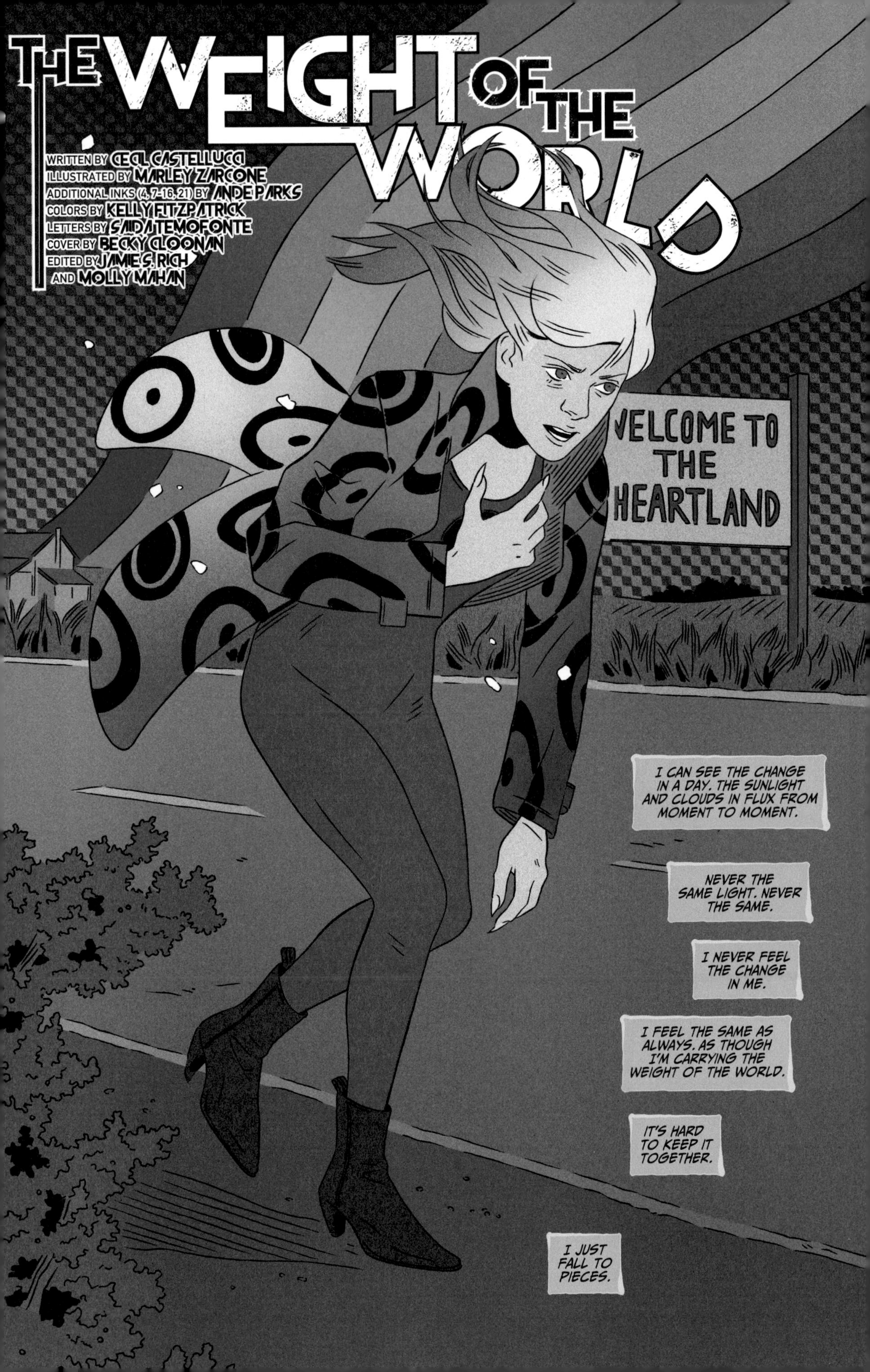

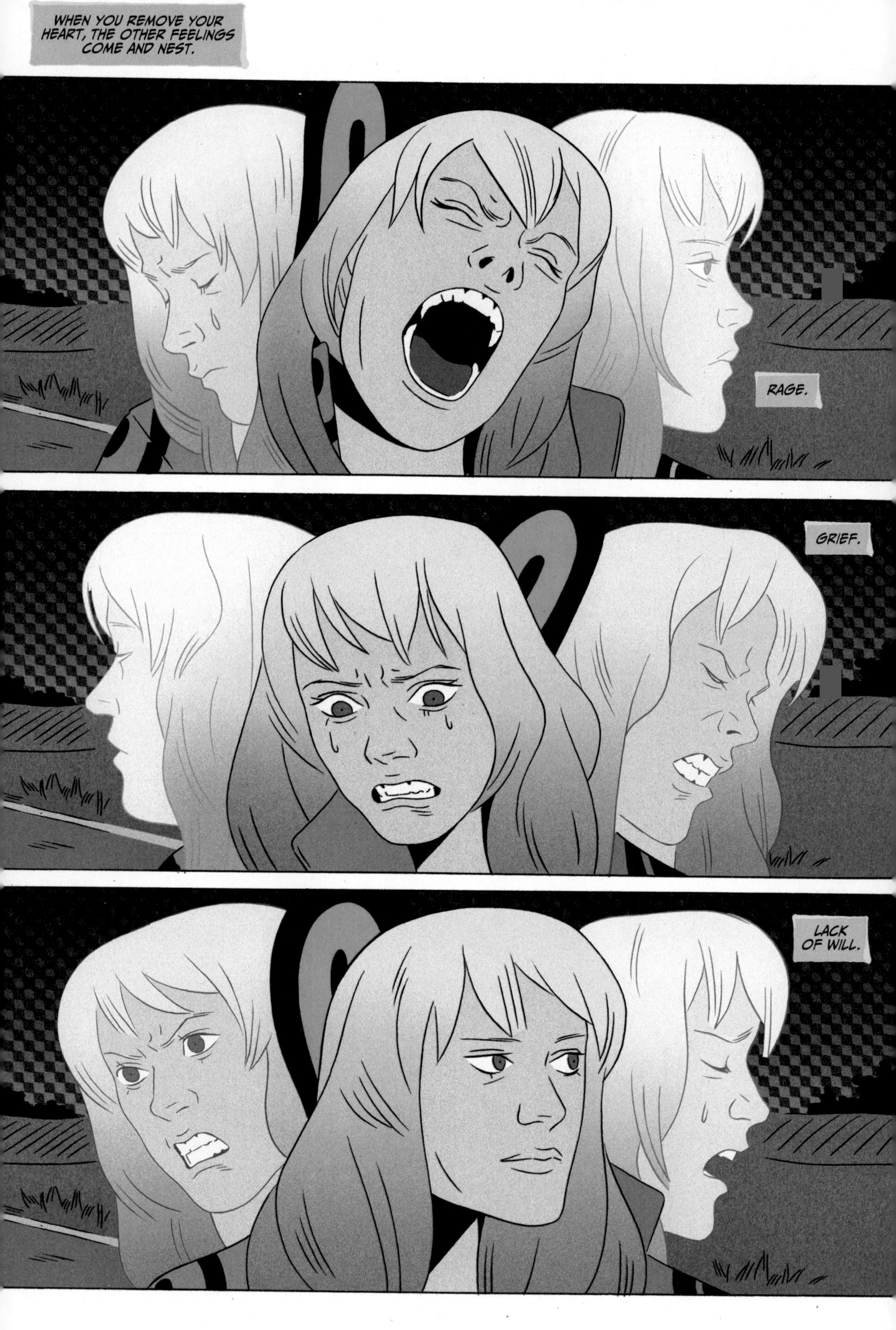
WHEN YOU REMOVE YOUR HEART, THE OTHER FEELINGS COME AND NEST.
RAGE.
GRIEF.
LACK OF WILL.

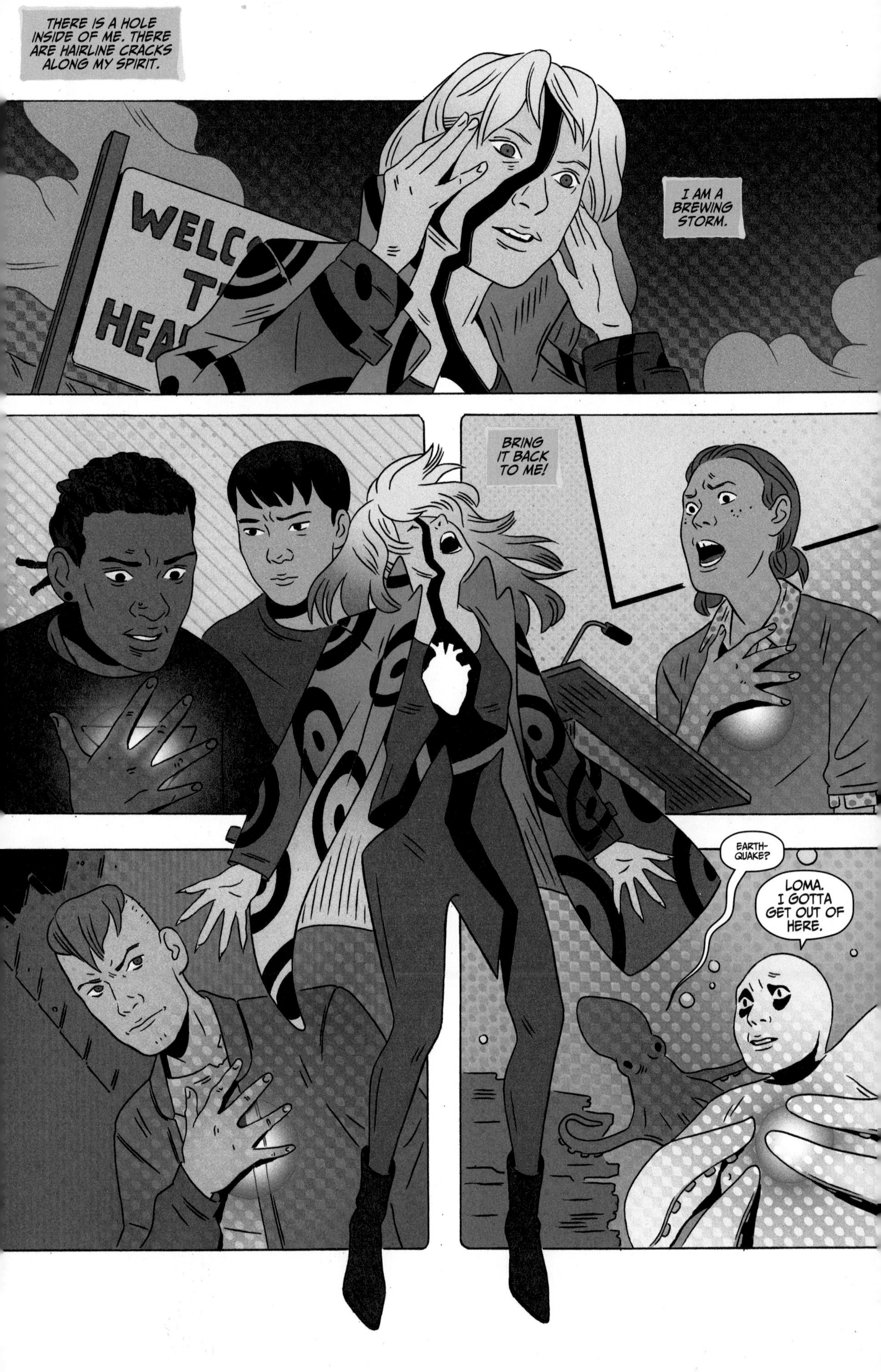
THERE IS A HOLE INSIDE OF ME. THERE ARE HAIRLINE CRACKS ALONG MY SPIRIT.
WELC
T
HEA
I AM A BREWING STORM.
BRING IT BACK TO ME!
EARTH-QUAKE?
LOMA. I GOTTA GET OUT OF HERE.

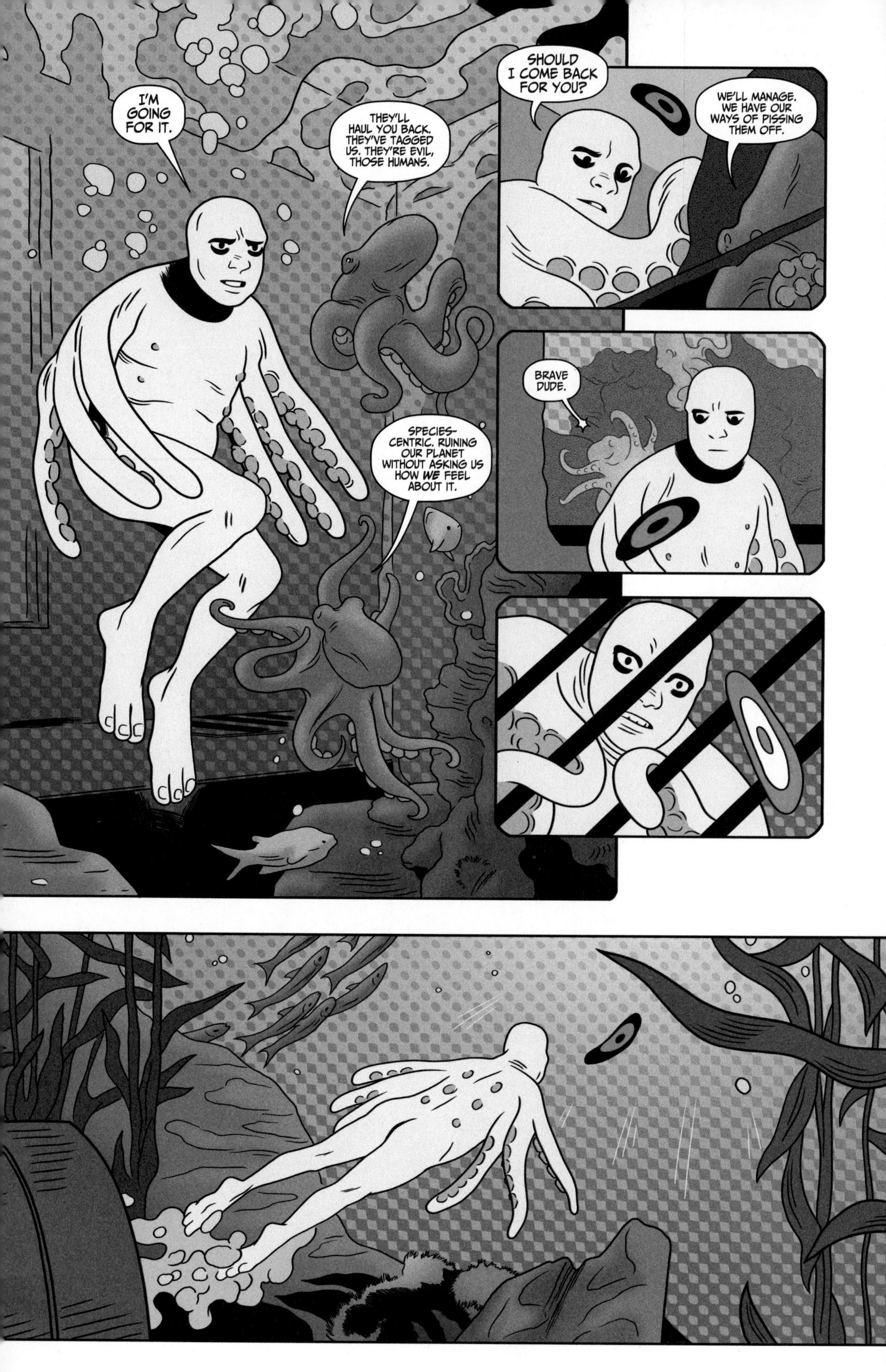
I'M GOING FOR IT.
THEY'LL HAUL YOU BACK. THEY'VE TAGGED US. THEY'RE EVIL, THOSE HUMANS.
SPECIES-CENTRIC. RUINING OUR PLANET WITHOUT ASKING US HOW WE FEEL ABOUT IT.
SHOULD I COME BACK FOR YOU?
WE'LL MANAGE. WE HAVE OUR WAYS OF PISSING THEM OFF.
BRAVE DUDE.

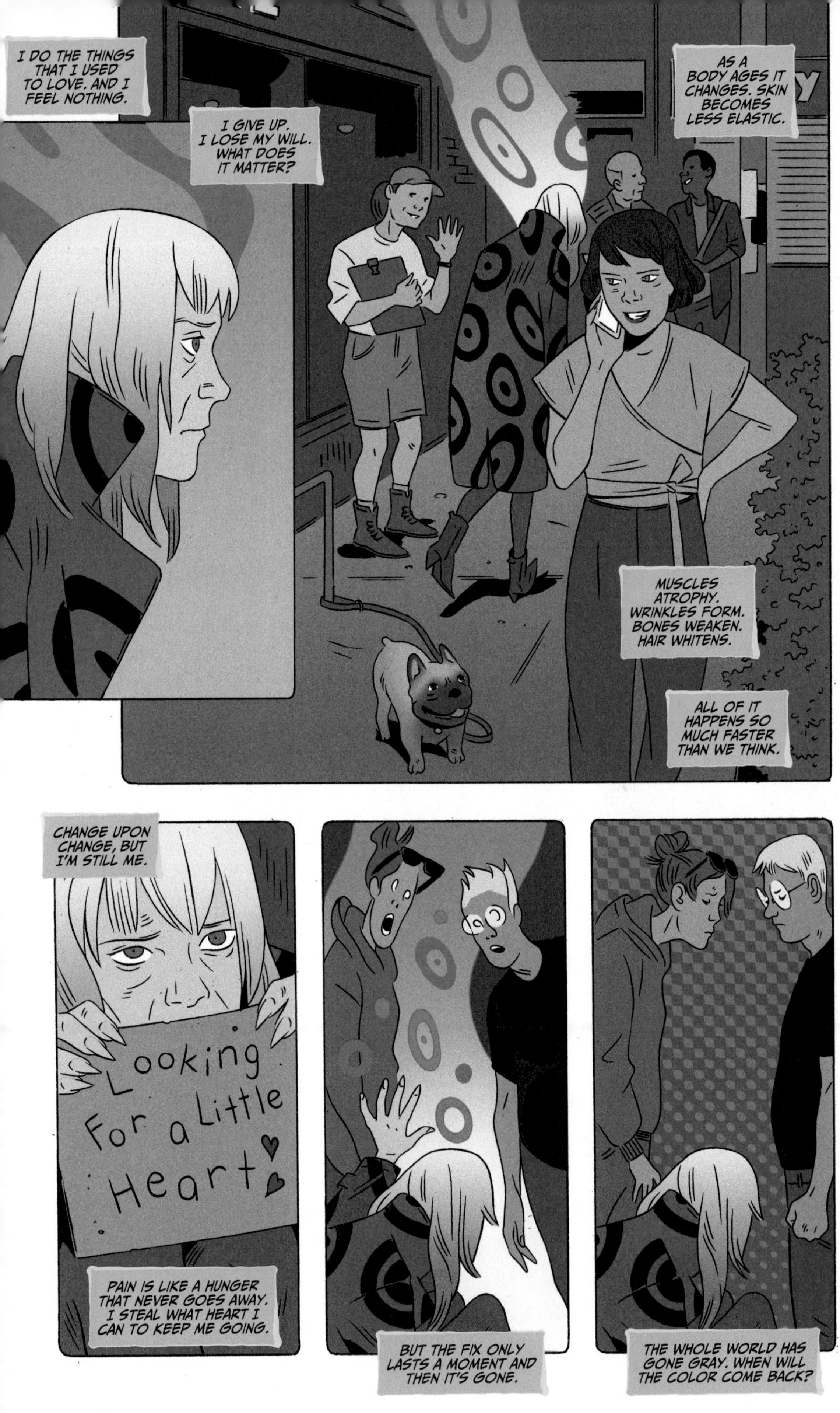
I DO THE THINGS THAT I USED TO LOVE. AND I FEEL NOTHING.
I GIVE UP. I LOSE MY WILL. WHAT DOES IT MATTER?
AS A BODY AGES IT CHANGES. SKIN BECOMES LESS ELASTIC.
MUSCLES ATROPHY. WRINKLES FORM. BONES WEAKEN. HAIR WHITENS.
ALL OF IT HAPPENS SO MUCH FASTER THAN WE THINK.
CHANGE UPON CHANGE, BUT I'M STILL ME.
Looking For a Little Heart
PAIN IS LIKE A HUNGER THAT NEVER GOES AWAY. I STEAL WHAT HEART I CAN TO KEEP ME GOING.
BUT THE FIX ONLY LASTS A MOMENT AND THEN IT'S GONE.
THE WHOLE WORLD HAS GONE GRAY. WHEN WILL THE COLOR COME BACK?

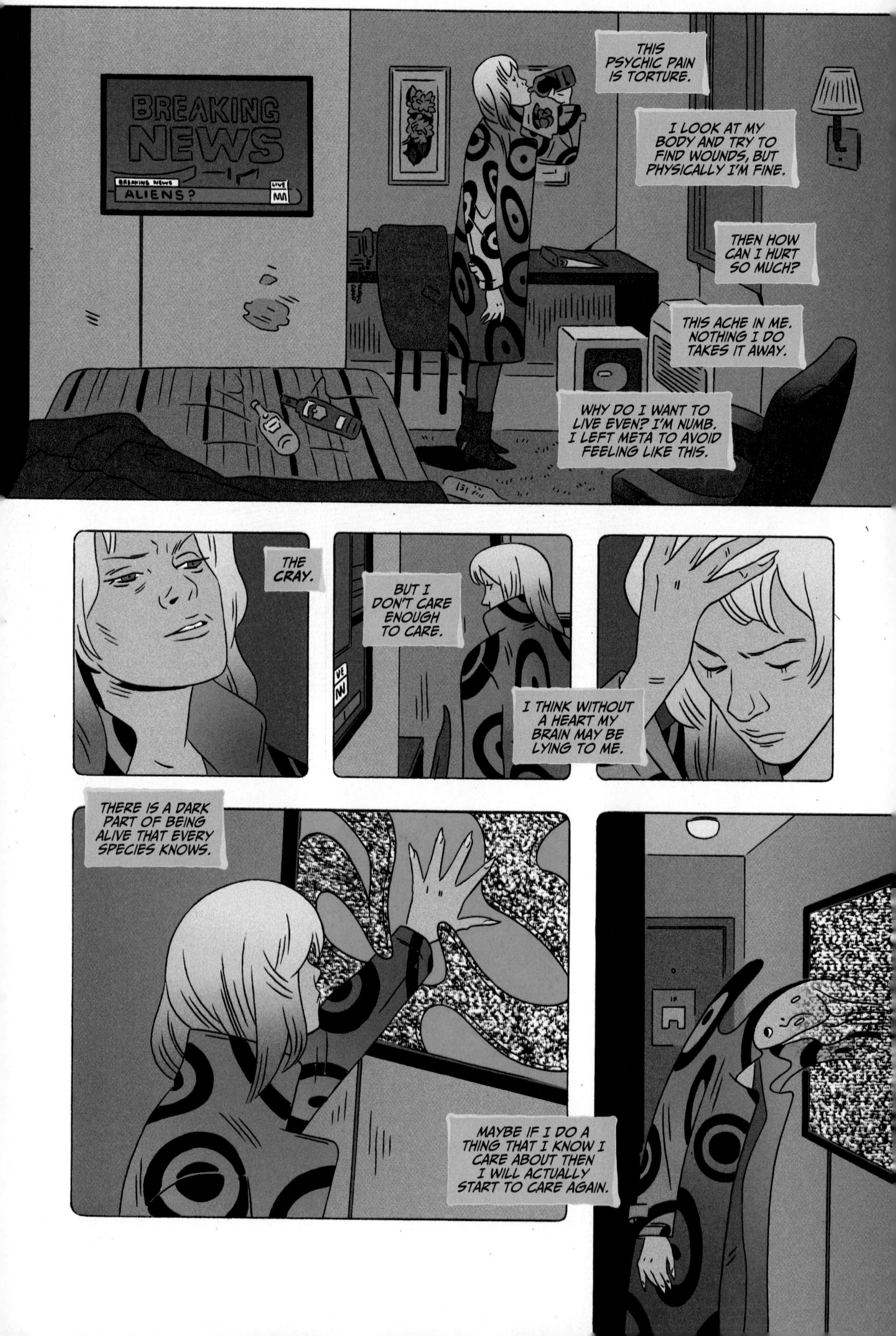

BREAKING NEWS
BREAKING NEWS
ALIENS?
LIVE
THIS PSYCHIC PAIN IS TORTURE.
I LOOK AT MY BODY AND TRY TO FIND WOUNDS, BUT PHYSICALLY I'M FINE.
THEN HOW CAN I HURT SO MUCH?
THIS ACHE IN ME. NOTHING I DO TAKES IT AWAY.
WHY DO I WANT TO LIVE EVEN? I'M NUMB. I LEFT META TO AVOID FEELING LIKE THIS.
THE CRAY.
BUT I DON'T CARE ENOUGH TO CARE.
I THINK WITHOUT A HEART MY BRAIN MAY BE LYING TO ME.
THERE IS A DARK PART OF BEING ALIVE THAT EVERY SPECIES KNOWS.
MAYBE IF I DO A THING THAT I KNOW I CARE ABOUT THEN I WILL ACTUALLY START TO CARE AGAIN.

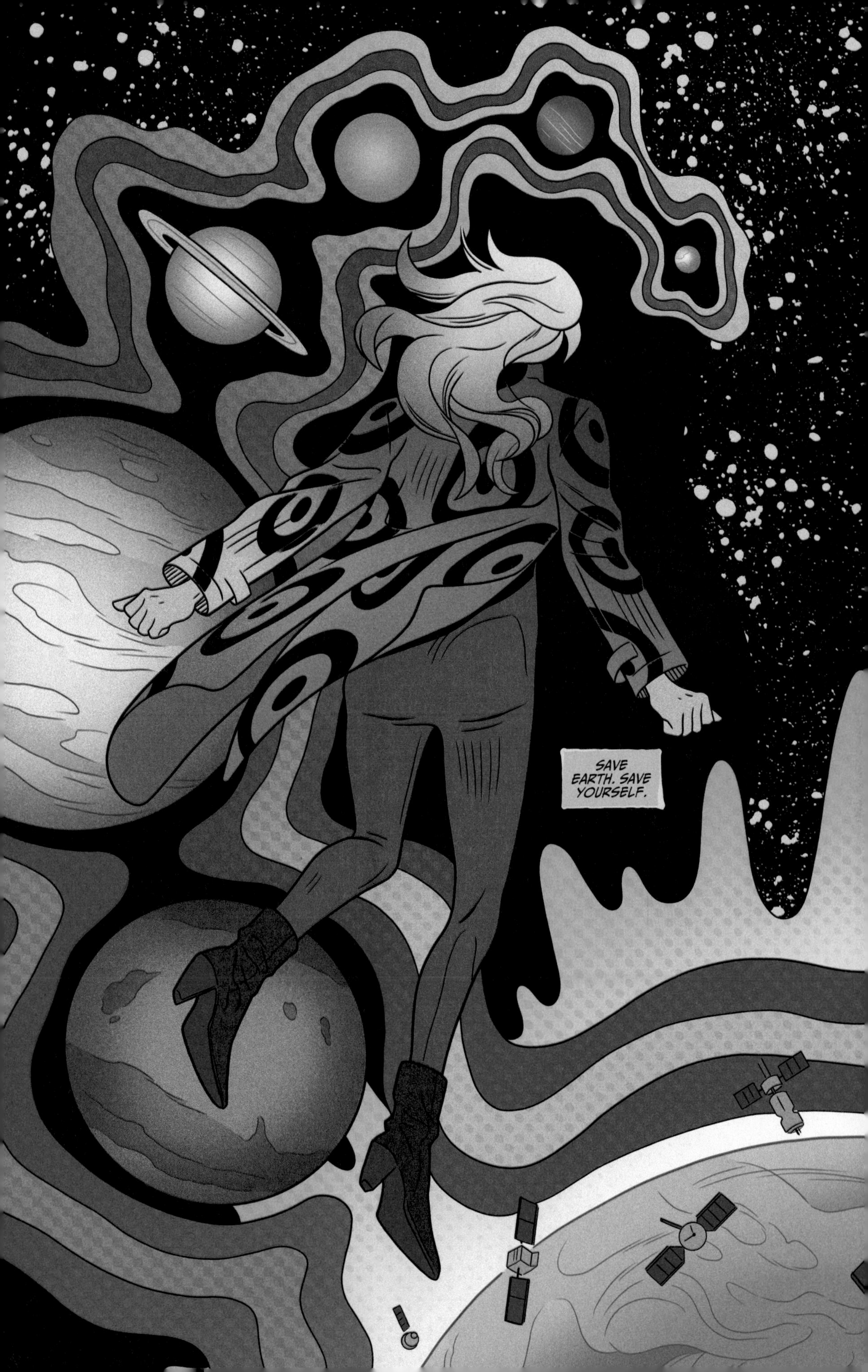
SAVE EARTH. SAVE YOURSELF.

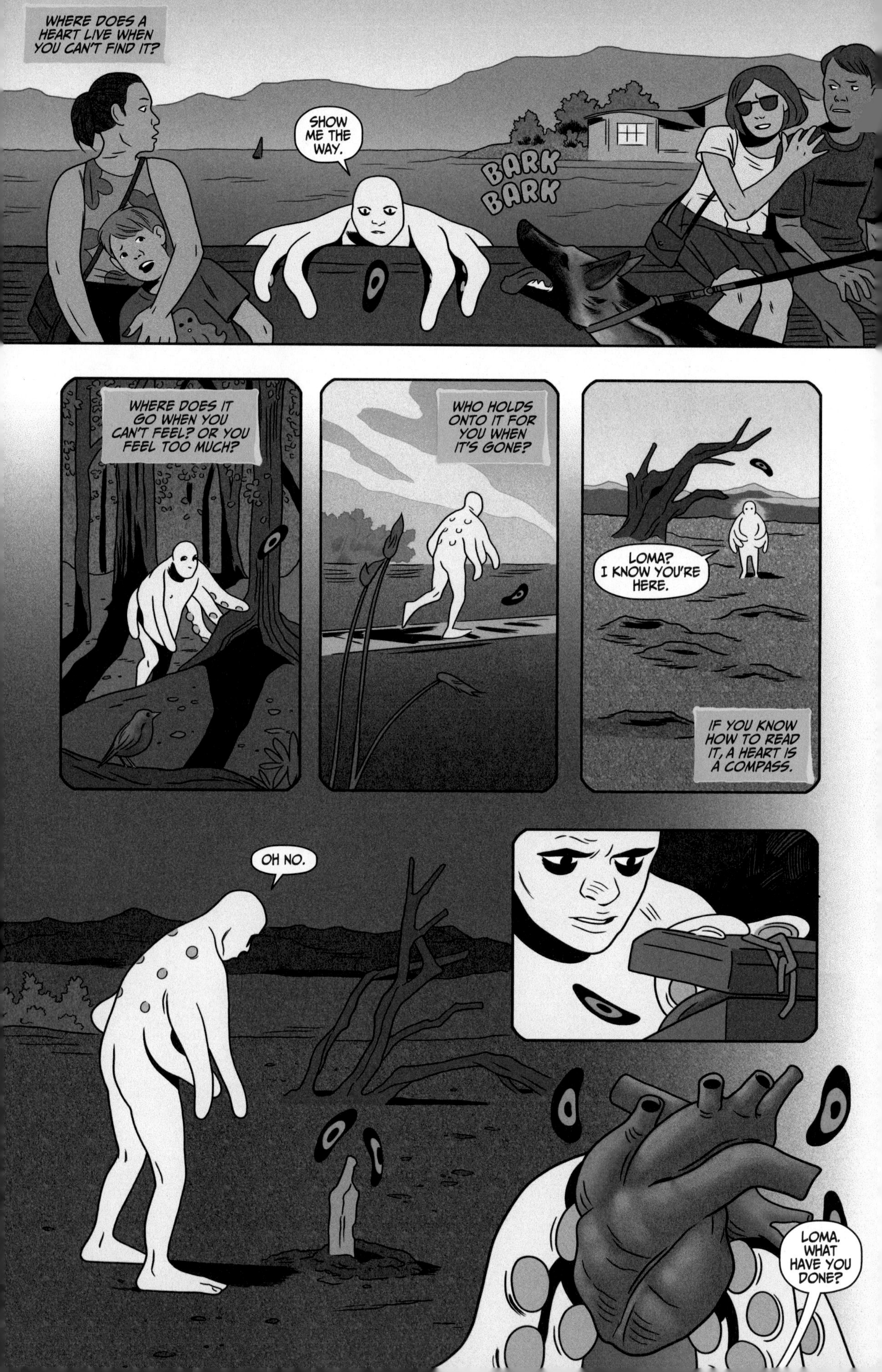
WHERE DOES A HEART LIVE WHEN YOU CAN'T FIND IT?
SHOW ME THE WAY.
BARK BARK
WHERE DOES IT GO WHEN YOU CAN'T FEEL? OR YOU FEEL TOO MUCH?
WHO HOLDS ONTO IT FOR YOU WHEN IT'S GONE?
LOMA? I KNOW YOU'RE HERE.
IF YOU KNOW HOW TO READ IT, A HEART IS A COMPASS.
OH NO.
LOMA. WHAT HAVE YOU DONE?

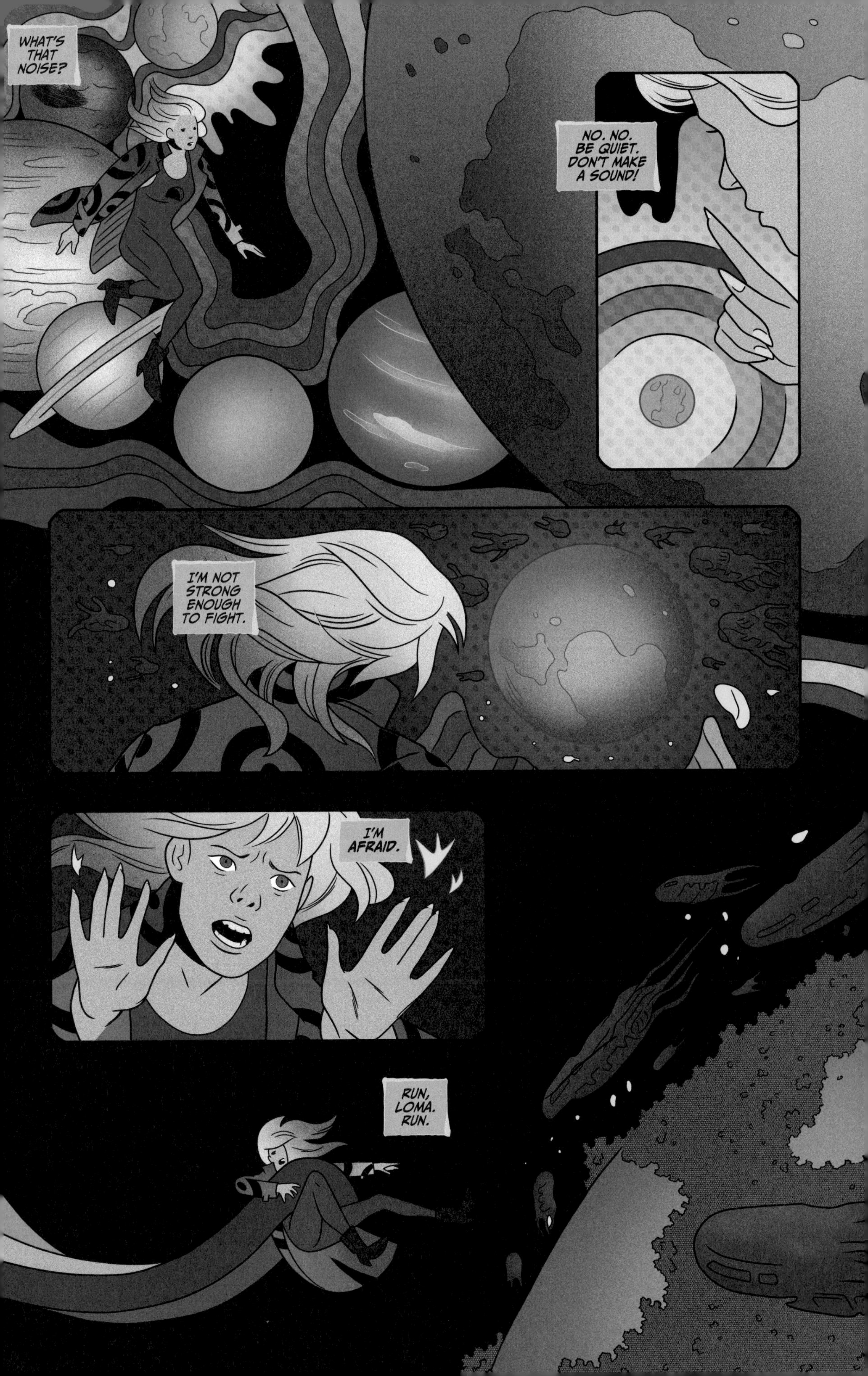
WHAT'S THAT NOISE?
NO. NO. BE QUIET. DON'T MAKE A SOUND!
I'M NOT STRONG ENOUGH TO FIGHT.
I'M AFRAID.
RUN, LOMA. RUN.

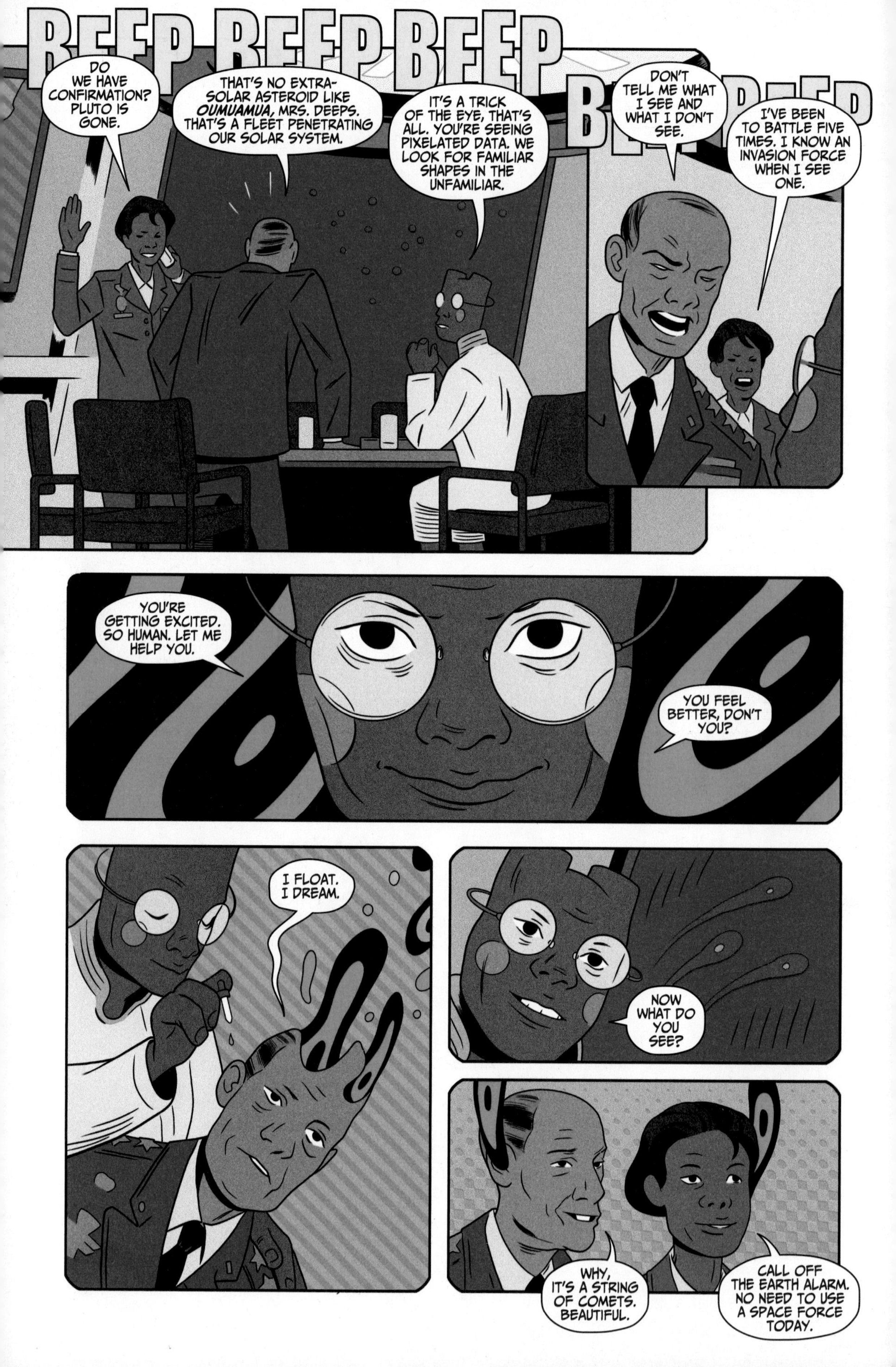
BEEP BEEP BEEP
DO WE HAVE CONFIRMATION? PLUTO IS GONE.
THAT'S NO EXTRA-SOLAR ASTEROID LIKE OUMUAMUA, MRS. DEEPS. THAT'S A FLEET PENETRATING OUR SOLAR SYSTEM.
IT'S A TRICK OF THE EYE, THAT'S ALL. YOU'RE SEEING PIXELATED DATA. WE LOOK FOR FAMILIAR SHAPES IN THE UNFAMILIAR.
DON'T TELL ME WHAT I SEE AND WHAT I DON'T SEE.
I'VE BEEN TO BATTLE FIVE TIMES. I KNOW AN INVASION FORCE WHEN I SEE ONE.
YOU'RE GETTING EXCITED. SO HUMAN. LET ME HELP YOU.
YOU FEEL BETTER, DON'T YOU?
I FLOAT. I DREAM.
NOW WHAT DO YOU SEE?
WHY, IT'S A STRING OF COMETS. BEAUTIFUL.
CALL OFF THE EARTH ALARM. NO NEED TO USE A SPACE FORCE TODAY.

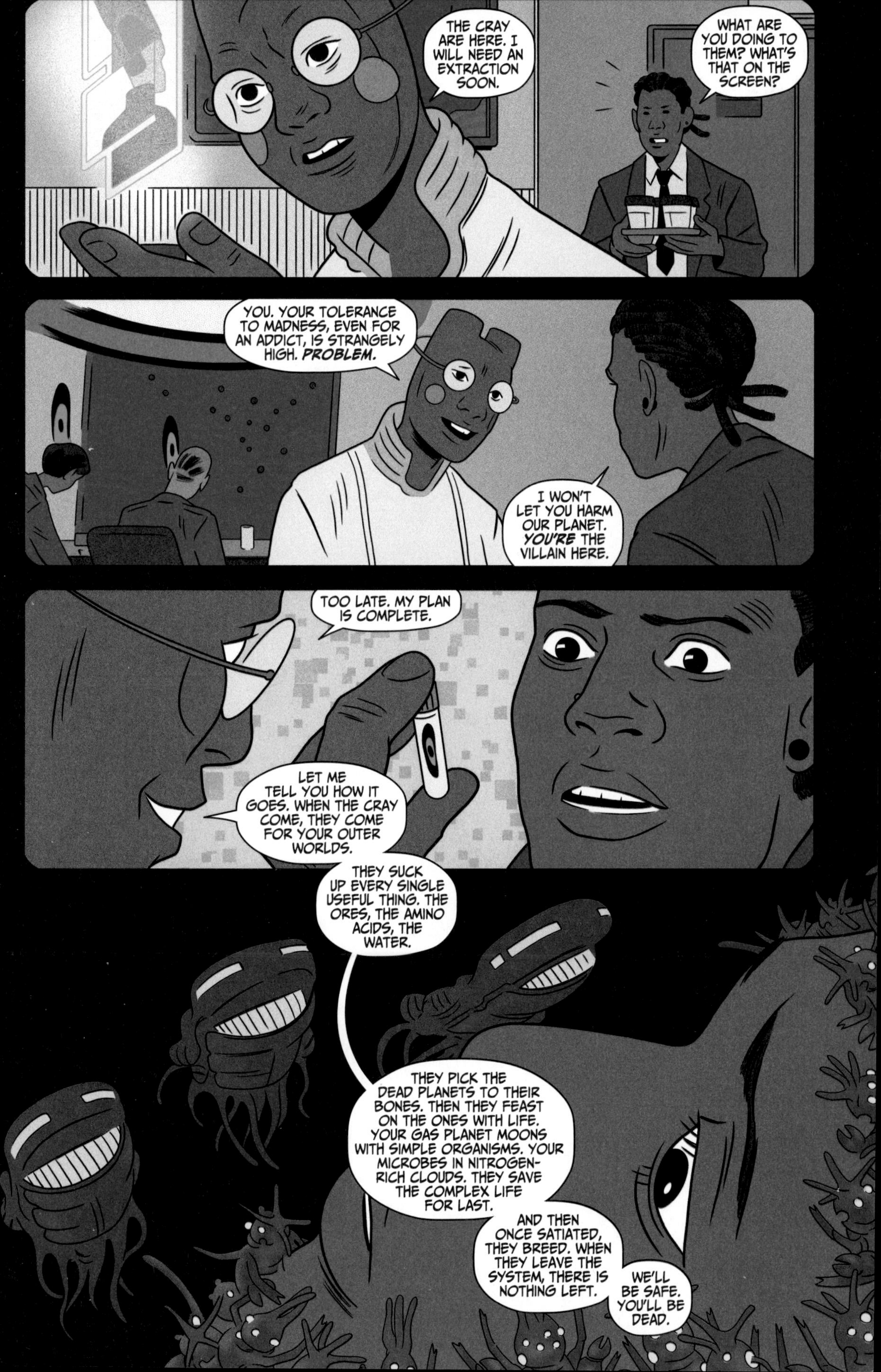
THE CRAY ARE HERE. I WILL NEED AN EXTRACTION SOON.
WHAT ARE YOU DOING TO THEM? WHAT'S THAT ON THE SCREEN?
YOU. YOUR TOLERANCE TO MADNESS, EVEN FOR AN ADDICT, IS STRANGELY HIGH. PROBLEM.
I WON'T LET YOU HARM OUR PLANET. YOU'RE THE VILLAIN HERE.
TOO LATE. MY PLAN IS COMPLETE.
LET ME TELL YOU HOW IT GOES. WHEN THE CRAY COME, THEY COME FOR YOUR OUTER WORLDS.
THEY SUCK UP EVERY SINGLE USEFUL THING. THE ORES, THE AMINO ACIDS, THE WATER.
THEY PICK THE DEAD PLANETS TO THEIR BONES. THEN THEY FEAST ON THE ONES WITH LIFE. YOUR GAS PLANET MOONS WITH SIMPLE ORGANISMS. YOUR MICROBES IN NITROGEN-RICH CLOUDS. THEY SAVE THE COMPLEX LIFE FOR LAST.
AND THEN ONCE SATIATED, THEY BREED. WHEN THEY LEAVE THE SYSTEM, THERE IS NOTHING LEFT.
WE'LL BE SAFE. YOU'LL BE DEAD.

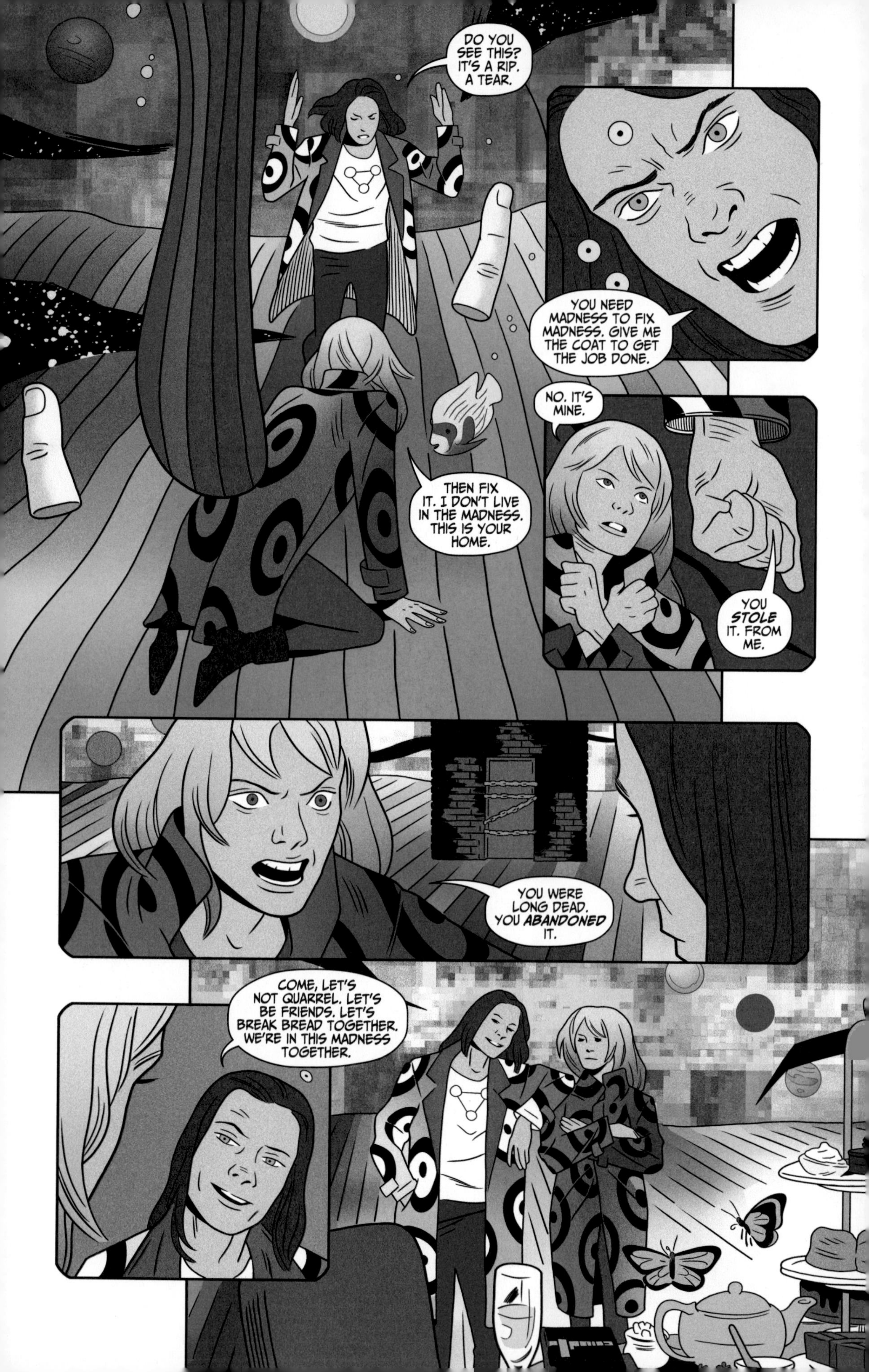
DO YOU SEE THIS? IT'S A RIP. A TEAR.
YOU NEED MADNESS TO FIX MADNESS. GIVE ME THE COAT TO GET THE JOB DONE.
THEN FIX IT. I DON'T LIVE IN THE MADNESS. THIS IS YOUR HOME.
NO. IT'S MINE.
YOU *STOLE* IT. FROM ME.
YOU WERE LONG DEAD. YOU *ABANDONED* IT.
COME, LET'S NOT QUARREL. LET'S BE FRIENDS. LET'S BREAK BREAD TOGETHER. WE'RE IN THIS MADNESS TOGETHER.

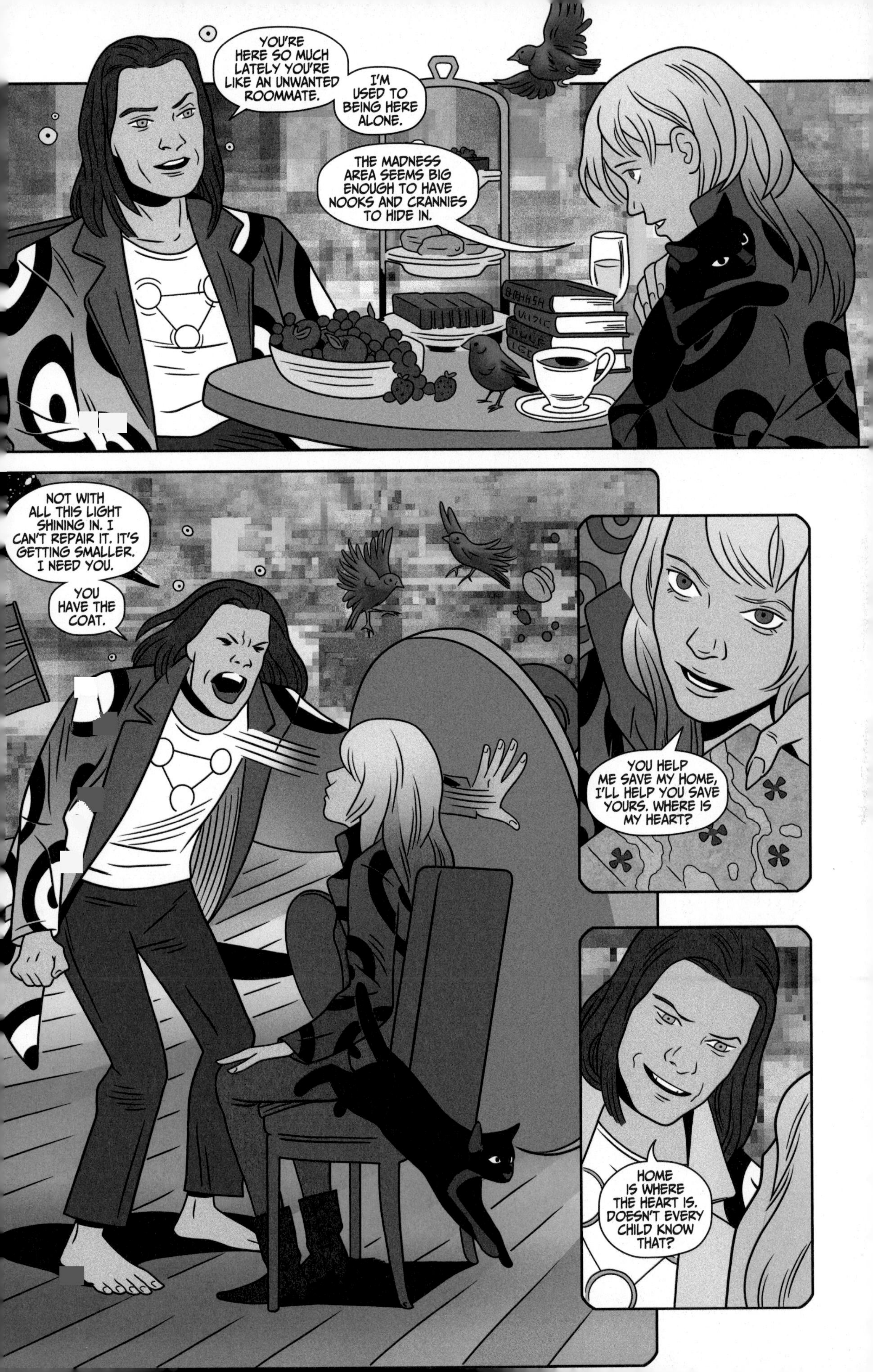
YOU'RE HERE SO MUCH LATELY YOU'RE LIKE AN UNWANTED ROOMMATE.
I'M USED TO BEING HERE ALONE.
THE MADNESS AREA SEEMS BIG ENOUGH TO HAVE NOOKS AND CRANNIES TO HIDE IN.
NOT WITH ALL THIS LIGHT SHINING IN. I CAN'T REPAIR IT. IT'S GETTING SMALLER. I NEED YOU.
YOU HAVE THE COAT.
YOU HELP ME SAVE MY HOME, I'LL HELP YOU SAVE YOURS. WHERE IS MY HEART?
HOME IS WHERE THE HEART IS. DOESN'T EVERY CHILD KNOW THAT?

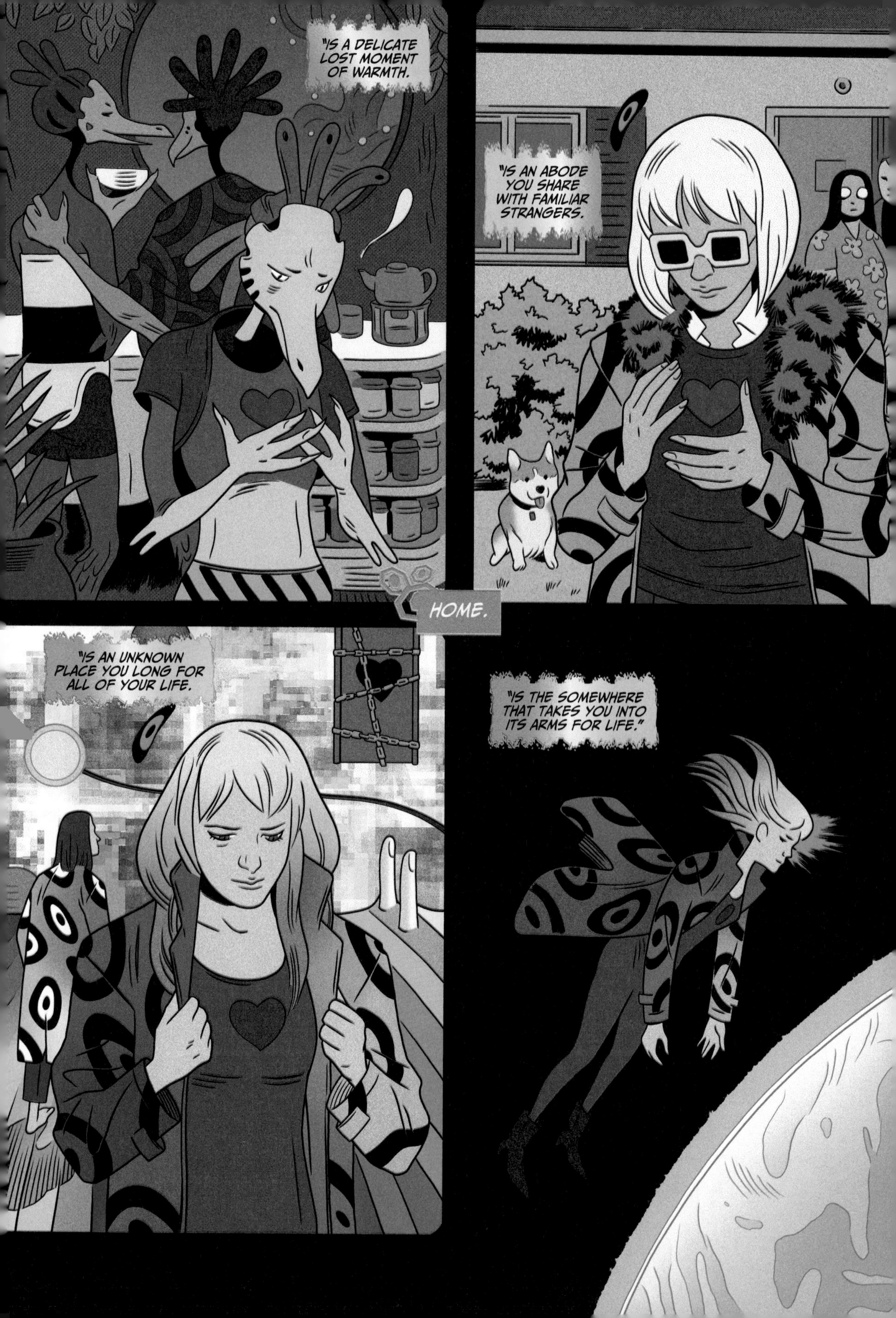
"IS A DELICATE LOST MOMENT OF WARMTH.
"IS AN ABODE YOU SHARE WITH FAMILIAR STRANGERS.
HOME.
"IS AN UNKNOWN PLACE YOU LONG FOR ALL OF YOUR LIFE.
"IS THE SOMEWHERE THAT TAKES YOU INTO ITS ARMS FOR LIFE."

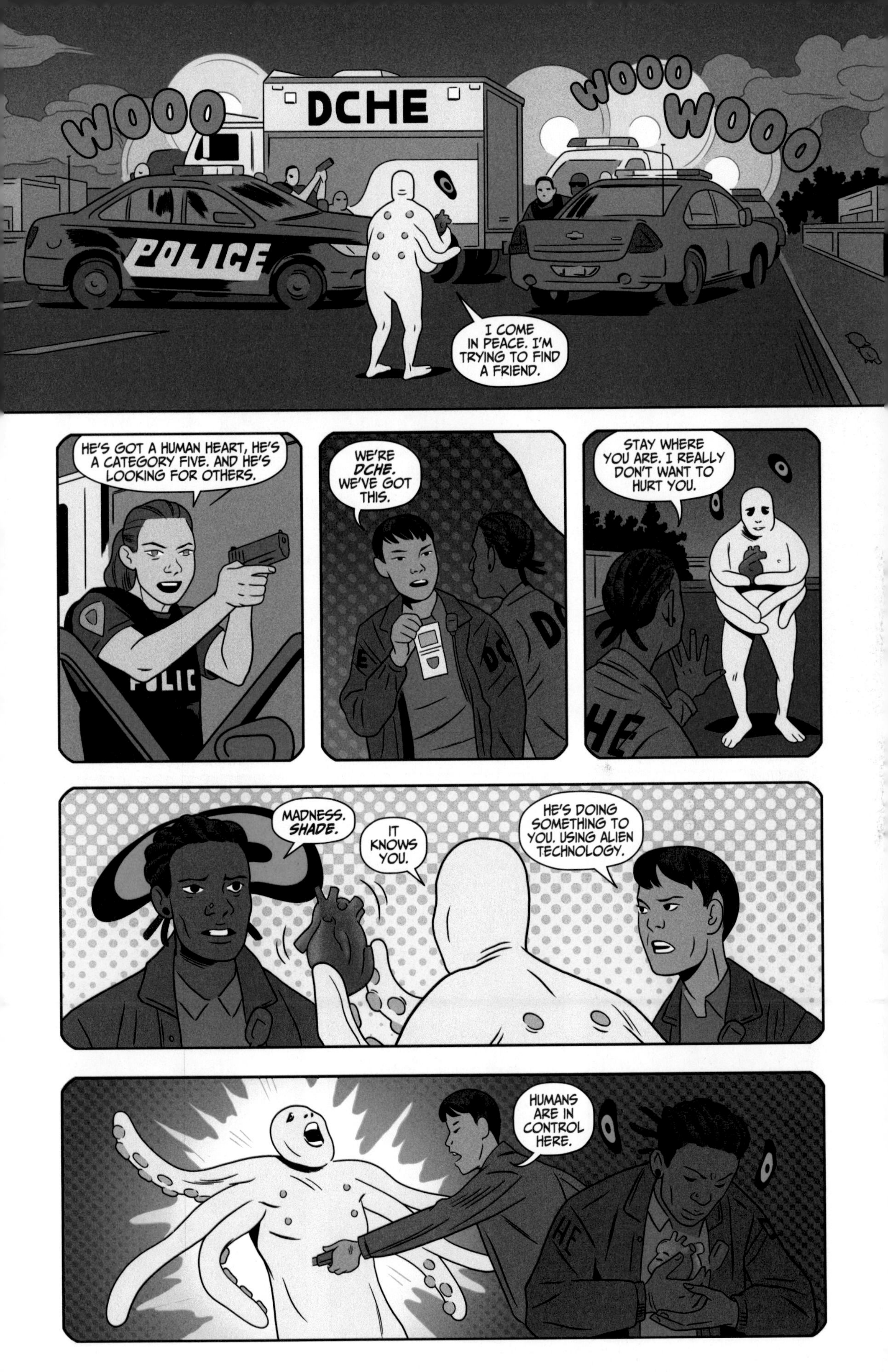
WOOO
DCHE
WOOO
WOOO
POLICE
I COME IN PEACE. I'M TRYING TO FIND A FRIEND.
HE'S GOT A HUMAN HEART, HE'S A CATEGORY FIVE. AND HE'S LOOKING FOR OTHERS.
WE'RE *DCHE.* WE'VE GOT THIS.
STAY WHERE YOU ARE. I REALLY DON'T WANT TO HURT YOU.
MADNESS. *SHADE.*
IT KNOWS YOU.
HE'S DOING SOMETHING TO YOU. USING ALIEN TECHNOLOGY.
HUMANS ARE IN CONTROL HERE.

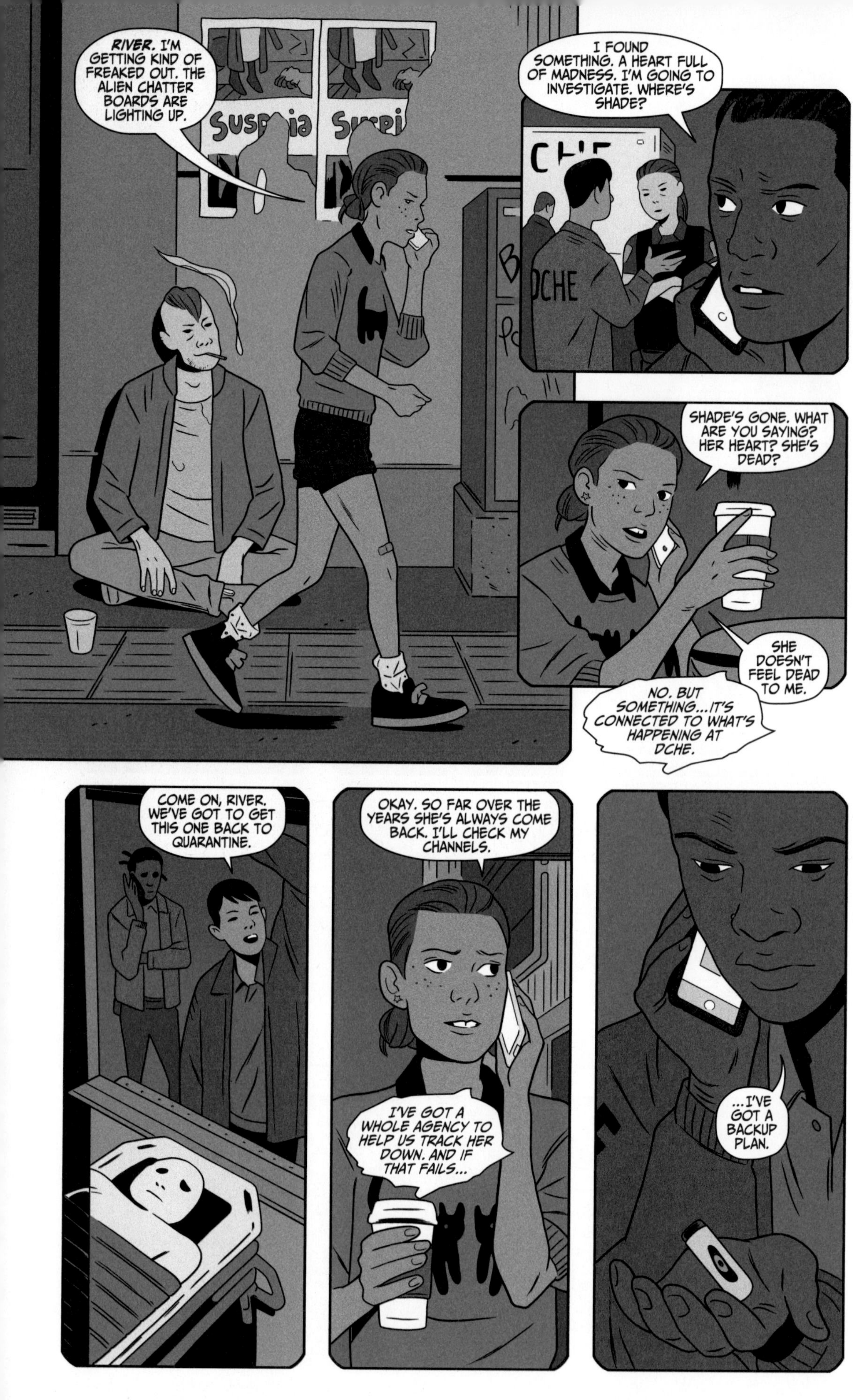
RIVER. I'M GETTING KIND OF FREAKED OUT. THE ALIEN CHATTER BOARDS ARE LIGHTING UP.
Suspiria
Suspi
I FOUND SOMETHING. A HEART FULL OF MADNESS. I'M GOING TO INVESTIGATE. WHERE'S SHADE?
DCHE
SHADE'S GONE. WHAT ARE YOU SAYING? HER HEART? SHE'S DEAD?
SHE DOESN'T FEEL DEAD TO ME.
NO. BUT SOMETHING...IT'S CONNECTED TO WHAT'S HAPPENING AT DCHE.
COME ON, RIVER. WE'VE GOT TO GET THIS ONE BACK TO QUARANTINE.
OKAY. SO FAR OVER THE YEARS SHE'S ALWAYS COME BACK. I'LL CHECK MY CHANNELS.
I'VE GOT A WHOLE AGENCY TO HELP US TRACK HER DOWN. AND IF THAT FAILS...
...I'VE GOT A BACKUP PLAN.

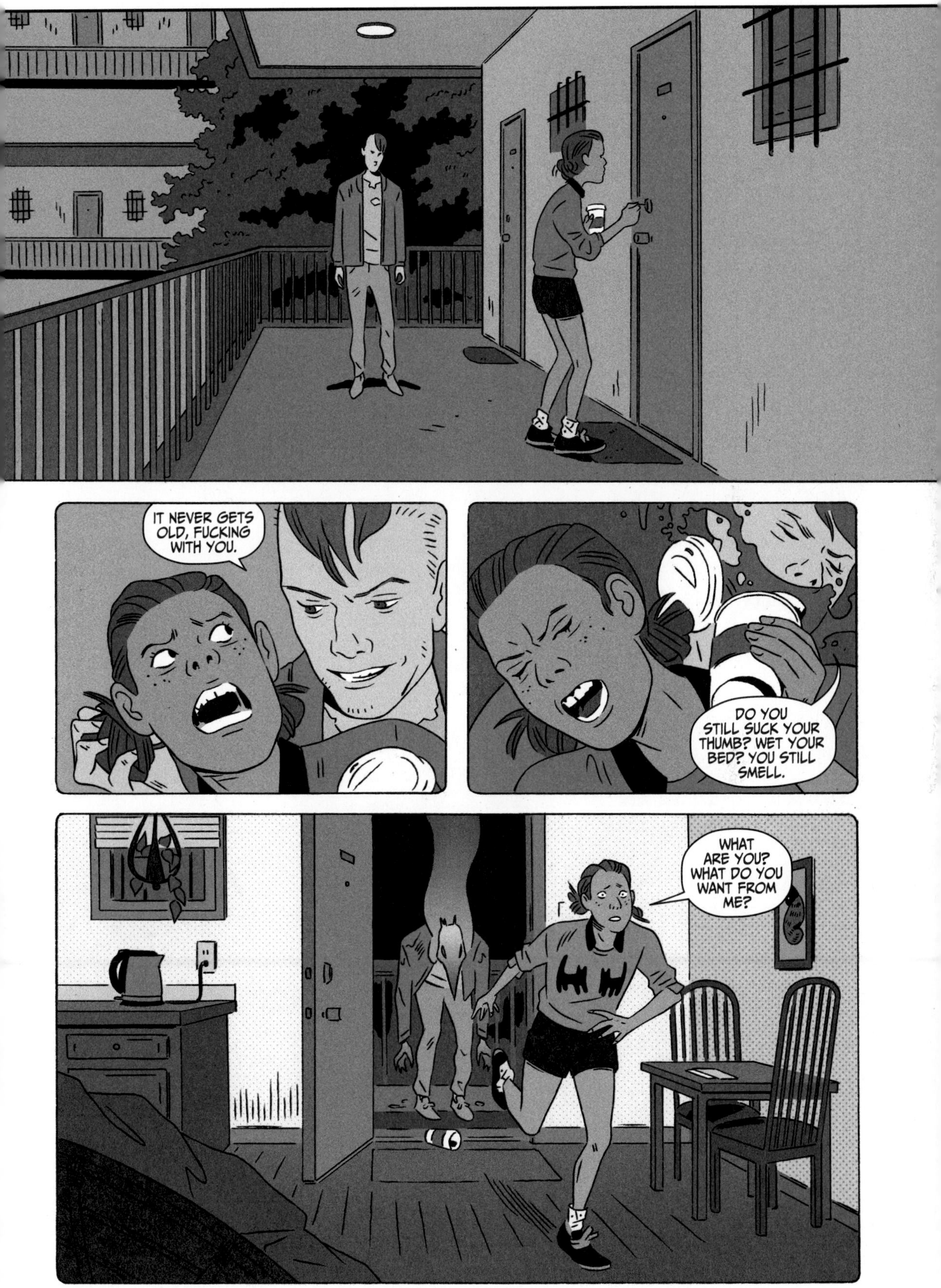
IT NEVER GETS OLD, FUCKING WITH YOU.
DO YOU STILL SUCK YOUR THUMB? WET YOUR BED? YOU STILL SMELL.
WHAT ARE YOU? WHAT DO YOU WANT FROM ME?

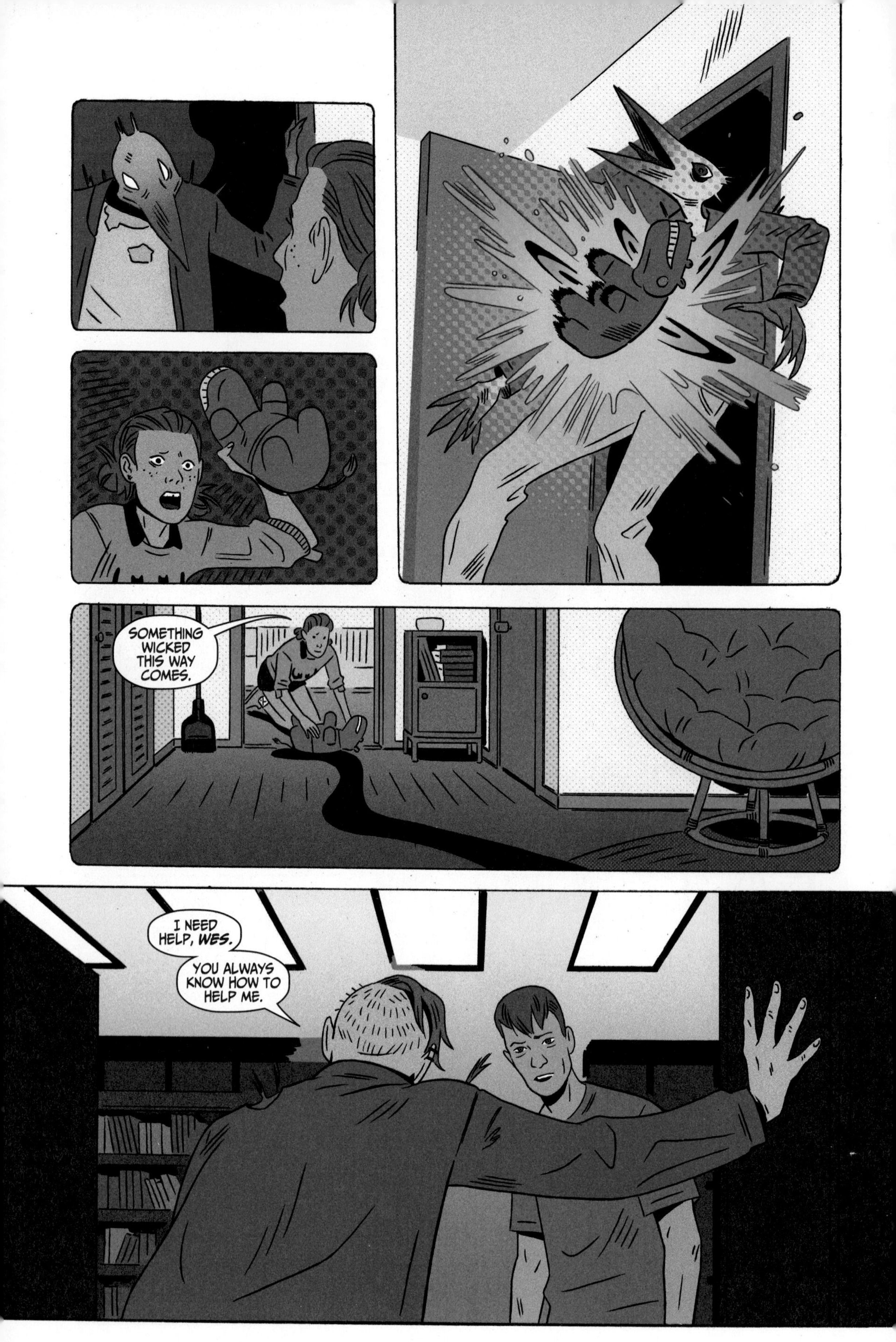
SOMETHING WICKED THIS WAY COMES.
I NEED HELP, WES.
YOU ALWAYS KNOW HOW TO HELP ME.

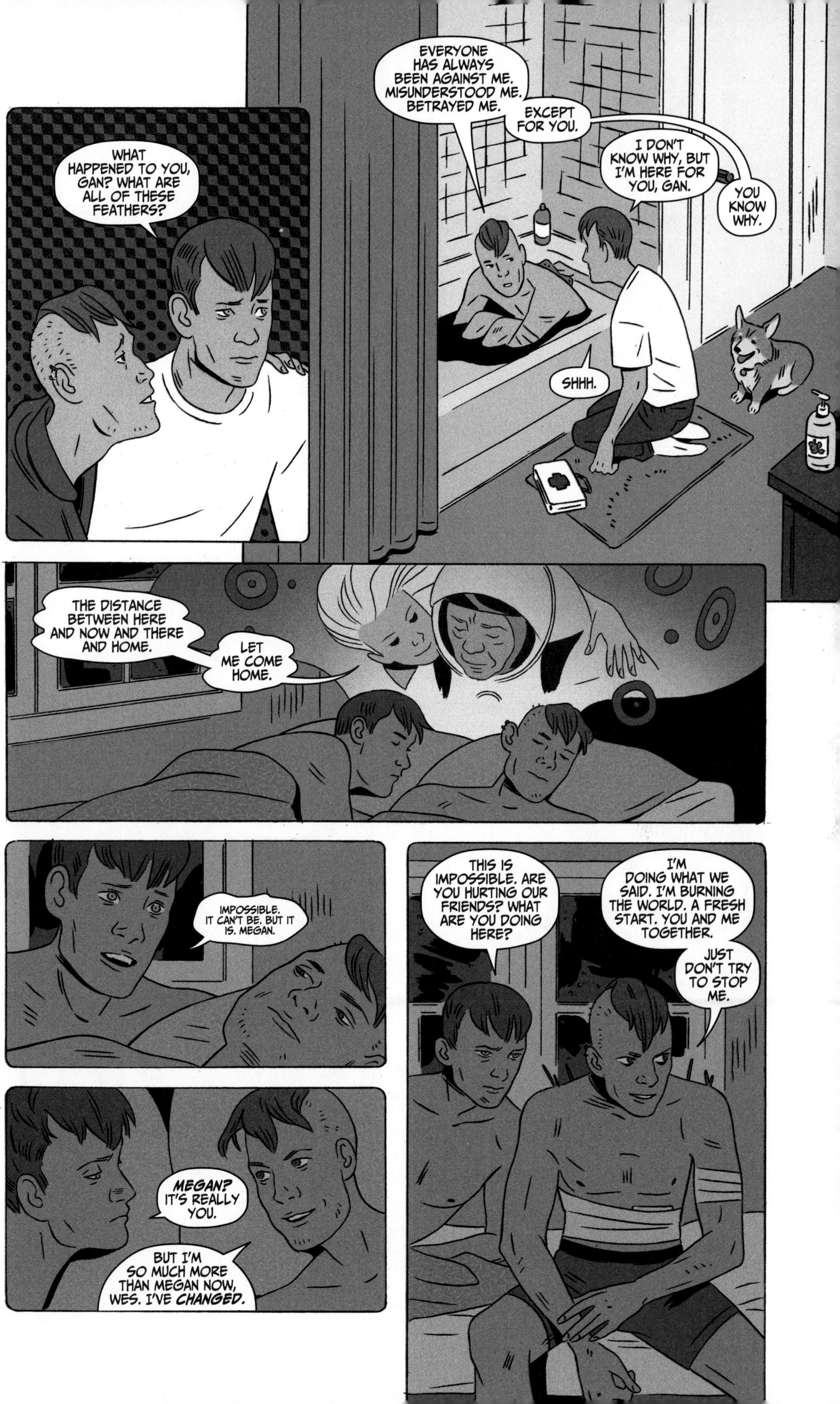
WHAT HAPPENED TO YOU, GAN? WHAT ARE ALL OF THESE FEATHERS?
EVERYONE HAS ALWAYS BEEN AGAINST ME. MISUNDERSTOOD ME. BETRAYED ME.
EXCEPT FOR YOU.
YOU KNOW WHY.
I DON'T KNOW WHY, BUT I'M HERE FOR YOU, GAN.
SHHH.
THE DISTANCE BETWEEN HERE AND NOW AND THERE AND HOME.
LET ME COME HOME.
IMPOSSIBLE. IT CAN'T BE. BUT IT IS. MEGAN.
MEGAN? IT'S REALLY YOU.
BUT I'M SO MUCH MORE THAN MEGAN NOW, WES. I'VE CHANGED.
THIS IS IMPOSSIBLE. ARE YOU HURTING OUR FRIENDS? WHAT ARE YOU DOING HERE?
I'M DOING WHAT WE SAID. I'M BURNING THE WORLD. A FRESH START. YOU AND ME TOGETHER.
JUST DON'T TRY TO STOP ME.

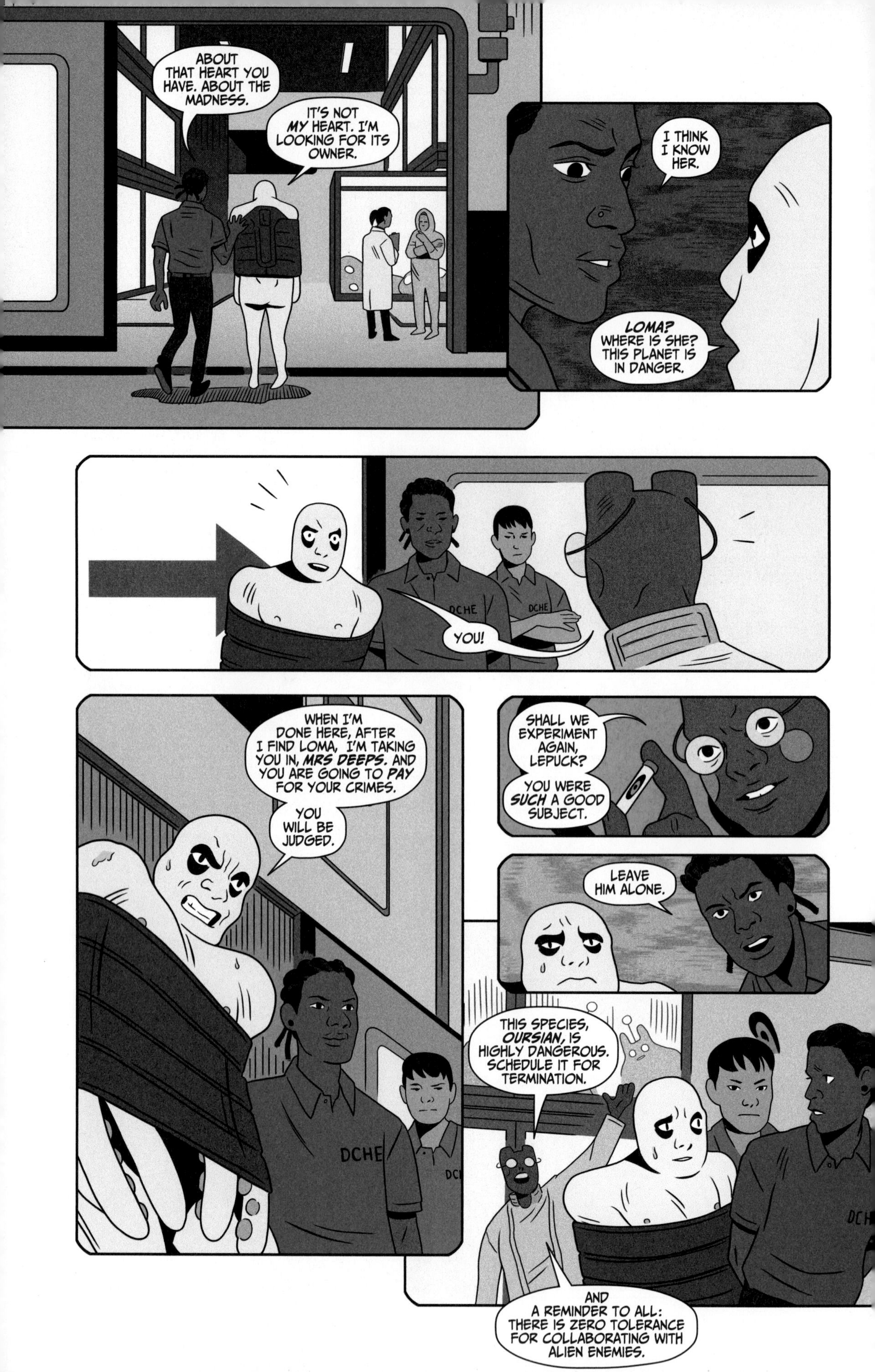
ABOUT THAT HEART YOU HAVE. ABOUT THE MADNESS.
IT'S NOT *MY* HEART. I'M LOOKING FOR ITS OWNER.
I THINK I KNOW HER.
LOMA? WHERE IS SHE? THIS PLANET IS IN DANGER.
DCHE
DCHE
YOU!
WHEN I'M DONE HERE, AFTER I FIND LOMA, I'M TAKING YOU IN, *MRS DEEPS.* AND YOU ARE GOING TO *PAY* FOR YOUR CRIMES.
YOU WILL BE JUDGED.
DCHE
SHALL WE EXPERIMENT AGAIN, LEPUCK?
YOU WERE *SUCH* A GOOD SUBJECT.
LEAVE HIM ALONE.
THIS SPECIES, *OURSIAN,* IS HIGHLY DANGEROUS. SCHEDULE IT FOR TERMINATION.
AND A REMINDER TO ALL: THERE IS ZERO TOLERANCE FOR COLLABORATING WITH ALIEN ENEMIES.

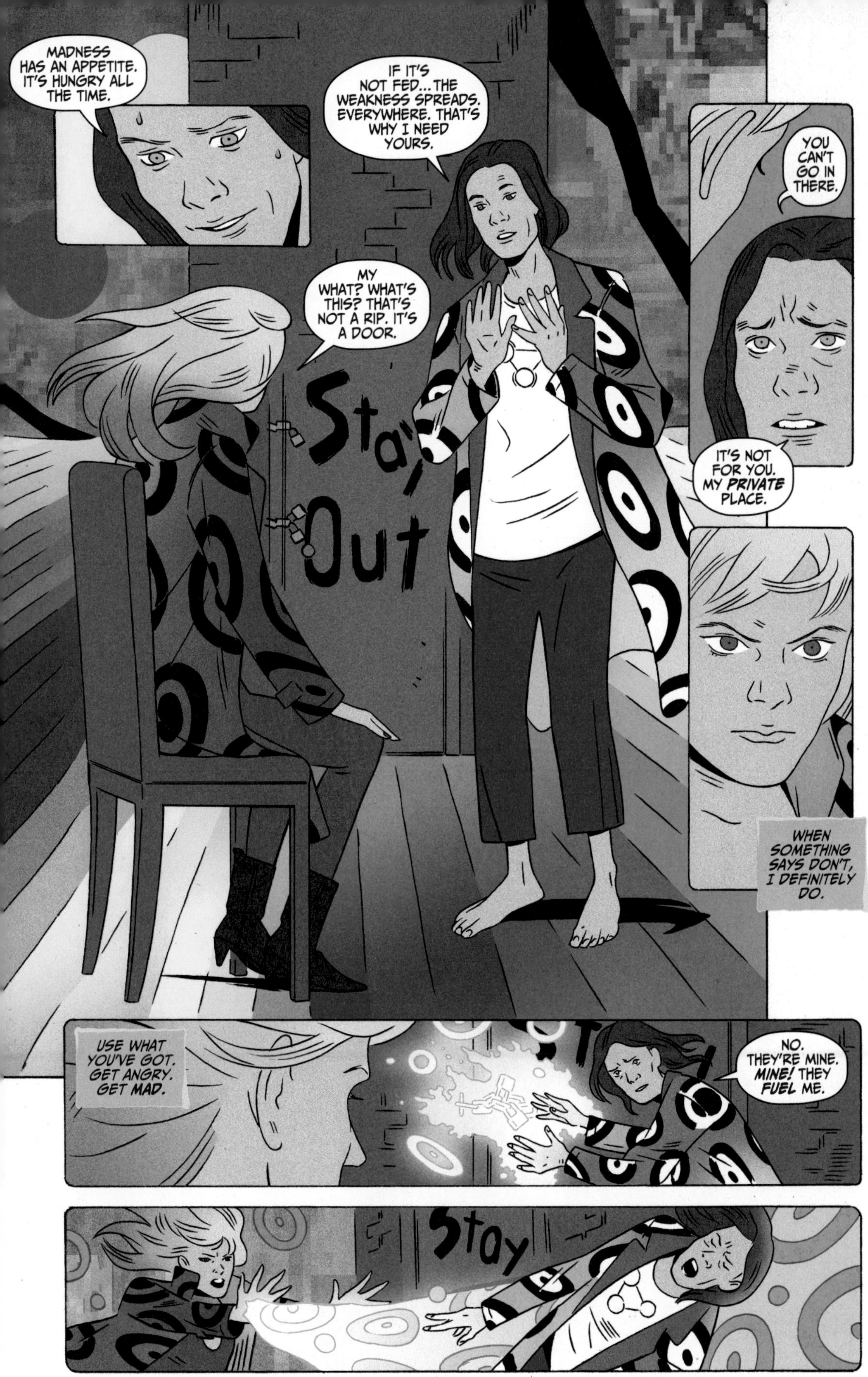
MADNESS HAS AN APPETITE. IT'S HUNGRY ALL THE TIME.
IF IT'S NOT FED... THE WEAKNESS SPREADS. EVERYWHERE. THAT'S WHY I NEED YOURS.
MY WHAT? WHAT'S THIS? THAT'S NOT A RIP. IT'S A DOOR.
Stay Out
YOU CAN'T GO IN THERE.
IT'S NOT FOR YOU. MY PRIVATE PLACE.
WHEN SOMETHING SAYS DON'T, I DEFINITELY DO.
USE WHAT YOU'VE GOT. GET ANGRY. GET MAD.
NO. THEY'RE MINE. MINE! THEY FUEL ME.
Stay

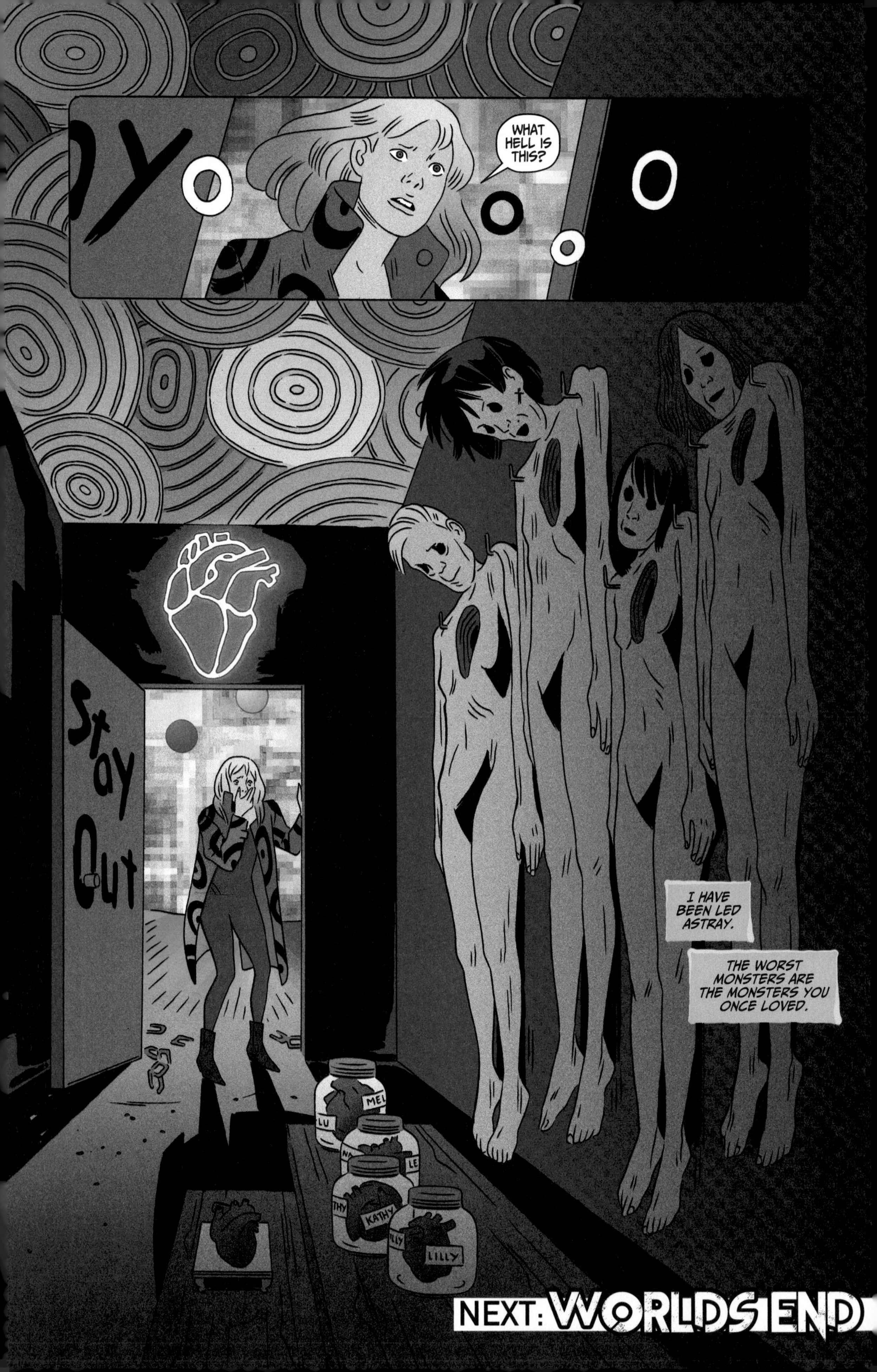
WHAT HELL IS THIS?
Stay Out
KATHY
LILLY
I HAVE BEEN LED ASTRAY.
THE WORST MONSTERS ARE THE MONSTERS YOU ONCE LOVED.
NEXT: WORLDS END

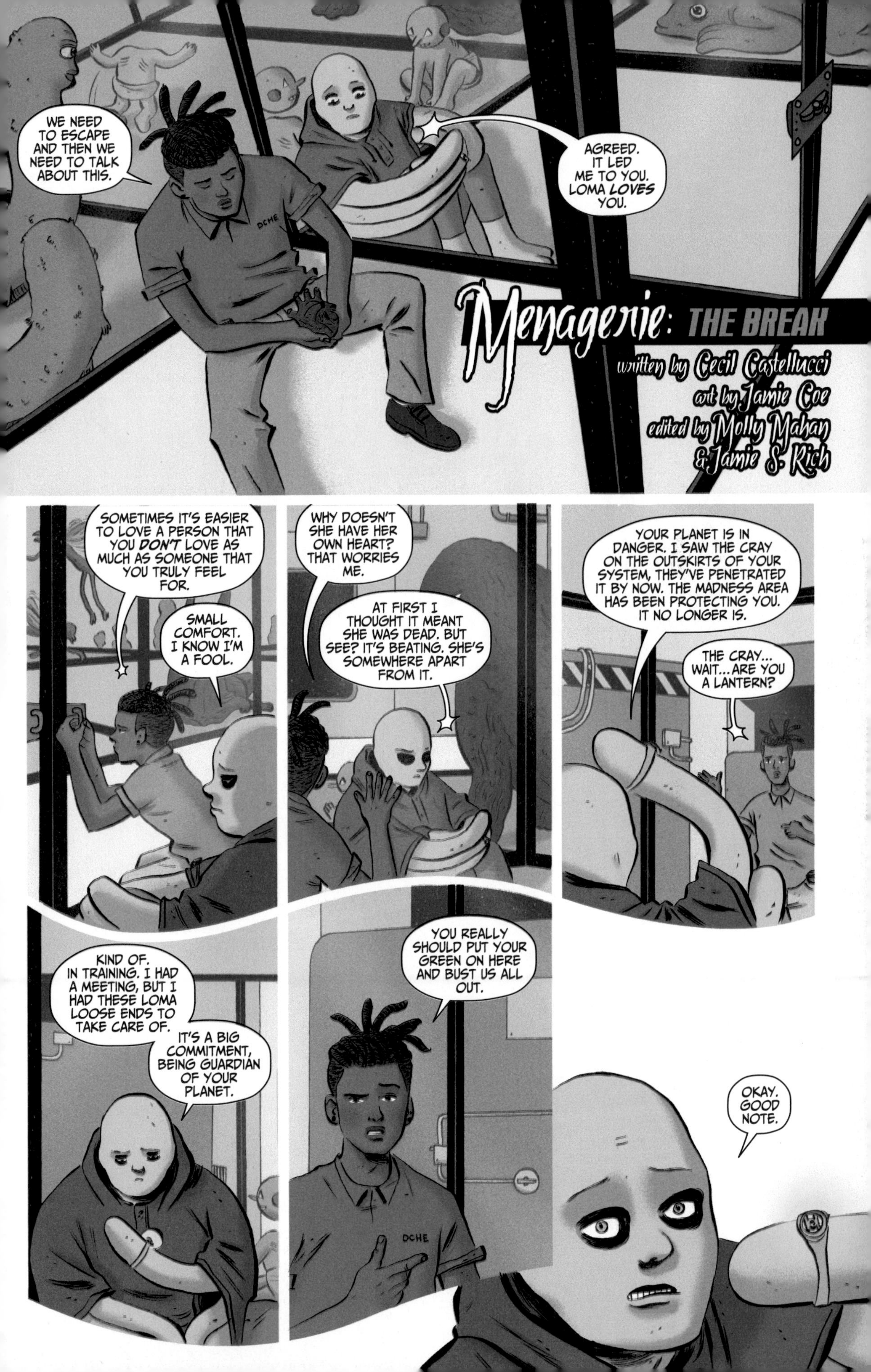
WE NEED TO ESCAPE AND THEN WE NEED TO TALK ABOUT THIS.
AGREED. IT LED ME TO YOU. LOMA LOVES YOU.
Menagerie: THE BREAK
written by Cecil Castellucci
art by Jamie Coe
edited by Molly Mahan & Jamie S. Rich
SOMETIMES IT'S EASIER TO LOVE A PERSON THAT YOU DON'T LOVE AS MUCH AS SOMEONE THAT YOU TRULY FEEL FOR.
SMALL COMFORT. I KNOW I'M A FOOL.
WHY DOESN'T SHE HAVE HER OWN HEART? THAT WORRIES ME.
AT FIRST I THOUGHT IT MEANT SHE WAS DEAD. BUT SEE? IT'S BEATING. SHE'S SOMEWHERE APART FROM IT.
YOUR PLANET IS IN DANGER. I SAW THE CRAY ON THE OUTSKIRTS OF YOUR SYSTEM, THEY'VE PENETRATED IT BY NOW. THE MADNESS AREA HAS BEEN PROTECTING YOU. IT NO LONGER IS.
THE CRAY... WAIT... ARE YOU A LANTERN?
KIND OF. IN TRAINING. I HAD A MEETING, BUT I HAD THESE LOMA LOOSE ENDS TO TAKE CARE OF.
IT'S A BIG COMMITMENT, BEING GUARDIAN OF YOUR PLANET.
YOU REALLY SHOULD PUT YOUR GREEN ON HERE AND BUST US ALL OUT.
OKAY. GOOD NOTE.

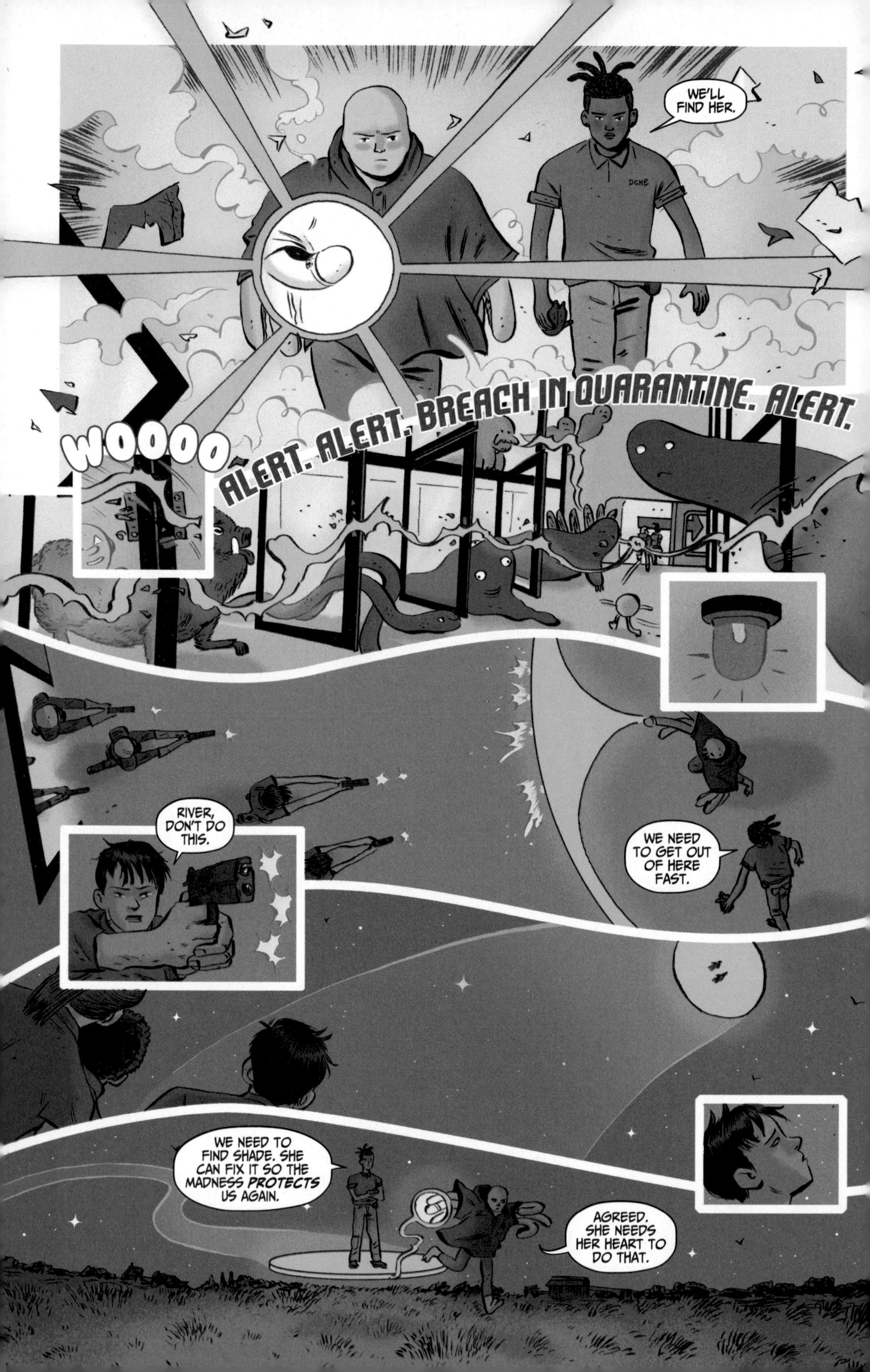
WE'LL FIND HER.
WOOOO
ALERT. ALERT. BREACH IN QUARANTINE. ALERT.
RIVER, DON'T DO THIS.
WE NEED TO GET OUT OF HERE FAST.
WE NEED TO FIND SHADE. SHE CAN FIX IT SO THE MADNESS PROTECTS US AGAIN.
AGREED. SHE NEEDS HER HEART TO DO THAT.

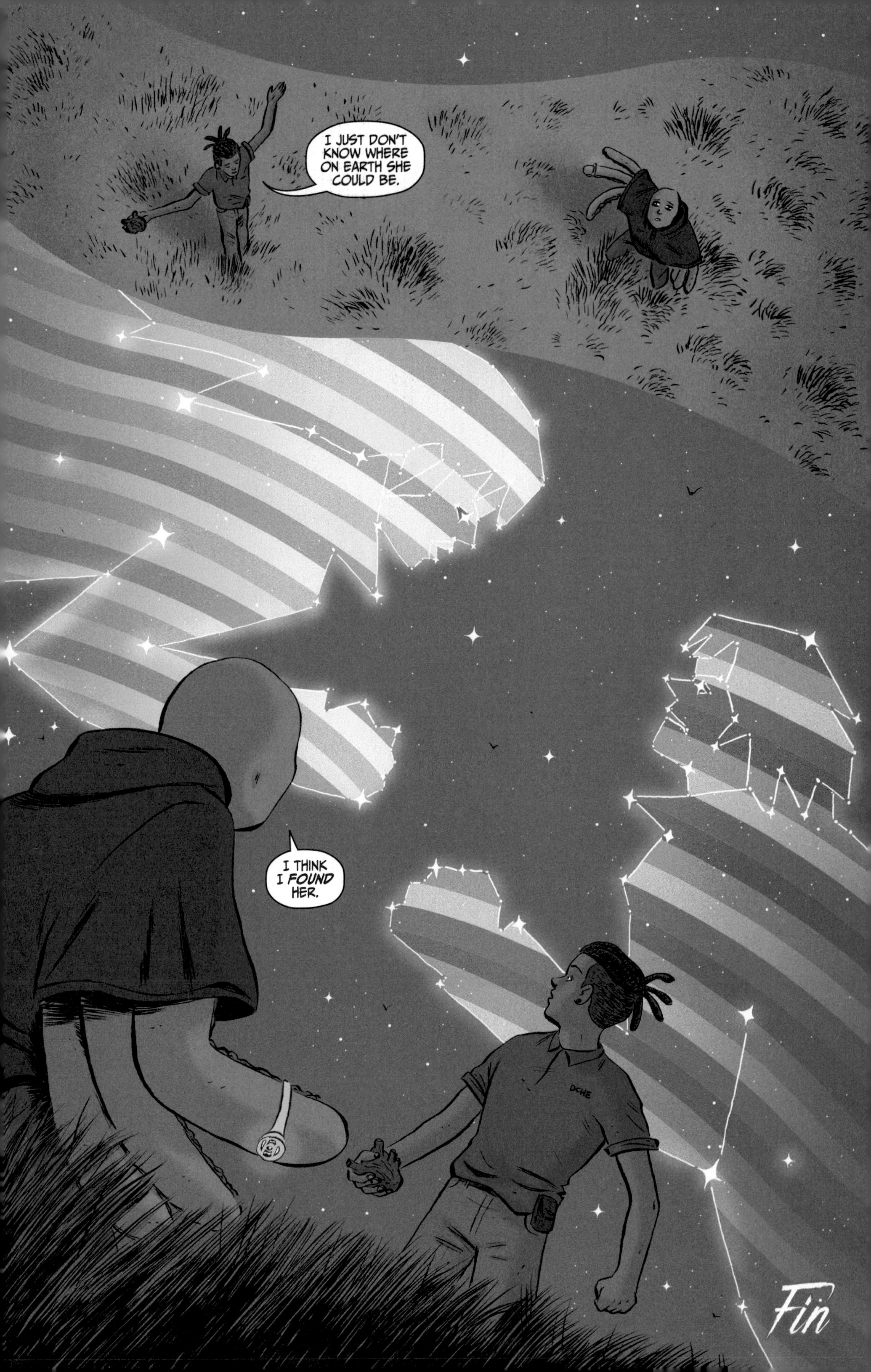
I JUST DON'T KNOW WHERE ON EARTH SHE COULD BE.
I THINK I *FOUND* HER.
DCHE
Fin

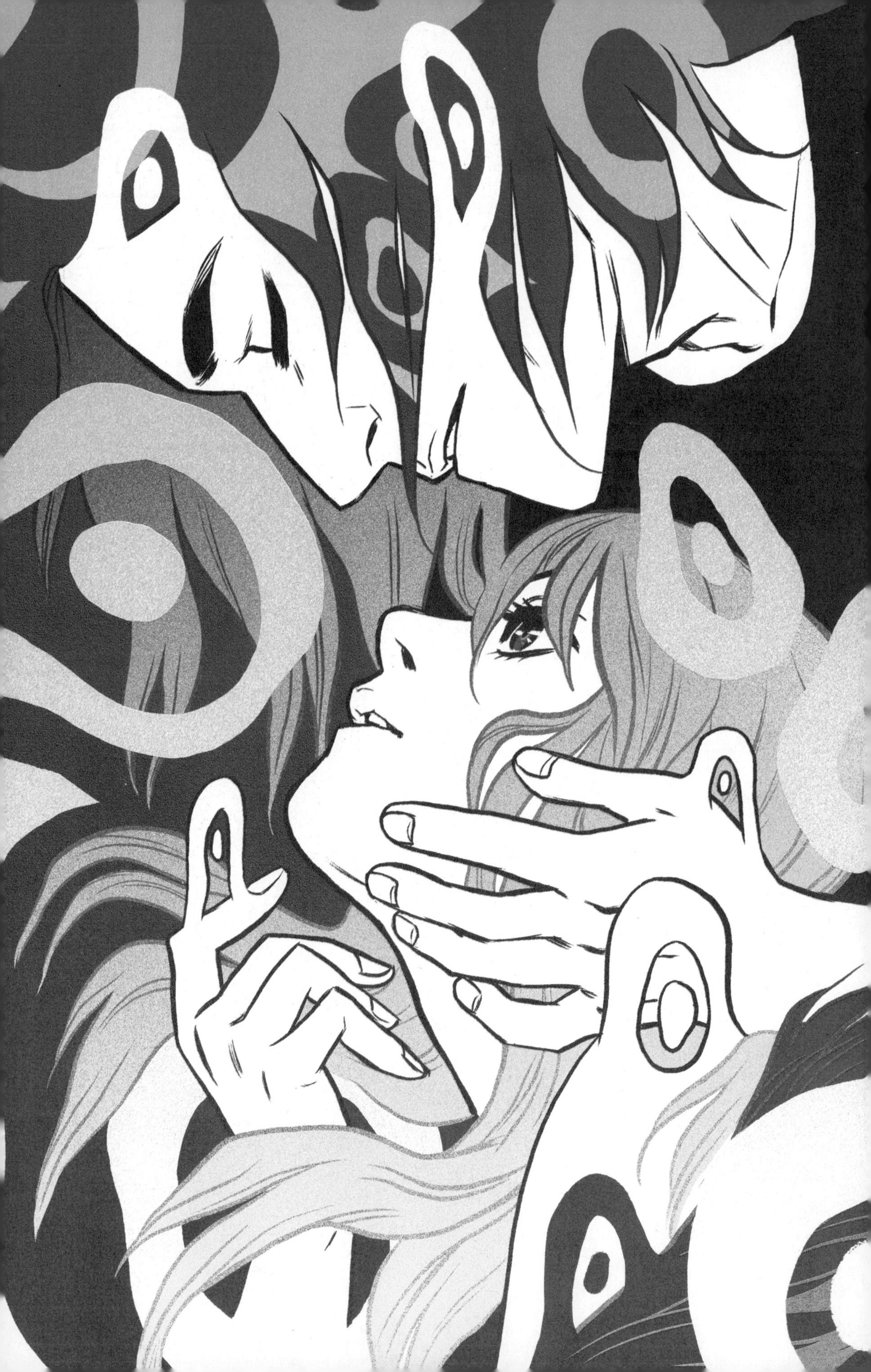

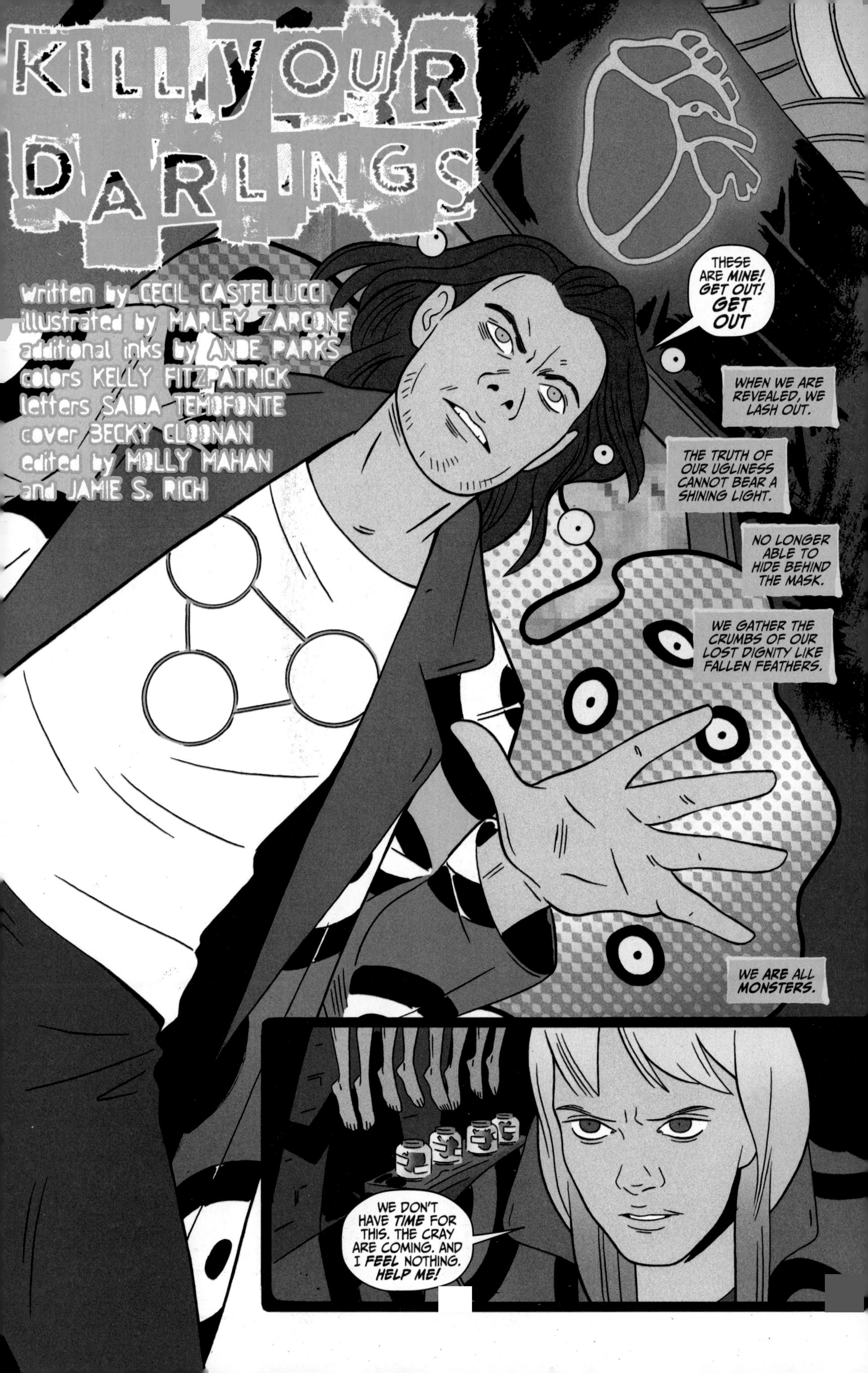

KILL YOUR DARLINGS
written by CECIL CASTELLUCCI
illustrated by MARLEY ZARCONE
additional inks by ANDE PARKS
colors KELLY FITZPATRICK
letters SAIDA TEMOFONTE
cover BECKY CLOONAN
edited by MOLLY MAHAN
and JAMIE S. RICH
THESE ARE MINE! GET OUT! GET OUT
WHEN WE ARE REVEALED, WE LASH OUT.
THE TRUTH OF OUR UGLINESS CANNOT BEAR A SHINING LIGHT.
NO LONGER ABLE TO HIDE BEHIND THE MASK.
WE GATHER THE CRUMBS OF OUR LOST DIGNITY LIKE FALLEN FEATHERS.
WE ARE ALL MONSTERS.
WE DON'T HAVE TIME FOR THIS. THE CRAY ARE COMING. AND I FEEL NOTHING. HELP ME!

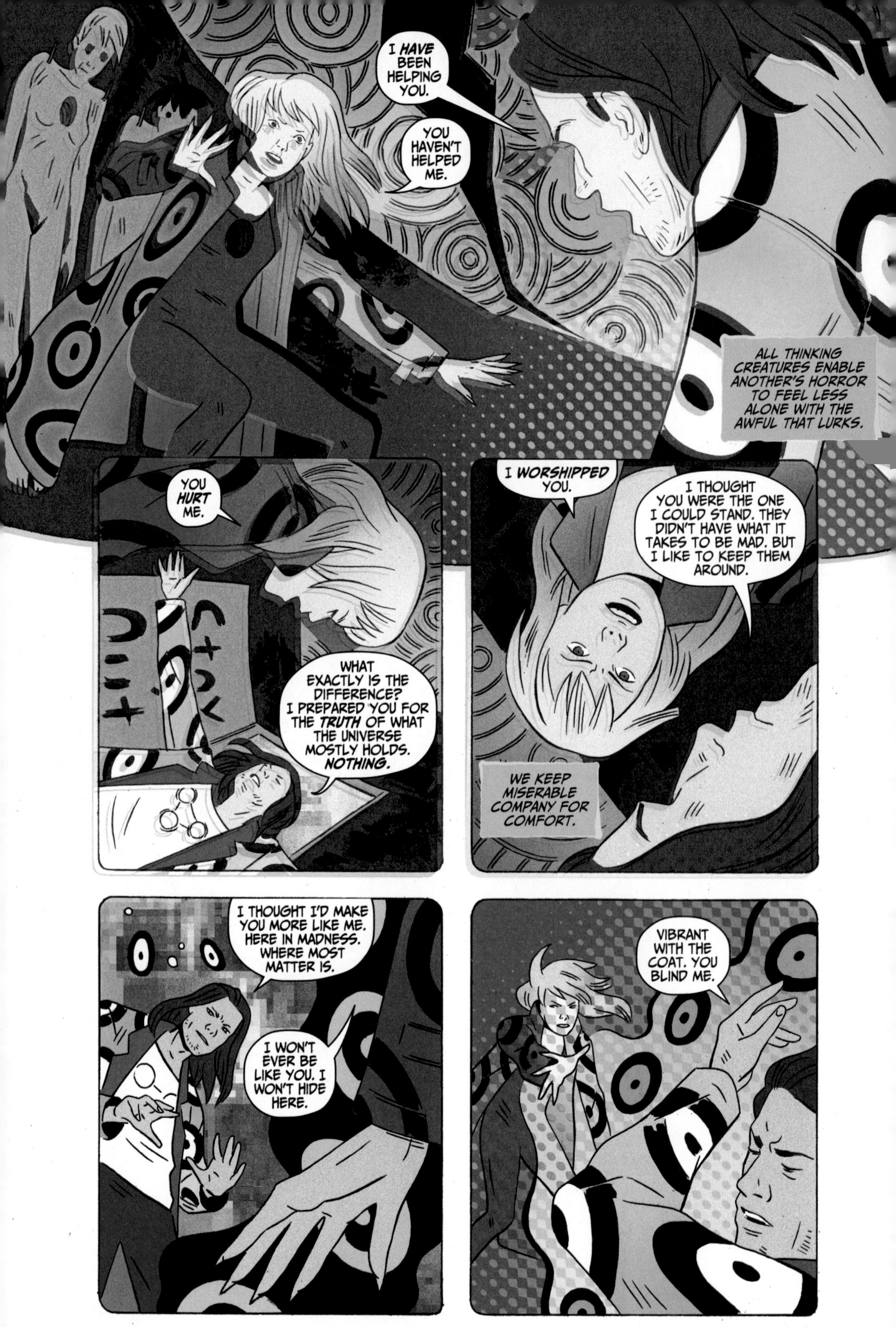

I *HAVE* BEEN HELPING YOU.
YOU HAVEN'T HELPED ME.
ALL THINKING CREATURES ENABLE ANOTHER'S HORROR TO FEEL LESS ALONE WITH THE AWFUL THAT LURKS.
YOU *HURT* ME.
WHAT EXACTLY IS THE DIFFERENCE? I PREPARED YOU FOR THE *TRUTH* OF WHAT THE UNIVERSE MOSTLY HOLDS. *NOTHING.*
I *WORSHIPPED* YOU.
I THOUGHT YOU WERE THE ONE I COULD STAND. THEY DIDN'T HAVE WHAT IT TAKES TO BE MAD. BUT I LIKE TO KEEP THEM AROUND.
WE KEEP MISERABLE COMPANY FOR COMFORT.
I THOUGHT I'D MAKE YOU MORE LIKE ME. HERE IN MADNESS. WHERE MOST MATTER IS.
I WON'T EVER BE LIKE YOU. I WON'T HIDE HERE.
VIBRANT WITH THE COAT. YOU BLIND ME.

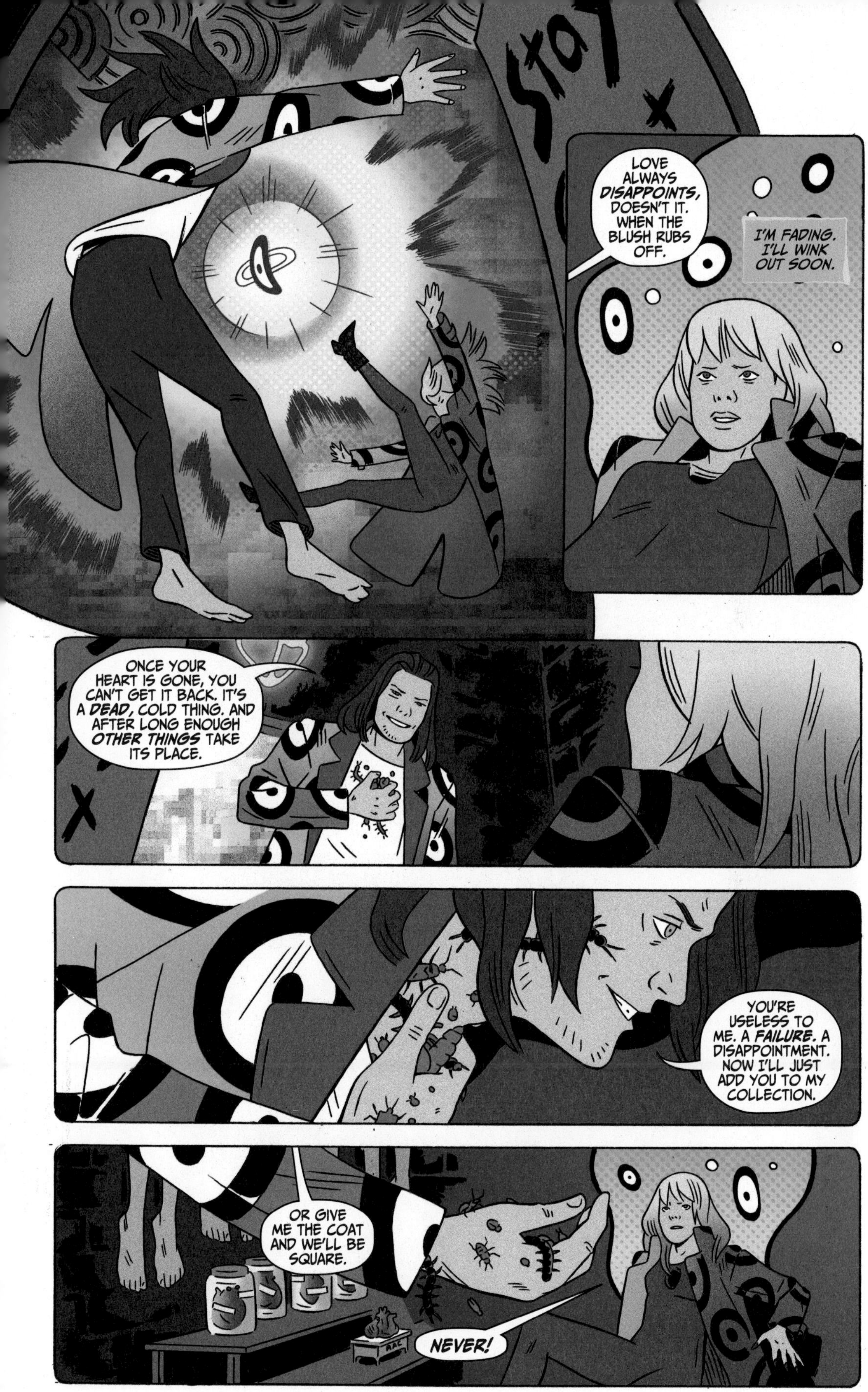
STAY
LOVE ALWAYS *DISAPPOINTS*, DOESN'T IT. WHEN THE BLUSH RUBS OFF.
I'M FADING. I'LL WINK OUT SOON.
ONCE YOUR HEART IS GONE, YOU CAN'T GET IT BACK. IT'S A *DEAD*, COLD THING. AND AFTER LONG ENOUGH *OTHER THINGS* TAKE ITS PLACE.
YOU'RE USELESS TO ME. A *FAILURE*. A DISAPPOINTMENT. NOW I'LL JUST ADD YOU TO MY COLLECTION.
OR GIVE ME THE COAT AND WE'LL BE SQUARE.
NEVER!

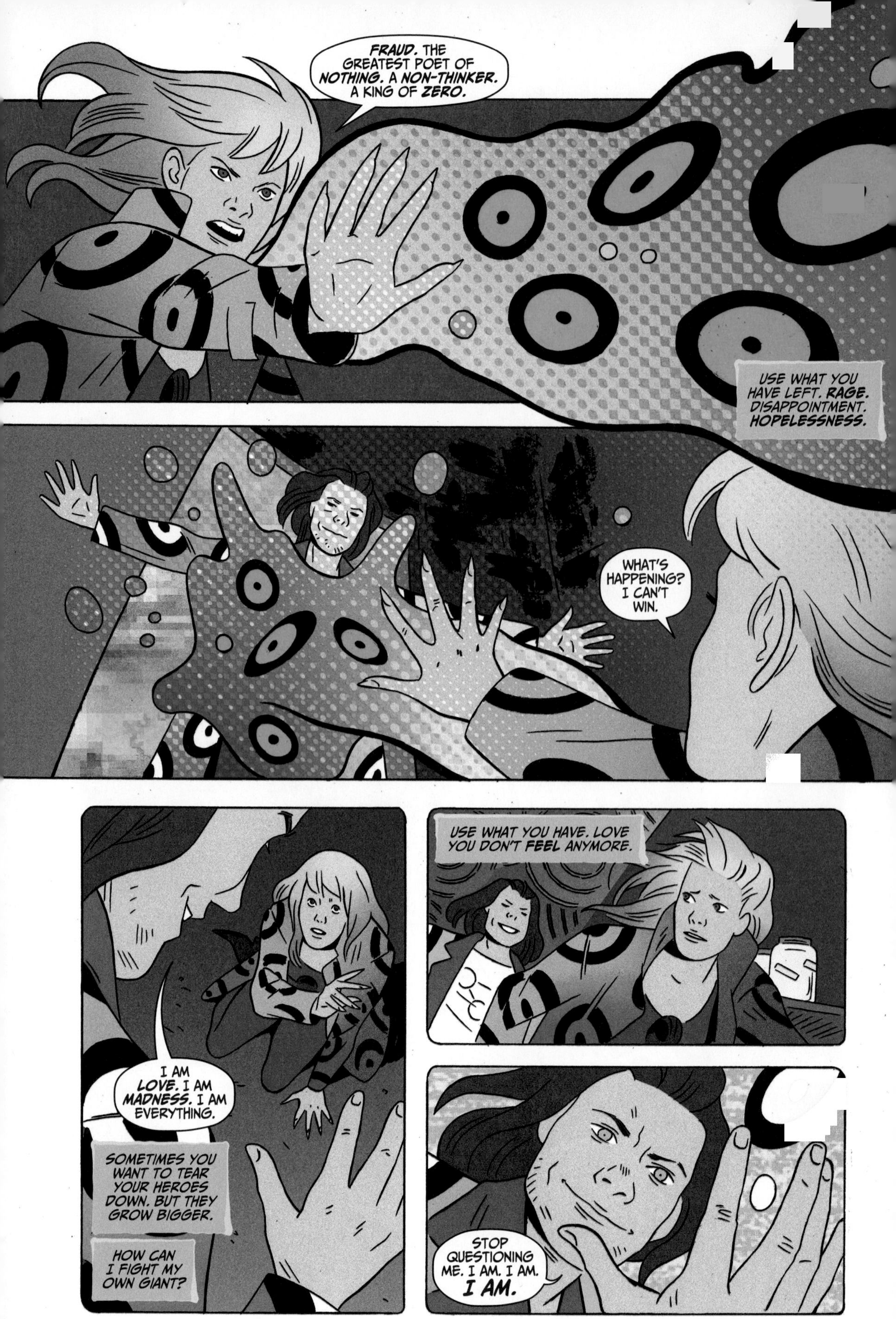
FRAUD. THE GREATEST POET OF NOTHING. A NON-THINKER. A KING OF ZERO.
USE WHAT YOU HAVE LEFT. RAGE. DISAPPOINTMENT. HOPELESSNESS.
WHAT'S HAPPENING? I CAN'T WIN.
I AM LOVE. I AM MADNESS. I AM EVERYTHING.
SOMETIMES YOU WANT TO TEAR YOUR HEROES DOWN. BUT THEY GROW BIGGER.
HOW CAN I FIGHT MY OWN GIANT?
USE WHAT YOU HAVE. LOVE YOU DON'T FEEL ANYMORE.
STOP QUESTIONING ME. I AM. I AM. I AM.

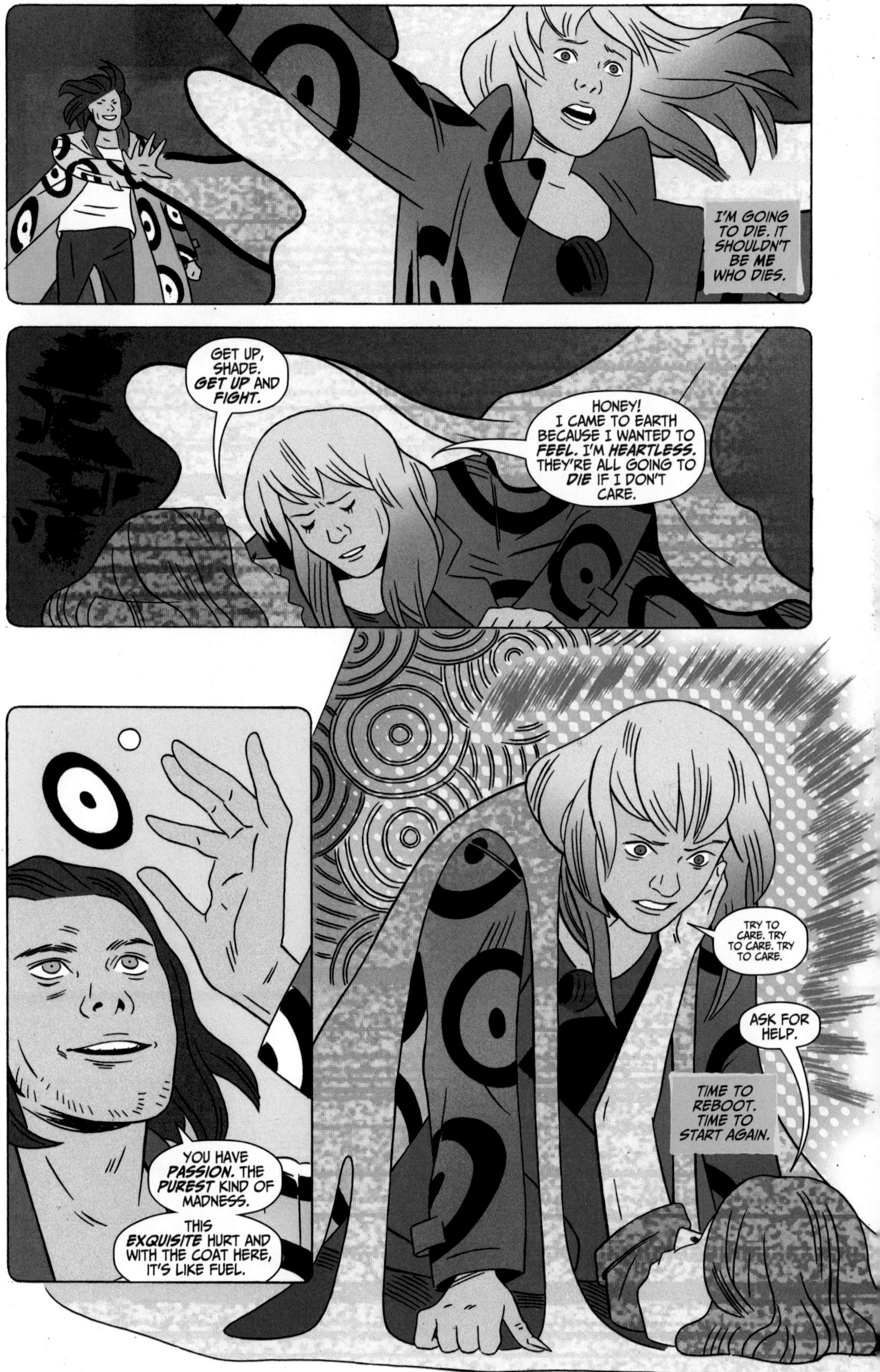
I'M GOING TO DIE. IT SHOULDN'T BE ME WHO DIES.
GET UP, SHADE. GET UP AND FIGHT.
HONEY! I CAME TO EARTH BECAUSE I WANTED TO FEEL. I'M HEARTLESS. THEY'RE ALL GOING TO DIE IF I DON'T CARE.
YOU HAVE PASSION. THE PUREST KIND OF MADNESS.
THIS EXQUISITE HURT AND WITH THE COAT HERE, IT'S LIKE FUEL.
TRY TO CARE. TRY TO CARE. TRY TO CARE.
ASK FOR HELP.
TIME TO REBOOT. TIME TO START AGAIN.

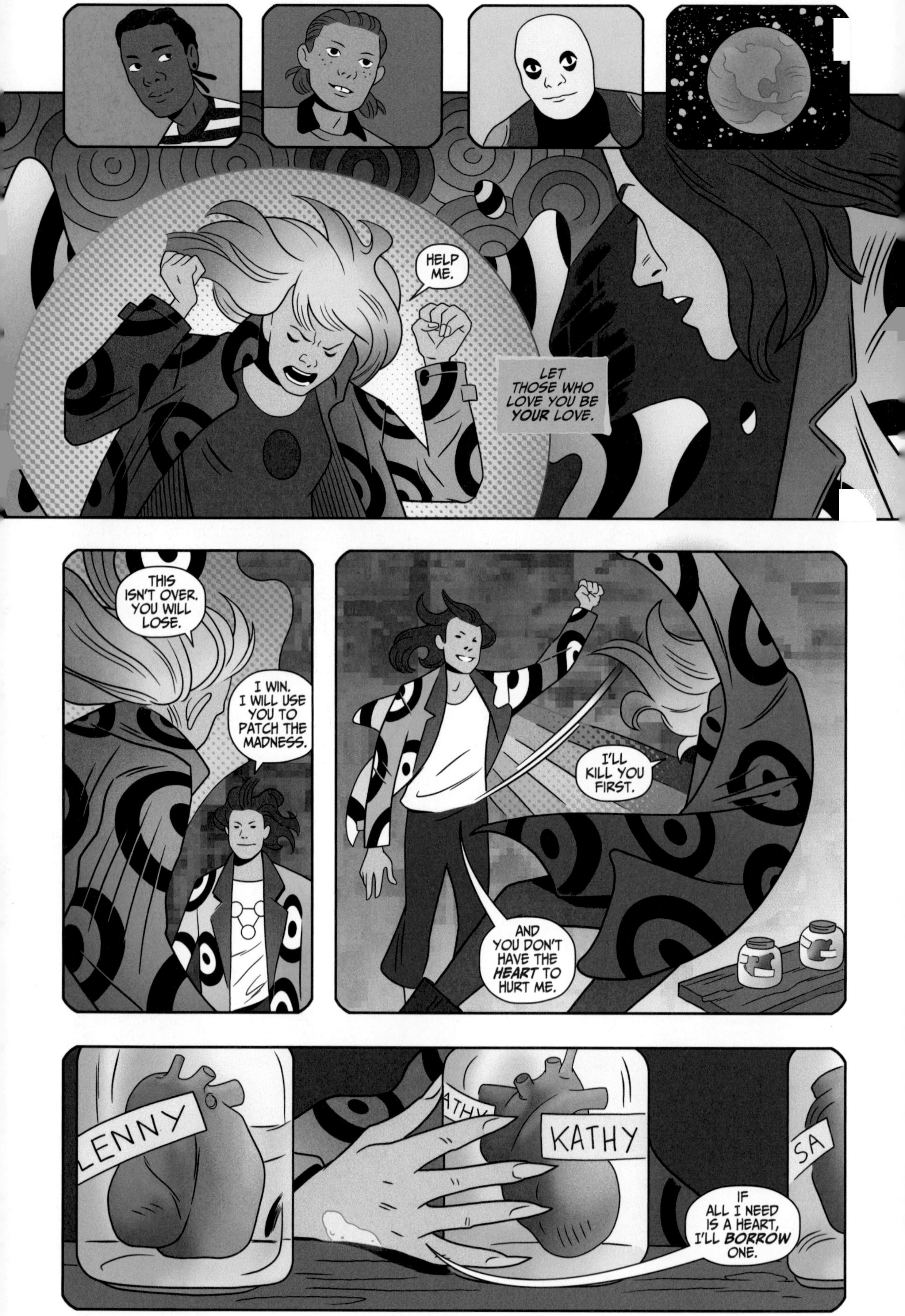
HELP ME.
LET THOSE WHO LOVE YOU BE YOUR LOVE.
THIS ISN'T OVER. YOU WILL LOSE.
I WIN. I WILL USE YOU TO PATCH THE MADNESS.
I'LL KILL YOU FIRST.
AND YOU DON'T HAVE THE HEART TO HURT ME.
LENNY
KATHY
IF ALL I NEED IS A HEART, I'LL BORROW ONE.

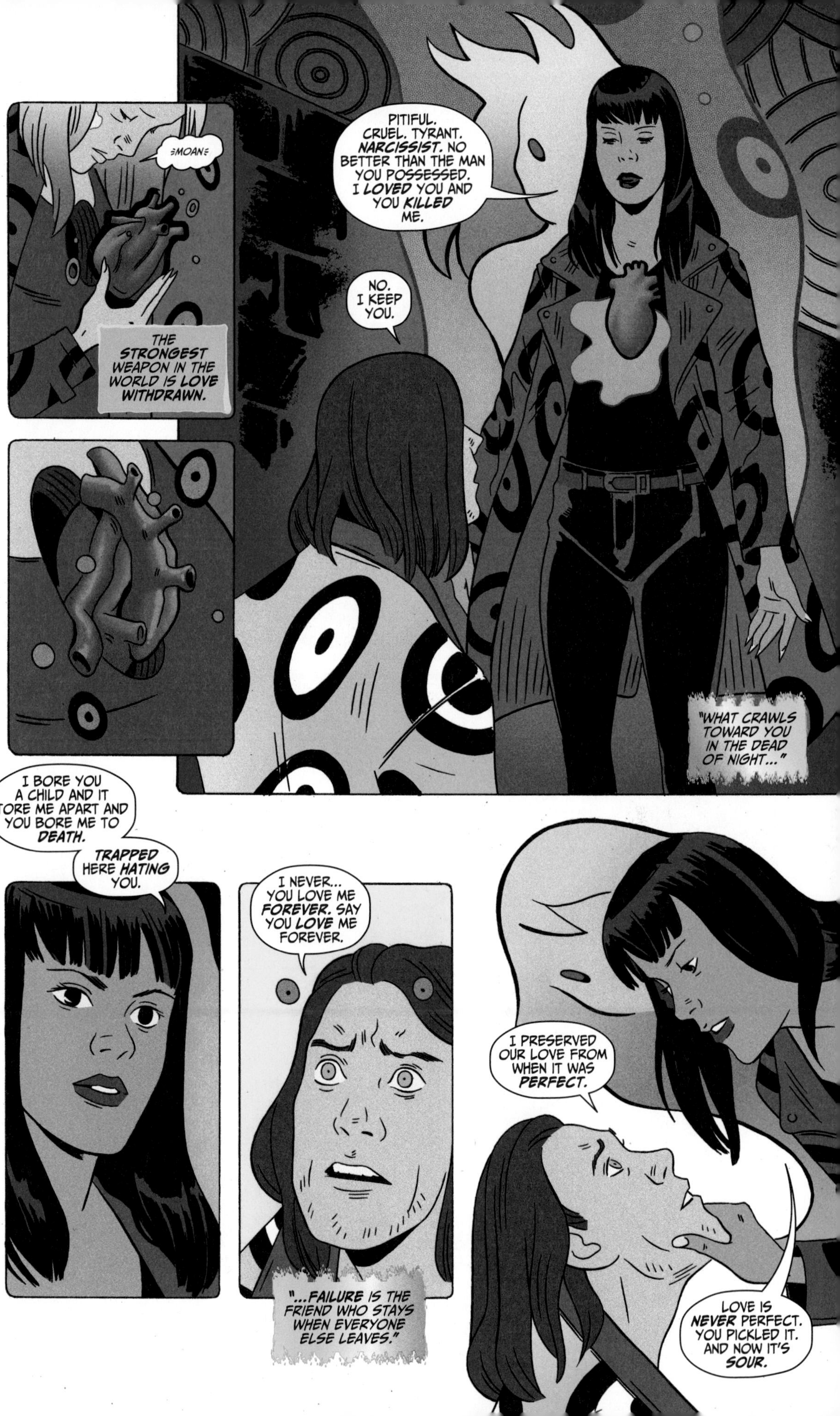

MOAN
THE STRONGEST WEAPON IN THE WORLD IS LOVE WITHDRAWN.
PITIFUL. CRUEL. TYRANT. NARCISSIST. NO BETTER THAN THE MAN YOU POSSESSED. I LOVED YOU AND YOU KILLED ME.
NO. I KEEP YOU.
"WHAT CRAWLS TOWARD YOU IN THE DEAD OF NIGHT..."
I BORE YOU A CHILD AND IT TORE ME APART AND YOU BORE ME TO DEATH.
TRAPPED HERE HATING YOU.
I NEVER... YOU LOVE ME FOREVER. SAY YOU LOVE ME FOREVER.
"...FAILURE IS THE FRIEND WHO STAYS WHEN EVERYONE ELSE LEAVES."
I PRESERVED OUR LOVE FROM WHEN IT WAS PERFECT.
LOVE IS NEVER PERFECT. YOU PICKLED IT. AND NOW IT'S SOUR.

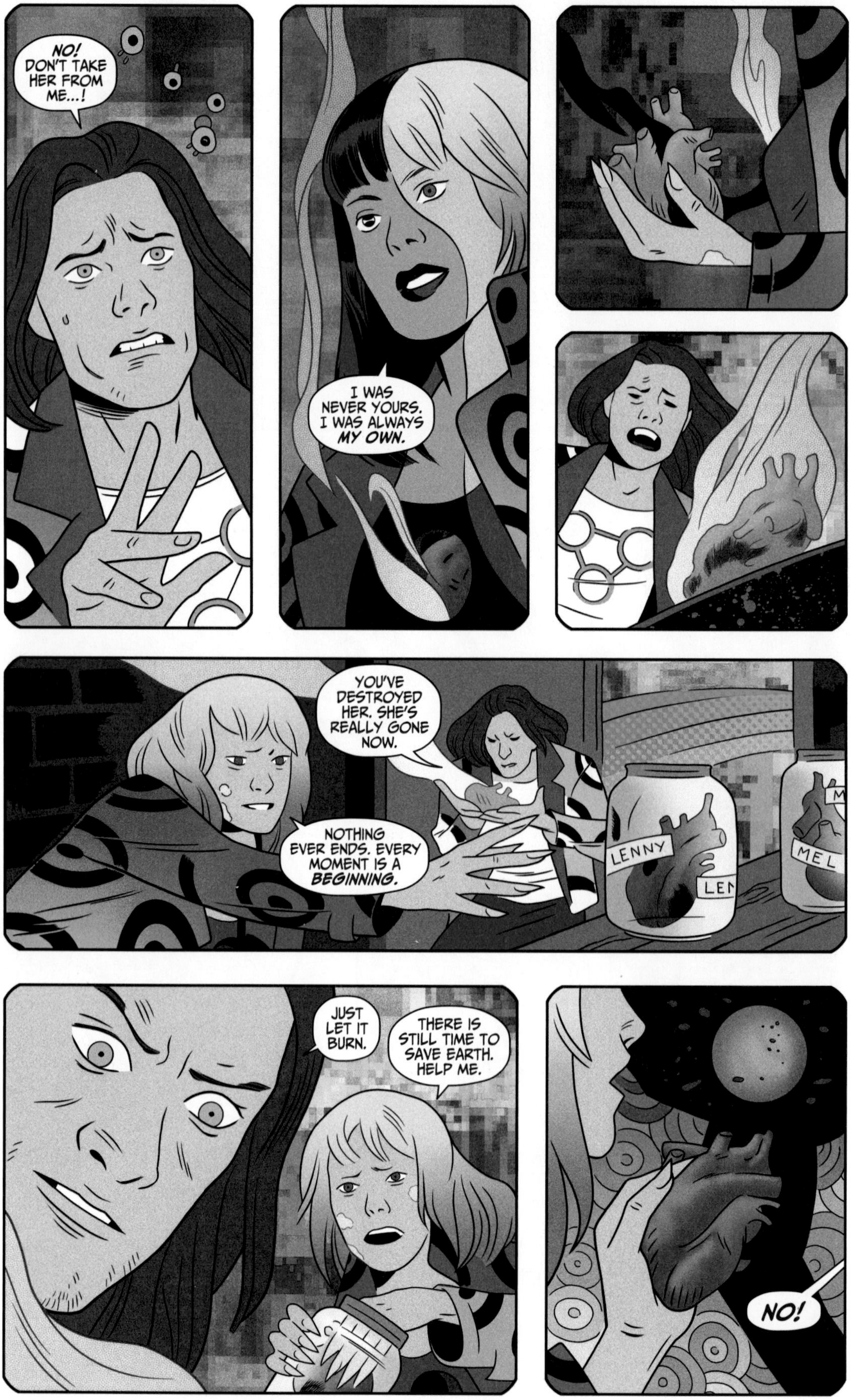
NO! DON'T TAKE HER FROM ME...!
I WAS NEVER YOURS. I WAS ALWAYS MY OWN.
YOU'VE DESTROYED HER. SHE'S REALLY GONE NOW.
NOTHING EVER ENDS. EVERY MOMENT IS A BEGINNING.
LENNY
JUST LET IT BURN.
THERE IS STILL TIME TO SAVE EARTH. HELP ME.
NO!

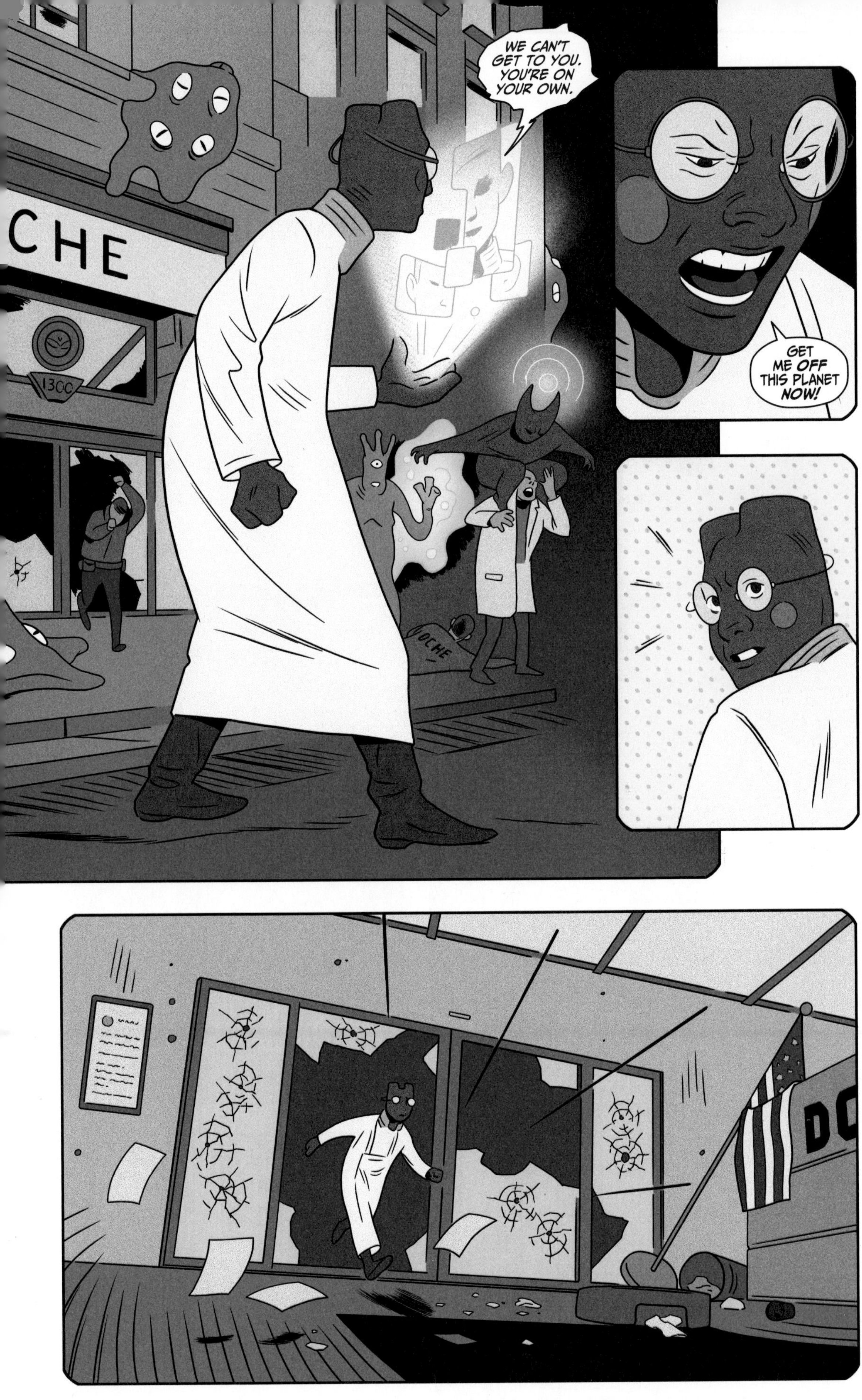

WE CAN'T GET TO YOU. YOU'RE ON YOUR OWN.
GET ME OFF THIS PLANET NOW!

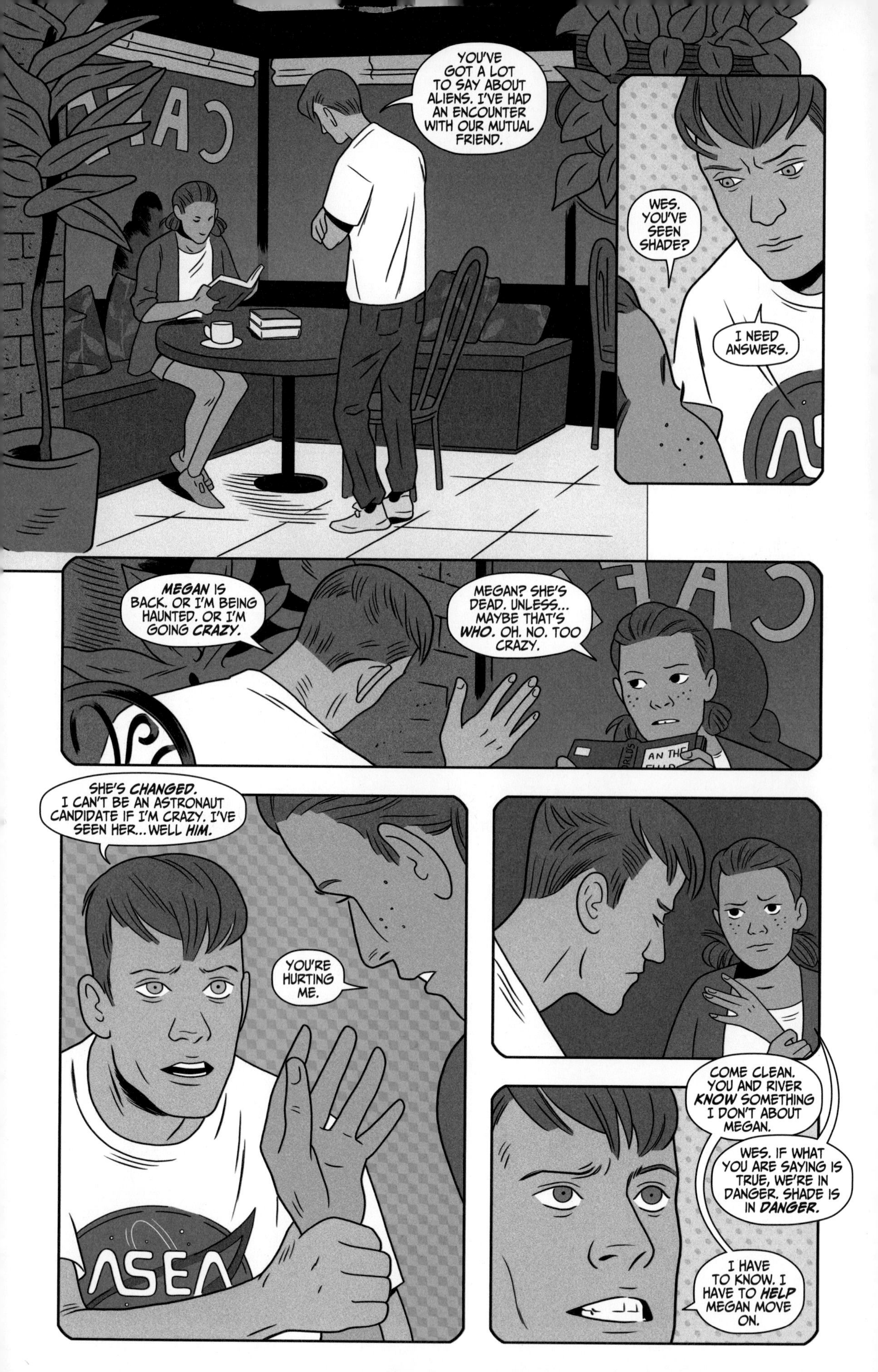

YOU'VE GOT A LOT TO SAY ABOUT ALIENS. I'VE HAD AN ENCOUNTER WITH OUR MUTUAL FRIEND.
WES. YOU'VE SEEN SHADE?
I NEED ANSWERS.
MEGAN IS BACK. OR I'M BEING HAUNTED. OR I'M GOING CRAZY.
MEGAN? SHE'S DEAD. UNLESS... MAYBE THAT'S WHO. OH. NO. TOO CRAZY.
SHE'S CHANGED. I CAN'T BE AN ASTRONAUT CANDIDATE IF I'M CRAZY. I'VE SEEN HER...WELL HIM.
YOU'RE HURTING ME.
COME CLEAN. YOU AND RIVER KNOW SOMETHING I DON'T ABOUT MEGAN.
WES. IF WHAT YOU ARE SAYING IS TRUE, WE'RE IN DANGER. SHADE IS IN DANGER.
I HAVE TO KNOW. I HAVE TO HELP MEGAN MOVE ON.

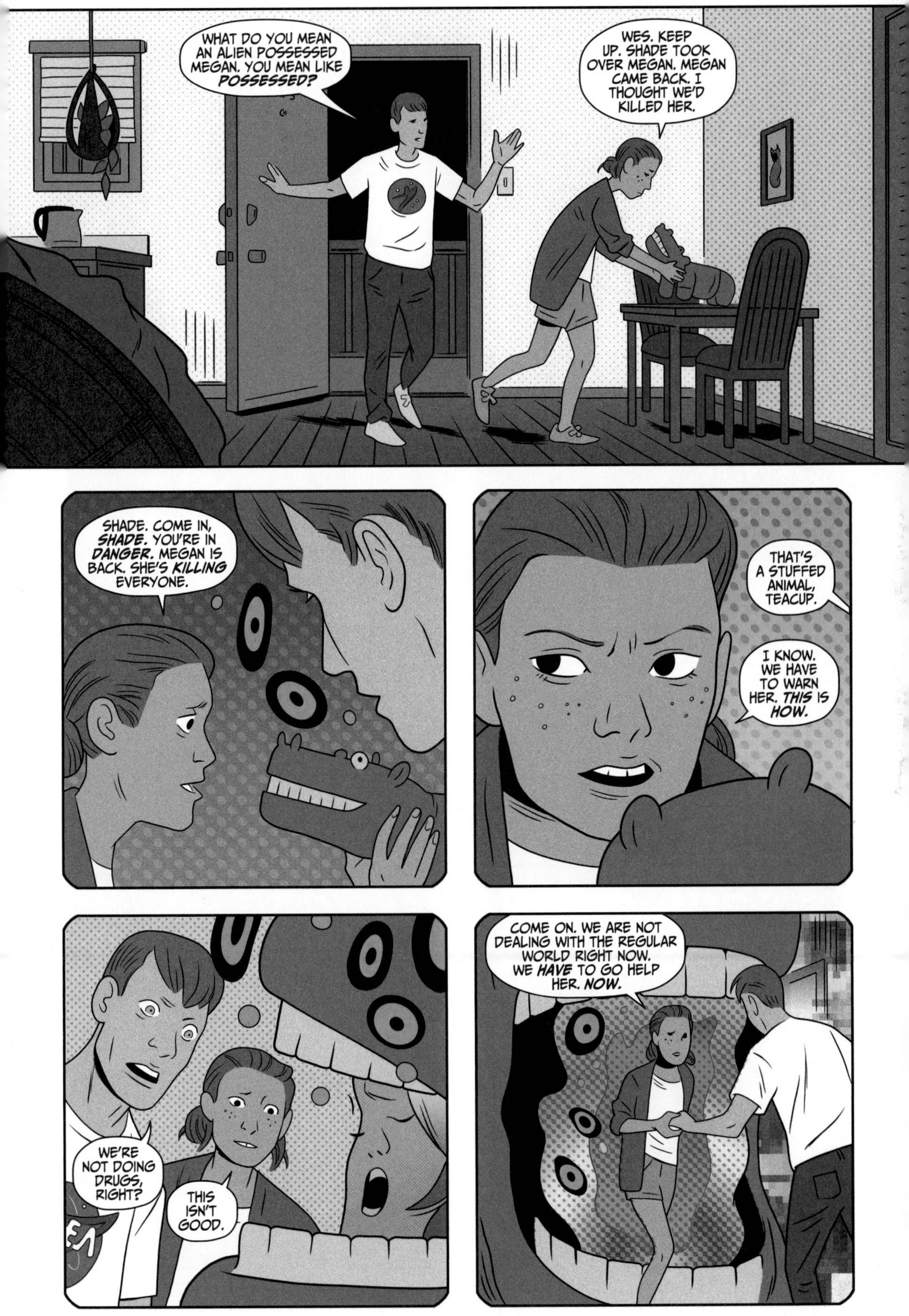
WHAT DO YOU MEAN AN ALIEN POSSESSED MEGAN. YOU MEAN LIKE POSSESSED?
WES. KEEP UP. SHADE TOOK OVER MEGAN. MEGAN CAME BACK. I THOUGHT WE'D KILLED HER.
SHADE. COME IN, SHADE. YOU'RE IN DANGER. MEGAN IS BACK. SHE'S KILLING EVERYONE.
THAT'S A STUFFED ANIMAL, TEACUP.
I KNOW. WE HAVE TO WARN HER. THIS IS HOW.
WE'RE NOT DOING DRUGS, RIGHT?
THIS ISN'T GOOD.
COME ON. WE ARE NOT DEALING WITH THE REGULAR WORLD RIGHT NOW. WE HAVE TO GO HELP HER. NOW.

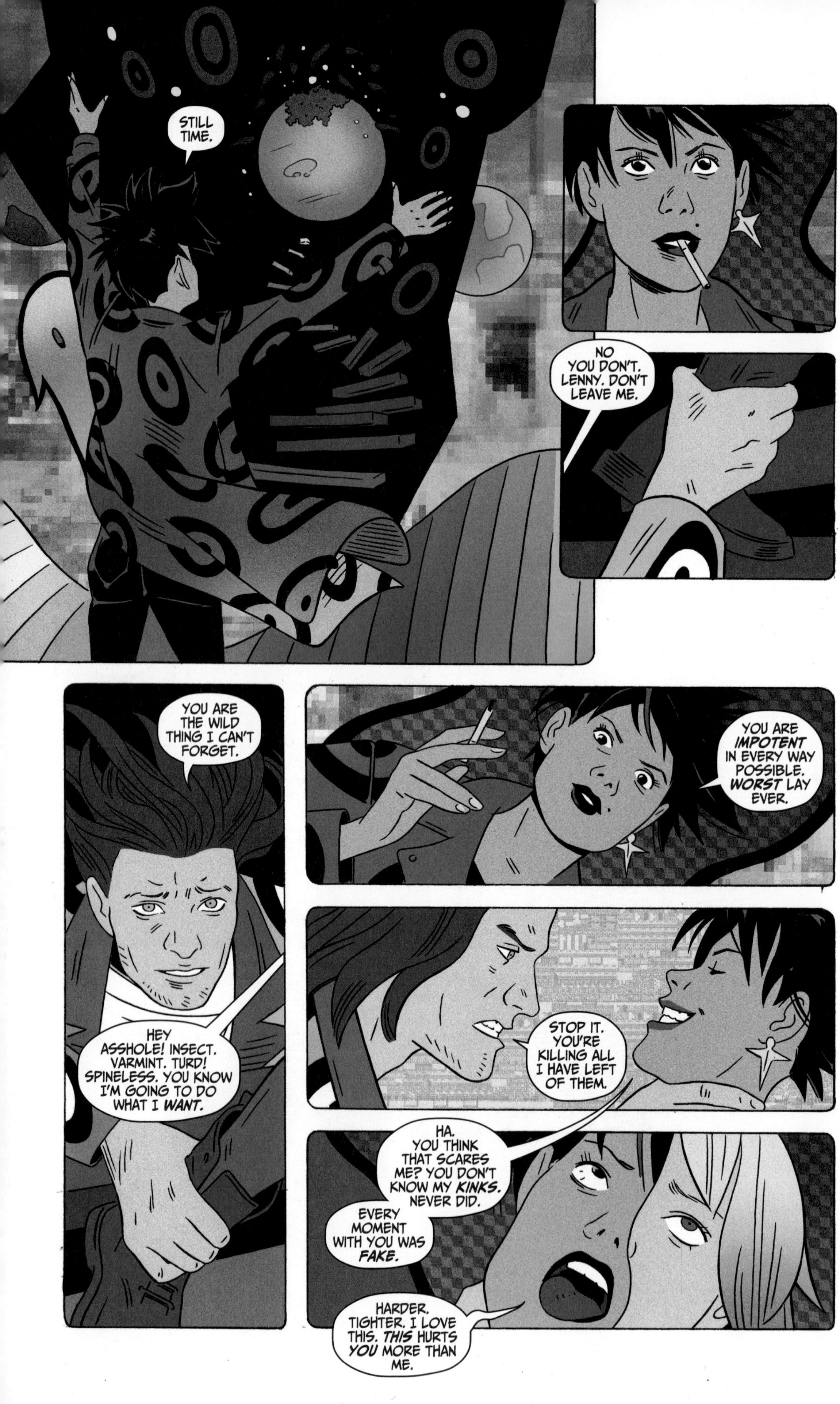
STILL TIME.
NO YOU DON'T. LENNY. DON'T LEAVE ME.
YOU ARE THE WILD THING I CAN'T FORGET.
YOU ARE *IMPOTENT* IN EVERY WAY POSSIBLE. *WORST* LAY EVER.
HEY ASSHOLE! INSECT. VARMINT. TURD! SPINELESS. YOU KNOW I'M GOING TO DO WHAT I *WANT*.
STOP IT. YOU'RE KILLING ALL I HAVE LEFT OF THEM.
HA. YOU THINK THAT SCARES ME? YOU DON'T KNOW MY *KINKS*. NEVER DID.
EVERY MOMENT WITH YOU WAS *FAKE*.
HARDER. TIGHTER. I LOVE THIS. *THIS* HURTS *YOU* MORE THAN ME.

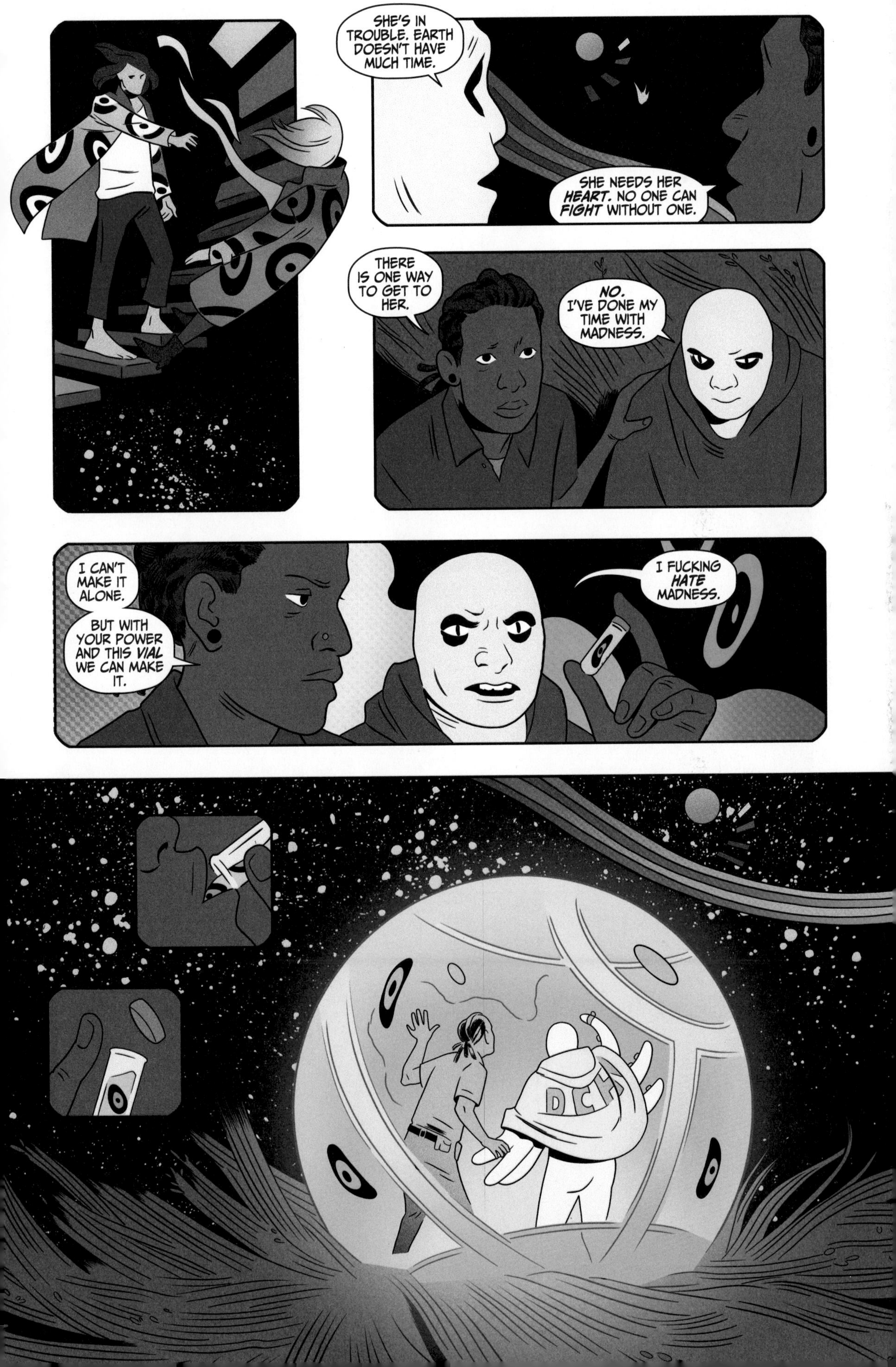
SHE'S IN TROUBLE. EARTH DOESN'T HAVE MUCH TIME.
SHE NEEDS HER HEART. NO ONE CAN FIGHT WITHOUT ONE.
THERE IS ONE WAY TO GET TO HER.
NO. I'VE DONE MY TIME WITH MADNESS.
I CAN'T MAKE IT ALONE.
BUT WITH YOUR POWER AND THIS VIAL WE CAN MAKE IT.
I FUCKING HATE MADNESS.
DCH

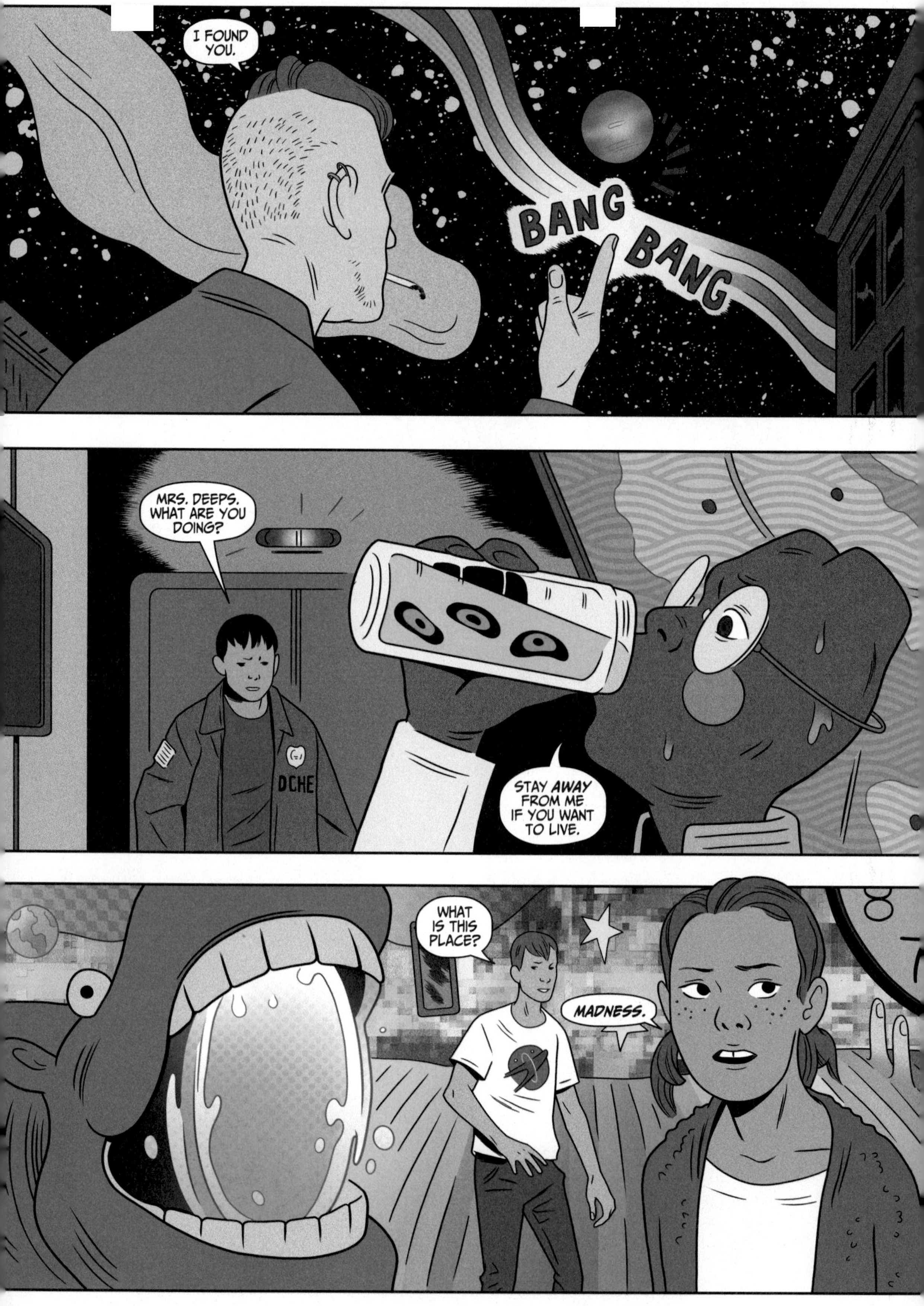
I FOUND YOU.
BANG
BANG
MRS. DEEPS. WHAT ARE YOU DOING?
DCHE
STAY AWAY FROM ME IF YOU WANT TO LIVE.
WHAT IS THIS PLACE?
MADNESS.

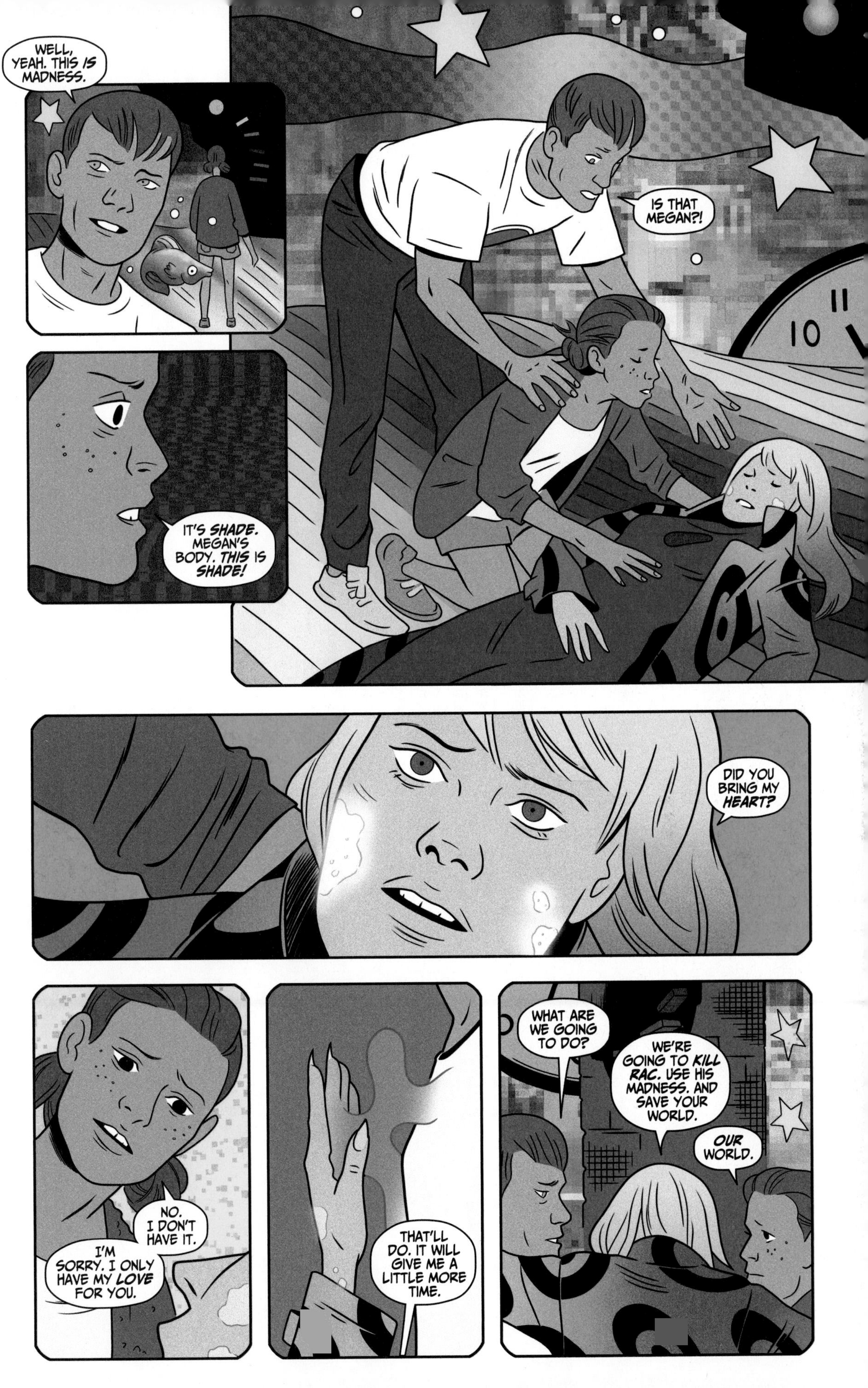
WELL, YEAH. THIS *IS* MADNESS.
IS THAT MEGAN?!
IT'S *SHADE.* MEGAN'S BODY. *THIS* IS *SHADE!*
DID YOU BRING MY *HEART?*
NO. I DON'T HAVE IT.
I'M SORRY. I ONLY HAVE MY *LOVE* FOR YOU.
THAT'LL DO. IT WILL GIVE ME A LITTLE MORE TIME.
WHAT ARE WE GOING TO DO?
WE'RE GOING TO *KILL RAC.* USE HIS MADNESS. AND SAVE YOUR WORLD.
OUR WORLD.

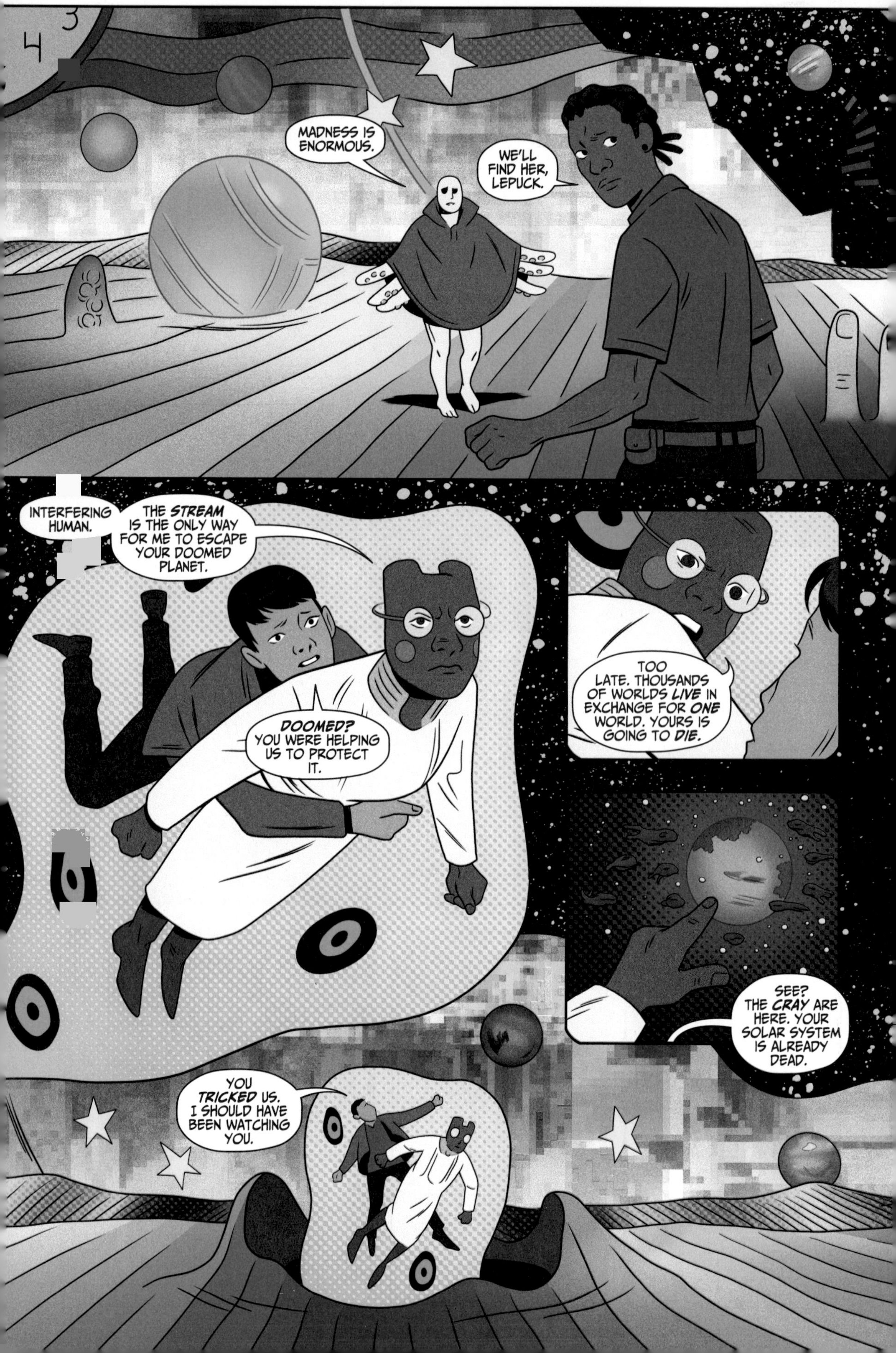
MADNESS IS ENORMOUS.
WE'LL FIND HER, LEPUCK.
INTERFERING HUMAN.
THE *STREAM* IS THE ONLY WAY FOR ME TO ESCAPE YOUR DOOMED PLANET.
DOOMED? YOU WERE HELPING US TO PROTECT IT.
TOO LATE. THOUSANDS OF WORLDS *LIVE* IN EXCHANGE FOR *ONE* WORLD. YOURS IS GOING TO *DIE.*
SEE? THE *CRAY* ARE HERE. YOUR SOLAR SYSTEM IS ALREADY DEAD.
YOU *TRICKED* US. I SHOULD HAVE BEEN WATCHING YOU.

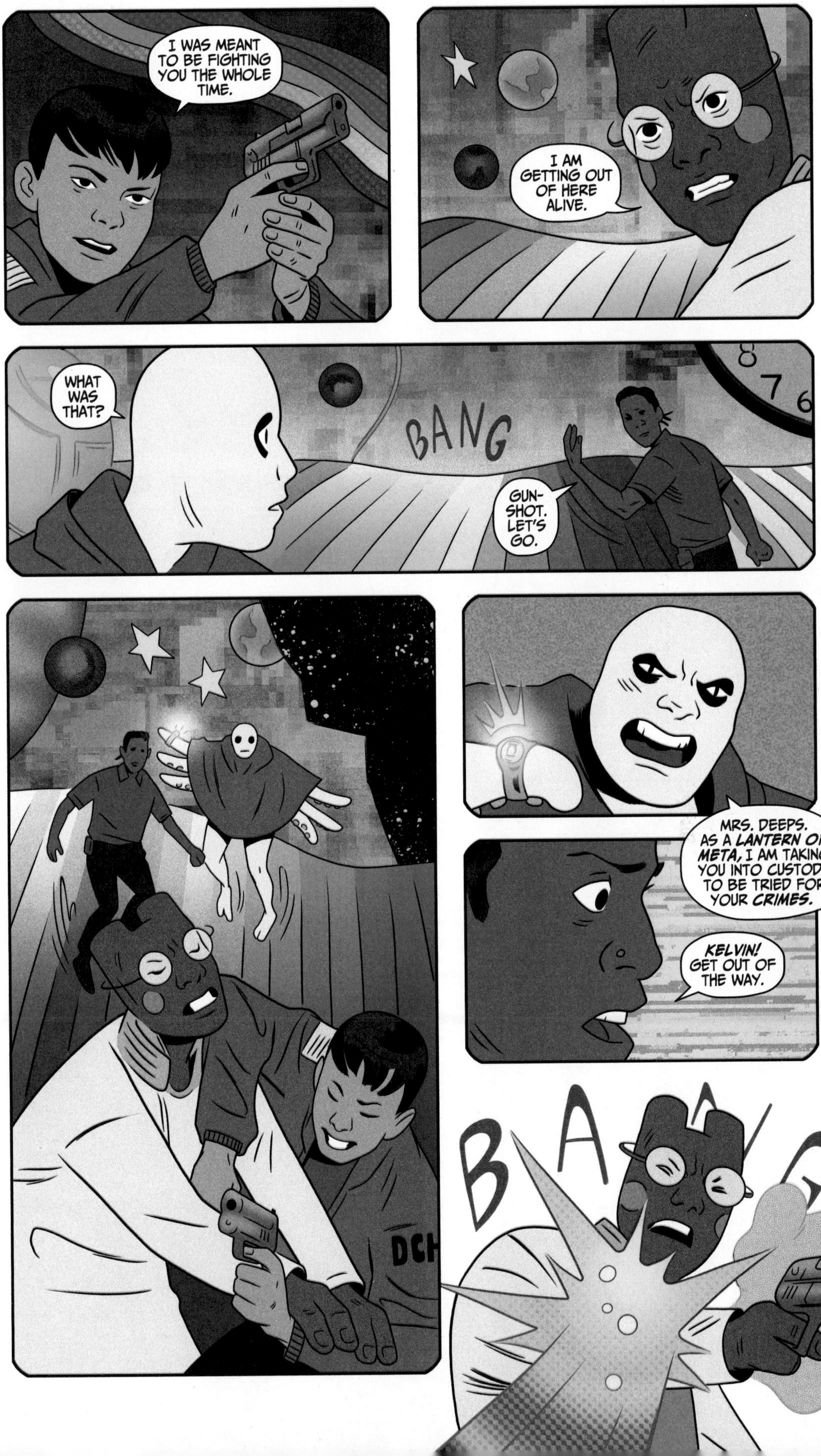
I WAS MEANT TO BE FIGHTING YOU THE WHOLE TIME.
I AM GETTING OUT OF HERE ALIVE.
WHAT WAS THAT?
BANG
GUN-SHOT. LET'S GO.
MRS. DEEPS. AS A LANTERN OF META, I AM TAKING YOU INTO CUSTODY TO BE TRIED FOR YOUR CRIMES.
KELVIN! GET OUT OF THE WAY.
BANG

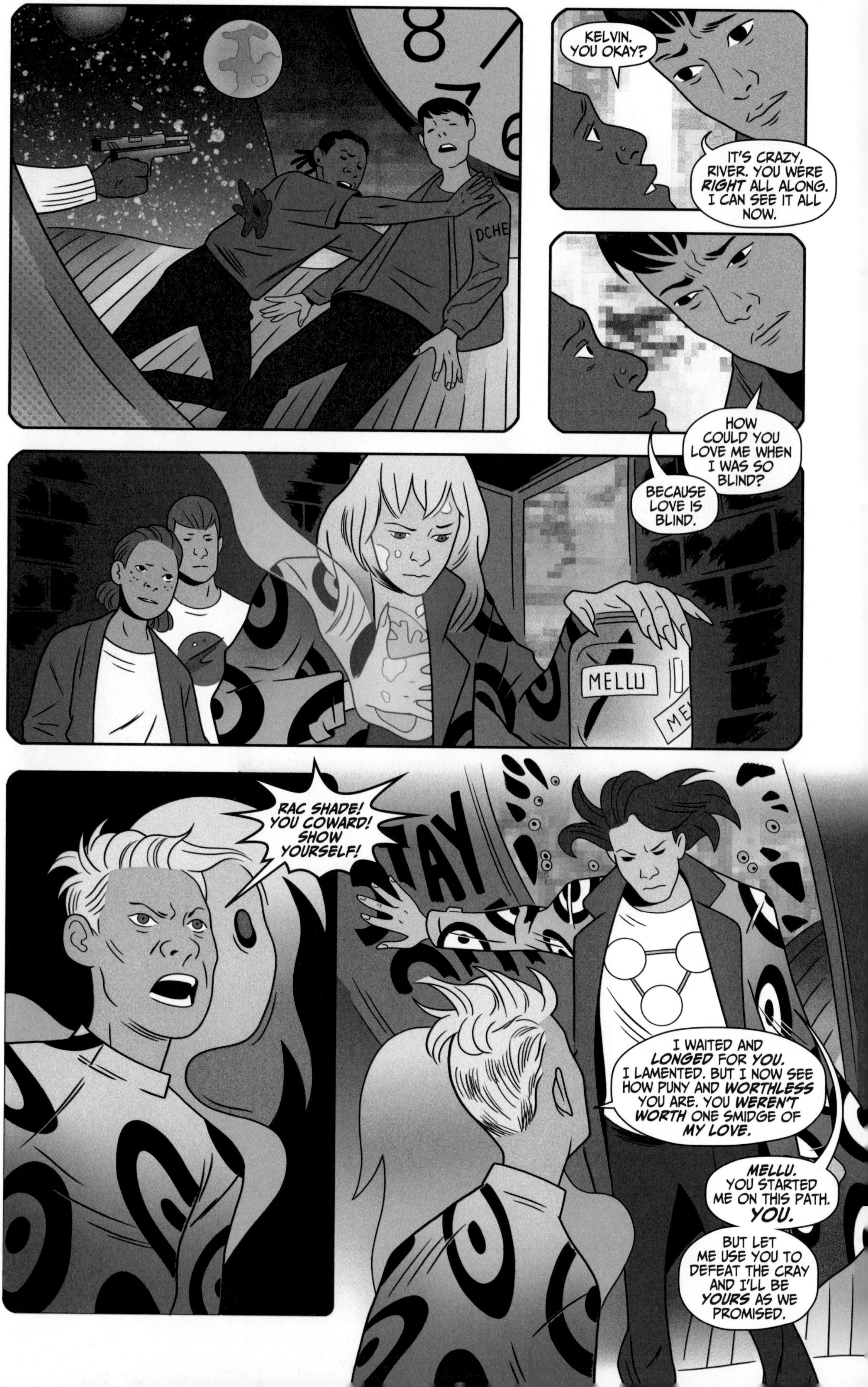
KELVIN. YOU OKAY?
IT'S CRAZY, RIVER. YOU WERE RIGHT ALL ALONG. I CAN SEE IT ALL NOW.
HOW COULD YOU LOVE ME WHEN I WAS SO BLIND?
BECAUSE LOVE IS BLIND.
MELLU
RAC SHADE! YOU COWARD! SHOW YOURSELF!
I WAITED AND LONGED FOR YOU. I LAMENTED. BUT I NOW SEE HOW PUNY AND WORTHLESS YOU ARE. YOU WEREN'T WORTH ONE SMIDGE OF MY LOVE.
MELLU. YOU STARTED ME ON THIS PATH. YOU.
BUT LET ME USE YOU TO DEFEAT THE CRAY AND I'LL BE YOURS AS WE PROMISED.

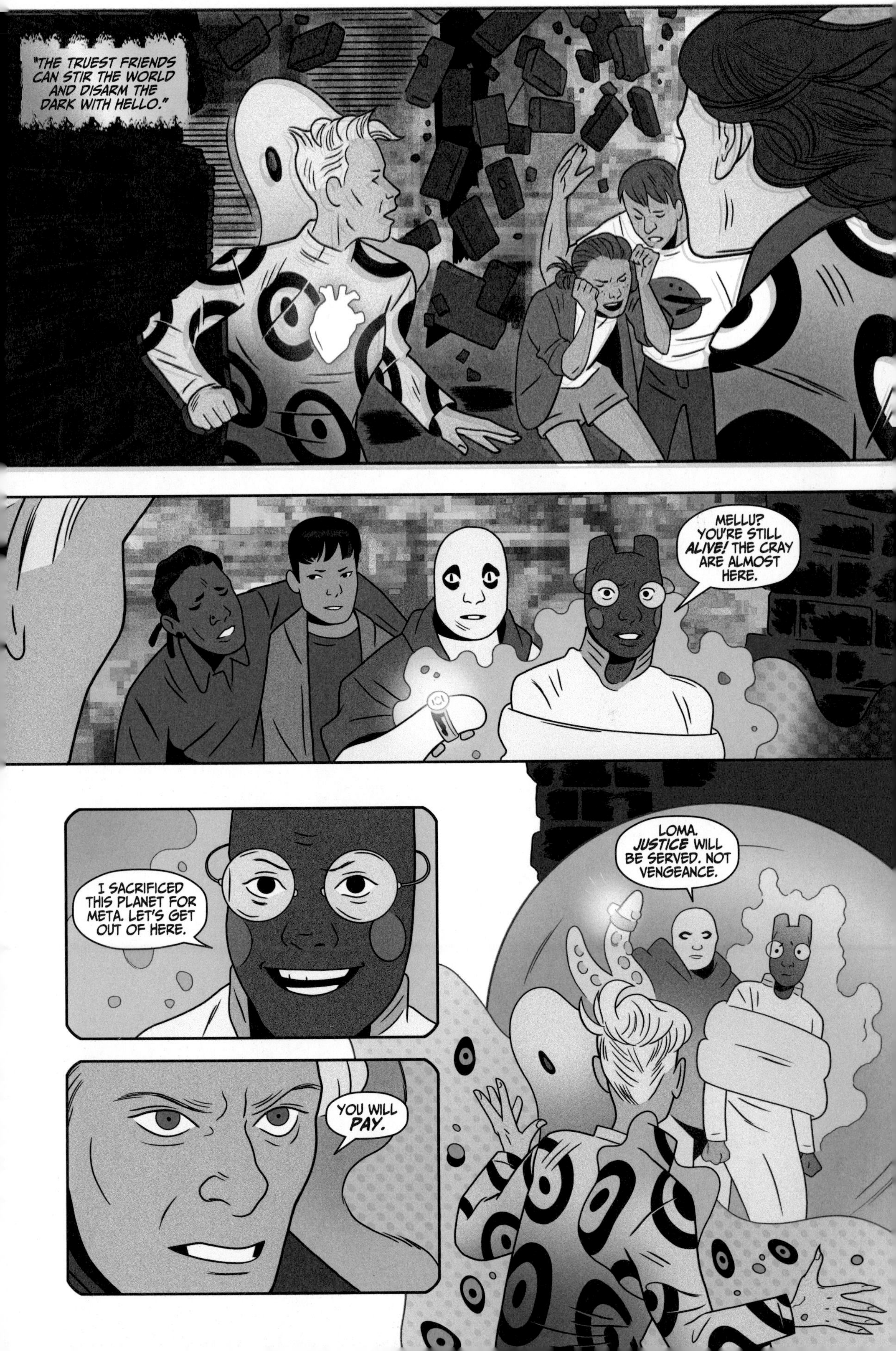
"THE TRUEST FRIENDS CAN STIR THE WORLD AND DISARM THE DARK WITH HELLO."
MELLU? YOU'RE STILL ALIVE! THE CRAY ARE ALMOST HERE.
I SACRIFICED THIS PLANET FOR META. LET'S GET OUT OF HERE.
YOU WILL PAY.
LOMA. JUSTICE WILL BE SERVED. NOT VENGEANCE.

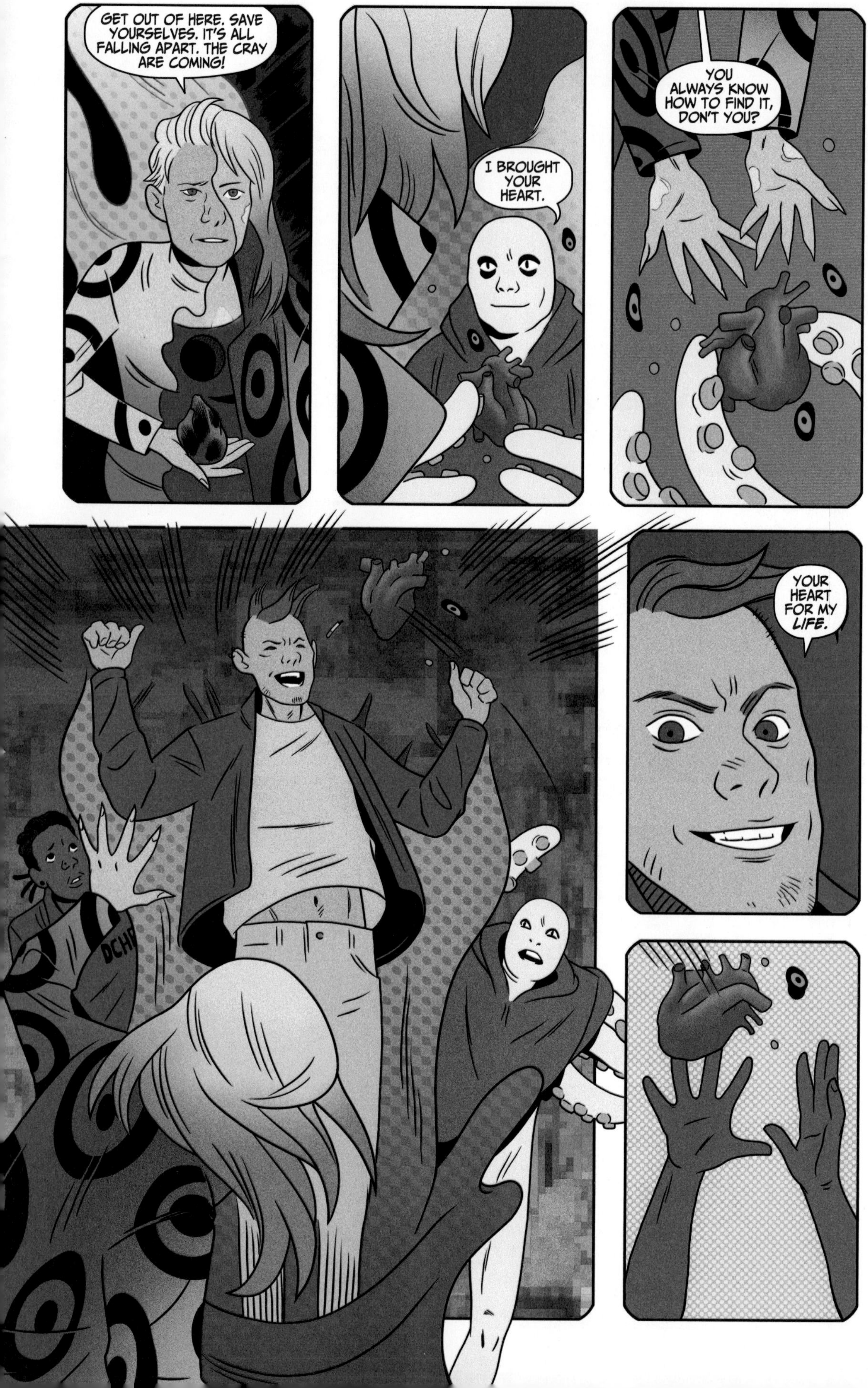
GET OUT OF HERE. SAVE YOURSELVES. IT'S ALL FALLING APART. THE CRAY ARE COMING!
I BROUGHT YOUR HEART.
YOU ALWAYS KNOW HOW TO FIND IT, DON'T YOU?
YOUR HEART FOR MY *LIFE.*
DCHP

YOU CAN'T HAVE YOURS IF I DON'T HAVE *MINE*.

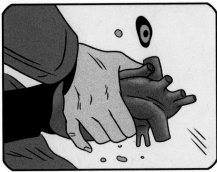

MEGAN. LET GO. IT'S *NOT* YOURS.

WHY DO YOU KEEP MEETING ME HERE? IS THIS MARS?

HERE? *MARS?* I'LL MEET YOU THERE. DEAL? GIVE HER THAT HEART. YOU'LL BE GIVING IT TO YOURSELF.

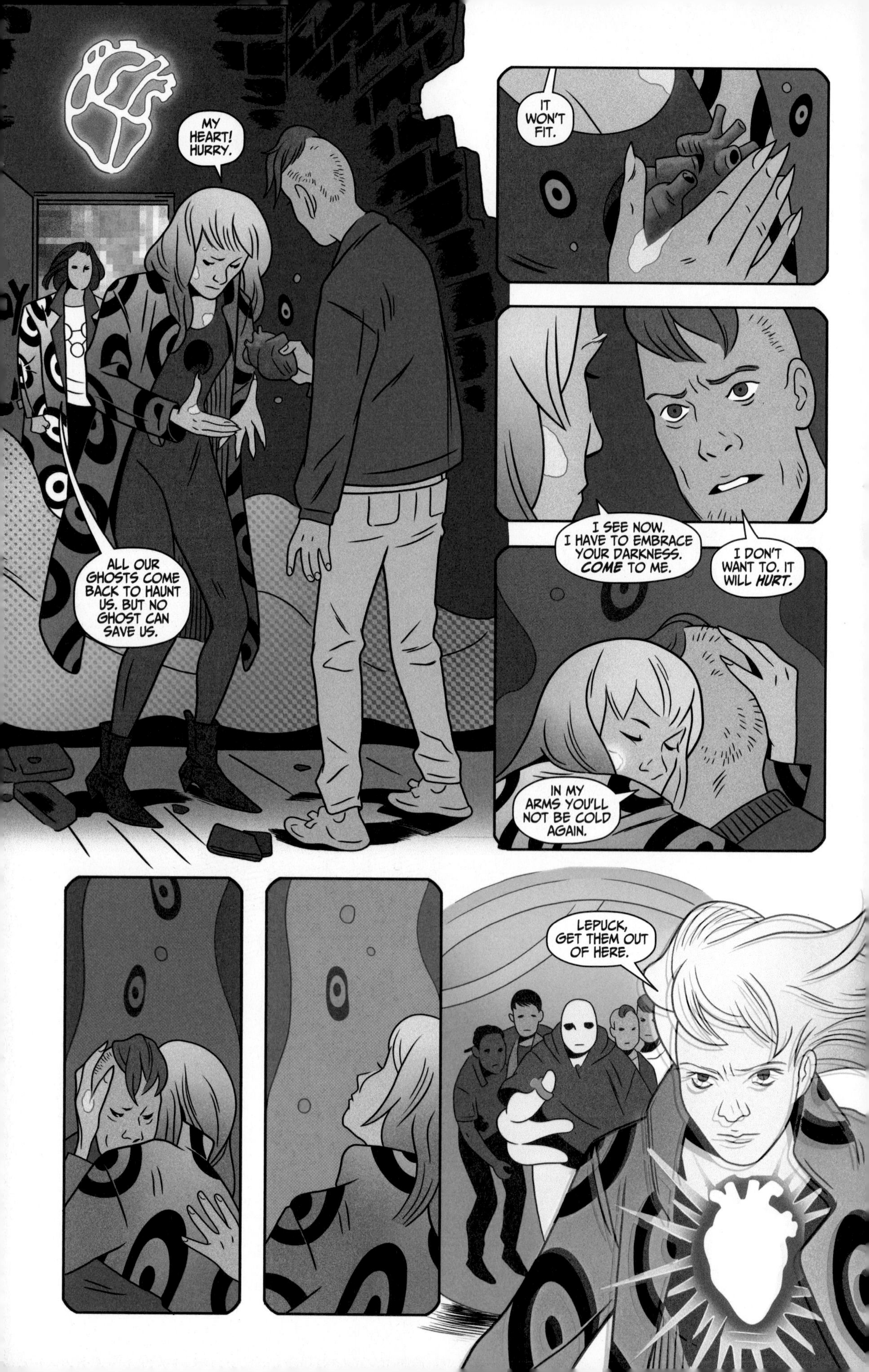
MY HEART! HURRY.
ALL OUR GHOSTS COME BACK TO HAUNT US. BUT NO GHOST CAN SAVE US.
IT WON'T FIT.
I SEE NOW. I HAVE TO EMBRACE YOUR DARKNESS. COME TO ME.
I DON'T WANT TO. IT WILL HURT.
IN MY ARMS YOU'LL NOT BE COLD AGAIN.
LEPUCK, GET THEM OUT OF HERE.

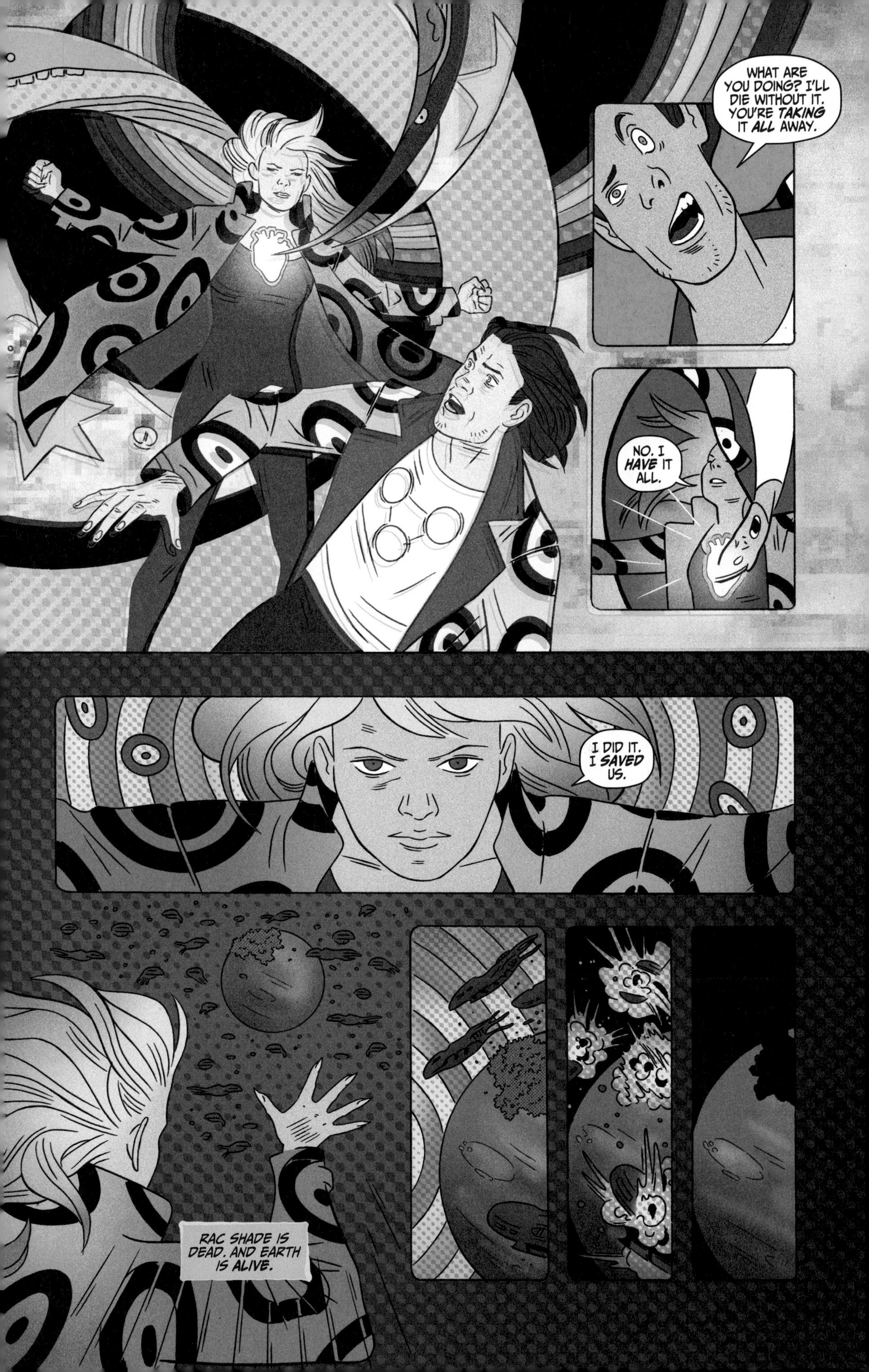
WHAT ARE YOU DOING? I'LL DIE WITHOUT IT. YOU'RE TAKING IT ALL AWAY.
NO. I HAVE IT ALL.
I DID IT. I SAVED US.
RAC SHADE IS DEAD. AND EARTH IS ALIVE.

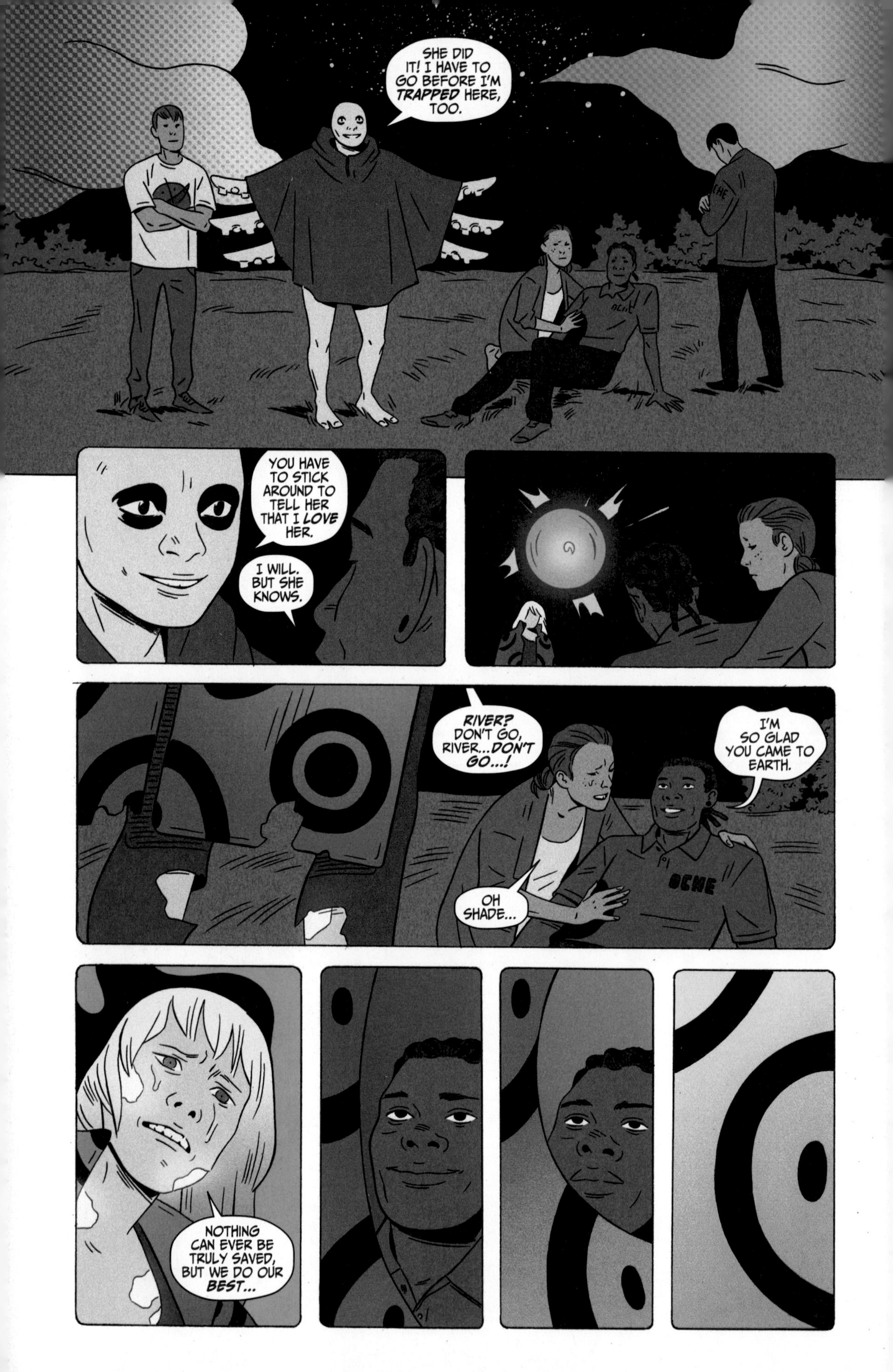
SHE DID IT! I HAVE TO GO BEFORE I'M TRAPPED HERE, TOO.
YOU HAVE TO STICK AROUND TO TELL HER THAT I LOVE HER.
I WILL. BUT SHE KNOWS.
RIVER? DON'T GO, RIVER...DON'T GO...!
I'M SO GLAD YOU CAME TO EARTH.
OH SHADE...
NOTHING CAN EVER BE TRULY SAVED, BUT WE DO OUR BEST...

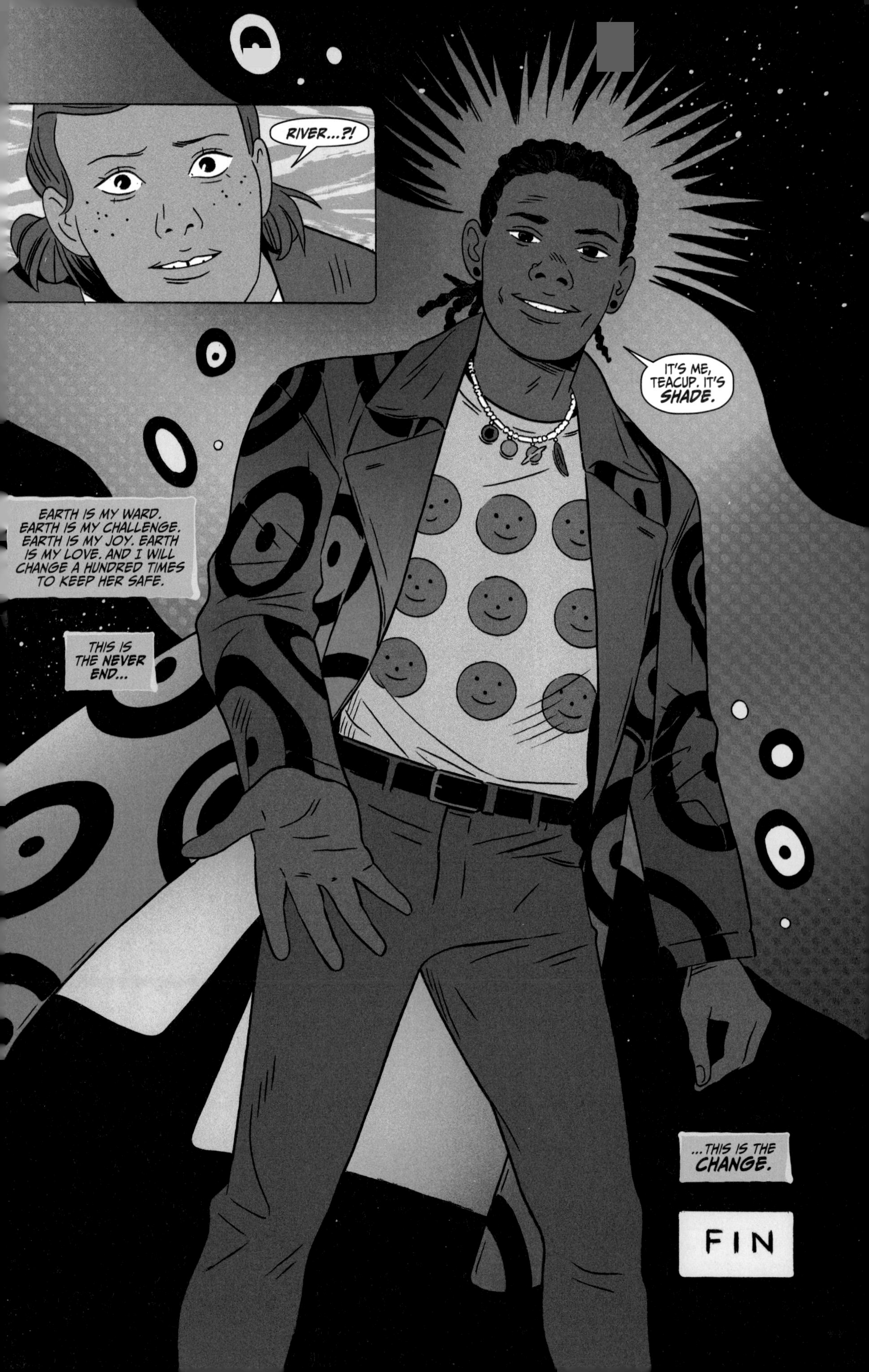
RIVER...?!
IT'S ME, TEACUP. IT'S SHADE.
EARTH IS MY WARD. EARTH IS MY CHALLENGE. EARTH IS MY JOY. EARTH IS MY LOVE. AND I WILL CHANGE A HUNDRED TIMES TO KEEP HER SAFE.
THIS IS THE NEVER END...
...THIS IS THE CHANGE.
FIN

KATHY GEORGE

Kathy George met Rac Shade when he entered the body of the serial killer Troy Grenzier, who had murdered her parents. The two were deeply connected through this trauma and the insanity that followed them. Complicated feelings of love developed between Rac and Kathy, and Rac came to depend upon her as a lifeline during his time on Earth. But Kathy was haunted by the deaths of her parents and boyfriend, and she self-medicated with alcohol. She eventually found comfort in the arms of her friend Lenny, but she was constantly drawn back to Rac. The trio became inseparable and made a strange threesome. After becoming pregnant with Rac's child, Kathy died giving birth to their son, George. Rac is now haunted by her death.

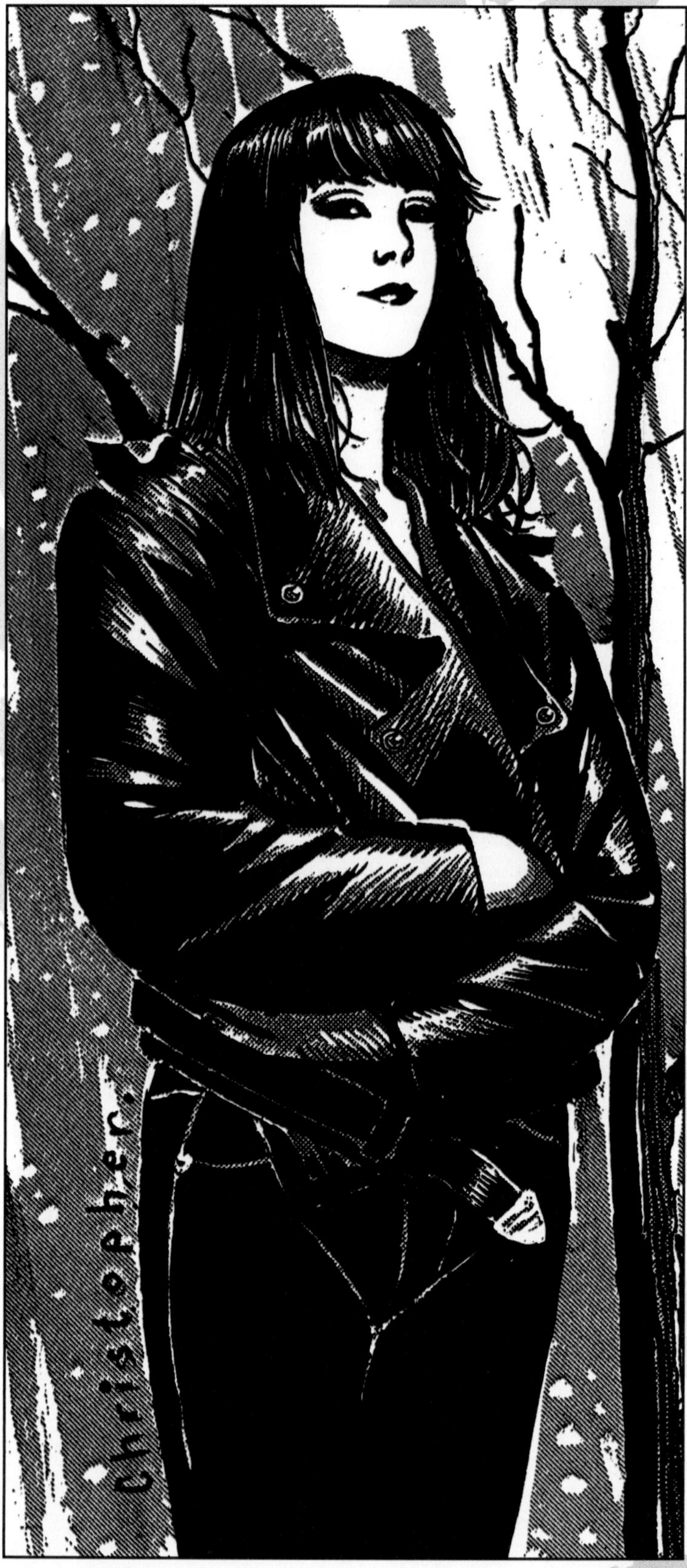
christopher.

Art by Chris Bachalo

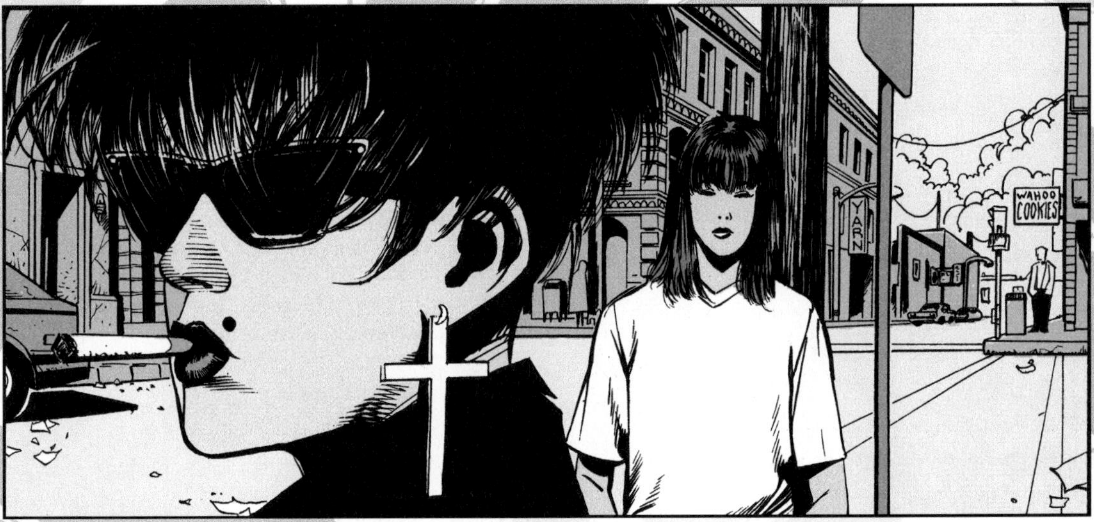
YARN
WAHOO
COOKIES

Art by Chris Bachalo and Mark Pennington

LENNY SHAPIRO

Lenny Shapiro is a sharp-witted, bisexual woman who likes sex and booze. Lenny is fearless and self-confident and was unafraid to call Rac Shade out on his bullshit. She became his best friend, staying with him all the way up to the end, and was also Kathy's lover. The three were an inseparable unit until Kathy's death in childbirth. Lenny always tells it like it is and never minced words with Rac. She abandoned her daughter Lilly, whose body was taken over by Rac and Kathy's son, George.

SHADES OF CHANGING

BY MARLEY ZARCONE

When I first took a stab at designing Loma Shade, I definitely took some inspiration from Gerard's drawing. I wanted to kind of bridge the energy of that drawing with the style from the Vertigo series of **SHADE, THE CHANGING MAN**. The drawing of Loma with the bag probably best channeled her excitable nature and alien curiosity. As the series continues, she definitely experiments more with different styles. I think that suits her character at the time. She's a newly human teenage girl, so there's no way she's sticking to a single uniform throughout the first two volumes of the series.

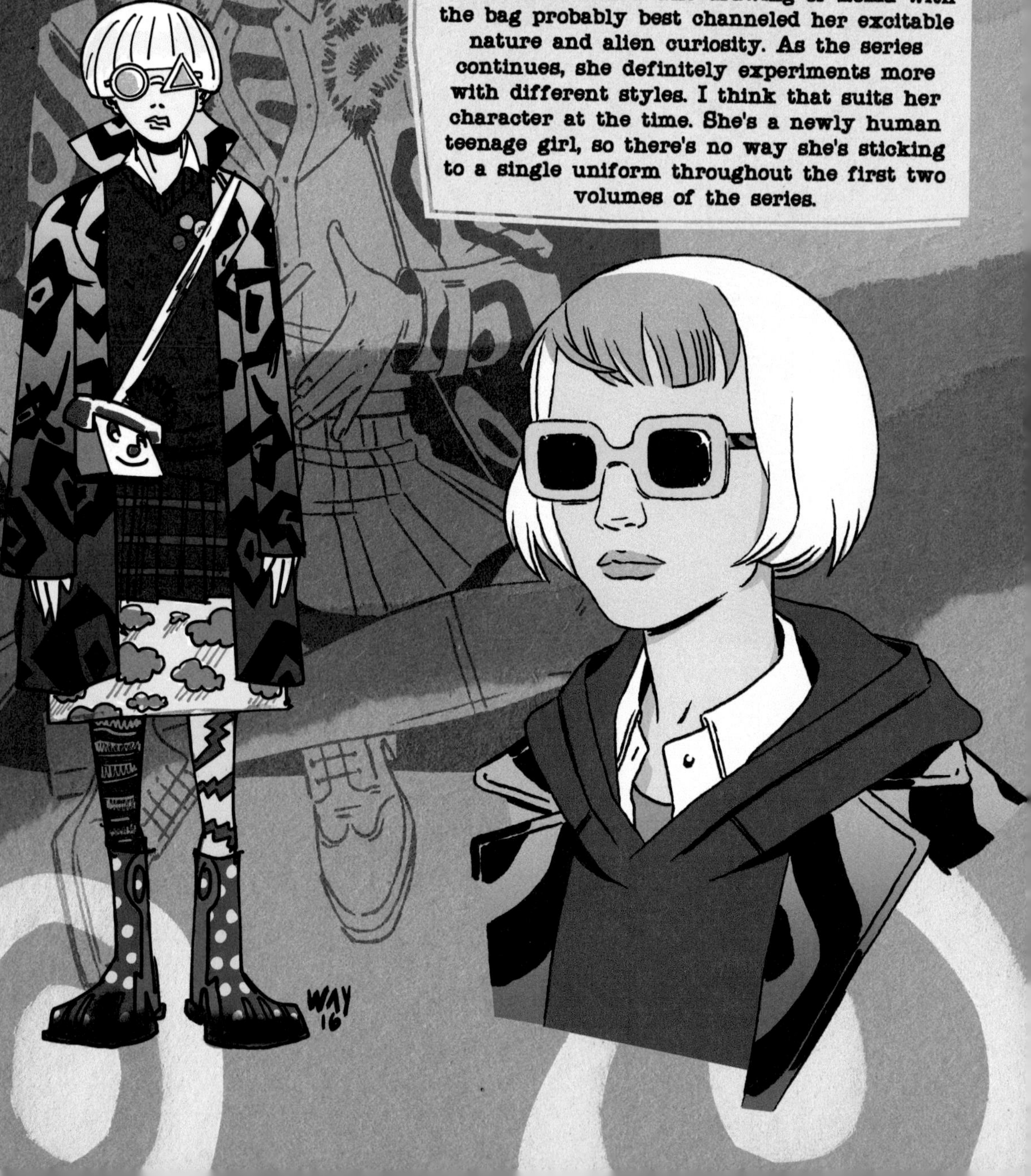
WAY '16

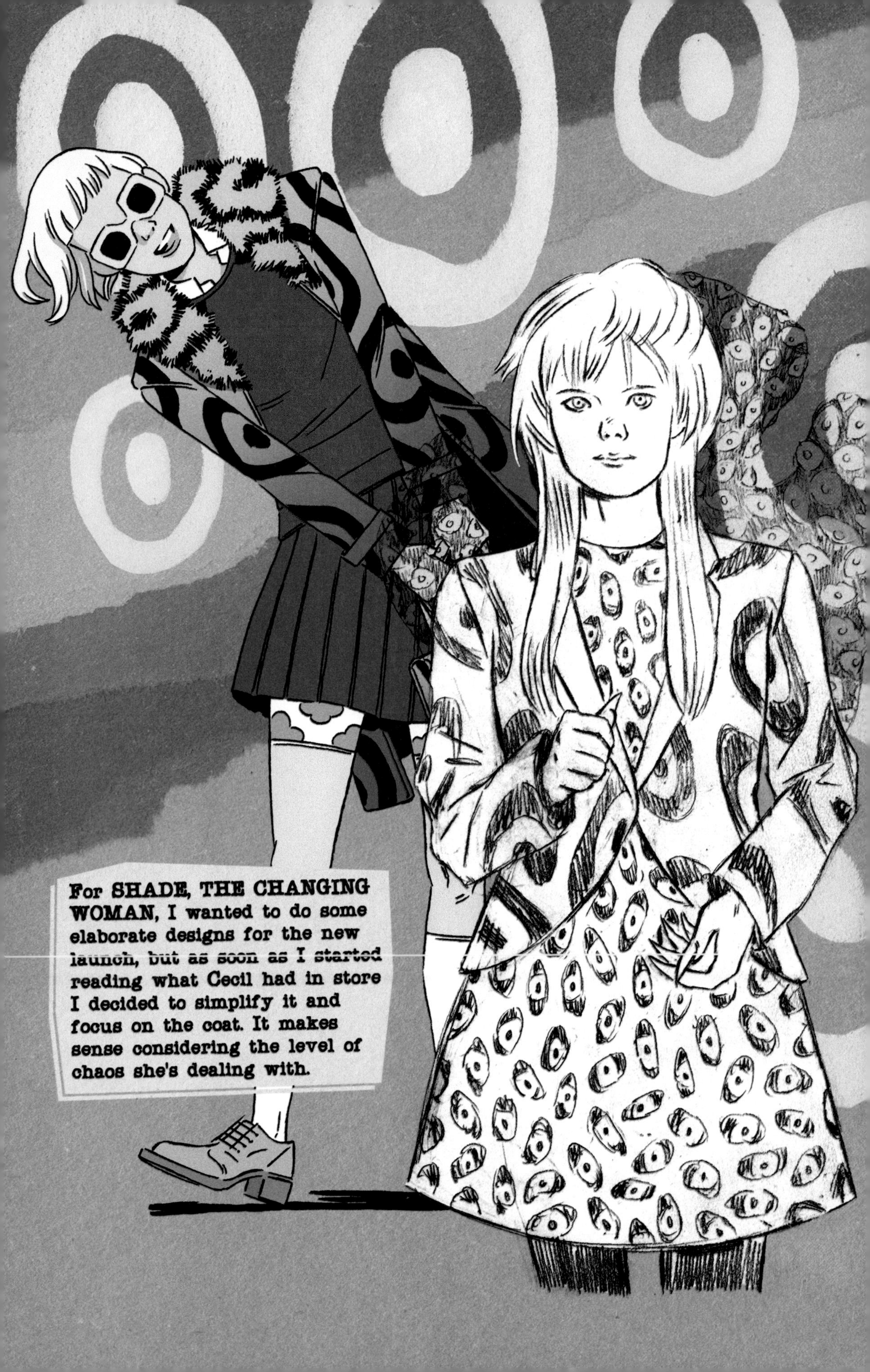
For SHADE, THE CHANGING WOMAN, I wanted to do some elaborate designs for the new launch, but as soon as I started reading what Cecil had in store I decided to simplify it and focus on the coat. It makes sense considering the level of chaos she's dealing with.

Variant cover art for issue #1 by Marley Zarcone

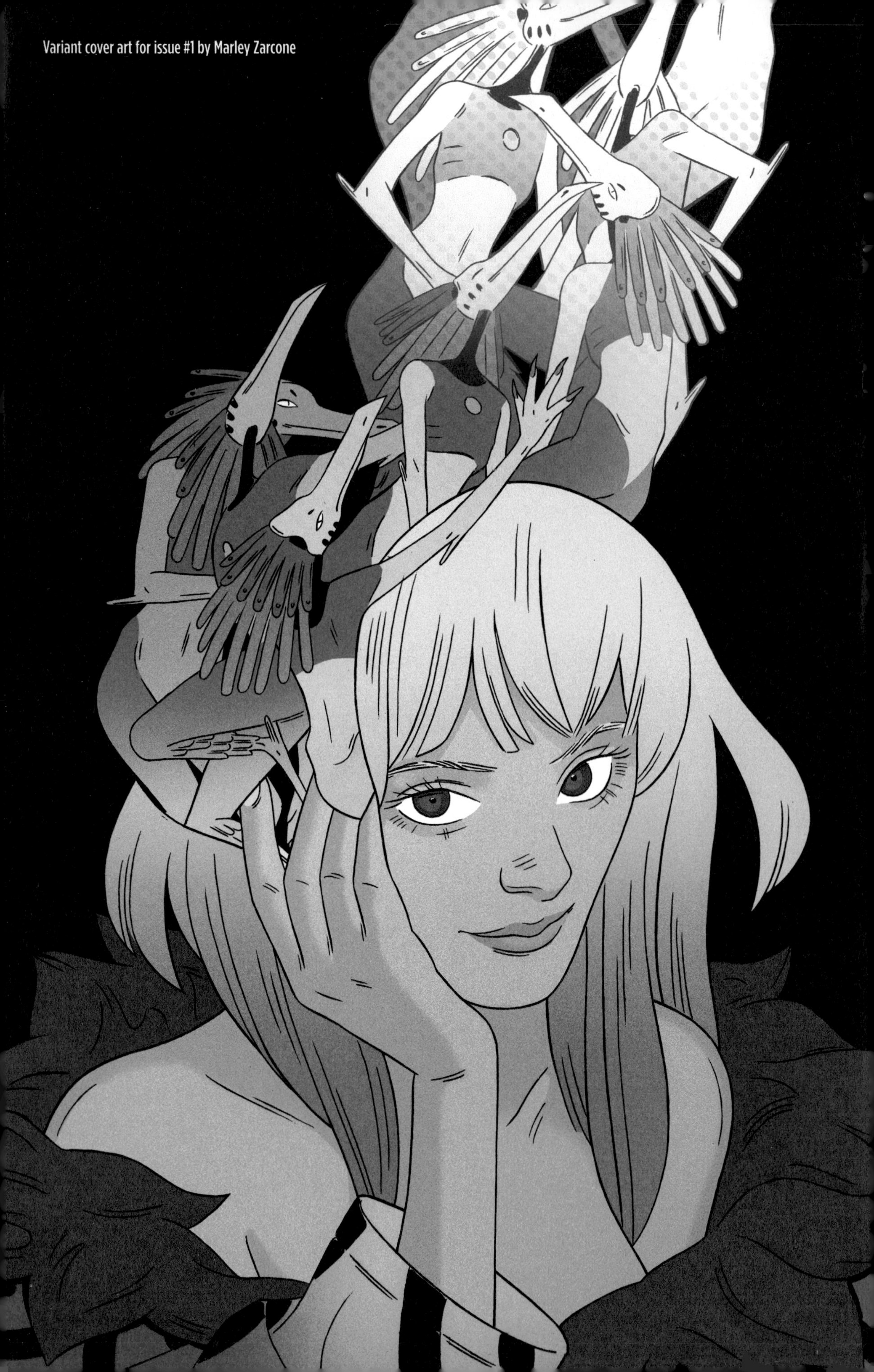